John Tyler Morgan

Belligerent Rights for Cuba

John Tyler Morgan

Belligerent Rights for Cuba

ISBN/EAN: 9783337379223

Printed in Europe, USA, Canada, Australia, Japan

Cover: Foto ©Suzi / pixelio.de

More available books at **www.hansebooks.com**

BELLIGERENT RIGHTS FOR CUBA.

SPEECHES

OF

HON. J. T. MORGAN,

OF ALABAMA,

IN THE

SENATE OF THE UNITED STATES,

January 29, February 5, 20, 24, 25, March 16, 17, 23, 24, and May 6, 1896;
April 6, 7, 8, 13, and May 4, 1897.

WASHINGTON.
1897.

SPEECHES

OF

HON. JOHN T. MORGAN.

January 20, 1896.

WAR IN CUBA.

Mr. MORGAN said:

Mr. PRESIDENT: I am directed by the Committee on Foreign Relations to report back a number of petitions on the subject of recognizing the belligerent rights of Cuba; also a joint resolution offered by the Senator from Florida [Mr. CALL], Senate joint resolution 4, declaring that a state of public war exists in Cuba, and that belligerent rights be accorded to the Cuban Government.

I report back as a substitute two resolutions, which I will read, accompanied by a written report. The report is brief, and explains the attitude of the committee toward these questions. I will read it:

The Congress of the United States, deeply regretting the unhappy state of hostilities existing in Cuba, which has again been the result of the demand of a large number of the native population of that island for its independence, in a spirit of respect and regard for the welfare of both countries, earnestly desires that the security of life and property and the establishment of permanent peace and of a government that is satisfactory to the people of Cuba should be accomplished.

And to the extent that the people of Cuba are seeking the rights of local self-government for domestic purposes, the Congress of the United States expresses its earnest sympathy with them. The Congress would also welcome with satisfaction the concession by Spain of complete sovereignty to the people of that island, and would cheerfully give to such a voluntary concession the cordial support of the United States. The near proximity of Cuba to the frontier of the United States, and the fact that it is universally regarded as a part of the continental system of America, identifies that island so closely with the political and commercial welfare of our people that Congress can not be indifferent to the fact that civil war is flagrant among the people of Cuba.

Nor can we longer overlook the fact that the destructive character of this war is doing serious harm to the rights and interests of our people on the island, and to our lawful commerce, the protection and freedom of which is safeguarded by treaty obligations. In the recent past and in former years, when internal wars have been waged for long periods and with results that were disastrous to Cuba and injurious to Spain, the Government of the United States has always observed, with perfect faith, all of its duties toward the belligerents.

It was a difficult task thus forced upon the United States, but it was performed with vigor, impartiality, and justice, in the hope that Spain would so ameliorate the condition of the Cuban people as to give them peace, contentment, and prosperity. This desirable result has not been accomplished. Its failure has not resulted from any interference on the part of our people or Government with the people or Government of Cuba.

The hospitality which our treaties, the laws of nations, and the laws of Christianity have extended to Cuban refugees in the United States has caused distrust on the part of the Spanish Government as to the fidelity of our Government to its obligations of neutrality in the frequent insurrections of the people of Cuba against Spanish authority. This distrust has often become a source of serious annoyance to our people, and has led to a spirit of retaliation toward Spanish authority in Cuba, thus giving rise to frequent controversies between the two countries. The absence of responsible government in Cuba, with powers adequate to deal directly with questions between the people of the United States and the people and political authorities of the island, has been a frequently recurring cause of delay, protracted imprisonment, confiscations of property, and the detention of our people and their ships, often upon groundless charges, which has been a serious grievance.

When insurrections have occurred on the Island of Cuba, the temptation to unlawful invasion by reckless persons has given to our Government anxiety, trouble, and much expense in the enforcement of our laws and treaty obligations of neutrality, and these occasions have been so frequent as to make these duties unreasonably onerous upon the Government of the United States.

The devastation of Cuba in the war that is now being waged, both with fire and sword, is an anxious and disturbing cause of unrest among the people of the United States, which creates strong grounds of protests against the continuance of the struggle for power between Cuba and Spain, which is rapidly changing the issue to one of existence on the part of a great number of the native population.

It is neither just to the relations that exist between Cuba and the United States, nor is it in keeping with the spirit of the age or the rights of humanity, that this struggle should be protracted until one party or the other should become exhausted in the resources of men and money, thereby weakening both until they may fall a prey to some stronger power, or until the stress of human sympathy or the resentments engendered by long and bloody conflict should draw into the strife the unruly elements of neighboring countries.

This civil war, though it is great in its proportions, and is conducted by armies that are in complete organization and directed and controlled by supreme military authority, has not the safeguard of a cartel for the treatment of wounded soldiers or prisoners of war.

In this feature of the warfare it becomes a duty of humanity that the civilized powers should insist upon the application of the laws of war recognized among civilized nations to both armies. As our own people are drawn into this struggle on both sides, and enter either army without the consent of our Government and in violation of our laws, their treatment when they may be wounded or captured, although it is not regulated by treaty and ceases to be a positive care of our Government, should not be left to the revengeful retaliations which expose them to the fate of pirates or other felons.

The inability of Spain to subdue the revolutionists by the measures and within the time that would be reasonable when applied to occasions of ordinary civil disturbance is a misfortune that can not be justly visited upon citizens of the United States, nor can it be considered that a state of open civil war does not exist, but that the movement is a mere insurrection and its supporters a mob of criminal violators of the law, when it is seen that it requires an army of 100,000 men and all the naval and military power of a great kingdom even to hold the alleged rebellion in check.

It is due to the situation of affairs in Cuba that Spain should recognize the existence of a state of war in the island, and should voluntarily accord to the armies opposed to her authority the rights of belligerents under the laws of nations.

The Congress of the United States, recognizing the fact that the matters herein referred to are properly within the control of the Chief Executive until, within the principles of our Constitution, it becomes the duty of Congress to define the final attitude of the Government of the United States toward Spain, presents these considerations to the President in support of the following resolution:

"*Resolved by the Senate* (*the House of Representatives concurring*), That the present deplorable war in the Island of Cuba has reached a magnitude that concerns all civilized nations to the extent that it should be conducted, if unhappily it is longer to continue, on those principles and laws of warfare that are acknowledged to be obligatory upon civilized nations when engaged in open hostilities, including the treatment of captives who are enlisted in either army; due respect to cartels for exchange of prisoners and for other military purposes; truces and flags of truce, the provision of proper hospitals and hospital supplies, and services to the sick and wounded of either army.

"*Resolved further*, That this representation of the views and opinions of Congress be sent to the President; and if he concurs therein that he will, in a friendly spirit, use the good offices of this Government to the end that Spain shall be requested to accord to the armies with which it is engaged in war the rights of belligerents, as the same are recognized under the laws of nations."

The VICE-PRESIDENT. The resolutions will be placed on the Calendar.

Mr. CAMERON. From the Committee on Foreign Relations I present the views of the minority, accompanied by a resolution.

Mr. LODGE. I ask that the views of the minority and the resolution may be read.

Mr. PLATT. I wish the Secretary, before he reads the views of the minority, would read the resolutions reported by the majority of the committee. They were not, I think, heard as read by the Senator from Alabama.

The VICE-PRESIDENT. The resolutions reported by the majority of the committee will be read.

The Secretary read the resolutions appended to the report of the majority of the committee.

Mr. CHANDLER. If the Senator from Pennsylvania has no objection, before the views of the minority are read I should like to hear the resolution which is proposed by the minority as a substitute.

Mr. CAMERON. That will be found at the end of the views of the minority.

The VICE-PRESIDENT. The resolution reported by the minority will be read.

The Secretary read as follows:

Resolved, That the President is hereby requested to interpose his friendly offices with the Spanish Government for the recognition of the independence of Cuba.

Mr. PLATT. Now let the whole minority report be read.

The VICE-PRESIDENT. The views of the minority will be read.

The Secretary read the views of the minority, as follows:

VIEWS OF THE MINORITY.

After the cessation of our civil war we were called upon to take notice of the struggle in Cuba against Spanish rule which broke out in October, 1868. It is said that early in the year 1869 a proclamation was actually signed by President Grant recognizing the Cubans as belligerents, although the fact was known to very few persons. This proclamation was not promulgated, owing to the opposition of Secretary Fish. In December, 1869, President Grant, in his first annual message, called the attention of Congress to this struggle. He said:

"For more than a year a valuable province of Spain, and a near neighbor of ours, in whom all our people can not but feel a deep interest, has been struggling for independence and freedom. The people and Government of the United States entertain those same warm feelings and sympathies for the people of Cuba in their pending struggle that they manifested throughout the previous struggles between Spain and her former colonies in behalf of the latter. But the contest has at no time assumed the conditions which amount to a war in the sense of international law, or which would show the existence of a de facto political organization of the insurgents sufficient to justify a recognition of belligerence. The principle is maintained, however, that this nation is its own judge when to accord the rights of belligerency, either to a people struggling to free themselves from a government they believe to be oppressive, or to independent nations at war with each other."

He concluded that in due time Spain must find it for its interest to establish its dependency as an independent power, which could then exercise its right of choice as regarded its future relations with other powers.

The Cuban war which broke out in 1868 had been in existence for only nine months when our Government felt the necessity of interference. Mr. Sickles was appointed our minister to Madrid in 1869, and instructions were given to him to submit propositions on the part of our Government, in order to bring to a close the "civil conflict" raging in Cuba. The part taken by our Government at that time in Cuban affairs is full of interest, not only as regards the engagement into which the authorities were willing to enter, but also as respects the status which the instructions gave to the Cuban conflict. Our minister was directed to impress upon the Spanish mind "the advancing growth of that sentiment which claims for every part of the American hemisphere the right of self-government and freedom from transatlantic dependence." The good offices of the United States were offered to the cabinet at Madrid for the purpose of bringing to a close "the civil war now ravaging the Island of Cuba." The bases of settlement were:

1. The independence of Cuba to be acknowledged by Spain.

2. Cuba to pay Spain an indemnity for her relinquishment of all her rights in the island.
3. The abolition of slavery.
4. An armistice pending negotiations of settlement.

Our minister was also authorized to state that if Spain insisted, our Government might guarantee the payment of the indemnity by Cuba.

His attention was called particularly to the expression used in the instructions, "the civil war now ravaging the island."

While this expression is not designed to grant any public recognition of belligerent rights to the insurgents, it is nevertheless used advisedly and in recognition of a state and condition of the contest which may not justify a much longer withholding of the concession to the revolutionary party of the recognized rights of belligerents. Should the expression, therefore, be commented upon you will admit what is above stated with reference to it, and may add in case of a protracted discussion, or the prospect of a refusal by Spain to accept the proposed offer of the United States, that an early recognition of belligerent rights is the logical deduction from the present proposal, and will probably be deemed a necessity on the part of the United States unless the condition of the parties to the contest shall have changed very materially.

Negotiations were at once entered upon by our minister with the Spanish Government, and the proposition of the United States was submitted to General Prim. the president of the council of state, who was then at the head of Spanish affairs, and practically dictator in Spain. Prim asked how much Cuba would give, and it was suggested that $125,000,000 might be arranged. Prim intimated that autonomy to Cuba would be conceded as soon as hostilities ceased, but that Spain could not entertain the question of the independence of Cuba as long as the Cubans were in arms against the Government. He also declined to consider the Cubans as parties to be consulted in the negotiation.

He was willing to assure Cuban independence if, after laying down their arms, the Cubans should vote for a separation, although he would not insist upon the necessity of such a vote. That for his part, if he alone were consulted, he would say to the Cubans, "Go, if you will; make good the treasure you have cost us, and let us bring home our army in peace, and consolidate the liberties and resources of Spain." He added that he had no doubt that whatever might be the result of the conflict, Cuba would eventually be free; that he recognized without hesitation the manifest course of events on the American Continent, and the inevitable termination of all colonial relations in their autonomy as soon as they were prepared for independence; but he repeated, that no consideration would reconcile Spain to such a concession until hostilities ceased. His language was:

"I do not flatter myself that Spain will retain possession of the island. I consider that the period of colonial autonomy has virtually arrived. However the present contest may end, whether in the suppression of the insurrection or in the better way of an amicable arrangement through the assistance of the United States, it is equally clear to me that the time has come for Cuba to govern herself; and if we succeed in putting down the insurrection to-morrow, I shall regard the subject in the same light, that the child has attained its majority and should be allowed to direct its own affairs. We want nothing more than to get out of Cuba, but it must be done in a dignified and honorable manner."

Our Government saw the futility of accepting the conditions suggested by Spain. They recognized that nothing could be effected by a plebiscite, and that the Cubans could not be induced to lay down their arms and trust the Spaniards to carry out their promises. Moreover, while the negotiations were in progress the public became informed of them. Immediately a great excitement arose, communicated by the press, which disinclined the Spanish administration to pursue the matter, and our Government, finding itself unable to effect any good purpose, withdrew its offer of mediation.

Mr. Sickles wrote Mr. Fish that Spain deprecated the expression of the sympathy of the Government and people of the United States for the cause of the revolutionists, as well as the President's declaration of the right of the Government of the United States to determine when it may rightfully proclaim its neutrality in the conflict between a colony struggling for independence and the parent state. It is remarkable, was the comment of Mr. Sickles, that in all these discussions the fact is overlooked that Spain conceded the rights of belligerents to the Confederates without waiting for the outbreak of hostilities.

"The Queen's proclamation of June, 1861, is forgotten; and the large and profitable commerce carried on between Habana and the blockaded ports of the South in enemies' ships, which changed their flags in Cuban waters, is quite ignored."

On the failure of negotiations, the logical result of our action was to recognize the Cubans as belligerents engaged in a "civil war." As was said by Secretary Fish, the mere offer on our part to mediate as between the contending forces was in itself a concession of belligerency and a recognition of

2777

that condition. But for various reasons this argument was not pressed by our Government. Although from month to month the aggressiveness of the revolutionists increased and their power extended, our Government, speaking through the State Department and the President, continued to inform the country that the Cubans had not reached such a condition as entitled them to be recognized as belligerents, although the Administration had already in instructions to our own minister to Spain recognized that condition at a time when the revolution had hardly attained any headway.

One of the reasons for this inconsistency was the expectation felt by our Government that Spain would voluntarily concede to the Cubans much that they were struggling for. Liberal ministries succeeded one another in Spain, each of which was more liberal than its predecessor in promises of reform and recognition of the rights of the Cubans. Civil war broke out in Spain, and its Government became involved in such difficulties that ours was loath to press the subject of Cuba or to insist upon a speedy solution of the question. Mr. Fish was irritated by the operation of the Cuban junta in this country, which at times infringed our neutrality laws. He thought they should have confined their activity to sending to the insurgents arms and munitions of war, which he says they might have done "consistently with our own statutes and with the law of nations." At home the Federal Administration had to deal with the pressing question of the reconstruction of the South. The negro problem in this country was of such importance that the Administration had no desire to add difficulties by undertaking to settle the negro question in Cuba.

The action of our Government was in striking contrast to that of Spain in recognizing the Confederates as belligerents. Mr. Fish refers to this in a letter to Señor Roberts, the Spanish minister, in 1869:

"The civil war in Cuba has continued for a year; battle after battle has been fought; thousands of lives have been sacrificed, and the result is still in suspense. But the United States have hitherto resisted the considerations which in 1861 controlled the action of Spain and determined her to act upon the occurrence of a single bloodless conflict of arms and within sixty days from its date."

Six years later, in 1875, this Government was again on the point of intervening. In a dispatch from Mr. Fish, Secretary of State, to Mr. Cushing, then minister to Spain, the Secretary said that the condition of Cuba was the one great cause of perpetual solicitude in the foreign relations of the United States. He informed the minister that the President did not meditate the annexation of Cuba to the United States, but its elevation as an independent republic—

"The desire of independence [the Secretary says] on the part of the Cubans is a natural and legitimate aspiration of theirs, because they are Americans. That the ultimate issue of events in Cuba will be its independence, however that issue may be produced, whether by means of negotiation, or as the result of military operations, or of one of those unexpected incidents which so frequently determine the fate of nations, it is impossible to doubt. If there be one lesson in history more cogent in its teachings than any other, it is that no part of America large enough to constitute a self-sustaining state can be permanently held in forced colonial subjection to Europe. Complete separation between the metropolis and its colony may be postponed by the former conceding to the latter a greater or less degree of local autonomy, nearly approaching to independence. But in all cases where a positive antagonism has come to exist between the mother country and its colonial subjects, where the sense of oppression is strongly felt by the latter, and especially where years of relentless warfare have alienated the parties one from another more widely than they are sundered by the ocean itself, their political separation is inevitable. It is one of those conclusions which have been aptly called the inexorable logic of events."

Thus we have shown that already, in 1869, when the revolution of the preceding year had attained but inconsiderable proportions, President Grant expressed his firm conviction that the ultimate result of the struggle for independence would be to break the bonds which attached Cuba as a colony to Spain. President Grant announced the determination of our Government to intervene if the struggle in Cuba was not speedily terminated. It was pointed out that while the Spanish authorities insisted that a state of war did not exist in Cuba, and that no rights as belligerents should be accorded to the revolutionists, they at the same time demanded for themselves all the rights and privileges which flowed from actual and acknowledged war. That Cuba exhibited a chronic condition of turbulence and rebellion was due to the system pursued by Spain and the want of harmony between the inhabitants of the island and the governing class. That should it become necessary for this Government to intervene it would be moved by the necessity for a proper regard to its own protection and its own interests and the interests of humanity.

The inhuman manner in which the war was waged and the shocking executions of natives and citizens of this country made an impression of horror on the world.

The nicest sense of international requirements can not fail to perceive that provocation from Spain was overlooked by our Government for a longer period and with greater patience than any other government of equal power would have tolerated. A writer in the London Times, in 1875, reflecting upon the possibility of Spain's overcoming the then insurrection, and on the prospect of our interference, said:

"Were Cuba as near to Cornwall as it is to Florida we should certainly look more sharply to matters of fact than to the niceties of international law. But everything, we repeat, depends upon these matters of fact. If Spain can suppress the insurrection and prevent Cuba from becoming a permanent source of mischief to neighboring countries, she has the fullest right to keep it. But she is on her trial, and that trial can not be long. When she is made to clearly understand that the tenure of her rule over Cuba depends upon her ability to make that rule a reality, she will not be slow to show what she can do, and the limits of her power will be the limits of her right."

In 1869 Gen. Martinez Campos, the greatest soldier Spain possessed, was sent to Cuba to make a final effort to bring hostilities there to a termination. He was not only a great soldier, but was believed to be a great administrator, and had the respect of all parties on account of his patriotism and integrity. He was afforded all the aid in the way of men and money which Spain could furnish. In 1878 he succeeded in the so-called pacification, for which service he was raised to the highest pinnacle in Spain and made prime minister. He did not conquer the insurgents, but induced them to lay down their arms on conditions of peace which, as the Spanish administrator, he undertook for his Government should be faithfully carried out.

A treaty of peace was negotiated with the leaders of the revolution. In 1879 General Campos wrote a long dispatch to his Government from the seat of his triumph, which at this day is extremely interesting, owing to the fact that the present war owes its origin to the same circumstances as caused the former outbreak. In this dispatch, stating the particulars of the pacification, General Campos gave an extended review of the situation in Cuba and of the terms of the treaty of peace and the negotiations which led thereto. This recital shows that General Campos believed, as was afterwards said by our minister, James Russell Lowell, that the reforms he stipulated were necessary if Cuba was to be retained as a dependency of Spain, and, Mr. Lowell remarked, all intelligent Spaniards admitted that the country could not afford another war. As a reason for according conditions to the Cubans, General Campos sketched the motives of his policy:

"Since the year 1869, when I landed on this island with the first reenforcements, I was preoccupied with the idea that the insurrection here, though acknowledging as its cause the hatred of Spain, yet this hatred was due to the causes that have separated our colonies from the mother country, augmented in the present case by the promises made to the Antilles at different times (1812, 1837, and 1845), promises which not only have not been fulfilled, but, as I understand, have not been permitted to be so by the Cortes when at different times their execution had been begun.

"While the island had no great development, its aspirations were confined by love of nationality and respect for authority; but when one day after another passed without hopes being satisfied, but, on the contrary, the greater freedom permitted now and then by a governor was more than canceled by his successor; when they were convinced that the colony went on in the same way; when bad officials and a worse administration of justice more and more aggravated difficulties; when the provincial governorships, continually growing worse, fell at last into the hands of men without training or education, petty tyrants who could practice their thefts and sometimes their oppressions because of the distance at which they resided from the supreme authority, public opinion, until then restrained, began vehemently to desire those liberties which, if they bring much good, contain also some evil. * * * The 10th of October, 1868, came to open men's eyes; the eruption of the volcano in which so many passions, so many hatreds, just and unjust, had been heaped up was terrible, and almost at the outset the independence of Cuba was proclaimed."

He showed the gains speedily made by the insurgents and the advantages they had by reason of the familiarity with the country, so that "they defeated large columns with hardly a battalion of men. They almost put us on the defensive, and as we had to guard an immense property, the mission of the army became very difficult." He recounted his efforts to reestablish the principle of authority, but said that he had against him a "public spirit without life. Nobody had higher aspirations than to save his crop of sugar. In official regions the enemy was thought inferior, but the commanders generally believed it unsafe to operate with less than three battalions; there was no venturing beyond the highways."

He said little was gained by beating the enemy. What he needed was to exterminate them, and that he could not do. That had his responsibility been free of the Cortes and the Government he would in the beginning have ventured everything to secure peace—the disembargo of estates, a general pardon, the assimilation of Cuba with Spain, orders to treat prisoners well—and to show that this was not weakness, but strength, there was "the argument of his 100,000 bayonets." He finally related the terms by which he induced the Cubans to lay down their arms. All desired reforms were promised. Municipal law, the law of provincial assemblies, and representation in the Cortes should be established; the jurisdiction of the courts defined, tax laws settled, the form of contribution and assessments determined, schools established, the people to be consulted through their representative as to all these reforms and others, and they were not to be left to the will of the Captain-General or the head of a department. This summary is sufficient to indicate what was stipulated between the parties. Said General Campos:

"I do not wish to make a momentary peace; I desire that this peace be the beginning of a bond of common interest between Spain and her Cuban provinces, and that this bond be drawn closer by the identity of aspirations and the good faith of both. Let not the Cubans be considered as pariahs or children, but put on an equality with other Spaniards in everything not inconsistent with their present condition. Perhaps [he concluded] the insurgents would have accepted promises less liberal and more vague than those set forth in this condition; but even had this been done, it would have been but a brief postponement, because those liberties are destined to come for the reasons already given, with the difference that Spain now shows herself magnanimous, satisfying just aspirations which she might deny, and a little later, probably, very soon, would have been obliged to grant them, compelled by the force of ideas and of the age. Moreover, she has promised over and over again to enter on the path of assimilation, and if the promise were more vague, even though the fulfillment of this promise were begun, these people would have a right to doubt our good faith, and to show a distrust unfortunately warranted by the failings of human nature itself. The not adding another 100,000 to the 100,000 families that mourn their sons slain in this pitiless war, and the cry of peace that will resound in the hearts of the 80,000 mothers who have sons in Cuba or liable to conscription, would be a full equivalent for the payment of a debt of justice."

This debt of justice has not yet been paid.

The highest Spanish authorities have been obliged to confess that the grievances of the Cubans are just and their aspirations for liberty legitimate.

Marshal Serrano, in his official report to the Spanish Government of the 10th of May, 1867, said:

"We are forced to acknowledge that in the last years the treasury of Cuba has been used abusively, which is partly the cause of the crisis the islands go through now and of the exhaustion of its resources."

Castelar, in 1873, while President, endeavored to convince Spain of the necessity of making reforms demanded alike by "humanity and civilization," and he deplored making Cuba a "transatlantic Poland." In 1874 our minister to Spain informed our Government that the entire unwillingness of Spain to do anything toward the amelioration of Cuba was shown by the fact that all the governments since the breaking out of the revolution in 1868 had promised to reform the administration, but that the situation of the island was worse than ever. And Secretary Fish informed the Spanish Government that most of the evils of which Cuba was the scene were the necessary results of harsh treatment and of the maladministration of the colonial government.

In 1875 Mr. Cushing, then minister to Madrid, communicated to our Government a large amount of evidence from Spanish sources showing the demoralization existing in the administration in Cuba. The Spanish journals of that date openly informed the central government that war in Cuba could never be ended until the vices of the ultramarine administration were corrected and its moral tone raised. Spain was exhorted to make one supreme effort for the pacification of Cuba and its moralization.

"The journals of all shades of opinion speak of the official corruption," said Mr. Cushing, "and peculations of the public employees in Cuba as a feature of the situation not less calamitous than the insurrection." He remarked that the burden of taxation had become intolerable, aggravated as it was by the frauds and wastes committed by almost everybody connected with the collection or expenditure of the public moneys; that the abuses of administration, of which so much was being said at that time, were old, chronic, deep-rooted, and impossible of eradication under the colonial régime. "It would seem that each of the ephemeral parties on attaining power, with a crowd of eager partisans behind it like troops of howling wolves, shakes off as many as it can upon Cuba."

Notwithstanding that the public press did not cease to advise the Government that the immorality of the public administration of the island offered a vast field to censure, nothing was done to improve its condition. It was thought by the central government that it was only necessary by force to save Cuba to Spain. It was common remark, however, that the Government ought to sustain two campaigns in Cuba—one against insurrection and the other against corruption. Said Mr. Cushing:

"So merely mercenary and so regardless of duty and the public weal are many of the public officers who go out to the island as to cause the saying to become current that on embarking they leave all sense of shame behind them in Cadiz."

And he observed that all testimony was unanimous as to the corruptions and the embezzlements of the administrations of Cuba.

The testimony of Mr. Cushing is of the most convincing character, as he has never been accused of being unfriendly to Spain. That he did not draw a too highly colored picture of Spanish misrule is shown by the declaration of the minister of transmarine affairs at Madrid in an official paper quoted by Mr. Fish in 1874:

"A deplorable and pertinacious tradition of despotism, which, if it could ever be justified, is without a shadow of reason at the present time, intrusted the direction and management of our colonial establishment to the agents of the metropolis, destroying, by their dominant and exclusive authority, the vital energies of the country and the creative and productive activity of free individuals. And although the system may now have improved in some of its details, the domineering action of the authorities being less felt, it still appears full of the original error, which is upheld by the force of tradition and the necessary influence of interests created under their protection. A change of system, political as well as administrative, is therefore imperatively demanded."

It is needless to say no such change has been made.

The Spanish Government to-day in Cuba is of the same character as it was when Richard Henry Dana visited the island in 1854, "an armed monarchy encamped in the midst of a disarmed and disfranchised people; an unmixed despotism of one nation over another." Dana warned the public against the testimony of Americans and other foreigners engaged in business in Cuba as to the condition of affairs there:

"Of all classes of persons I know of none whose situation is more unfavorable to the growth and development of sentiments of patriotism and philanthropy and of interest in the future of a race than foreigners temporarily resident, for purposes of money-making only, in a country with which they have nothing in common in the future or the past. This class is often called impartial. I do not agree to the use of that term. They are indeed free from the bias of feeling or sentiment, but they are subject to the attractions of interest. It is for their immediate advantage to preserve peace and the existing order of things."

That the condition of Cuba had not improved prior to the present war is shown by a report of our consul-general at Habana to the State Department in 1885. This stated that the entire population, with the exception of the official class, was living under a tyranny unparalleled at this day on the globe.

"There is a system of oppression and torture which enters into every phase of life, eats into the soul of every Cuban, mortifies, injures, and insults him every hour, impoverishes him and his family from day to day, threatens the rich man with bankruptcy and the poor man with beggary. The exactions of the Spanish Government and the illegal outrages of its officers are in fact intolerable. They have reduced the island to despondency and ruin. * * * The Government at Madrid is directly answerable for the misery of Cuba and for the rapacity and venality of its subordinates. * * * No well-informed Spaniard imagines that Cuba will long continue to submit to this tyranny, or at least that she will long be able to yield this harvest to her oppressors. Spain cares nothing whatever for the interests, the prosperity, or the sufferings of her colony. The Government does almost nothing to ameliorate any of the evils of the country. The police are everywhere insufficient and inefficient. The roads are no roads at all. Every interest which might enrich and improve the island is looked upon by the officials as one more mine to exploit. * * * Cuba is held solely for the benefit of Spain and Spanish interests, for the sake of Spanish adventurers. Against this all rebel in thought and feeling if not yet in fact and deed. * * * They wish protection from the grasping rapacity of Spain and see no way to attain it except by our aid."

He concluded that from the general misery war must ensue of such a savage character that the world would be shocked and the United States would be compelled from sheer humanity to interfere and save a country which Spain would be unable either to control or to preserve. He had learned from many quarters that in any future attempt to change the condition of affairs all the inhabitants would go hand in hand; "it is generally understood that the permanent white population is of one mind."

While some of the reforms stipulated for by the Cubans and engaged to be carried out by General Campos in 1879 were nominally granted, they were all substantially withheld. The central government did not feel itself bound, after the cessation of hostilities was secured, to perform the conditions by which that result was brought about. Our consul-general reported (1885) "that the island is worse governed than at any previous period of its history."

2777

"Cuba, it was determined, must pay the entire cost of the war. At the time when the fostering care of the Government was most needed to heal the wounds inflicted by the war, when every interest was prostrate and every business suffering, new and enormous taxes were imposed. * * * A war tax of the most exaggerated character was laid. Every business, trade, art, or profession is taxed in the proportion of from 25 to 33½ per cent of its net income. * * * All ordinary mercantile business and all the petty trades and employments of the country are separately suffering. All participate in the common distress."

He stated that the absolute legal tax imposed on the island was only a part of what the wretched and impoverished inhabitants were compelled to pay.

"It is a matter of notoriety that illegal charges are constantly made and then taken off for a bribe. The hordes of officials who batten like hungry beasts on the vitals of Cuba make no pretense of honesty except on paper. The highest officers, when they chance to be better than their subordinates, admit the character of their inferiors; more often they share it. * * * The present state of things can not continue. Some change amounting almost to revolution is inevitable. What with governmental oppression and illegal tyranny, emancipation, brigandage, low prices for sugar and high taxes on everything, the ruin of the island is already almost consummated. She is absolutely incapacitated for rendering the revenue demanded or supporting the army of officials who keep her prostrate in her agony."

Shortly after Mr. Blaine became Secretary of State, in the Administration of President Harrison, it was the subject of consideration whether Spain could be induced to acknowledge Cuba as independent should the United States agree to guarantee the sum to be paid by Cuba for the relinquishment of all Spanish rights in the island. This movement was made by the sugar planters, and it was thought that the entire sugar interest would support it. Mr. Blaine announced himself warmly in favor of the project, but after long conferences it was ascertained that the consent of Spain could not be obtained.

In truth, the pacification effected by Martinez Campos in 1878 was hardly efficient even as a truce. The reports of our consular agents, the testimony of travelers, the avowals made in the Spanish press, and the constant evidence almost daily recurring in the Cuban press, show that between 1878 and 1895 Cuba enjoyed little peace or repose. Brigandage, which was merely one form of public discontent, never ceased. Only the presence of a very large Spanish army prevented organized war.

The danger and the scandal of the Cuban situation have been such as can be compared with nothing but the condition of Armenia. So serious did they become, and so imminent was the peril, that in 1894-95 the Spanish Government at last adopted measures looking to the partial satisfaction of Cuban demands. These measures we need not discuss. They were held by the old insurgent party to be illusory and deceptive. Another attempt at independence was decided upon, and in February, 1895, the present "sanguinary and fiercely conducted war" broke out, "in some respects more active than the last preceding revolt." In thus characterizing the situation in Cuba as a state of war, President Cleveland, like Secretary Fish, has cleared the subject of all preliminary doubts. A state of war exists in Cuba. With that, and with that alone, we have to deal.

The precedents are clear, and if our action were to be decided by precedent alone, we should not be able to hesitate. The last great precedent was that of the civil war which broke out in the United States in the spring of 1861. In that instance, without waiting for the outbreak of actual hostilities, further than the bloodless attack on Fort Sumter and its surrender April 13, 1861, the British Government issued its proclamation of neutrality on the 13th of May following, before it had received official information that war existed, except as a blockade of certain insurgent ports. The French Government acted in concert with Great Britain, but delayed the official announcement until June. The Spanish Government issued its proclamation of belligerency June 17, and the first battle of our war was not fought until July 21, or known at Madrid until August.

In this great instance the outbreak of insurrection and the recognition of belligerency were simultaneous. The United States protested against the precipitancy of the act, and have never admitted its justice or legality, Neither in 1869 nor in 1895 did the President enforce the precedent against Spain in regard to the insurrection in Cuba. Not even in 1873, when the insurgents held possession of a great part of the island and seacoast, with no restraint but the blockade, did the United States recognize their belligerency.

Yet belligerency is a question of fact, and if declared at all it should be declared whenever the true character of neutrality requires it or the exigencies of law need it. The nature of such action may be political or legal, or both. As a political act, impartiality requires that belligerency should be recognized whenever, existing in fact, its denial is equivalent to taking part with one of the belligerents against the other. In such cases the unrecognized belligerent has just ground for complaint. The moral support of the neutral government is given wholly to its opponent. That the Cuban insurgents were belligerents in fact as early as 1869 was expressly stated by Mr. Fish when he explained the meaning he attached to his phrase regarding "the civil war now ravaging the island." The word "war" in such conditions necessarily implies the fact of belligerency. President Cleveland, in his annual message of last month, informs us that the present war is more active than the preceding one.

Nevertheless, our Government has still refrained from what Mr. Fish called "any public recognition of belligerent rights to the insurgents." No legal necessity arose to require it, and the political exigency was not absolute. Yet, after the victory of Bayamo, in the month of July last, when the insurgents defeated and nearly captured the Captain-General, Martinez Campos, and gained military possession of the whole eastern half of the island, the fact of their belligerency was established, and if further evidence was needed it was fully given by the subsequent victory at Coliseo, on the 24th of December, when the insurgents drove the Captain-General back to Habana and gained military control of the western provinces.

If the Government of the United States still refrained from recognizing the belligerency of the insurgents after this conclusive proof of the fact, the reason doubtless was that in the absence of any legal complications the question became wholly political, and that its true solution must lie not in a recognition of belligerency, but in a recognition of independence.

In 1875, when the situation was very far from being as serious as it is now, President Grant, after long consideration of the difficulties involved in public action, decided against the recognition of belligerency as an act which might be delusive to the insurgents and would certainly be regarded as unfriendly by Spain. He decided upon a middle course. The documents above quoted show that he proposed to the Spanish Government a sort of intervention which should establish the independence of Cuba by a friendly agreement. In doing so he not only necessarily recognized both parties to the conflict as on an equal plane, but he also warned Spain that if such mediation should not be accepted, direct intervention would probably be deemed a necessity on the part of the United States.

Spain preferred to promise to the insurgents terms so favorable as to cause for a time the cessation of hostilities. Since then twenty years have passed. The insurrection, far from having ceased, has taken the proportions of a war almost as destructive to our own citizens as to the contending parties. The independence of Cuba was then regarded by the President of the United States as the object of his intervention, and has now become far more inevitable than it was then. Evidently the Government of the United States can do no less than to take up the subject precisely where President Grant left it, and to resume the friendly mediation which he actually began, with all the consequences which necessarily would follow its rejection.

Confident that no other action than this accords with our friendly relations with Spain, our just sympathy with the people of Cuba, and with our own dignity and consistency, I recommend the following resolution to the consideration of the Senate:

"*Resolved*, That the President is hereby requested to interpose his friendly offices with the Spanish Government for the recognition of the independence of Cuba."

Mr. ALLEN. What order was made concerning the report of the Committee on Foreign Relations with reference to Cuba?

Mr. MORGAN. It goes to the Calendar.

Mr. ALLEN. And will be printed?

The VICE-PRESIDENT. The report will be printed, as well as the views of the minority.

* * * * * *

February 5, 1896.

Mr. MORGAN. On the 29th day of January I had the honor to report certain concurrent resolutions from the Committee on Foreign Relations relating to Cuba. That committee now direct me to report a resolution as a substitute for the previous report. I take the liberty of saying that I concur in the substitute of the committee, which I ask to have read.

The concurrent resolution reported as a substitute was read, as follows:

Resolved by the Senate (the House of Representatives concurring), That, in the opinion of Congress, a condition of public war exists between the Government of Spain and the government proclaimed and for some time maintained by force of arms by the people of Cuba; and that the United States of America should maintain a strict neutrality between the contending powers, according to each all the rights of belligerents in the ports and territory of the United States.

Mr. MORGAN. The report heretofore made as a declaration of facts, of course, will remain as a part of this report.

The VICE-PRESIDENT. What disposition does the Senator from Alabama ask to have made of the resolution now reported?

Mr. MORGAN. I merely ask that it be placed on the Calendar.

The VICE-PRESIDENT. The resolution will be placed on the Calendar.

Mr. CALL. I desire to give notice that I shall ask the Senate to take up for consideration the report made by the Committee on Foreign Relations in regard to Cuba as soon as I can get the attention of the Senate to the matter.

*   *   *   *   *   *   *

February 20, 1896.

Mr. MORGAN. Mr. President, this is an occasion which requires from Congress and the President the utmost degree of deliberation and circumspection. Great events may hinge upon our action here, events of great magnitude, considered with reference to the national expenditures of money and lives in the possible occurrence of war.

In the opening of my remarks I wish to say that after a calm and almost a reluctant examination of this very serious situation I believe the possibilities of a war with Spain growing out of our action ought to be discarded from our consideration, as affecting our action, because we shall not give to Spain any just cause of offense in anything that we may do, whether it is the recognition of the belligerency of Cuba or whether it is the recognition of the independence of that republic. We can neither abate nor avoid nor run away from duties that are incumbent upon us by considering what impression they may make upon any other country, provided the motive of our action is such as is required and justified by the demands of our own country by its historical facts and the reminiscences, traditions, and sentiments of our people.

We have not heretofore occupied, nor do we now occupy, an inimical position toward the Government of Spain. I do not use the word "hostile," because there is nothing approximating that thought in our present attitude or in our past history, except upon occasions when we have had cause of special complaint against her or she against us. We do not occupy now a position that is even inimical to Spain, and yet it must be admitted that Spanish monarchy is not a form of government, or that it has ruled in its colonial possessions in Cuba or elsewhere in South America, when it had sovereign powers on this hemisphere, in a way that is agreeable to our people. We do not, of course, admit that the Spanish monarchy, in its rule of its colonies, had the approbation or the affectionate regard of the American people in the past, or that it is likely in the future to meet with the approbation of a government like that of the United States and of people such as we have. We have our own institutions, our own surroundings, our own destiny, and our own means of accomplishing that destiny under the providence of God, and our responsibility as a nation is to the Great Ruler of Events, and secondarily to the opinion of the other nations of the earth.

So, in the consideration of this question, I hope it will be perfectly understood that the Committee on Foreign Relations, whose resolution I have the honor to advocate at this moment, have not been animated in the slightest degree by any sense of wrong or injustice intentionally done by the Spanish Government to the Government of the United States now or heretofore. There is nothing in our action that partakes in the least degree of retaliation. Our action is controlled, as far as we are able to shape it, entirely, as I have remarked, by the consideration of what is due to our own Government and our own people under a very peculiar relation that we hold to the government and people of Cuba.

In the consideration of this question the Committee on Foreign Relations have found themselves able to separate themselves entirely from all considerations except those which I have indicated as the basis of our action. When this Congress met, petitions and memorials from different persons and communities, from societies and legislatures of the States, flooded in upon the Senate and upon the House. They reached the table of the Senate and were referred to the Committee on Foreign Relations until they amounted to a great number.

The pressure of these various proceedings on the part of the people of the United States was very heavy upon both Houses, and doubtless upon the Executive also. The Committee on Foreign Relations of the Senate, not desirous of repressing or resisting these demands from the people of the United States, have still felt that the gravity of the occasion required them to give a very careful investigation to the whole question as far as we were in the possession of means to understand it. I must confess that the information which we possess on that subject is not perhaps official. It is in a large sense accurate; in my opinion, it is altogether credible. Yet it has been gathered from various sources, an important part of it from certain persons delegated by the government of the Republic of Cuba to visit the United States and to present to the Executive and to Congress a full statement of the actual situation in Cuba, both as to civil affairs and the military situation.

After patient examination of these various documents and comparing them with such information as we could gather from the statements in the public prints, to which credit was given by the press and the United States almost without dissent, the committee feel that they have reached a ground upon which they can stand firmly in presenting for the consideration of the Senate the action that is proposed in the resolution which has been presented to the Senate in behalf of the majority of the committee.

I think the demands of duty have been growing more serious upon the committee, as they have upon the Senate and upon the country, from day to day by a fuller and a better understanding of the actual situation as between Cuba and Spain. Surrounded as that island is by the Spanish navy and under the censorship exercised over all communications which have been permitted to come to the United States, it has only been occasionally that we have had the means of access to those private sources of information from which, after all, we can derive the truest view of the real situation in Cuba.

This embarrassment has retarded the committee in its action very properly; but we have not come before the Senate without being persuaded, fully persuaded, that we have quite sufficient

2777

information of an authentic and reliable character upon which to base the report that we have made.

Before going into the argument of that report I wish to make some statements in regard to the law upon this question. I would begin, Mr. President, by defining what is a state of belligerency when it is recognized by one government in favor of another, and what are the consequences of it. When any insurrection has grown to the magnitude of a public civil war and has so impressed itself upon other nations of the world as to convince them that they would be justified in recognizing the existence of a civil war, it then becomes the privilege and, in the Christian sense and in the sense of modern international law, the duty of civilized governments to recognize the state of belligerency as existing.

No nation can proceed against its own people in such a way as to hold them amenable to the pains and penalties of felony or piracy or ignominious punishment after those people, animated by a desire for liberty, have concentrated their efforts in the assemblage of large masses for the purpose of achieving liberty and independence, and have so far been able to concentrate and organize their power as to present important armies in the field of military exploit, such armies organized regularly under military law, divided into corps and other subordinate divisions of an army, reaching down to the company organization, and controlled by supreme military authority, as the ruling power and law of these collections of armed men are capable of conducting war and are entitled to the recognition that is accorded to regular armies in the laws of nations. When these things have attained to that degree, a man engaged in those ranks by enlistment changes his character from that of a felonious rebel or insurrectionist into the higher character of a soldier, and the civilized nations of the earth feel it incumbent upon them, in honor and in duty, to recognize that man as a soldier, entitled to the protection of the laws of civilized war. This is a direct purpose of the resolutions under discussion, and it has every sanction of justice and benevolence.

It must be remembered, Mr. President, that armies are composed, after all, not of officers alone, but of soldiery as well. They are led and commanded by officers, but the soldiers do the marching, bear the guns, do the fighting, fill the graves and the hospitals, and when they are captured fill the prisons.

It must also be remembered that governments de facto exist and are recognized the world over, and have been recognized for many ages, and that governments de facto, whether they are considered in the military or in the civil sense, while they have rule and supremacy in a certain area of country, have the right to demand the services of the people over whom they are instituted and to impose duties upon them to the extent of enlisting them in the armies, to the extent of taking their property for military purposes or government purposes, and even to the extent of commanding their allegiance and their support; and that the civilized nations of the earth extend to people thus put under the dominion of de facto power the correlative right of protection in their persons and property, without being held liable criminally for their acts of obedience to that government.

That is the same law, sir, that applies in civil and military establishments, and where any body of citizenship have collected together and armed and organized themselves into a military power, and they have dominion over a given area of country, the people who are within the influence of that dominion are justified, under the laws of nations everywhere, in rendering obedience and even support to that power. When a man enlists in an army thus constituted, which has the power of supreme authority in his vicinity, and he puts upon himself the insignia of a soldier, and takes his arms and makes his enlistment and swears his allegiance to the flag that is over him, as he can be compelled to do by a power that he can not resist, that man's character, in the eye of the laws of nations, changes from the private rebel or insurrectionist into that of a soldier, and he has the right to the protection that the laws of civilized warfare give to soldiery. The world has too much need of the services of the soldier to permit that service to subject him to the penalties of infamous punishment when he is captured in open war.

What is the consequence of the position I have just been attempting to discuss, if it be true? It is, of course, that a Cuban taken in arms, under the existing state of affairs in that island, is not amenable to trial and execution, we will say, by drum-head court-martial or by any summary proceeding, or any other proceeding. He can not be justly considered as being a felon—a man who has compromised his relations with his former Government to that extent that he is entitled only to bear the ignominy of a felonious conviction, with imprisonment for the remainder of his life, and his children doomed to follow him in wearing this stained garment of reputation.

This is the condition that Spain imposes upon native citizens who resist tyranny, in obedience to God, rather than endure it through fear of terrible personal sufferings. Driven to war by relentless oppression, the world is asked to deny them the rights that belong to armies in the field, because Spain chooses to denounce them as robbers.

If the Government of Spain could make up its mind to recognize the existence in Cuba of an insurrection, if they please to call it such, which has reached the proportions of a general civil war with organized armies, by that act they would place themselves in line with the opinion and conduct of other Christian powers and they would concede to the soldiery who might be in the Cuban army the rights of belligerency, just as was done during the period of the civil war in the United States. Neither party suffered from that course of civilized warfare. But Spain obstinately refuses to do this.

Is there any doubt, Mr. President, can there be any doubt, that the war in Cuba has attained to that magnitude in which it becomes the duty and the wisest policy of Spain to make this acknowledgment in behalf of the Cuban insurrectionists? There can be no doubt about it.

The President of the United States, in his last annual message to the Congress, describes this as a bloody war, a public war, no longer a mere insurrection, no longer a mob or an embroilment of citizens without organization, for the purpose of wreaking some revenge or for the purpose of displacing some officer who may be offensive to them in the civil or military government of Cuba; nothing of that kind. It is an open, public war, and the fact is so plain, so manifest, in the history of which we are perfectly cognizant, that the question does not admit of debate.

We, therefore, in the progress of our consideration of this question, can advance to that ground with absolute confidence that this is a public war, and that in this public war it is the duty of

Spain to make a concession in favor of the other belligerents to the effect that the people who are engaged in that army by regular enlistment are soldiers and shall have the treatment of soldiers.

If Spain should do such a thing as that, Mr. President, that would be a recognition by the sovereign of the belligerent rights of these people who are fighting against her flag and fighting for their independence; and in that view there would be no occasion, certainly no necessity, for the Government of the United States or any other government to interfere for the purpose of securing to the soldiery in those armies the benefits, whatever they may be, of civilized warfare. Spain has not done this; Spain does not intend to do this. Spain fills to repletion her prison in Africa with persons captured out of the army of the rebels; she fills Morro Castle, Puerto Cabaños, and all other prisons of which she has the control with these victims caught from the other army, who are taken when caught and by a summary process are condemned to life servitude in these terrible prisons, if, indeed, they are permitted to live.

If we are ever called in question for making a humane declaration in favor of these victims, we shall be, fortunately, supported by an array of facts that will call forth the sympathies of all Christendom. As the action we propose is based on justice and our regard for human rights, our sympathy for the oppressed needs not to be justified at this time by a recital of all their wrongs and sufferings.

Spain inflicts upon them penalties under the name of law which their crimes would not deserve, even if they were individuals engaged separate and apart, or in little squads, in insurrection against the Government of Spain; but being soldiers, and having enlisted in a place and at a time and under circumstances and for purposes which recommend them to the fair and favorable consideration of mankind, it becomes the duty of the civilized governments of the world, so far as they are able to effect or accomplish anything in that direction, to say to Spain: "We recognize the belligerent rights of the people under arms in that country who call themselves citizens of the Republic of Cuba."

I trust that I have brought out in this way, in rather simple form, the real ground upon which the United States and every other country has the right to intervene to the extent, at least, that this resolution proposes. It is in behalf of mercy: it is in behalf of justice; in this particular case it is in behalf of liberty, and, more than that, it is in behalf of the kind of liberty which we enjoy; it is in behalf of that kind of liberty where the people themselves furnish the governing power and where they dispute the right of monarchy to govern them at will and pleasure. So there is everything in the situation of the case which is attractive to the American people to induce us to occupy that ground which is justified, not merely by our predilections or our sympathies, but that ground which is justified by the laws of warfare; modern, civilized war, as it is described in the books on international law.

I therefore assume, Mr. President, without stopping to debate it particularly, that the Government of the United States has the right, and that it is our duty, and that it accords with our sentiments, and that it justly stirs the blood in our veins when we make this declaration and say to Spain: "You have long enough lacerated these people in your efforts to destroy them under the plea of quelling insurrection. Now they are entitled to belligerent rights, and we intend, so far as we are concerned, to give them that recognition by expressing our opinion here that they are so entitled; and when we have made that recognition, we intend to be bound hereafter, just as we have been in the past, by our own laws and also by the laws of the nations of the earth—the international law—to maintain perfect neutrality between these recognized belligerents, doing no favor to either that is not permitted by the laws of war, by international law, and denying to neither of them the privileges which they have the right to enjoy as belligerent powers." That is our attitude.

I now come back to the first proposition with which I started out: Can Spain rightfully assume that in our taking that course on an occasion like this there is any menace against her or any act which is inimical to her dignity and power, her jurisdiction, or her sovereignty? No; and if she desires to take offense where none is intended, and none is really given, all that we can say is, "You will have to take offense; but we had rather that you would take offense at our attitude as a Government than that the God of nations and the human family should take offense at our silence and our indifference in the presence of this wrong. We have got to choose an attitude here which you have forced upon us by your misgovernment in Cuba, or otherwise we shall not take that position which is becoming to a great Republic and an honest, upright, and courageous people; and, having taken that attitude without enmity toward you, if you choose to embroil us on that account, why, simply we can not help it. You embroil us, if you ever do so, because we do our plain duty, and no more."

We must determine for ourselves whether it is just that we should accord, on our part, and under our laws, the rights of civilized warfare to a great body of people in Cuba who have resisted the whole power of Spain for more than a year and increase in numbers and military strength with every day that passes.

I now come to the consideration of what would be our position when we recognize the belligerency of the Cuban Republic, for that is what I style it, that is what they style it themselves, and I think, before I get through with my argument, I shall show that they have ample reason for calling themselves, with proud satisfaction, the Republic of Cuba, for, if it be not now a republic in full development and in the majesty of power which it seems destined to enjoy some day, it may be another Moses in his basket among the bullrushes, and after a while it will come to light, and the world will rejoice in the presence of that new republic.

We have a number of remarkably stringent statutes upon our statute book for the protection of other countries surrounding us, by enforcing upon our people the doctrines of international law, which are called neutrality. One who reads our statute book and compares it with that of almost any other country in the world, I think, will be surprised at the stringency with which we guard against the interference of our people in any war which may take place in any country foreign to us. We have had on both sides of us nations which we have been compelled to protect by these statutes—Canada on the north, Mexico on the southwest, and more particularly Cuba on the south. This code of laws, strong and urgent and stringent as it is, was never suggested to the Congress of the United States by the enmity of our people toward any other nation in the world.

It is not our inherent trouble, it is not the drift of our people in the direction of maraud and robbery and interference with foreign governments which has caused this legislation to be placed upon the statute book. We have a conservative people, a law-abiding, lawmaking, law-loving people; and when you place a question of foreign relations or foreign troubles or difficulties before the mind of an American, you always find him looking at it with cool circumspection, ready to participate when duty demands it, but not ready to participate as a mere filibuster or as a mere aggressor upon the rights of foreign people. That is not a characteristic of our people that these statutes were put upon the statute book to hold in check or to correct. If we had been as insular as Great Britain, we should have needed none of those statutes with which to control our people. These laws have been put upon our statute book for the protection of our neighbors.

It has been, I think, only on one occasion, or perhaps two, that we have had any necessity for resorting to them in reference to our relations with Canada. We have had more frequent necessity to appeal to those laws in our relations with Mexico, but a still more frequent and still more painful necessity of appealing to them with reference to our relations with Cuba. This graduation of the necessity we have been under of applying these laws is a sufficient indication of our appreciation and that of our people at large of the characteristics of those Governments.

People who conduct good government have the friendship of the American people, while those who rule tyrannically incur their displeasure.

Canada is self-governing; she has a race of people very much like ourselves, very close akin to us. Mexico differs from Canada in that respect; and in consequence of some misfortunes, which crept into her constitution, and which she has only recently gotten rid of, Mexico has been so often in such a state of turbulence that it was necessary that the Government of the United States should exercise extraordinary supervision over her own people to keep them from going down there and participating in the insurrections and rebellions which have so often occurred.

When we get to Cuba, Mr. President, an island which is accessible only by the sea, guarded by a great monarchy, our people, when they have invaded or attempted to invade that island, have not gone there for the purpose of robbery. They have not gone there because they wanted to impose our institutions upon Cuba. Very few Americans, indeed, even the wildest of them, and in the most exaggerated condition of what I might call their covetousness of power and wealth, have ever thought about going to Cuba for the purpose of acquiring it and annexing it to the United States. While our people desire the independence of Cuba, very few of them desire its annexation.

Why is it, then, that we have had to keep these laws on the statute book, and that every time an outbreak has occurred in Cuba the first thing which has been done by the President of the United States was to issue a most radical proclamation, warning our people and forbidding them in the strongest possible manner from going into the Island of Cuba and from violating our laws intended to prevent them from doing so? What has caused this? It has been, on every occasion, some wrong done by Spain to the Cuban people, the recognition of which we could not shut out from our own consciences and our own hearts. We have stood here as a guard, as a picket post, as an outline of defense of the Monarchy of Spain through the medium of these laws and the proclamations of Presidents of the United States for very nearly a century, during which period of time five great insurrections or revolts have occurred in Cuba.

What has it cost us thus to guard a people whose resentments have been so justly excited, but are reluctant to interfere with foreigners or with foreign Governments? What has it cost us to keep in check and hold down the Cuban refugees who have come to the United States from time to time, driven out of the islands by the stress of persecution? Think of the lives of American citizens that have been sacrificed; think of the men who have been leaned up against adobe walls before sunrise in the morning and shot to death by Spain because, following their sympathies, they felt that they could go to Cuba and give a helping hand to their relatives, their own blood kindred, in the Island of Cuba, who went there, as Lopez did, for the purpose of relieving his own relatives from these barbarities.

What has it cost us? In money, Mr. President, a very large sum; in blood, a very great treasure; in anguish of feeling, an unutterable thing; in national distress, great discomfort; in our commercial relations with Cuba, and even with other parts of the earth, immense losses; in the honor of our flag, frequent searches and visitations, outrageous wrong, which we have put up with for the time being rather than to resent, because we preferred peace to war, although there might have been an occasion when we should have been entirely justified in going to war. That is what it has cost us; that is what it is costing us now. The record of our losses and of our sufferings and of our wrongs, wrongs to our own people which have been inflicted upon them through the cruelties of Spanish dominion in Cuba, is a record which, if it were written up consecutively, would astonish the world.

Mr. President, if the Island of Cuba were as close to Great Britain as it is to the United States and the same wrongs had been done there that have been perpetrated against our neighbor, who can fail to understand what would have been the fate of Cuba? Great Britain would have absorbed her a century ago or more. She would have said to herself as she has said in respect to Ireland, but with extreme injustice with regard to Ireland, "You have a rich country that we need; you have a people who are incapable of self-government, refractory, turbulent, and rebellious, and the best thing that Great Britain can do is to take you into the Kingdom and govern you, discrown your king, hang your martyrs, break down your constitution and the traditions of the past, and take you into our lordly bosom." If Cuba had occupied the geographical relation to Great Britain, France, or Germany that she occupies to the United States, long ago she would have disappeared from the list of Spanish colonies, and she would have belonged to some great ruling, energetic, Christian power.

Mr. GRAY. Does the Senator from Alabama like our policy better?

Mr. MORGAN. The Senator from Delaware asks me if I like our policy better. I like it better, provided that our temporizing is not to be protracted until Cuba is destroyed and until our self-respect is gone. I think there is a moment of time—perhaps that moment has arrived—when we have to determine that question for ourselves. Perhaps the moment now is when the American people ought to say to themselves: "It is high time that those people in Cuba had a government under which they could at least exist."

Now, our attitude toward Cuba and toward Spain has been one entirely innocent. It has been forbearing; it has been just and upright, and there is no ground for accusation against us. The only ground of accusation that exists in regard to our attitude toward Spain and Cuba is that we have forborne to do perhaps in the past what we should have done, to the great wrong of the people of Cuba and particularly to that large and respectable class of people who have been driven by those revolutions into the United States seeking hospitality.

I wish to speak a moment about those people who have come to the United States under the invitation of this Government upon its doctrines of expatriation and of naturalization. They have in good faith united in our citizenship; they have adopted our flag as the flag of their country; they have sworn allegiance to the Constitution of our country, and when war has prevailed here, or the exigencies of the Government have demanded any other great sacrifice, they have come along as willingly as any of us, and have contributed to the power and the honor and the glory of the United States. As citizens in time of peace, the Cubans, who, perhaps, mostly reside in the larger cities of the United States, have been citizens of eminent respectability and propriety of conduct.

I do not remember any Cuban who has been called to account in the courts of the United States or elsewhere for disloyalty to the Government of this country. They are not to be accounted among the rabble or the outcasts of society. Many of them have transferred their property to this country—what remnant of it was left—and have started in upon business engagements here of an honorable character. Many of them have left behind the titles that they wore under the Spanish Monarchy and in Cuba, and have cheerfully abandoned the distinctions which made them prominent among their own class of people, in order to accept the plain equality of the democracy and the republicanism of the United States. They have come in great numbers, and not one of them has set his foot upon these shores who has not had extended to him a hand of welcome and a heart beating with cordial regard, for this is the land of the persecuted refugee. It is a land to which all the oppressed of the earth may come with perfect assurance that when they have planted their feet upon our soil they have got home to the land of liberty.

These people have come in great numbers. Some of the most eminent men, not politically, but in science and in business and in law, are found among the Cuban circles who have been driven out of Cuba and who have taken refuge in the United States. I have great respect for them. Martin Kozsta had no firmer hold upon the heart of Daniel Webster than a man like Menocal has upon my heart to-day. When those people have ventured to go back to their own country occasionally, they have been subjected to violence and imprisonment and confiscation and the like by the Spanish Government out of a spirit of mere anger, resentment, and retaliation. That is not among the least of the evils that we have had to put up with or overlook on behalf of the Cubans who have been here.

To-day Spain has more animosity toward us on their account than on account of everything else. These men can traverse this country from one end to another; they can raise money for the relief of the people of Cuba; they can send it to them. They can discuss the situation in Cuba with perfect freedom. They can discuss and understand the restrictions of our laws upon them and render cheerful and perfect obedience to them. But the Spanish Government regards the liberty that we have accorded to them in holding their meetings and conventicles and in passing their resolutions or adopting their programmes in behalf of the people of Cuba as an offense that is intolerable to the mind and heart of a Spanish ruler. For that reason they, of course, grow more and more angry toward us continually, and that is the true ground of the opposition of Spain to the United States.

Spain would be the best friend to us that we have in the world if whenever a Cuban refugee undertakes to land in one of our ports we should drive him back to the sea and tell him to seek a home elsewhere. But we open our doors to him; he comes in here, and when he gets here he comes, it is true, as an enemy of Spain, but Spain becomes our enemy because we tolerate in our midst somebody who does not happen to like her. That is the situation. We give no encouragement to any ill feeling toward Spain, but accord to our citizens, native or adopted, the right to love Spain or to abhor her according to their free will. Justice, as it is enforced by public opinion, will temper such feelings, but force can not crush them out.

Now, Mr. President, these laws to which I have referred, after we have passed the concurrent resolution, will remain precisely what they are now. They will not be changed in the least, nor will any other law of the United States be changed, although there will be a new application of some of the international laws to a situation created by this act of recognition. That is all. The laws will not be changed anywhere, but a new application of them will thus be made.

Mr. PLATT. Will the Senator from Alabama allow me?

Mr. MORGAN. Certainly.

Mr. PLATT. Does the Senator understand that the passage of the pending concurrent resolution by the two Houses without its sanction by the President amounts to anything? Does he understand that it amounts to a recognition of belligerent rights?

Mr. MORGAN. I think it does, if the concurrent resolution is adopted. I do not deny the delicacy of that question, nor do I deny the fact that we have never settled it by a statute in the United States. That question is left open simply as a constitutional question, and the measure of the rights of Congress and of the President of the United States in respect to it is found only in the Constitution. What the proper interpretation of that instrument is as bearing upon the particular right or matter that the Senator from Connecticut suggests is something not really necessary in this debate, because the form of the resolution is not such as to evoke the question.

Nevertheless, if it becomes necessary, or if the Senate of the United States desires to pass a resolution of the actual recognition of the independence of Cuba on this occasion, then we would have to give consideration necessarily to the question whether a recognition by a concurrent vote of the two Houses would be a full recognition or whether the President of the United States must participate in the act before it becomes a full recognition.

Mr. HALE. Does the Senator from Alabama have any doubt that the passage of such a resolution as he has indicated, recognizing the independence of this assumed republic, would result immediately in a suspension of friendly diplomatic relations, the withdrawal of the Spanish minister, with the near probability of being involved in hostilities? Does not the Senator think that such a resolution would be a distinctive act in the direction of a probable war?

Mr. MORGAN. I remarked in the opening of my speech that this question had grown upon us, that we had approached it, I confessed I approached it, reluctantly because of its magnitude, because of the ultimate consequences that might follow it, and I think I will take the liberty of saying to the Senate what I said to the Committee on Foreign Relations on that question when this matter came up.

Mr. HALE. I am sure we will be glad to hear the Senator from Alabama.

Mr. MORGAN. Here was a great mass of petitions and memorials to which we had to make some answer. We had to report them back adversely and ask to be discharged from the further consideration of the question, or else we had to do something in the direction at least of the recognition of the belligerent rights of the Cubans. How far we should go was, of course, a matter left for after consideration.

Mr. HOAR. The Senator from Alabama has yielded to other Senators, and I should like to ask him a practical question. Suppose the pending resolution is passed by the concurrent action of the two Houses, not going to the President, what right or duty appertains to an American citizen after its passage which does not appertain to an American citizen before its passage, and what right belongs to a Cuban insurgent after its passage that he did not possess before?

Mr. MORGAN. It is a part of my duty, before I can lay this matter properly before the Senate, although it may require some prolixity of speech to do so, to take up the question suggested by the honorable Senator from Massachusetts [Mr. HOAR], and also the one suggested by the honorable Senator from Connecticut [Mr. PLATT].

Mr. PLATT. I do not think I made myself exactly clear. The question which I wish to have answered is whether the passage of this resolution by the two Houses of Congress, without the action of the Executive, amounts to according to the insurgents or patriots, as they may be called, in Cuba belligerent rights?

Mr. MORGAN. That will depend on the wording of the resolution. The question put to me by the Senator from Maine [Mr. HALE] involves the very consideration of the question whether——

Mr. PLATT. If I may be permitted still further, we understand that when the President, under such circumstances, issues a proclamation of neutrality, which is the ordinary form in which belligerent rights are accorded, certain rights attach to the people who are struggling, and certain obligations attach to the United States.

Now, what I wish to know is whether those same rights attach to the Cuban people and the same obligations attach to the people of the United States and the Government of the United States upon the passage of this resolution just as if it were an Executive act, performed by the President.

Mr. MORGAN. I can not leave the floor without answering, if I am able to do so, the questions propounded by each of the honorable Senators.

Mr. CALL. Mr. President——

Mr. MORGAN. I hope the Senator from Florida will let me go on without further interruption, inasmuch as I have before me a large field of questions to answer.

Mr. FRYE. I hope the Senator from Alabama will preserve the distinction between the question asked by my colleague and the one asked by the Senator from Massachusetts [Mr. HOAR].

Mr. MORGAN. The question propounded to me by the colleague of the honorable Senator from Maine [Mr. FRYE] is the one I propose to answer first. I was proceeding to do so by a statement of the attitude which I held on this question when it was first presented to the Committee on Foreign Relations.

When the petitions had to be considered and had to be reported adversely, with a request that we might be discharged from their further consideration, or else we had to take the other side of the question and find that we could and should pass a resolution in some form recognizing belligerency in Cuba, I said to the Committee on Foreign Relations: "I contemplate war at the end of any resolution that we pass in that direction, not that it would be just, not that there would be the slightest excuse for it, but because Spain is in such a condition, her animosities against us are so excited, her jealousy and her pride are so extreme, and I will add also absolutely inexcusable in the light of reason, that I feel that it makes no difference what steps we take, Spain will make it the occasion of belligerent action toward us." I therefore accepted the situation, whenever I took a step in that direction—it made no difference how long or how short it was—that it would ultimately result in war.

I said then, and I repeat, that I believe Spain to-day would be under obligations to us for giving her a cause of war in regard to Cuba. Why? Because Spain knows just as well as the rest of mankind knows that the fetters with which she has bound Cuba since Columbus made the discovery of it, and particularly in the last century or century and a half, have corroded until they are rusting off the limbs of those people. They have got to be inconvenient in the respect of the civilized world.

To give an illustration of it I will say there was a certain sort of shackle in use at the time when Christopher Columbus was occupying the Spanish provinces which he discovered here. The shackles were particularly heavy, and were worn upon the limbs of Spaniards when they were in durance under the law, military or civil. A very eminent Spanish artist painted Columbus as he was wearing those shackles when he was being taken from the Island of Cuba bact to Spain to answer for imaginary offenses. He was taken back a prisoner upon a Spanish ship to answer at the Spanish court for supposed offenses against the Crown of Spain. The shackles were painted there.

That picture was brought here to be exhibited at the World's Fair in Chicago, and the men who controlled the exhibitions from the Government of Spain refused to let the picture go on exhibition unless the artist would paint out the shackles. Why? Because it was an evidence of what barbarism existed in Spain at the time when Columbus was taken and put on that ship. He painted them out. The picture went back to Cuba, and the friends of this artist rose upon him and denounced him for his cowardice. He admitted it, but said: "Who is not a coward who stands in front of the Monarch of Spain? Give me a brush and I will paint them back." And he did, and there they are now, but they are only in paint.

Now, the very shackles that Spain has laid upon the limbs of the Cubans have become disreputable even in the contemplation of Spain herself, but her pride causes her to hold this poor slave by the throat. She can not consent, with her imperious and monarchic ideas, to lift her bloody hands from the neck of this victim and accord to that poor slave the rights of man, sanctified in the name of constitutional liberty. She can not afford to do it, and she is not going to do it, and yet she can not hold Cuba. If this revolution does not free the Cubans from the grasp of Spain, the next one will, or the next.

The revolutions have gone on now during all of this century, increasing in proportions and in power, each one making a step further in the direction of this happy release. There will be one more if this does not succeed, or one more if that does not succeed, and Cuba will come forward, amidst the pæans of the nations, free, sovereign, and independent. Spain knows it. Spain feels it. She is bound to recognize it. She would rather lose Cuba at the point of the sword when in conflict with the United States than to have us pay for it or to have those Cubans achieve their independence. She would thank us to take it off her hands with the point of the sword.

That is the reason why I say I have believed that any step in this direction would only anticipate the results that are bound to come in a very short time when Spain will find herself dismantled of her colonial strength on the American Hemisphere, as she has heretofore been by the combination of the great republics from Mexico to Patagonia from 1810 to 1830.

Spain has had no real, legitimate right to hold the province of Cuba and deny to her a voice in her own government after Mexico and Venezuela and Colombia and the South and Central American States were free. If Cuba had been occupied by people who in their hearts were as free and as strong as the people of Mexico, or the Central Americans, or the people of Colombia, or the Venezuelans were at the time they declared their independence, it is impossible to conceive that Cuba would have remained in the clutches of Spain. Why did she not? It was because at the time the revolutions took place in the other countries around Cuba she was dominated by a very few men who had their large plantations filled with slaves. She had no free population and none that were capable of aspiring to liberty at that time.

Mexico, when she achieved her independence, and every State down to the Antarctic Ocean, declared in their original constitutions, and held to their declaration irrevocably, that slavery should never exist in those countries. All declared it. Cuba could not make that declaration. She did not have the people. Her population were not up to the idea because the vast mass of her people then were slaves, else at the time these other Republics escaped from bondage to Spain Cuba would have released herself.

Now the situation is different. Now the slaves have been emancipated. The ten years' war of which we have been speaking here to-day was chiefly for the emancipation of those slaves. The very men emancipated at the end of that war have become soldiers in the Cuban army. They are fighting for higher liberties and to increase the standard of that liberty so that it shall amount to the right of self-government. That is the situation.

Therefore I hope the Senator from Maine will understand that in all I have done about this Cuban imbroglio I have acted with great reluctance. I have acted with the reluctance of a man who with his associates is compelled to take a very important position, what under ordinary circumstances might be called a very hazardous position, in the contemplation of actual war, without giving any just cause of offense to Spain. I have acted in full view of the fact that at the beginning of this controversy it was our business to discount the future, and to draw our sword and lay it upon the table and say to Spain, "If you want to take it up, take it up."

Mr. President, I think it is incumbent upon me as the Senator in charge of this measure on behalf of the committee to enter somewhat more fully than I have been able to do this afternoon upon a consideration of the facts, particularly those that relate to the organization of the Republic of Cuba and the progress of the war. I feel that I am scarcely able—I have had a very hard day's work—to complete this task this evening.

Mr. HOAR. If the Senator is going to yield the floor for to-day——

The PRESIDING OFFICER (Mr. BACON in the chair). Does the Senator from Alabama yield to the Senator from Massachusetts?

Mr. MORGAN. I am perfectly willing to yield for to-day.

Mr. HOAR. If the Senator is desirous to continue another day, as he has intimated, I should like to call his attention to what I had in mind when I put him the question before. No man can read the story of a Spanish war against anybody without having his whole nature stirred by the emotions which were so eloquently uttered by my colleague. No American, no decent man on the face of the earth, can help that feeling. But after all, when the Congress of the United States is to do something on such a matter with such consequences as the Senator conceives, we ought to do it with a full comprehension of what we are about, and we look to the great committee of which that eminent Senator was so long chairman, and of which he is now so influential a member, to instruct us practically and exactly in what we are doing.

The Senator from Pennsylvania [Mr. CAMERON] in his very quiet speech (but into which a great deal of meaning was crowded in a very few sentences) said that this declaration, supposing it takes effect, according belligerent rights to the Cubans, is to have two effects, and two only. One is that it gives Spain belligerent rights at sea, so that not merely being at war in putting down a rebellion that is a little too strong for the constable, but being at war with another power which we have admitted is an equal power to her in the rights of war, she may search our ships under the right of a belligerent, under certain circumstances, at sea. Of course such a right would also belong to the Cubans, but they have not got any ships and it is valueless to them. Next, as I understood the Senator from Pennsylvania, he said the further effect is to release Spain from any obligation for injuries caused to the very large property of the numerous American citizens in Cuba.

Mr. MORGAN. After the declaration.

Mr. HOAR. After the declaration. The Cuban belligerents can not pay for such injuries if they inflict them, and they never would be expected to do it hereafter if they gained their independence.

Mr. TELLER. The Cubans are as able to do so as Spain.

Mr. HOAR. Whether they are as able as Spain or not is another question. So she is released; because this happened to our citizens in a war and not by acts of lawlessness in a country with whom we are at peace. Now, those two things the Senator from Pennsylvania——

Mr. TELLER. Mr. President——

Mr. HOAR. I wish the Senator from Colorado would pardon me.

Mr. TELLER. I should like to ask the Senator a question.

Mr. HOAR. No; I do not want to answer a question; I want to put one.

Mr. TELLER. Very well.

Mr. HOAR. The Senator from Pennsylvania said with great force that those are the two things which are to come from a recognition of belligerency. Now, is there anything else which is to come from it?

Mr. MORGAN. Yes; one very important matter.

Mr. HOAR. Is there anything which is going to do those Cubans, those insurrectionists, any good? I do not speak now of an expression of good will, but I speak of the practical result. What help is it to be?

In the next place, the other question which has arisen in my mind—and it has also occurred to several other Senators—is, What is the effect on the obligations, duties, or rights of an American citizen, or on the obligations, duties, or rights of a Cuban insurrectionist, of a recognition of belligerency by the two Houses of Congress not signed or agreed to by the President of the United States?

In putting these questions I am not expressing my own opinion. I put them as a learner, and I put them with a very earnest desire to agree with the Senator from Alabama and those of his colleagues who have spoken on this subject. I wanted to call the attention of the Senator from Alabama to them now, so that when he goes on, if he thinks they are worth dealing with he may do so. They are things that are, in my mind at least, points for instruction.

Mr. MORGAN. I will interpose a very brief answer.

Mr. TELLER. Will the Senator allow me to ask him a question?

Mr. MORGAN. Allow me to answer the one put to me by the Senator from Massachusetts, and then I will hear the Senator's.

Mr. TELLER. In this connection I wanted the Senator from Massachusetts to add the further question whether the recognition on our part of belligerent rights changes the obligations of Spain with reference to, say, our own people who may be there. Is it not a question of fact to be determined, whether it is flagrant war or not?

Mr. CALL. Will the Senator from Alabama——

Mr. MORGAN. I can not afford to yield to the Senator from Florida—I am something more than a mere target for interrogatories.

Mr. CALL. In this connection I think the Senator from Alabama would like to read what I have in my hand here.

Mr. MORGAN. I have my own answer, which I will undertake to give in a very few words, with a view of elaborating it when I next take the floor; but I want now to present my answer in a few words to the Senator from Massachusetts, which he has courteously asked me for.

The last question asked by the Senator from Massachusetts he will find answered in the form and language of the resolution which we have reported. It is fully answered in the form and language of the resolution of the Committee on Foreign Relations.

As to the preceding question, as to the right of search, I will state that the right of search exists on the part of any country that is engaged in open war with an adversary. If the Spanish Government found that an American ship was destined for a Cuban port, it would have the right, outside of the 3-mile limit, to make a certain search of that ship.

Mr. HOAR. In case of war?

Mr. MORGAN. In case of a recognition of belligerency, as if they were at war. Now, what would that search be? It would be controlled by two things. Spain would have a responsibility about that search; she must make no mistake about it; just as a private man can not arrest another one for felony, and if he is mistaken about it he can not escape damages. There is more than that about it. We have got our own statutes here for the protection of our customs. We send ships out by our statutes 12 miles to sea to examine and search ships that are destined for ports in the United States, and that is considered to be not only a civil remedy, but a very excellent one, for protection against smuggling. Spain would have the belligerent right, under the laws of nations, to send her ships out and search our ships or any ships destined to Cuban ports, if you please, and see whether they were carrying contraband of war. If they are found not to be carrying contraband of war, they are not amenable to arrest, yet the search may be rightful under the laws of war.

Now, another element comes in there which I beg to call to the attention of the Senator from Massachusetts, and that is the reason why I am making these remarks now, for I want to call the Senator's attention to our treaty relations with Spain. Under the treaty of 1795, a general treaty of commerce which is now in full force in the particular to which I am alluding, there is a restriction put upon her right of search of our ships in time of war. It does not make any difference who the war is with, whether with one of her own provinces or some foreign country. What is that restriction? It is that she shall not approach an American ship nearer than within gunshot, and there she shall stop and call the American ship to stop and send a boat out with not more than a definite number of persons—I think it is three or four—to examine the cargo of that ship to see whether or not there is anything contraband upon it.

Now, that treaty obligation remains, our treaty obligations with Spain remain, notwithstanding we may recognize the belligerency of the Cubans. That same treaty of 1795 outrode her recognition of the Confederate States and is still valid. It had no impression on it. So there it stands and regulates, so far as Spain is concerned, as between her and the United States, her right of search. That is now the limitation which is placed upon it by the treaty as well as by the international law, and that, I think, is an answer to the Senator.

Mr. HOAR. If the Senator will pardon me, I am afraid I did not quite make my question clear. My question was not whether the right of search was a severe, onerous one or not. My question was whether the recognition of belligerency did not give it to Spain, whatever it was, and she did not have it without——

Mr. MORGAN. It certainly has not.

Mr. HOAR. And what else it gave to anybody. That is, what is there, except the sentimental side of it, by which a recognition of belligerency operates, except to give two things to Spain? One is the right of search, which she had not before, and the other the

2777

exemption from the obligation for her mischief done on the Island of Cuba to our citizens' property, which she might, as the Senator from Colorado well suggests, be responsible for in a clear case of flagrant war.

Mr. TELLER. She might escape responsibility.

Mr. HOAR. She might escape responsibility. In other words, if we go to Spain and say, "Mr. Atkins's sugar plantation, worth $250,000 or $1,000,000, was destroyed in the Island of Cuba, and your police and authorities did not protect it as you should; now pay up," Spain would have the right to say, "You have admitted yourself a condition of things which exonerated me from any obligation to protect that property," while, if we do not declare the belligerency, it is a question of fact to be inquired into hereafter.

Mr. TELLER. She would have to prove it.

Mr. HOAR. She would have to prove it. What I want to know is not the extent of these two rights—I think we all probably understand those—but whether there is anything else under the sun that this resolution is operative to produce, supposing it to be binding on the Government of the United States without the assent of the President? That is my question.

Mr. MORGAN. There is one thing: At the present time, while that island is held by Spain to be in insurrection, she can prohibit the entry of our vessels into the island, and she can punish our people if she finds them there trading with these belligerents, and the laws of the United States would prohibit our people from trafficking with the people of Cuba in articles of contraband. We make the declaration of neutrality, and our people using these articles as merchandise and for mercantile purposes, powder, shot, cannons, wagons, or what not, would have the perfect right to leave our shores and proceed to Cuba and trade with the Cuban rebels if they can escape the blockade and escape detection, and Spain could not do anything with them. Spain could not arrest our people after they had gone in there and sold the product, whatever it might be.

In other words, the declaration of neutrality between these two powers, or assumed powers, would give to the people of the United States the free right of traffic, subject only to be caught by Spain. That is a very great advantage. It is not an advantage that I would give to the rebels in Cuba at all if they were a mere set of insurrectionists and the question was how much money we could make out of them, but it is an advantage which when moved by my sympathies I would not withhold from them.

Mr. PLATT. The Senator is very kind; but if he will permit me once more, it seems to me that the question I asked goes deeper than all these questions as to what the rights of the parties would be after belligerency. It is whether the passage of this resolution in itself amounts to according belligerent rights. If it is a mere resolution of sympathy, we might do that by saying that the two Houses of Congress sympathize with the Cuban patriots in their efforts to establish the independence of Cuba. Now, if it means only that, it is one thing. If it means that we, the two Houses of Congress, can by this action, in fact, recognize on the part of the Government of the United States the belligerency of those parties, then it is a very much more serious thing.

Mr. MORGAN. I will refer the Senator again to the language of this resolution, which has been very carefully drawn. If he will refer to that language, I think he will discover that the action of the House and Senate, if the resolution shall be adopted just as it is, amounts to an absolute and irrevocable declaration in favor of belligerency and neutrality, and in favor of the Republic of Cuba.

Mr. PLATT. Then the question arises whether the two Houses can do that.

Mr. MORGAN. Then that would be a question as to whether the two Houses in passing a bill have the right to instruct the President of the United States as the Commander-in-Chief of the Army and Navy to see that its will in regard to war is executed, and that would throw it back to where I suggested when I first set out—to a question which, not being regulated by statute, as it ought to be regulated by statute, is a question which must look for its solution alone to the Constitution of the United States; and there is no other source of law or power and no regulator in that case except the Constitution of the United States.

Mr. PLATT. I wish to say that I think there is, to say the least, very great doubt as to whether the action of the two Houses alone can change in any sense our relation with other countries.

Mr. MORGAN. Perhaps the Senator from Connecticut will be prepared to admit that there is still greater doubt as to whether the action of the President of the United States, Congress being in session, can change the relation of the people of the United States to Spain. There might be still greater doubt. It is a question, after all, that has to be settled, I will remark again, by a proper consideration of the bearing of the Constitution of the United States upon it; and there is no other law that controls it.

Mr. FRYE. What is the Senator's own opinion?

Mr. MORGAN. My opinion is that Congress has the perfect, independent, absolute right to make this recognition of belligerency or a declaration of independence, and if it is necessary to enforce it by any military movement at sea or on land, it has the right to command the Commander-in-Chief of the Army and Navy to go on the field if it is necessary and in person to see to the execution of that order. That is my opinion. [Applause in the galleries.]

The PRESIDING OFFICER. The occupants of the galleries must preserve order.

Mr. MORGAN. I do not understand, after the Congress of the United States declares that war exists between this country and Spain, for instance, that the President of the United States by vetoing that declaration can make it peace.

Mr. PLATT. There is no doubt but that Congress can declare war. There is no doubt about that.

Mr. MORGAN. If it can, then there is great doubt whether the President, by vetoing that declaration, can make it peace. It is either peace or war, the one or the other. But I never have thought that the Commander-in-Chief of the Army of the United States could refuse to go into the field and lead the armies because he did not want to fight, if we ordered him to do it. I never have thought that. This resolution, however, is in such form that if it is passed, the President of the United States will be required to communicate to these two Governments, and then the subsequent question may possibly concern us no more. I do not know.

Mr. PLATT. But this is not a declaration of war.

Mr. MORGAN. No; it is not a declaration of war. There is no war in it.

Mr. PLATT. It is a declaration that war exists somewhere else.

Mr. MORGAN. That is right; and all that Congress can do is

to declare that war exists. Congress can not make war by joint resolution, nor can Congress and the President make war by joint resolution. War is first of all a legal situation; secondly, it is belligerency. It divides itself into two separate and distinct parts. One gives an attitude to the people and Government of the United States, and the other gives an attitude to the Army of the United States.

When Congress is said in the Constitution to have the power or the right to declare war, it means that Congress has the right to put the people of the United States and its Government in the attitude of war, and to make the laws of war applicable to this people. That is what it means. But a declaration of war, broadly considered or narrowly considered, when it is announced by the Congress of the United States, is the declaration of an existing status; that is all. We do not create it; we declare its existence. Now, if Congress can declare war and declare that it exists in the United States, it can declare it exists anywhere else, and the relations of this Government toward that foreign country where war exists must be governed by the laws of nations as they apply to war. That is the whole matter as I understand it. Our declaration does not create a war, does not create belligerency; it merely recognizes a certain condition which we decide to be a condition of war.

More than that, it would be very improper for the Senate of the United States to consider this question in the light of its being a war measure, in any other sense than as merely giving us an opportunity for determining what are our own powers as compared or contrasted with those of the President, for the reason that there is nothing done in this resolution, nor will anything be done in a declaration of the independence of Cuba, if such a resolution should pass, that has in it one breath of war. When the independence of the United States was recognized by Holland and by Belgium and by France in the Revolutionary times, that was not considered an act of war, nor did that declaration make any of those governments an ally of the United States. France went further. She declared our independence and made herself an ally by assisting us.

France came into our war by an act of her own and in the contribution of ships and soldiers and money; but these other governments, recognizing our independence quite as fully as France had done, committed no act of hostility toward anybody by the declaration, nor do we. We did not get into a war with Spain when we recognized the independence of Mexico or any of the South American States. There was no partisanship on our part at all, no inclination toward partisanship or an affiliation or an alliance with them, but an act of simple right on our part, prompted by motives which were honorable to our country and designed for purposes which were countenanced in international law.

I am now ready, Mr. President, to yield to an adjournment.

* * * * * * *

February 24, 1896.

The Senate resumed the consideration of the following concurrent resolution, reported by the Committee on Foreign Relations:

Resolved by the Senate (the House of Representatives concurring), That, in the opinion of Congress, a condition of public war exists between the Government of Spain and the government proclaimed and for some time maintained by force of arms by the people of Cuba; and that the United States of

America should maintain a strict neutrality between the contending powers, according to each all the rights of belligerents in the ports and territory of the United States—

The pending question being on the amendment submitted by Mr. CAMERON, to substitute for the concurrent resolution the following:

Resolved, That the President is hereby requested to interpose his friendly offices with the Spanish Government for the recognition of the independence of Cuba.

Mr. MORGAN. Mr. President, on the 29th of January, by order of the Committee on Foreign Relations, I reported from that committee a concurrent resolution on the subject of the recognition of belligerency in Cuba. Afterwards the committee chose to change their ground, with my concurrence (I was pleased with the change), and they reported the resolution which is now before the Senate. That was on the 5th day of February. I now ask unanimous consent that the resolution reported on the 5th day of February shall be substituted for the resolution reported on the 29th of January from the same committee.

The PRESIDING OFFICER (Mr. BURROWS in the chair). The Senator from Alabama asks unanimous consent that the resolution reported from the Committee on Foreign Relations on February 5 may be substituted for the one reported from that committee on the 29th of January. Is there objection? The Chair hears none, and it is so ordered.

Mr. MORGAN. Mr. President, on last Thursday, when I had the honor of occupying the floor upon the resolution which is now before the Senate, several questions of a very grave and important nature were asked me by Senators, which I said at the time I should endeavor to answer before I finally left the floor upon this resolution. Before doing so, however, I shall present in order, and as concisely as I can, a statement of our relations with Spain in connection with Cuba, based upon the utterances of our predecessors in the Senate and of some of the wisest statesmen who have filled the highest places in our Government. I shall be painstaking in this and other presentations of the facts and opinions of the various American statesmen, because the committee have not seen proper to present a formal report in which they have displayed the whole ground of their action upon this very important subject.

Mr. Adams, in April, 1823, while Secretary of State, in a letter to Mr. Nelson writes as follows:

In the war between France and Spain, now commencing, other interests, peculiarly ours, will in all probability be deeply involved. Whatever may be the issue of this war as between those two European powers, it may be taken for granted that the dominion of Spain upon the American continents, North and South, is irrevocably gone. But the islands of Cuba and Puerto Rico still remain nominally, and so far, really, dependent upon her, that she yet possesses the power of transferring her own dominion over them, together with the possession of them, to others. These islands, from their local position, are natural appendages to the North American continent, and one of them (Cuba) almost in sight of our shores, from a multitude of considerations, has become an object of transcendent importance to the commercial and political interests of our Union. Its commanding position, with reference to the Gulf of Mexico and the West India seas; the character of its population; its situation midway between our southern coast and the Island of Santo Domingo; its safe and capacious harbor of the Habana, fronting a long line of our shores destitute of the same advantage; the nature of its productions and of its wants, furnishing the supplies and needing the returns of a commerce immensely profitable and mutually beneficial, give it an importance in the sum of our national interests with which that of no other foreign territory can be compared, and little inferior to that which binds the different members of this Union together. Such, indeed, are, between the interests of that island and of this country, the geographical, commercial, moral, and political relations formed by nature, gathering, in the process of time, and even now verging to maturity, that, in looking forward to the probable course of events for the short period of half a century, it is scarcely possible to resist the conviction that the annexation of Cuba to our Federal Republic will be indispensable to the continuance and integrity of the Union itself.

The same great statesman from the Northeast, on the 28th of April, 1823, writing also to Mr. Nelson, says:

The transfer of Cuba to Great Britain would be an event unpropitious to the interests of this Union. The opinion is so generally entertained, that even the groundless rumors that it was about to be accomplished, which have spread abroad, and are still teeming, may be traced to the deep and almost universal feeling of aversion to it and to the alarm which the mere probability of its occurrence has stimulated. The question both of our right and of our power to prevent it, if necessary by force, already obtrudes itself upon our councils, and the Administration is called upon, in the performance of its duties to the nation, at least, to use all the means within its competency to guard against and forefend it.

On the 11th of June, 1823, Mr. Jefferson, in writing to President Monroe on this same subject, said:

I had supposed [when writing a former letter] an English interest there (in Cuba) quite as strong as that of the United States, and therefore that to avoid war and keep the island open to our own commerce it would be best to join that power in mutually guaranteeing its independence. But if there is no danger of its falling into the possession of England, I must retract an opinion founded on an error of fact. We are surely under no obligation to give her gratis an interest which she has not; and the whole inhabitants being averse to her, and the climate mortal to strangers, its continued military occupation by her would be impracticable. It is better, then, to lie still, in readiness to receive that interesting incorporation when solicited by herself, for certainly her addition to our confederacy is exactly what is wanted to round our power as a nation to the point of its utmost interest.

Mr. Clay takes up the subject in a letter to Mr. King, of October 17, 1825, and says:

Instructions were sent, under direction of the President (Mr. J. Q. Adams), by Mr. Clay, when Secretary of State, to the ministers to the leading European governments to announce "that the United States, for themselves, desired no change in the political condition of Cuba; that they were satisfied that it should remain open, as it now is, to their commerce, and that they could not with indifference see it passing from Spain to any (other) European power."

In writing to Mr. Brown on the 25th of October, 1825, Mr. Clay said:

You will now add that we could not consent to the occupation of those islands (Cuba and Puerto Rico) by any other European power than Spain under any contingency whatever.

Mr. Webster, Secretary of State, writing to Mr. Campbell, on the 14th day of January, 1843, says:

The Spanish Government has long been in possession of the policy and wishes of this Government in regard to Cuba, which have never changed, and has repeatedly been told that the United States never would permit the occupation of that island by British agents or forces upon any pretext whatever; and that in the event of any attempt to wrest it from her, she might securely rely upon the whole naval and military resources of this country to aid her in preserving or recovering it.

On the 15th of July, 1840, Mr. Forsyth, Secretary of State, writing to Mr. Burwell, says:

The United States will resist at every hazard an attempt of any foreign power to wrest Cuba from Spain. "And you are authorized to assure the Spanish Government that in case of any attempt, from whatever quarter, to wrest from her this portion of her territory, she may securely depend upon the military and naval resources of the United States to aid her in preserving or recovering it."

While Secretary of State, Mr. Buchanan wrote to Mr. Saunders, on the 13th of June, 1847, as follows:

The United States will not tolerate any invasions of Cuba by citizens of neutral states.

Mr. Crittenden, of Kentucky, while Acting Secretary of State, in writing to Mr. Sartiges, on the 22d of October, 1851, says:

> The geographical position of the Island of Cuba, in the Gulf of Mexico, lying at no great distance from the mouth of the River Mississippi, and in the line of the greatest current of the commerce of the United States, would become, in the hands of any powerful European nation, an object of just jealousy and apprehension to the people of this country. A due regard to their own safety and interest must therefore make it a matter of importance to them who shall possess and hold dominion over that island. The Government of France and those of other European nations were long since officially apprised by this Government that the United States could not see without concern that island transferred by Spain to any other European state.

Mr. Webster again, while Secretary of State, writing to Mr. Ballinger, on the 26th of November, 1851, says:

> The colonies of Spain are near to our own shores. Our commerce with them is large and important, and the records of the diplomatic intercourse between the two countries will manifest to Her Catholic Majesty's Government how sincerely and how steadily the United States has manifested the hope that no political changes might lead to a transfer of these colonies from Her Majesty's Crown. If there is one among the existing governments of the civilized world which for a long course of years has diligently sought to maintain amicable relations with Spain, it is the Government of the United States. Not only does the correspondence between the two Governments show this, but the same truth is established by the history of the legislation of this country and the general course of the executive government. In this recent invasion Lopez and his fellow-subjects in the United States succeeded in deluding a few hundred men by a long-continued and systematic misrepresentation of the political condition of the island and of the wishes of its inhabitants. And it is not for the purpose of reviewing unpleasant recollections that Her Majesty's Government is reminded that it is not many years since the commerce of the United States suffered severely from armed boats and vessels which found refuge and shelter in the ports of the Spanish islands. These violators of the law, these authors of gross violence toward the citizens of this Republic, were finally suppressed, not by any effort of the Spanish authorities, but by the activity and vigilance of our Navy. This, however, was not accomplished but by the efforts of several years, nor until many valuable lives, as well as a vast amount of property, had been lost. Among others, Lieutenant Allen, a very valuable and distinguished officer in the naval service of the United States, was killed in au action with these banditti.

I now read from the third annual message of President Fillmore in 1852:

> The affairs of Cuba formed a prominent topic in my last annual message. They remain in an uneasy condition, and a feeling of alarm and irritation on the part of the Cuban authorities appears to exist. This feeling has interfered with the regular commercial intercourse between the United States and the island, and led to some acts of which we have a right to complain. But the Captain-General of Cuba is clothed with no power to treat with foreign Governments, nor is he in any degree under the control of the Spanish minister at Washington. Any communication which he may hold with an agent of a foreign power is informal and a matter of courtesy.

Mr. Marcy, when Secretary of State, writing to Mr. Buchanan, on July 2, 1853, said:

> Nothing will be done on our part to disturb its (Cuba's) present connection with Spain, unless the character of that connection should be so changed as to affect our present or prospective security. While the United States would resist at every hazard the transference of Cuba to any European nation, they would exceedingly regret to see Spain resorting to any power for assistance to uphold her rule over it. Such a dependence on foreign aid would in effect invest the auxiliary with the character of a protector and give it a pretext to interfere in our affairs, and also generally in those of the North American continent.

This review of the opinions and statements on these particular topics indicates a very firm and thoroughly understood attitude of the Government of the United States toward Spain in reference to the Island of Cuba. The subject of the acquisition of the Island of Cuba as one of our possessions, we see, was first brought in direct form to the attention of the people of the United States by President Adams, and he then took ground, which was stated as a prophecy, that in fifty years from the time he wrote he expected that Cuba would be in the possession of this country as one of our States or Territories. This subject gained such a hold upon public attention that our ministers at foreign courts in the year 1854, Mr. Buchanan, Mr. Mason, and Mr. Soulé, were instructed by the President of the United States to meet at some place in Europe, and there confer upon the best method of acquiring Cuba as one of our possessions, and their meeting was called the Ostend Conference. They met at Ostend, and in Lawrence's Wheaton the result of their meeting is stated, which I will read:

In the summer of 1854 a conference was held by the ministers of the United States accredited at London, Paris, and Madrid, with a view to consult on the negotiations which it might be advisable to carry on simultaneously at these several courts for the satisfactory adjustment with Spain of the affairs connected with Cuba. The joint dispatch of Messrs. Buchanan, Mason, and Soulé to the Secretary of State, dated Aix-la-Chapelle, October 18, 1854, after remarking that the United States had never acquired a foot of territory, not even after a successful war with Mexico, except by purchase or by the voluntary application of the people, as in the case of Texas, thus proceeds: "Our past history forbids that we should acquire the Island of Cuba without the consent of Spain, unless justified by the great law of self-preservation. We must, in any event, preserve our own conscious rectitude and our self-respect. While pursuing this course, we can afford to disregard the censures of the world, to which we have been so often and so unjustly exposed. After we shall have offered Spain a price for Cuba far beyond its present value, and this shall have been refused, it will then be time to consider the question, Does Cuba, in the possession of Spain, seriously endanger our internal peace and the existence of our cherished Union? Should this question be answered in the affirmative, then by every law, human and divine, we shall be justified in wresting it from Spain, if we possess the power; and this upon the very same principle that would justify an individual, in tearing down the burning house of his neighbor if there were no other means of preventing the flames from destroying his own home. Under such circumstances, we ought neither to count the cost nor regard the odds which Spain might enlist against us. We forbear to enter into the question whether the present condition of the island would justify such a measure."

President Buchanan, in his second annual message, speaking on the subject of the Island of Cuba, says:

The Island of Cuba, from its geographical position, commands the mouth of the Mississippi and the immense and annually increasing trade, foreign and coastwise, from the valley of that noble river, now embracing half the sovereign States of the Union. With that island under the dominion of a distant foreign power, this trade, of vital importance to these States, is exposed to the danger of being destroyed in time of war, and it has hitherto been subjected to perpetual injury and annoyance in time of peace. Our relations with Spain, which ought to be of the most friendly character, must always be placed in jeopardy whilst the existing colonial government over the island shall remain in its present condition.

And in his third annual message Mr. Buchanan said:

I need not repeat the arguments which I urged in my last annual message in favor of the acquisition of Cuba by fair purchase. My opinions on that measure remain unchanged. I therefore again invite the serious attention of Congress to this important subject. Without a recognition of this policy on their part it will be almost impossible to institute negotiations with any reasonable prospect of success.

General Grant, in his special message of June 13, 1870, to the Congress of the United States, seems to have encountered a development of feeling of hostility and jealousy on the part of Spain on account of our relations to Cuba, and possibly on account of all these utterances of our great and leading men, which gave him very deep concern and caused him to send a special message to the Congress of the United States, from which I will make a liberal extract, for the purpose of showing the progress of opinion and of sentiment in the United States, and in Spain also, upon subjects which seem now to have driven us very wide apart. He said:

In my annual message to Congress, at the beginning of its present session, I referred to the contest which had then for more than a year existed in the Island of Cuba between a portion of its inhabitants and the Government of Spain, and the feelings and sympathies of the people and Government of the United States for the people of Cuba, as for all peoples struggling for liberty and self-government, and said that "the contest has at no time assumed the conditions which amount to war, in the sense of international law, or which would show the existence of a de facto political organization of the insurgents sufficient to justify a recognition of belligerency."

During the six months which have passed since the date of that message the condition of the insurgents has not improved; and the insurrection itself, although not subdued, exhibits no signs of advance, but seems to be confined to an irregular system of hostilities, carried on by small and illy-armed bands of men roaming, without concentration, through the woods and the sparsely populated regions of the island, attacking from ambush convoys and small bands of troops, burning plantations and the estates of those not sympathizing with their cause.

But if the insurrection has not gained ground, it is equally true that Spain has not suppressed it. Climate, disease, and the occasional bullet have worked destruction among the soldiers of Spain; and, although the Spanish authorities have possession of every seaport and every town on the island, they have not been able to subdue the hostile feeling which has driven a considerable number of the native inhabitants of the island to armed resistance against Spain, and still leads them to endure the dangers and the privations of a roaming life of guerrilla warfare.

On either side the contest has been conducted, and is still carried on, with a lamentable disregard of human life and of the rules and practices which modern civilization has prescribed in mitigation of the necessary horrors of war. The torch of Spaniard and of Cuban is alike busy in carrying devastation over fertile regions; murderous and revengeful decrees are issued and executed by both parties. Count Valmaseda and Colonel Boet, on the part of Spain, have each startled humanity and aroused the indignation of the civilized world by the execution, each, of a score of prisoners at a time, while General Quesada, the Cuban chief, coolly, and with apparent unconsciousness of aught else than a proper act, has admitted the slaughter, by his own deliberate order, in one day, of upward of 650 prisoners of war.

A summary trial, with few, if any, escapes from conviction, followed by immediate execution, is the fate of those arrested on either side on suspicion of infidelity to the cause of the party making the arrest.

Whatever may be the sympathies of the people, or of the Government of the United States for the cause or objects for which a part of the people of Cuba are understood to have put themselves in armed resistance to the Government of Spain, there can be no just sympathy in a conflict carried on by both parties alike in such barbarous violation of the rules of civilized nations, and with such continued outrage upon the plainest principles of humanity.

We can not discriminate in our censure of their mode of conducting their contest between the Spaniards and the Cubans; each commits the same atrocities and outrages alike the established rules of war.

The properties of many of our citizens have been destroyed or embargoed—

That means confiscated—

the lives of several have been sacrificed, and the liberty of others has been restrained. In every case that has come to the knowledge of the Government, an early and earnest demand for reparation and indemnity has been made, and most emphatic remonstrance has been presented against the manner in which the strife is conducted, and against the reckless disregard of human life, the wanton destruction of material wealth, and the cruel disregard of the established rules of civilized warfare.

That was in the message of June 13, 1870. Even at the end of the brief period which has passed since the delivery of that message by General Grant, one of the most heroic men who ever lived, inured to warfare, and understanding all about its effects and dire results, the people of the United States read this message now again, and reflect upon it, and they wonder how it ever happened that the Government of the United States could stand idly and indifferently by and permit such outrages to go on in the Island of Cuba as those perpetrated there. It was done, Mr. President, in the hope and in the expectation that the Crown of Spain would be enabled to subjugate what was then considered to be a riotous mob, not amounting to a great army in the field, and would by reconciliation bring the people who were natives of this island back to the love of their flag and country, and would cause them to embrace the monarchy of Spain when it held out to them the gentle hand of promise and made the faithful pledge that in the future their political and personal situation should be better than it had ever been.

I will take occasion here to remark that those pledges were given by the Government of Spain to the people of Cuba, and in consequence of the fact that the Government of the United States at that time turned its back upon the slaughter of more than 600 prisoners by a general who ordered them to be shot down like cattle in a slaughter pen, those people, seeing that the circumstances of their situation were such that they could have no sympathy and comfort from the outside world, turned again to Spain and yielded to her their submission. What has been the result of it? The fruit of it, Mr. President, is now too obvious and distinct to admit of question. The persecutions were renewed because we did not force upon Spain a more humane policy. The promises thus made by Spain to procure the submission of the people of Cuba under the circumstances recited in the message of General Grant have been broken in every possible form, as the Cubans assert, and it has renewed the spirit of revolution, the desire for emancipation, and the love of liberty more potently than it has ever existed heretofore in the Island of Cuba. It may be very well said that our forbearance toward Spain and our omission to do a duty which even then turned our nerves almost into steel with anxiety to perform it have been one more inciting cause of the present lamentable condition of affairs in that island.

This war kept on during President Grant's two terms in office and then during the term of Mr. Hayes in office, and during a part of the term of Mr. Arthur in office, before it could be ended, and it was not until his Administration had proceeded for more than a year, I believe, that Mr. Arthur congratulated the Congress of the United States and the people of the United States on the termination of hostilities in Cuba, under circumstances which promised relief to those people from the oppressions which they had theretofore endured, through the firm, distinct promises of the Government of Spain, all of which Cubans insist have been broken and about which I think there can not be any possible doubt.

The Cubans allege that Spain has broken faith with her own people—that breach of faith which is treason to honor and cruelty added to deliberate deception. Vattel describes civil war and its incidents and results on pages 424 and 425, which I will not now stop to read, and on page 423 of his wonderful book he treats of the obligations of the sovereign to keep faith with the subjects whose submission he has obtained through promises. I refer to these pages for the purpose of getting the attention of Senators to the fundamental law which is laid down by that great writer on the subject of the duty of a government to keep faith with its own citizens when they have once risen in rebellion against that government and at the end of strife or war have yielded their submission to the government upon certain published and agreed conditions. When the submission of the people is obtained by promises of reform, or the conception of new guaranties of liberties to them, there can be no dispute about the justice of their resistance.

If the people of Cuba had been at war with the United States and had surrendered to us, if you please, on a pledge given by treaty that we would grant to them certain rights and privileges, and afterwards we had wickedly and unjustly refused to comply with our promise, that would be a cause of complaint as between two nations which would be classed among that great, almost innumerable, category of causes of complaint which have so frequently brought the nations of the earth into antagonism on battlefields. But in a case of that kind there would be no breach of moral faith toward men of your own blood and your own kindred who had a quarrel, admitted to be righteous and just, to a large extent, because of the reformation which was promised, which quarrel was settled by a submission on the grounds that they would return to all their duties to that government if the government would promise to secure them certain rights and privileges which were thereupon agreed to.

Such agreements between the subject and the crown, between the party who must submit to the superior force of his own government and the ruling authorities, are attended with a sanction that does not belong to any of the ordinary agreements between nation and nation. They are rested upon the supposition that the monarch has a friendship, a regard, and even a love for his subjects; that he is not their natural enemy; that he is not in office for the purpose of breaking faith with them and robbing them of privileges and rights which he has solemnly granted to them.

But, Mr. President, the history of Cuba from 1717 to the present time is almost a continuous record of complaints, riots, attempted revolutions by the natives on account of alleged oppressions of Spanish rulers and the breach of the promises with which they were compelled to buy their peace from time to time. The measures of repression by which those complaints were stifled and the insurrections were suppressed were extremely cruel and destructive. President Grant has recited some of those things in his message to the Congress of the United States, which I have just read, to which no tongue and no pen could add anything by way of emphasis or to darken the picture.

Twelve men were hanged by Captain-General Guazo in 1723, nearly two centuries ago, and a state of siege was then authorized to be declared throughout the island whenever the Captain-General wished it as a precautionary measure. The Island of Cuba from 1723 down to the present time has been left in an attitude where a captain-general at his will and pleasure at any moment of time can declare a state of siege and the existence of martial law. Now, it is impossible to conceive that any people in the world can be under a more strenuous, disagreeable, and dangerous restraint and threat than that which results from the power of their ruler, without consulting anybody else at all, at any moment of time to declare a state of war.

Mr. FRYE. Has the Captain-General ever been a Cuban?

Mr. MORGAN. Oh, no. That was never within the contemplation of the Government of Spain so far as I have ever heard.

In 1851 fifty men of the Lopez expedition were shot in Habana. These are not referred to by General Grant except in general terms. In 1854 Pinto and his associates to the number of 100 men were shot or deported. Then followed the ten years' war from 1867 to 1878, during the progress of which these enormities occurred to which General Grant refers. Spain had more than 90,000 troops in the field in that war. In 1869 the Spanish troops committed atrocities that shocked the civilized world in the wholesale slaughter of men, women, and children in Habana at the Villa Nueva Theater, at the Louvre, and in the sacking of the house of Aldama.

The number of these cruelties is almost beyond comprehension, and the loss of life is appalling. Spain marched into the war 80,000 troops and brought out 12,000. It is stated on high authority that "according to official reports forwarded from Madrid, by the United States minister, 13,600 Cubans had been killed in battle up to August, 1872, besides 43,500 prisoners whom the Spanish minister admitted to have been put to death."

We, Mr. President, have been so blessed with the kindly fruits of liberty in this country, we have had so much of national enjoyment, we have had so much of pleasant occupation in taking care of the affairs of our own great Government and our wonderfully increasing population and our developing wealth and our glorious prestige among the nations of the earth and in illustrating by our conservative and industrious and virtuous example the blessings to mankind of this wonderful form of government which has been established and conducted here, that it seems we have forgotten the sufferings of those so close to ourselves. Now, can it be possible that a mistake is made by an accurate and able historian when he says to us that the Spanish minister admitted that in that war, in addition to 13,600 Cubans who had been killed in battle, 43,500 prisoners had been put to death?

I confess that when I came across that statement in an authentic history to which we give credit, I read it over and over to ascertain whether it could have been possible that such a multitude of humanity had been slaughtered within 90 miles of the coast of the United States during that ten years' war; and I inquired of myself, What has Christianity been doing in the world if in this age, the nineteenth century, it has been possible that such things could be done in an island like Cuba, and that this great and free Republic could stand indifferently by, knowing the facts, and not unsheath its sword and strike the brutal monarch to death who inflicted them?

The cost of that war was all shouldered upon Cuba. It must have been $500,000,000.

The close of such a war was surely a sufficient consideration for the promises made to Gomez and Cisneros and their compatriots, upon faith of which they again submitted their fate into the hands of the Spanish monarchy.

Mr. FRYE. Mr. President——

The PRESIDING OFFICER (Mr. BURROWS in the chair). Does the Senator from Alabama yield to the Senator from Maine?

Mr. MORGAN. Certainly.

Mr. FRYE. I failed to catch the name of the authority for the wonderful, the horrible statement which the Senator from Alabama has just made in relation to the slaughter of prisoners to the number of over 40,000.

Mr. MORGAN. I am sorry that for the moment I can not recall his name. I will hand it to the Senator.

Mr. FRYE. It is from history?

Mr. MORGAN. Yes; deliberately written, and written by a Spaniard.

Mr. FRYE. Does the Senator credit it?

Mr. MORGAN. For a long time I hesitated to credit it, but I had to credit it or else deny the evidence of a deliberate statement made by a historian in a book of universal acceptance, one of reliable authority.

Mr. GRAY. Will the Senator from Alabama state the name of the historian or the book?

Mr. MORGAN. It is in the American Encyclopedia, under the title of Cuba.

Mr. CALL. If the Senator from Alabama will allow me, I will read a very short extract from a publication by Mr. Clarence King.

Mr. MORGAN. I shall be very glad to have it read.

Mr. CALL. Jesus Rivocoba, one of the officers on duty in the service of Spain in the Island of Cuba, under date of September 4, 1869, writes this letter:

> We captured 17, 13 of whom were shot outright. On dying they shouted, "Hurrah for free Cuba!" "Hurrah for independence!" A mulatto said, "Hurrah for Cespedes!" On the following day we killed a Cuban officer and another man. Among the 13 that we shot the first day were found three sons and their father; the father witnessed the execution of his sons without even changing color; and when his turn came he said he died for the independence of his country. On coming back we brought along with us three carts filled with women and children, the families of those we had shot; and they asked us to shoot them, because they would rather die than live among Spaniards.

Pedro Fardon, another officer, who entered perfectly into the spirit of the service, writes on September 22, 1869, as follows:

> Not a single Cuban will remain in this island, because we shoot all those we find in the fields, on the farms, and in every hovel.

On the same day the same officer sends the following:

> We do not leave a creature alive where we pass, be it man or animal. If we find cows, we kill them; if horses, ditto; if hogs, ditto; men, women, or children, ditto; as to the houses, we burn them. So everyone receives his due—the men in balls, the animals in bayonet thrusts. The island will remain a desert.

Mr. WHITE. I should like to inquire of the Senator from Florida from what he has read? What is the paper he has in his hand?

Mr. CALL. I read from a pamphlet published by Clarence King. The article appeared in The Forum for September, 1895, and purports to contain a literal copy of the letters of those officers themselves.

Mr. MORGAN. The President of the United States at the close of the war to which I have been referring, the war which preceded the one in which the incidents occurred to which the Senator from Florida [Mr. CALL] now alludes, sent to the Senate the papers which relate to the submission of the Cuban insurgents in 1878. I find in that paper, which I have not had the opportunity of examining with care, a statement of the terms and conditions upon which the surrender took place.

Mr. Antonio Mantillo, who, I think, was then the representative at this legation of the Government of Spain, writes as follows to the Secretary of State, Mr. Evarts:

> In the decree in question the phrase is to be noted with which its preamble begins: "The war being now near its end" (not a regular war in the sense in which it is defined by international law, but an intestine struggle, civil contest, or armed rebellion, which, in the military parlance of the Spanish language, is commonly called war); which phrase shows that said military authorities do not consider the contest to be entirely at an end, although its termination is very near. The first sentence in the second paragraph of the same preamble is also noteworthy, in which it is declared that, had it not been for this contest, "Cuba would long since have enjoyed, according to the constitution of the State, the advantages which must necessarily accrue to her from a possible assimilation to the peninsula," which shows that the prevailing sentiment in Spain is in favor of treating Cuba as Puerto Rico has been treated; that is to say, like a Spanish province, although she could not grant to rebellious subjects what they demand with arms in their hands, namely, absolute independence, during a time of trial for the mother country, nor even what she was always ready to grant them voluntarily, and

what she has now granted, at a time of greater prosperity for herself, to them, now that they have repented and sued for peace, which is an act of generosity and a guaranty of reconciliation.

A decree of the general in chief of the army of operations in the Island of Cuba was also inserted in the Habana Gazette of the 3d.

This was issued at Puerto Principe on the 10th of March, and will be found in Appendix F. It guarantees the freedom which was offered in article 3, of the capitulation of all slaves who were in the ranks of the insurgents on the 10th day of February, and who have surrendered or who shall surrender before the 31st day of the current month of March.

Articles 5, 6, 7, and 8 of the capitulation have been fulfilled already, or are now in course of fulfillment, toward all who are willing to take advantage of their benefits. Article 4 requires no immediate action, and article 2 has always constituted the distinguishing trait of the Spanish policy in Cuba. Forgetfulness of the past, pardon of political crimes, release of property embargoed for the same cause, mitigation of the effects of these embargoes as regards the innocent members of the families of those whose property has been embargoed, and even the furnishing of means of subsistence to repentant rebels—all this has been frequently offered or granted by the Government and authorities of Spain from the time of the decree of amnesty, issued on the 12th of January, 1869, by the governor, captain-general of the island, Don Domingo Dulce, who was sent by the revolutionary government of 1868 to establish in Cuba the same liberties and franchises that were enjoyed by the peninsula, until the royal decree of October 27, 1877, by which the unimproved public lands, certain forests belonging to the State, and town lands not used, are ordered to be divided among various classes, viz:

1. Licentiates and volunteers, who have been mobilized or who have taken part in a battle.

2. Inhabitants of the towns of the island, who have remained loyal to the Government and who have suffered considerable losses of property in consequence of the war.

3. Persons who have voluntarily surrendered to the authorities and forces of the Government.

The reproduction and analysis of all these general acts, and many other private ones, of pardon, clemency, and generosity, would render this note interminable, which had no other object, as remarked at the beginning, than to satisfy the desire of the honorable Secretary of State to become accurately acquainted with the present situation of Cuba, but which the undersigned, in his wish to correct false impressions which have been circulated by the conspirators against Spain in this country, has thought proper to extend sufficiently to indicate succinctly the policy of Spain in Cuba and the causes that have given rise to the recent events. Although the Government of Spain does not recognize the right of any foreign power to interfere in the internal affairs of that country, it values too highly the opinion of the sensible people of the United States and the friendship of its Government for its representative at Washington to neglect an opportunity like the one now offered to present in their true aspect the acts, intentions, and constant policy of Spain in her relations with the Island of Cuba.

He then proceeds:

If it were necessary, or the honorable Secretary of State should desire it, the undersigned would amplify and prove by means of trustworthy documents the assertions which he has just made, and he proposes shortly to show that the only obstacle that can now retard, not absolutely prevent, the complete pacification of Cuba, is the war cry and the false promises of immediate aid which are once more sent from New York by the Cuban conspirators, who urge in public meetings the continuation of the struggle which is now so near its end. And it is a remarkable fact that in this struggle, by a sad fatality for the liberators of Cuba, a fatality which would not escape, and which has not escaped, the observation of the American people and the perspicacity of its enlightened press, foreigners have been its principal leaders—those who have most zealously maintained it, and who have most distinguished themselves in it. Jordan and Reeve, Americans; Maximo Gomez and Modesto Diaz, Dominicans; Roloff, a Pole; Caoba and Maceo, the one an African and the other a semi-African; Prado, the captor of the Moctezuma, a Peruvian; and finally, not to mention any more names, Gonzales, a Mexican, who was deputed by the revolutionary committee of Camaguey to announce the dissolution of the legislative chamber and of the government of the republic to its representatives in the United States.

Even the diplomatic commissioner of Cuba abroad, Echevarria, who less than a month ago proclaimed throughout the length and breadth of this great country, by a circular telegram from the Washington agency of the Associated Press, that the news of the submission of the greater part of the insurgent leaders was false, and that they would accept no terms not based upon the recognition of Cuban independence—even that diplomatic agent, whom the honorable Committee on Foreign Relations of the House of Representatives of the United States, having charge of Cuban affairs, received and listened to with interest in the belief that he was a son of Cuba, is no Cuban at all, but a Venezuelan.

If an insurrection composed of such antagonistic elements as the Latin, African, Mongolian, and Anglo-Saxon races, led on by officers of all known nationalities, could have triumphed, the confusion of tongues at the Tower of Babel and the memorable catastrophe which took place in the formerly French portion of the island of Santo Domingo would have been cast into the shade by the spectacle which victorious, free, and Africanized Cuba would have presented to the civilized world.

* * * * * *

ANTONIO MANTILLA.

Now, there is the Spanish side of that statement. The Cuban side of the statement comes later. It comes out now in the declarations which have been read in the newspapers, in declarations which I will place in the RECORD without reading, because it is not necessary to take the time of the Senate in reading them, which show that the terms and conditions which were agreed upon in that submission of the Cubans to the Spanish Government at that time have been flagrantly violated, and that the people of Cuba have received from it not only none of the advantages promised, but the very machinery which was set on foot by that submission and the articles which followed it have been employed by the Spanish monarchy for the purpose of continuing to rob them more flagrantly than ever.

These articles of submission, so far as I can gather from this paper, seem to have been drawn up at several places and at several times, and after a portion of the people of Cuba through their representatives had signed these articles or assented to them new adhesions to this capitulation were obtained from others. I will hereafter put in the RECORD enough of this paper to show the exact nature, as far as it can be found from this document, of the capitulation that was made, the promises which have been broken, as the Cubans allege.

They and their associates, then and now, assert that Spain has broken these promises in all respects, and has greatly aggravated her persecutions of the people of Cuba since these promises were entered into. That was one of the grounds upon which their present revolution is predicated—a breach of national promise.

It is not ours to decide such controversies, since the action we propose to take on this occasion is not dependent in the least degree on the facts that led to the revolt, but upon its existence and progress to the state of open, public war.

If the United States should be forced into the espousal of the cause of the Republic of Cuba as an ally, the facts are not wanting to justify our people in fighting, if need be, for the principles of our own Government against a despotic monarchy and for the sacred rights of man that are being destroyed and exterminated in sight of our coasts.

But this is not our purpose. We do not intend to interfere in that matter unless we are forced to do so from supreme necessity. The present proposed action of the Congress of the United States has not the slightest bearing one way or the other upon that question. We are for peace, security, and good neighborship with Cuba, if we have to fight for it.

No Cuban army has fought as yet for a single leader who was ambitious for place or honors under the Spanish Monarchy, or for the spoils of war, or the liberty of pillage, or even for revenge. Their leaders are patriots and men of great abilities. Gomez is an old man, said to be fatally stricken with consumption. No earthly station could induce him to endure the labor and suffering to which he is subjected. His ambition is only that he may live to see Cuba free, or, dying, that he may bequeath its liberty to the people.

In all these belligerent movements, extending through two centuries, the Cubans have not fought merely for redress of grievances, though these were a just cause of war; they have at all times resisted and resented the despotism of the Spanish Monarchy, and their battle cry has always been "God and liberty."

The freedom of Cuba has been always the undying aspiration of the native people.

One of these struggles is but the renewal of those that preceded it. Either from workings of military power or under the inducement of false promises, a truce has been, from time to time, on frequent occasions adopted. But when the oppression has been renewed, and strength to resist it has been regained, these people have come forth in that native strength which belongs to a liberty-loving people and have renewed the battle for independence. And now Gomez returns to his command, and Cisneros, who was president at the time that the surrender took place of which I have been reading, comes back to his presidency, and the Cubans fall into the ranks and take up their arms to renew the war of 1867 to 1878.

The civil government then disbanded upon false assurances, and the military power and organization that then laid aside its arms are again renewed upon a basis that is good in law throughout all Christendom, that a right surrendered to fraud upheld by force may be justly reasserted whenever the power exists to reclaim it.

In these battles fought in this protracted war of independence the blood of patriots that Cuban soil has drunk has not been shed in vain—

> For freedom's battle, once begun,
> Bequeath'd by bleeding sire to son,
> Though baffled oft, is ever won.

That we have witnessed this struggle for so many years, during which our ears have not been deaf to the appeal for liberty and independence and our hearts have not refused their sympathy to the suffering Cubans, is enough for us to have done in order to prove our faithful adhesion to our national duty.

We can go no further in our forbearance without a stain upon our national honor and without doing injustice to our Government and our people.

If the war in Cuba should end in disaster to the republic they have organized there, even within a week, our duty would be ill performed if we did not declare that this war is and has been a public war for independence, and has been so admitted by Spain in declaring that war exists in four Cuban departments.

This declaration should be made promptly on our part, for it will stand us in hand when we are again forced to call Spain in question for her treatment of our citizens captured during this struggle. It should be made also to warn Spain that she can not impose the Weyler code, following the Balmaceda code, upon our people or their property, and that when the war for independence again breaks out, its character and purposes will not be misunderstood by the United States. The future wars in Cuba will not be mere civil insurrections when it requires 150,000 men and the navy of Spain to hold the people in check.

Our rights and duties in regard to this war in some sense depend upon its purposes and its magnitude, but not upon its ultimate success or failure. The purposes commend this war to our respect at least. Its magnitude is equal to the territorial control of more than half the area of Cuba and more than half the people of the island.

In this war, unlike that of the war of 1867 to 1878, few native troops have fought in the field under the Spanish flag. Some of them have been enlisted as volunteers, quite a number of them probably under duress, but they have put a condition in the enlistment that they were to be home guards; that they were not to enter the field; that they were to guard the plantations and the railway stations and towns, villages, and cities.

The great body of the native people are in sympathy with the republic, though the repression of any such avowal, in act or word, is the relentless purpose of Weyler's cruel code. This code may again smother the fires of liberty, of which Gomez speaks in his letter of November 13, 1895, in which he says:

We can truthfully say that, even if Spain sends thousands of her children to their death, we have already established the basis of the Cuban Republic, and that republic will be a fact, no matter how many of us may fall.

There are few Americans who do not accept that result as inevitable, and the Weyler code will serve only to remind him hereafter that no grasp of tyranny can be strong enough to repress the fires of liberty, though it may silence the tongues of its votaries for the time.

The victories won over the Spaniards by the Cubans at Los Negros, at Iobito, at Bayamo, where Campos and his staff sought safety in flight, on foot and in the nighttime, at Cascorra, at Sao Del Indio, and in many minor engagements, and the splendid march through Cuba from east to west and from north to south are lessons of skill and evidences of military power, and proofs of valor and endurance that do not presage the ultimate defeat of the Cuban army. Spain has sent to this conflict up to this time 61 vessels of war, all heavily armed, but in the 2,200 miles of Cuban coast there are 200 harbors and sheltered places of landing, and in all the guns sent there by Cuban agents not one rifle has yet been lost. Spain has sent to Cuba 110,000 men, and has 80,000 volunteers for garrison duty, yet with this enormous force she has not been able to keep Gomez out of hearing of the morning and evening guns that are fired at Habana. Their armies grow while the armies of Spain perish and decrease from losses in the field and hospital.

The organization of the Cuban army was conducted in eastern Cuba, and the first and hardest battles were fought there. Then Gomez and Maceo invaded western Cuba to burn cane fields and to recruit their forces.

A comparison of the statements of our consuls, made from time to time, shows a tremendous rapidity of increase of the forces and war material of their commands.

It is through the reports of the consuls of the United States sent in by the President to Congress that we derive that better statement of facts to which Gomez refers and which will be referred to in a paper that I will presently have read at the desk, in which it is said that doubtless the Government of the United States knows more of the actual facts of the progress and development of the war than the Captain-General of Cuba or the Government of Spain. These consuls, situated in Cuba at three of the most important points, all of them being men of intelligence, ability, and faithful public service, have from time to time sent the best information available to them in respect to the condition of the country surrounding them and the progress of the armies in that country.

I therefore read extracts from these reports to the Senate with a view of getting what I conceive to be an authentic statement upon this subject of the magnitude of the war, the character of the war, the progress of the war, the character of the army that conducts the war, and the policy of the men in rule and authority there who manage and control the army. It is from these facts that we are to derive a sound and solid judgment upon which we will feel authorized to act.

I have mentioned already in the speech I made last Thursday the reluctance with which I proceeded to investigate this question, because of the uncertainty of the evidence upon which we had to rely. I was not aware how very certain, how very strong it was, until I took up these consular reports and was able to compare them also with the reports in newspapers and reports from private sources; and I find that we are in possession of an authentic history of the rise and progress of the present revolution.

On the 23d of February, 1895, just a year ago, Mr. Pulaski F. Hyatt, writing to Mr. Uhl, says:

CONSULATE OF THE UNITED STATES,
Santiago de Cuba, February 23, 1895.

SIR: I have the honor to advise you that grave apprehensions are felt of a revolution breaking out here. Rumors are rife, and it is difficult to get at exact facts.

The people are very much frightened, and those of the country are moving to the city in large numbers for safety. The banditti element in the mountains is being augmented by certain parties hostile to the Spanish Government.

Information has come to the consulate that the Government has notified certain Cubans, known to have been prominently in favor of the island's freedom, that if there is trouble they will be held responsible and shot, and a number, said to be 27, of the members of leading families who were spotted have left for parts unknown.

The military governor, Lachambre, has had his home in the country guarded by 250 soldiers, and he gave notice to a number of American engineers and workingmen, living in a house close by, and here for the purpose of constructing railroad bridges, that if they had cause to go to their yard in the night, to carry a lantern as a preventive against being shot.

That is the outbreak of it a year ago; that is the form in which it presented itself to Mr. Hyatt, who was living in the country where the first organization took place and where the feeling of the Cubans was most intense. On the 26th day of the same month he says:

The insurrectional movements that have given rise to the measures of the governor-general seem to be limited to a very small number of persons, as shown by the prompt action of the three political parties above mentioned engrossing the major part of the population, and which really represent the entire planting, industrial, and commercial interests, as well as the professional classes of the island, though it can not be denied that poverty, induced by the cumulative effects of the erroneous economic system long established here, has brought about discontent among the working classes since the principal exportable products of the island, sugar and tobacco, are very depressed in their exchangeable values. This has brought on low and precarious wages, while at the same time imported provisions and clothing are very high and in unfavorable disproportion to the earnings of the workmen.

Those workmen, starving men, got to thinking and feeling, and they bared their shoulders to the burdens of the revolution; really they started it.

Now, writing again on March 1, he says:

On the 27th ultimo the governor-general of the island issued a decree, copy inclosed being extract from official bulletin, declaring this province in a state of war, giving the military authorities control of all matters appertaining to public order, and giving insurgents eight days to present themselves and be exempt from punishment.

Now, I wish to connect that statement with one that I made in the opening of my remarks, when I called attention to the fact, which nobody has denied or can deny, that for more than two centuries the Captain-General of Cuba has had the power to put any province in that whole island into a state of siege, to declare military law as prevailing, and to declare a state of war as existing. In this province our consul affirms that the governor of this particular province has declared that a state of war exists. What kind of a war is that? An insurrection? An émeute? A mere rebellion? A mob? A sedition? No; he declared that war existed; and he put the laws and powers of war at work there by changing the whole legal situation from one of peace to that of war. I should like to know, after that declaration on his part, followed up, as it has been, by declarations of a like kind by the Captain-General in three of the provinces of eastern Cuba, more recently made, how they can hold up their heads and look the world in the face and say to us that we have no right to recognize that a war exists when they proclaim it and enforce it? Our consul says, further on in the same article:

> There have been a number of scrimmages with troops in the province, and several on both sides killed and wounded. The insurgent element so far is confined mostly to the negro population, which predominates. The whites and property owners hope that the reforms promised by the Government will be put into effect and that the movement will be suppressed before much property is destroyed and lives lost.
>
> A strong reenforcement of Spanish troops is daily expected.

The last letter was on the 1st of March. Thirty days later, on the 30th of March, he says:

> I have the honor to report further on the situation in the province of Santiago as follows: On Monday, March 24, 900 troops were landed from Spain, which, with the 2,437 recruits which landed last week, make a total of 3,337 additional Spanish forces landed at this port. After arrival these troops were newly uniformed in linen suits and straw hats.
>
> A battle occurred near Manzanillo on Sunday between 300 Government troops and 560 Cubans. The Government claims 50 of the enemy killed, while the Cubans claim a victory.
>
> * * * * * * *
>
> That same evening—

That was on Thursday, the 28th—

> (a dark night) about 9 o'clock sharp musketry firing was distinctly heard from this consulate, which lasted forty-five minutes, when a heavy rain set in. I afterwards learned that a body of insurgents were waiting in ambush for the outgoing troops and fired on them from behind rocks and trees, causing a loss of 50 killed on the Spanish side, including one captain.
>
> * * * * * * *
>
> Men are constantly leaving the large centers of population to join the insurgents, and public opinion is rapidly in their direction.

Then again he writes on April 4:

> With starvation facing them on one side; with relations, friends, and companions on the other, fighting for the independence of their country, it will readily be seen how the present uprising may become one that will defy the efforts of Spain to subdue.
>
> It is safe to say that there are at present large bodies of insurgents under arms in the jurisdiction of Santiago de Cuba. Spain must have to meet these twice their number, as the country is an ideal one in which to harass regular troops who are not familiar with the country.
>
> Another important factor to be considered is the ravages that will be made among the Spanish soldiers during the summer months by yellow fever, which will far exceed their losses in action.
>
> To check and end the present uprising it will be necessary for Spain to concentrate all her forces at Santiago de Cuba, Puerto Principe, and to act promptly and decisively, for as each day the rebellion continues lessens her

chances for subduing the same, and, as before stated, she must accomplish the subjugation of those in revolt before the present crop is finished, or their accessions will be so great that her dominion over this island will be in great jeopardy, if not lost.

Then, on the 5th of April, he writes again:

On April 2 the insurgents entered the town of Carney, about 6 miles from here, where they captured about 50 guns, some horses, and, it is said, about 2,500 cartridges.

On April 3 the Government forces met the insurgents at Socorro, about 18 miles from here. The insurgents are said to have been defeated with 10 lost and many wounded.

The Spanish Government is now employing Cubans at $30 per month to join the guerrilla forces against the insurgents, and naturally these accessions against the cause of the revolutionists are looked upon with great hatred by the other Cubans.

Private advices from parties capable of speaking are to the effect that the territory between here and Manzanillo and along the Canto River is alive with insurgents. Their cavalry are said to be in a very excellent condition, well armed, and well mounted. Pending the arrival of Martinez Campos, the war seems to be in a quiescent state.

Campos had not yet landed. Then again he writes on the 13th of April:

On Thursday a battle was fought near Bayamo. The number of troops and results are not definitely known. The work of the insurgents seems to be more along the line of gathering arms and ammunition rather than seeking conflict, while the Government troops do not seem desirous of forcing a fight, but rather to guard important points from attacks while they await the arrival of Martinez Campos, who is expected to land at this port on the 16th instant. Preparations are in progress to give him a big reception.

The sugar planters complain that whenever they pay off their hands large numbers leave to join the insurgents, thus crippling work. It is estimated that the population of Santiago has been increased by 15,000 people, mostly old men, women, and children, who have left the country and are quartered on anybody that will keep them. Beggars are very numerous. The death statistics for the first fifteen days of March was 82, and jumped to 62 for the last half of the month, there being 8 deaths from yellow fever, 5 deaths from paludal fever, and 1 from diphtheria. I am informed by a physician that smallpox in a mild form has also appeared.

Now, on the 28th of April he writes:

SIR: I have the honor to report that on Sunday, the 21st instant, a fight took place near Songo, this province, between about 500 Cubans and 800 Spanish troops, which resulted eventually in the Cubans retiring from the field. A major and chaplain of the Spanish forces were killed. Other losses unknown.

Two thousand and fourteen new Spanish recruits arrived at this port from Spain on the 22d instant, and it is reported that 20,000 more will arrive during the next six weeks.

Rebels burned the town of Ramon de Yaguas on Monday last, killed Captain Miranda of the Spanish forces, took 16,000 rounds of ammunition and a quantity of arms from the fort.

Lieutenant Gallego, on the part of the Spanish troops, surrendered the fort, for which he was court-martialed and ordered to be shot. The sentence was commuted to life imprisonment by cablegram from the Queen.

Then he adds as a postscript:

Lieutenant Gallego was shot at Habana on May 1, after having attempted suicide on the passage from Manzanillo to Habana.

This consul goes on to speak of other battles from time to time. May 11 he says:

Monday night the rebels attacked Cristo, a town 10 miles distant, on the Sabanilla and Maroto Railroad, derailed an engine, and burned two bridges. The road is operated and owned mostly by American citizens. Martinez Campos has recommended Government aid to this road for the purpose of extending the same and furnishing employment to the many men who will soon be thrown out of employment by the shutting down of sugar mills, and it is feared that without work the men will drift into the rebel army. * * * Friends of the insurrection claim that they are as far advanced now at the end of three months as they were at the end of three years in the former rebellion. They claim now to have 10,000 men under arms in the province of Santiago, and to have 4,000 more doing effective work.

That is from the time of this first dispatch, which was February 23, 1895, down to the date of this letter, which is May 11, 1895, a rise in their power from nothing to 14,000 troops in the field. In my observation, few countries have ever been able to recruit an army as rapidly out of their own legitimate resources, arm them and equip them, and put them in the field as these Cuban rebels have done during that period from the 23d day of February down to the 18th day of May—three months! Again, he says on the 18th of May:

On Monday, the 13th, 400 men are said to have left Holquin in a body to take up arms against the Government.

Four hundred leaving one place.

Perhaps the most sanguinary battle that has taken place up to the present time occurred on the 13th and 14th instant, near Guantanamo. The Spanish authorities claim that with 400 men they put to rout the enemy, 3,400 strong, inflicting severe loss on the rebels.

The rebels claim that there were over 2,000 Spaniards engaged in the first day's battle, and that they punished them severely, driving them into the town and inflicting a loss of over 200 in killed and wounded, including among the killed the commander, Colonel Bosch, and several other officers, while their own loss was insignificant; but finding that on the second day the Government forces had been strengthened, they thought it prudent to retire.

* * * * * * *

It is reported—

He says in the same letter—in fact, it turned out to be true—

that 400 convicts are enlisted in the next shipment of soldiers to arrive at this place from Spain.

These convicts and others from Africa have been pardoned for the worst of crimes committed in Cuba and armed as bands of guerrillas to destroy the people they had formerly assailed with brigandage, robbery, and murder. Yet it is not more surprising that convicted robbers should be turned loose to war against Cuba than that unconvicted and titled robbers should use them for like purposes.

I will omit to read quite a number of these reports, although they all contain very strong corroborative testimony to the continual and steady progress of this revolution. On July 13 Mr. Hyatt says:

I have the honor very respectfully to report in reference to the further uprising in the eastern end of Cuba that Saturday, July 6, a battle of considerable importance occurred near Manzanillo, in which it appears that the Government forces, made up mostly of "guerrillas" (home guards), were, to the number of 100 or more, cut to death with machetes.

Continuous fighting between Manzanillo and this place has been kept up all of the week, with uncertain results.

The case of Dr. Joaquin Castillo, reported in my dispatch of July 6 (No. 149), is a peculiar case, and is, perhaps, worthy of further mention. The Doctor, a man of commanding appearance, is one of a numerous and highly respectable family, born on this island, but who have sought and obtained naturalization in the United States, and by marriage related to Spanish officers of high rank. The Doctor served as surgeon to our *Jeannette* polar expedition.

It appears that some five years ago Gen. Antonio Maceo (who was famous in the previous insurrection) came to Santiago, and was quietly feasted and toasted by a number of prominent people, among them Dr. Castillo. In the hilarity of the occasion they promised Maceo that when he came to Cuba again on business they would be with him. On Maceo's return to the present conflict he notified these gentlemen that he was here, and expected them to remember and keep their promise. Some of them were slow to respond, and the Doctor among the number, because a lucrative practice and the large possessions of his wife made it inconvenient to respond. A second notice is said to have been sent, which contained no threats, but interpreted by those capable of reading between Cuban lines that it would not be well for the Doctor to delay his coming, and he went.

Numerous young men have left lucrative positions and cast their lots with the insurgents.

It is estimated by men of judgment that the revolution is now three times as strong as it was at its height during the previous insurrection.

Any insurgent force that now attempts to enter Santiago will have to jump over, climb through, or cut down a three-stranded barbed wire fence which now surrounds the city.

For a fortification, I suppose.

Yellow fever, though still bad among Spanish soldiers, has not seemed quite so virulent during the past week. Deaths for week, 109. Yellow fever, 41; smallpox, 1.

Mr. GRAY. From whom is that?

Mr. MORGAN. That is from our consul at Santiago. I pass over a number of places which I had marked for the purpose of calling attention to them, but it would protract the story too much for me to undertake to give all these incidents as the narrative proceeds. On the 21st of August he writes to Mr. Adee:

SIR: I have the honor to report the situation in Cuba to be deeply interesting.

With perhaps the exception of Santa Cruz, the Government forces hold every important seaport town and a few large towns in the interior, while from Cienfuegos east, which constitutes three-fourths of the island, the insurgents hold the balance of the territory and some territory farther west.

Cuban leaders claim 25,000 men, mostly under arms, in the province of Santiago and 10,000 farther west. I think the number overstated by at least eight or ten thousand men, but I am inclined to the opinion that there are many more ready to join them when assured that they will be supplied with arms and ammunition.

That arms and ammunition are now coming quite freely to Cuba there seems little room for doubt. A paper published here called The Public Opinion has recently declared that if the Government would look more carefully after the large carrying companies and less for filibustering expeditions they would find the source of trouble.

Those who desire to see the island restored to peace are much depressed, as there is at present three times as large a force of insurgents as at any time in the previous insurrection.

Then he gives an account of more battles which occurred in his vicinity. Then, under date of October 10, writing to Mr. Uhl, he says:

SIR: Judging by results that tend to terminate a war, the situation in Cuba, from an American standpoint, might aptly be termed one of "masterly inactivity." But few engagements have occurred up to the present time that should be dignified by a higher title than a skirmish.

Cuban tactics are to fight only when they have the Spaniards at a disadvantage, and at other times small attacking parties will fire from ambush on the Government forces for the purpose of demoralization, or to induce the troops to follow them to a more advantageous place for battle; but the Spaniards seem to understand this, and thus far have declined to accept battle on such terms.

The Cubans assert that they can not afford to make a stand in an open field, or even behind ordinary breastworks, with their present quota of arms and ammunition, as every shot must count; while being themselves acclimated and thoroughly inured to Cuban climate, diet, and modes of living and traveling, they can kill more Spaniards by fatigue, exposure, and disease, and at less sacrifice to themselves, than by hand-to-hand battles, and by such tactics can continue the war indefinitely.

* * * * *

The Spanish forces can not long remain away from their base of supplies, as their quartermaster, commissary, ordnance, and hospital supplies are all carried on the backs of pack mules. No tents or shelter of any kind are provided for soldiers on the march, nor any ambulance service for the sick and exhausted.

The Red Cross tendered their services to go in there, but they have never heard from the Spanish Government upon the subject.

Up to the present time Spain has put into the field about 80,000 soldiers, probably a little more than one-half of which are now available for active operations. The best-informed persons here estimate the active Cuban force at 25,000 or 23,000.

* * * * *

Spanish agents, Spanish newspapers, as well as American newspapers, have for months openly declared that certain vessels carrying the British flag and conveying iron ore from Cuba to the United States have on their return trips carried articles contraband of war, which they have disposed of through persons connected with the mines and landed at certain points along the coasts.

And thereupon the Government of Spain, through the Captain-General, established fortifications at those American iron mines upon the avowed pretense of prohibiting or preventing those men from receiving what they called "contraband of war." They were obliged to receive powder in large quantities for the purpose of conducting their iron works and their regular business; but inasmuch as the Captain-General said there was a possibility of such things falling into the hands of the insurrectionists, they forbid their importation, under the doctrine of their being contraband. There is something which needs inquiry. I do not mean the special instance, for perhaps not much loss has occurred on that account, but as to a Government with which we are at peace, and that peace secured by treaty guaranteeing to us wide commercial privileges and providing rules and regulations by which contraband of war in time of war may be excluded from the island, how can that Government, while saying that peace prevails, contend that there is contraband of war when a merchant in the United States ships a keg of powder to his consignee in Cuba?

What right have they in a time of peace to interpose and examine the cargoes of our ships upon principles of war and declare these things contraband? They can not do it except when they make a declaration of war against the ports or places at which these articles are to be landed, establish a blockade, and interpose that declaration as creating the rights which are given by war of inspecting a vessel to see whether its cargo is contraband. But here. while they declare that a state of war exists in four provinces of Cuba, and put out their proclamation to that effect, and in virtue of that fact insist upon the existence there of war—while they are in that condition in regard to their own people, for the purpose of putting down a rebellion that they can not subdue, they hold out to us the relations of peace and amity and friendship, and say, "You must not import into Cuba powder or shot or any munitions of war, because they have become contraband."

That is a position which can not possibly be submitted to by the Government of the United States, and when they insist, as they do insist, that war obtains in their own provinces in Cuba, and so proclaim to the world, and follow it up by seizures of the cargoes of vessels because they are contraband, then of course what we have got to do, and all we can do, is to declare, along with them, that a state of public war exists in that country, and that these things are contraband; but that if our people can get through their blockaders, it is all right and no longer illegal to sell them to the recognized belligerents. Spain can not declare that one of our merchants shall have his property, his ship and his cargo, confiscated in time of peace by imposing upon that vessel a hostile characteristic because it has on board articles contraband. Spain must say that she is at war with another power, which is a part of her own provinces, and being at war, she has a right to declare those imports contraband which would assist the enemy in waging war.

Mr. Hyatt proceeds again on the 16th of October to say:

SIR: The Cubans assert that they could quickly double or treble their forces in the field if they could only equip them for service, in which case they would take the aggressive; but as it is they are obliged to husband their resources to the fullest extent to meet the Government forces that are armed with Mauser rifles and well supplied with ammunition, while they, the insurgents, are confined largely to such resources as by "hook or crook" they can obtain from the Spaniards.

On the 11th instant the insurgents captured between Santiago and Manzanillo 17 soldiers with personal arms and 4,000 cartridges, which were being conveyed to a fort 2 leagues from the coast. The Spanish soldiers were set free, but I learn that the lieutenant in command has been court-martialed and will be shot for surrendering.

Then he speaks of the coming in of certain cargoes on board of ships that were landed surreptitiously on the coast.

Then Mr. Casanova writes that the war had included his consulate at Cienfuegos, and speaks of it as follows:

The destruction of sugar estates has been principally directed against buildings of strategic value to the Government troops or that might serve them as shelter; generally buildings of abandoned sugar estates, though occasionally of late the dwellings and labor quarters on "colonias," or cane farms, have been destroyed. Some of these cases are due to political rancor toward the proprietors who have made themselves conspicuously hostile to the insurgents.

As the most important measure proclaimed by the revolutionary government (leaders?) is the prevention of sugar making, with a view to crippling the resources of the Spanish Government, it is likely that more extensive destruction will follow, as threatened by the insurgents. In the approaching crop season unless this Government is able to afford needed protection by garrisoning the plantations with sufficient forces to enable planters to work in safety. As the insurgents up to the present time to so great extent control the surrounding country, the prospect for preventing the consummation of their plans is not very reassuring, and in consequence great despondency prevails in all classes of the community, so largely interested and dependent on the sugar crop. In fact, on this vital question is involved the gravest problem to the life of this district, and the same applies to the rest of the island.

On the 16th of November, Mr. Hyatt, writing from Santiago de Cuba, says:

SIR: I have the honor to very respectfully offer a brief résumé of the situation in Cuba as it appears to one who has watched it carefully from its inception to the present, a period of nearly eight months.

The total strength of the insurgents at present is between thirty-five and forty thousand men, 10,000 of which are not well armed, but are useful in other directions, which number would be quickly increased if arms and ammunition were available.

Their generalship has been neither brilliant nor dashing, and it has indeed been questionable whether they have not allowed important advantages to get away from them for want of well-directed heroism, yet, on the whole, well calculated to conserve their cause.

Their settled purpose is to fight only when they have advantage in position and numbers; but to harass the Government troops, mostly with small detachments, and depend upon their better knowledge of the country and greater powers of endurance to avoid punishment, and by the aid of yellow fever, dysentery, etc., to finally wear out the Government forces.

Discipline is maintained better than might be expected, and desertions are infrequent, owing to the great difficulty in escaping from the island, so the deserter must either go to the enemy or go home and face Cuban scorn.

As a rule the Cuban army is healthy, their powers of endurance are great, and they show not the slightest disposition to give up the fight.

When prisoners are taken, if they can not be induced to change their allegiance, they are disarmed and released.

They have levied and collected heavy assessments on every industry possible, and seem to have plenty of money.

I am unable to say how much success has attended their attempts to establish a local and permanent government. I think, however, it is of a movable nature.

They respect American property and rights much more than those of other nations.

On the part of Spain there is no lack of disposition to supply all the men and means necessary to subdue the rebellion; but the first 30,000 troops sent to the island were largely boys, too young and inexperienced to take proper care of themselves, and many of them have succumbed to exposure and disease. The later arrivals were more mature men and are able-bodied soldiers. They have also several thousand volunteer natives and acclimated Spaniards, making the number placed in the field up to the present time nearly 100,000, 30,000 of which are dead or unavailable, leaving for service about twice as many as the Cubans have, and are better armed and equipped. About one-third of this number are kept on guard duty, a portion of which may be called off in emergencies, so that fifty-five or sixty thousand are available for field service.

Up to the present writing most of the Spanish forces continue to occupy mostly the cities and large towns near the seacoast, or about the mines, railroads, and large plantations. Transportation of troops and supplies is by steamships along the coast.

In the person of her captain and governor-general, Martinez Campos, Spain possesses a soldier and statesman of marked ability, who tempers justice with mercy to a large extent.

With the exception of iron mining, nearly every industry on the island is going rapidly to destruction, and nothing but a sudden termination of the war can prevent the island from becoming a waste that will require many years to repair.

Native-born Americans have but little cause to complain in regard to their treatment by Spanish officials, and even our naturalized Cubans are treated with far more consideration than those of other nationalities. So apparent is this distinction that it has become a subject of complaint on the part of citizens and consuls of other nations, and has been met by the reply that their treaty with the United States differed with that of other nations, and a counter reply has been made that they were entitled to the "most-favored-nation clause."

On the 2d of December Mr. Casanova says:

The prevention of sugar making is the most settled and determined policy of the insurgents. There have been already cases of partial burning of plantations in this consular district, some of them owned by Americans.

In this connection I deem it proper to submit to the Department the following data of the property represented by Americans in the sugar industry in this consular district alone, either residents here or owned by corporate companies in the United States. These plantations are of the most valuable here, yielding an aggregate yearly production of over 600,000 bags, or 86,000 tons, of sugar, at an estimated value of over $4,600,000 at present low prices. There are, besides, large American interests invested in cultivation of cane for supplying the sugar factories.

The effect of the present business depression and the impoverishment of the country that is becoming evident, all largely attributable to the crop difficulties, manifests itself in the lessened importation of goods, the shrinkage of consumption already affecting trade very seriously.

Mr. Casanova writes, under date of December 12, an interesting statement, as follows:

The larger part of the effective insurgent forces that heretofore operated in the eastern department of the island have gradually invaded the department of Las Villas and are now operating in this and the neighboring districts. These forces comprise some 16,000 to 20,000 men, both cavalry and infantry, fairly well armed, under command of Maximo Gomez, as general in chief of all the insurgent forces, and Antonio Maceo, his second in command, with other less noted leaders. This army, the largest that has so far in this war been gathered together in a body, has maneuvered to evade any pitched battle with the various large columns of Government troops acting in combination against them. Several partial engagements have taken place, but without any important results.

The evident purpose of the insurgents is to penetrate further into the heart of this section with large forces and carry the war eastward into the richest and most productive districts. At last accounts the main insurgent army above referred to was in the vicinity of Santa Clara, the capital of the department of Las Villas, one detachment being sent to the vicinity of Trinidad, under command of a colored leader, to destroy the few sugar estates that remain there, the largest of which belongs to an American company. Aside from the above-mentioned forces, there are the numerous bands in larger or smaller numbers that continue to infest every part of the country, harassing the troops and carrying on the usual guerrilla warfare.

The laying waste of all the country and prohibition to the farmers to market their produce or move cattle is causing great hardship and privation. But chief in gravity, in its fearful import to the community, is the impending failure of the sugar crop. This is being effectually prevented by the insurgents in this district, and no attempts are being made by planters to manufacture sugar. Even this passive acceptance of ruin by the planters does not obtain for them immunity from the destruction of their property. The firing of cane fields is assuming alarming proportions; thousands of acres of valuable cane fields are daily being burned, and, notably, on three of the largest sugar estates in this consular district, owned by Americans, the cane fields have been devastated. The machinery and buildings on sugar estates are of great value, costing from half a million to more than one million dollars. The Government, on application, grants a squad of soldiers to guard

2777

those buildings, but not in sufficient force to be entirely effective. Many planters prefer to take the chances of mercy from the insurgents by being ungarrisoned rather than draw on themselves their certain hostility and revenge unless effectively protected.

The recent reenforcements of 25,000 men from Spain will be mostly required for active field service, and not available for the defense of the sugar estates. Thus the existence and future of this valuable industry is threatened with complete annihilation.

I must not detain the Senate by matters which can possibly be omitted from this statement and yet give to the country a fair and just statement of the actual situation in Cuba. Writing on the 7th of January, 1896, Mr. Ramon O. Williams, our consul-general at Habana, says:

With reference to the proclamation of the Captain-General of the 2d instant, declaring a state of war to exist in the provinces of Habana and Pinar del Rio, copy and translation of which accompanied my dispatch No. 2695, of the 4th instant, I have to inform you that the newspapers, now under military censorship, report the burning of the sugar-cane fields throughout a large portion of this province by the insurgents, who entered it, as variously estimated by popular rumor, numbering all the way from 4,000 to 12,000 men, on foot and horse.

Besides the burning of the cane fields, the newspapers report cases of damage to railroads by the displacing of rails, the cutting of telegraph and telephone lines, the blowing up of culverts, burning of bridges and stations; also the pillaging of country stores, the carrying off of horses, saddles, and bridles from farms on their line of march for the mounting of their men, and the slaughter of cattle for food. Among the railroad stations destroyed are those of Ginvican and Guira de Melena, distant from here, respectively, about 28 and 40 miles on the line from Habana to Güines, and that of Gabriel, about 25 miles on the railroad from Habana to Pinar del Rio; the villages also were burned.

The trains on the first-named road only ran yesterday as far as Bejucal; on the Western Road from Habana to Pinar del Rio, only about 30 miles out, and on the Habana Bay and Matanzas no train goes beyond the latter city. All the railroads have handed in their rolling stock as much as possible to prevent its destruction.

Mr. WHITE. From what page does the Senator read?
Mr. MORGAN. Page 52, January 7, 1896.
On the 15th the same officer gives an account of the capture of a village on the Bay of Habana. Then, on the 15th of January, he writes:

In continuation of my dispatch No. 2707, of the 11th instant, reporting the doings of the insurgents in the Provinces of Habana and Pinar del Rio, I have now to say that, according to the newspapers and private accounts, the only sources of information at the disposal of this office, the insurgents have still continued in their marches and countermarches to leave havoc throughout their train.

They have wrought so much destruction on the Western Railroad, an English company, that the directors have resolved to stop their running. They also burned a large part of the important town of Bejucal, on the Habana and Güines Railroad, because of the resistance made there by the local authorities and volunteers. At the present writing there is no immediate prospect of their being driven out of the two mentioned provinces.

He then gives an order of Maximo Gomez dated January 10, in which he says:

Considering that the operations of the sugar crop have become suspended in the western districts, and it being no longer necessary to burn the cane fields, I therefore issue the following order:

ARTICLE 1. The burning of the sugar-cane fields is hereby absolutely prohibited.

ART. 2. The severest penalties of the military and civil jurisdictions of the revolution will be visited, regardless of rank and station in the army, upon each and all who contravene this order.

ART. 3. The buildings and machinery will be destroyed of all plantations that, despite this humane order, resume work.

ART. 4. All the inhabitants of the Island of Cuba, of whatever nationality, will be respected in their persons and agricultural occupations.

MAXIMO GOMEZ, *General in Chief.*

Mr. President, I have now laid before the Senate only a part of the testimony found in these consular reports which bears upon this question, but nobody can take up these official reports, sent in by our consuls, and, unless they impeach the consuls themselves, deny this consecutive array of facts, which proves absolutely the proposition that this rising of the Cuban people has reached the extent of a great public war, and that the likelihood is very strong that in the end the Cubans will achieve their liberty. I wish to make no prediction about it, because our action does not depend in the slightest degree upon our ability to forecast the result or upon the probability of it; but, at the same time, from the facts which are given by our own consuls to our own Government, it is impossible to believe but that the whole body of the Cuban people, the native population of Cuba, are in thorough sympathy with Cisneros, the president of the republic, with Gomez and Maceo, and their other leaders.

After a little while, in the course of my argument, I shall come to the attitude of President Cisneros, and I shall show, not by reading the constitution, but by bringing it into an appendix which I will hereafter lay before the Senate, that he has formed a government upon excellent principles and after due deliberation, and as well calculated to carry on civil administration in time of war in a country like Cuba, it seems to me, as any constitutional arrangement could do.

A letter from a gentleman whose character for veracity and good sense can be most thoroughly avouched by members of this body was written from Cuba on the 14th of February, 1896. It incloses a copy of an article written by another gentleman in Cuba, which was published in a New Orleans paper on February 8, 1896. The writer of the letter says that the author of the article is an American citizen "and is probably the best posted man in the island on Cuba and its affairs." This article, which I will have read at the desk, accounts for the military situation in Cuba, and shows how Gomez and Maceo have been able to make their splendid campaign to the west, and how it is impossible to hold Cuba much longer in chains.

The VICE-PRESIDENT. The Secretary will read as requested.

The Secretary read as follows:

REVIEW OF THE SITUATION IN CUBA.

EDITOR LOUISIANA PLANTER: Recent events here have clearly proven that the estimate of the situation in the Island of Cuba made in my last letter was in no wise exaggerated. The possibilities and probabilities indicated have all been as fully realized as the short time elapsed could permit. Spain has failed in obtaining another loan abroad, and has been obliged to take from one of her own banks the insufficient sum of $10,000,000 to begin the new campaign. Instead of the 50,000 new troops, evidently required to enable planters to harvest the present sugar crop, but 25,000 have been sent. These two facts, whatever may be said to the contrary with the intent of disguising the truth, would seem to indicate the weakening and proximate exhaustion of the resources of the Government, both military and pecuniary.

As I anticipated, the reenforcements arrived too late to enable the sugar factories to begin work in due season, and the detachments of troops protecting their buildings have, as was to be expected, been of no avail to save their cane fields from destruction when attacked. The anticipated inefficiency of the raw levees composing the new regiments seems to have been made quite as evident. Not only one line of troops has been broken through, as I suggested might happen, but, judging by the official reports, three in succession hastily formed, and the insurgents have invaded the provinces that have heretofore been comparatively safe, leaving behind them a broad path filled with smoking ruins and burnt cane fields, where local bands are completing more at leisure the hasty work of the invaders. Before this reaches you Gomez will in all likelihood have reached the other end of the island, devastating the district of Pinar del Rio, hitherto wholly exempt from the scourge of civil war and always considered perfectly secure.

Although this raid was announced months ago in the New York papers, Maximo Gomez, who during the last war always advocated this plan, has either completely outgeneraled Martinez Campos, or this general's orders have not, as I believe sometimes happens, been strictly obeyed by his subordinates. He does not seem to realize the radical differences there are between this and the former rebellion. Since the last war the Cubans have learned much—the Spaniards almost nothing.

I suppose that the reenforcements would have been used to form a cordon across the island to prevent the projected raid, gradually advancing and clearing the richest districts of the smaller bands, strengthening the line as it progressed by the detachments which would become unnecessary in the rear, a plan difficult in execution, but decisive if successful. The old system adopted during the last war, which lasted for ten years, has been preferred, and the dry season, so anxiously awaited to begin the sugar crop, upon which the fate of the island depends, after a victorious campaign, has principally served not to ripen the cane fields for the expectant planter, but to prepare them for the firebrand of the incendiary, quite as impatiently lying in wait to burn them. In answer to Martinez Campos's promise to enable the estates to grind early in the season, the rebels have obliged those that had commenced to suspend, and deprived a very large number of all means for future work.

He has evidently been led into two grave mistakes for a commander of his rank, by the exaggerated or false reports, perhaps, of his subordinates, against which he was obliged, some months ago, to issue a general order, which is discreditable to the army and his patriotic desire to economize Spain's limited resources. He has also overrated the efficiency of his own troops and underestimated the capabilities of his adversaries. It is quite likely that the President of the United States is better informed through the consular reports of what is really passing here than the governor-general of Cuba is by those upon whom he is obliged to depend. The vandalic raid of the insurgents was evidently planned with a full appreciation of the defects of the Spanish army, and to all appearances thoroughly carried out by their principal chief, born and brought up in the guerrilla warfare of the island of Santo Domingo, of which the army officers know little or nothing.

At the start he collected all the best of the insurgent bands and leaders, to the number of from 5,000 to 8,000, a body strong enough to cope with any two divisions of troops he might meet, trusting to rapidity of movement to outmaneuver the Government forces, destroying communication by wire and rail as he progressed to prevent those left in the rear from being brought again to the front. To do this he avoided his usual forest refuges and struck boldly down upon the open country, along the railways, through an almost continuous plain covered with cane fields. With no infantry nor impedimenta but ammunition to delay his movements, he advanced night and day at a trot, taking but few hours' rest, and keeping scouring parties in front and upon his flanks, collecting fresh horses to replace those that gave out, together with arms of all kinds for those who might rise to join him. When the supply of horses proved insufficient, the men mounted as "voltigeurs," the fresh horses carrying double. It is said, and it is quite probable, that he was accompanied by a full band of musicians of 22 pieces, who deserted in a body some time ago from one of the Spanish volunteer regiments.

He appears to have kept a strong vanguard under one of his best leaders to engage the bodies of troops as he met them (these are seldom of more than 1,200 men, with one field piece), while his main body passed in two columns, and then to retreat rapidly and fall into the rear. His force was estimated by one of the Spanish generals at 12,000 when he reached Matanzas, and is probably, with those who have joined him, now about 17,000.

Gomez's success is not surprising when, in an army of 120,000 troops, there are here but 13,000 troopers, either because cavalry is considered too expensive, or because no amount of experience in Cuba will convince the Government that Spaniards afoot can not overtake Cubans horseback—one of the old persistent errors. Even the Cuban rural "gendarmes," or police, are mostly infantry, although the robbers they are expected to pursue are always mounted, and a force of cavalry half as large as that employed would be more efficient for the purpose.

Orders have now been given to remedy this glaring defect by bringing cavalry from Spain and by a general requisition for horses throughout the island to mount infantry, giving in return promises to pay at low prices. Like all Government measures in Cuba, this comes too late for its purpose and will probably be converted into an abuse, as it was during the last war. There are already reports that the troops oblige all the poor country people they meet upon the highway, bringing their produce to the towns, to unload at the wayside and give up their horses to the soldiers. This course will probably, by depriving this class of their means of support, do more to swell the rebel ranks than to serve the Government. The infantry make very poor riders, and the few men who have been mounted heretofore upon horses taken from the insurgents look as though they would topple off at the slightest provocation and are unfit to fight in the saddle against Cubans, who have ridden since they were 6 years old.

Even the dearly bought experience of the last month (among the dearest that Cuba has had to pay) will not teach the Government that America is not Europe. The insurgents have already appropriated nearly all the best animals in the island, and the infantry, officers as well as men, seem to have no knowledge whatever of the care of horses, consequently they soon become unfit for service in their hands. In any case the insurgents can take horses quicker than the army can buy (even without paying for them), and this tardy measure seems likely to add little to the efficiency of the troops in this campaign. With the insurgents riding them to death upon the one hand, and the Spanish infantry killing them by ignorance and neglect upon the other, there is a very strong probability that the island will soon become quite as horseless as it was when unhappy Columbus discovered it, and if the rebels live upon other people's cattle much longer, quite as beefless.

Success in the field for either side seems now to depend upon celerity of movement, to which the army is little adapted, so far as can be judged from what is to be seen in the garrison town where this is written, one that has been in the midst of the war for over a year, and where bodies of troops from 200 to 1,500 are almost daily arriving and departing. The slothfulness with which the detachments are formed to go in search of the enemy is simply unaccountable to an American, and in a measure justifies the supposition of nonsympathizers that they are gaining time for the rebels to get away before they do. The looker-on becomes worn out waiting to see them start, and finally gives it up in despair. The dilatoriness of all the movements, the easy leisure of the officers, the stolid, apathetic indifference with which the men loll upon their rifles in carelessly formed ranks, apparently waiting first for one thing and then for another hour after hour, no one seeming to know why, offer little hope for the conversion of such material into that kind of "light horse infantry" the tactics of the Cubans so eminently demand.

The men, as a rule, are of low stature, a square, thick-set, stooping, short-legged, stiff-jointed race, evidently taken from a class of stolid, illiterate carriers of wood and drawers of water, to whom an adverse fate has denied all those boyhood pastimes, which give agility and suppleness of limb. Their wabbling attempts at running and clumsy ascent of the ladders to the small forts which surround the town are often ludicrous in the extreme. The bayonet exercise, so indispensable against the Cuban attack with the sword, seems entirely unknown to these poor victims of misrule, and, contemplating their awkwardness, one is filled with pity imagining what the futility of their defense must be with a lithe and wiry Cuban hanging over them from his saddle, slashing the deadly "machete" with nothing between its sharp edge and their devoted heads but the sultry atmosphere of Cuba and her cheapest straw hats. Ignorant all their lives of the use of arms until recruited, and without target practice, they fire in platoons at the word of command, taking little aim, if any at all, and the amount of ammunition wasted is something beyond belief.

I have myself heard almost continuous discharges of small arms, with 23 shots of a field piece, lasting from noon until after dark, and by a force said to number 700 troops, and the official report claimed only eight or ten of the enemy killed and as many wounded, ascertained solely by observing at long range the movements in the Cuban ranks. If such wild work is as general as the published accounts of engagements would indicate, it will do infinitely more to exhaust the financial resources of the Government than to deplete the ranks of its adversaries. There are more good marksmen among the insurgents, but fewer cartridges to waste, and casualties are on both sides generally few and far between. When any considerable execution is accomplished, it is at close quarters with cold steel—the bayonet and "machete."

There are undoubtedly good men among the Spanish officers, who fulfill their duties so far as they know them and the customs of the army permit, but a large proportion have, apart from their uniforms, nothing apparently that would commend them as soldiers, and the general standard seems very far below that of England and the United States. They appear to pay no attention to the health, food, comfort, or cleanliness of their men.

All but the most unavoidable duties seem to be left to the sergeants, and to bring the army to greater efficiency these would need the knowledge and capacity of general officers. If such defects are as common throughout the island, the recent successes point to a long war, and there is as yet no certainty that the crop of sugar will reach even 200,000 tons. The home Government has already called for volunteers, which in Spain shows a scarcity of troops, while as yet there is no evidence of weakening on the part of the insurgents; and if they have by their recent raid succeeded in effecting the rebellion of as large a proportion of the inhabitants of the heretofore undisturbed half of the island, which is much the more populous, very heavy reenforcements will be required, and there is little prospect of peace this year.

The Government allows little or no news about Gomez's movements, but rumor says that he has evaded the line formed across the island where it is but 21 miles, with 40,000 troops, in the hope of intercepting him upon his return. This concentration has left unprotected important districts, and the small bands of insurgents free to continue burning, collecting arms, and raising more men. There is no promise at present that any estate that did not pay subvention to the revolutionists last year will dare grind for a long time. In the solution of all-important political or race questions the unexpected is what generally happens; a change may nevertheless take place either way. It is also reported that Martinez Campos is going home, and the fear among Cubans that his withdrawal will give room for the repetition of the excesses of the last rebellion is having a deleterious effect.

Scant love of exactitude makes all statistics uncertain, and it is impossible to form any exact calculation of the real damage so far done. Maximo Gomez has shown much "method in his madness," and some generosity. Estates have been spared upon promising not to grind, one owner in Habana having been asked and given it by telephone. Others have been respected because the proprietors are more popular or had given money to the "cause." The cane fields of Spaniards have had a very decided preference, including those of a recent member of the present ministry. This is not surprising when it is remembered that many Spaniards are still in favor of summarily shooting all nonsympathizers at sight, and have been deadly enemies of the more civilized policy of Martinez Campos, to whom Cuba and humanity owe so much. Some still living went so far during the last war as to claim that all Cubans of the male gender over 10 years of age should be treated with the same tender mercy. Though not so drastic a remedy as that humorously proposed for the solution of the Irish question—by putting the sister island under water for fifteen minutes—it was fortunately not found admissible in the nineteenth century.

Among the estates of Spaniards there is one remarkable exception, the proprietor being famous for his unscrupulous dealings. Although the neighboring ones were burned, nothing upon his was harmed. This wily owner is supposed to have patriotically put up last year a golden lightning rod, which prevented his plantation from being struck. It is said that one American who had begun his crops was twice ordered to stop, and finally, seeing consequences more clearly under the lurid light of Gomez's firebrands, he accepted the inevitable and obeyed the revolutionary mandate. The insurgents, of course, excuse depredations which are beyond the pale of civilized warfare and at the same time a confession of impotence for better, though less effective, means, upon the ground that Spain with money can get men, and that they are not going to allow Cuba to give her, as she did during the last war, the means for cutting their own throats. The fact that rich Cubans who then gave money for the rebels have during this struggle refused all aid has also influenced feeling against the native planters. And incendiarism, besides depriving the Government of taxes, also obliges further outlay to save the homeless victims from starvation by supplying them with army rations. Meanwhile the misery it is spreading will probably soon begin to have its effect in strengthening the ranks of the perpetrators.

Where all this will end there is no foretelling. Nevertheless, considering that most of the insurgents and many of the most prominent leaders are of the African race, the state of demoralization to which the country has been brought, the dense ignorance of the lower classes, and the long provocation, we have so far to be thankful that results are no worse, and however much the system of warfare is to be condemned, justice should be done to the rebels by a fair statement, in spite of all the calamities their deeds entail.

So far as I have been able to ascertain, from the commencement women have been respected, and this, under the circumstances and in a country where the passions are strong and so frequently unbridled, says a great deal in favor of the sense of right in the chiefs, and shows a better control of their men than could have been hoped for or expected. The soldiers who have fallen prisoners have been well treated and released after depriving them only of their arms, ammunition, and accouterments. The rebels have respected towns where they were not fired upon after a call to surrender, and pillage has generally been limited to the grocers' or bodegueros' shops, and this exception is due partly to the necessity of supplying their most pressing wants and partly to the fact that men of this class—almost exclusively Spaniards—have generally made themselves so obnoxious to the poor, and even to the troops, by their extortions, that their very names in Cuba have become a byword and term of opprobrium. Estates have been spared where there was no attempt to grind, and one petty leader, at least, has been sentenced to death for extorting $6,000 from a planter.

Not the least beneficent of their good acts is that of hanging by the wayside, whenever caught, the "Plateados" or "silver-plated" insurgents, criminals, who, under the garb of patriotism, have committed thefts and murders. That this conflict has not degenerated into a war of pitiless extermination upon both sides is, in truth, due to the sterling common sense and humanity of Martinez Campos and the better instincts of the Cuban chiefs. They have committed none of those indiscriminate butcheries which characterized the other side during the last rebellion, though in some few cases they have killed defenseless men. They appear to have been provoked to it by some act on the part of the unfortunate victims, or these were volunteer officers and killed in reprisal because their own are shot when caught. If reports be true, many defenseless prisoners and unarmed peasants have been put to death secretly and against orders by the troops, and as this is generally believed in the rebel ranks, there is less of such work to lament than could be expected. If the small garrisons of the towns had delivered up their arms, it is to be supposed that no towns would have burned. They probably obeyed orders, whether rightly or wrongly given I leave others to decide. No right-minded person can sympathize with or approve atrocities by either side, but strict justice should be done to both in the opinion of the world, and to this end extenuating circumstances should not be hidden.

Those who are unacquainted with Cuban history may well ask, Who are responsible for all this havoc and bloodshed? There is no room left for doubt or discussion upon this point. Liberal Spaniards themselves admit the truth; centuries of error and misrule and the influence of the old local Spanish party opposing those indispensable reforms which would put an end to the spoliation to which its wealth is due. England by the independence of her best colonies learned a great lesson which has been often worth to her all its cost. Spain, on the contrary, has been taught nothing by the loss of hers; and Cuba is simply going the way of all the rest. Her inadequate rulers have nothing now to complain of but their own folly—the Cubans in revolt are what they themselves have made them, and innocent and guilty alike are now reaping the well-known fruit of the seed that political turpitude has so long been sowing.

The bane, the blight, the curse, and the scourge of Cuba from the days of her discovery to the present time have been blind, unbridled egotism and insatiable greed. We find the pages of her history soiled by injustice, extortion, and fraud, or crimsoned by man's inhumanity to man in an all-pervading and conscienceless haste to be rich. Many good men have come to her from Spain, contributing to her advancement and welfare, but unfortunately these were but a minority. The rest have been a band of spoilers who have hung their consciences when they had any upon the walls of the Morro upon entering Cuba's principal harbor, forgetting, so far as her interests were concerned, to take them down again when they left. If Spain had always been represented here by a majority of the better elements of her different classes, Cuba would have been one of the most tranquil, prosperous, and happy countries in the world.

Unfortunately for both, much immigration has come from Spain's very dregs. Priests and prelates have come, not to preach charity and practice morality, but to extort fortunes from the gross superstitions of rich and poor, living openly with their concubines, surrounded by their ill-begotten children, and have passed away without leaving a single good work to perpetuate their names. Judges have been sent with their scales, not to weigh out even-handed justice, but gold received for iniquitous decisions, bartering with wealth upon the one hand and selling freedom and immunity to the thief and life to the assassin upon the other. Thousands of avaricious shopkeepers have come to fill their coffers by smuggling, extortion, and robbery of the poor, going back in peace with their ill-gotten gains, or to shoal without them, leaving demoralized descendants, often as illegitimate as the fortunes they made, to squander them. Thousands upon thousands of corrupt officials have come to pervert the laws and customs, returning ladened with bribes. A badly paid and illy organized police have encouraged vice to live upon subornation. Every function of government has been perverted by greed for wealth, and not one single element in the whole body politic has been used to elevate the moral standard of the people or to induce respect for law.

With such antecedents it is not surprising that one looks in vain about this island for endowed schools, hospitals, asylums, or other charitable mementos of the vast fortunes that generation after generation have been made and spent or preserved in miserly egotism: that the rich have felt that they owed nothing to the country which gave them their wealth, and have often shifted the burdens of taxation to the shoulders of the poor; that the poor feel neither respect for nor gratitude to the rich, to whom they owe nothing; that the laborer has been considered unworthy of his hire and too often defrauded of his pittance without redress. Disregard of natural rights has never begotten a sense of justice, nor are extortion and the illicit distribution of wealth the best means for inculcating the sacredness of property rights or to prevent their possession being looked upon by the ignorant masses as being an injustice nearly allied to crime.

Among those who have joined this revolt there are few who had anything to lose but their lives, their liberty, or their good names; and, educated in such a school, it is not to be wondered at that they should think themselves justified by their aims in desolating their own country as though it were that of the enemy in a barbarous age, looking upon their fatal work as the well-merited spoliation of their despoilers. There are naturally in the dregs of this revolution anarchistic tendencies which, if it is unsuccessful, will become more apparent in the future. Meanwhile, with over 200,000 men (including the volunteers), the Government seems utterly unable, for the present, to put any check to this destruction.

Spain's rule is being weighed in its own unbalanced scales, measured with its own false, unequal measures, and found most lamentably wanting. Long-delayed retribution has come at last with red-handed avengers, Spain's own begetting, falling alike upon the just and the unjust and the innocent and the guilty—"Mene, tekel, upharsin," is being written in letters of fire from Cape San Antonio to Point Maisi, upon the black clouds of smoke from Cuba's blazing crops and villages, and the end is not. The fertile plains of the brightest jewel of the Spanish crown are once again being devastated by fire and sword; her rich soil is once again being fructified by human blood, while her verdant hills, silent witnesses of all the long, eventful story of sardonic nepotism, injustice, and misrule, seem to echo back the old war cry of the crusaders, "It is the will of God; it is the will of God."

Mr. MORGAN. If I had had this letter read in the beginning of my remarks I would not have needed to say much else; but it is due to the committee, whose action I am endeavoring to justify, that I should present to the Senate this and other authentic evidence upon which its action is based.

The committee have made no mistake in declaring that—

A condition of public war exists between the Government of Spain and the government proclaimed, and for some time maintained by force of arms, by the people of Cuba.

This Cuban government rests upon the civil power of the people who support it and recognizes, as we do, that the military power is subordinate to the civil power. The government of the Republic of Cuba, through its accredited agent, has sent to our Government a statement of their claims for recognition as belligerents, in which there is no apparent misrepresentation as to existing facts and conditions in Cuba.

I will hereafter lay before the Senate so much of that document as relates to the organization, constitution, and some general laws of the Republic of Cuba.

These papers are carefully prepared and bear witness to a remarkable aptitude and ability in the organization of a new republic, born in the throes and travail of internecine war.

We find, then, the actual existence of an open civil war for independence, waged by a great number of the people of Cuba who sanction it and give to it their support through the powers of civil government, and support it also with large, well-organized, and brave armies in the field, which have already overrun and are in control of more than half the territory of Cuba.

This situation fully justifies the United States in giving recognition to the Cuban Republic as a belligerent power and to the people of Cuba our recognition of their rights under the laws of civilized warfare.

If this resolution is adopted, it will impose upon the United States certain duties to which we must give careful consideration.

1. What is the attitude of the United States toward Spain if the belligerent rights of Cuba are recognized?

It is an attitude of peace and friendship, without either the intent to give offense or to challenge or dispute the sovereignty of Spain over the Island of Cuba. Spain did not offend the United States when she recognized the Confederate States as belligerents, nor do we offend Spain by recognizing the Cuban Republic or the Cuban people as belligerents in an open public war.

We do not conceal the earnest sympathy of our people with the people of Cuba in their struggle for independence, but until we are compelled we will not raise a hand to assist them.

General Grant, in his special message to the Congress of the United States on the subject of recognizing the belligerency of Cuba in the then existing war with Spain, on the 13th of June, 1870, says as follows:

> The question of belligerency is one of fact not to be decided by sympathies for or prejudices against either party. The relations between the parent state and the insurgents must amount, in fact, to war in the sense of international law. Fighting, though fierce and protracted, does not alone constitute war; there must be military forces acting in accordance with the rules and customs of war—flags of truce, cartels, exchange of prisoners, etc.—and to justify a recognition of belligerency there must be, above all, a de facto political organization of the insurgents sufficient in character and resources to constitute it, if left to itself, a state among nations capable of discharging the duties of a state, and of meeting the just responsibilities it may incur as such toward other powers in the discharge of its national duties.

That was a statement made by General Grant in his message, upon which he predicated a refusal to recognize the belligerent rights of Cuba in the preceding war. The present situation in Cuba has brought those people entirely within the strictest construction of all the doctrines and principles stated in the message of General Grant. I deem it unnecessary to read any further from the great number of authorities, many of them American, in which this same doctrine is stated, oftentimes with greater liberality, in favor of according belligerent rights than it is here stated by General Grant.

If we act in good faith and from proper motives in recognizing the belligerent rights of the Cubans and of the government they set up, Spain has no claim upon us, by treaty or otherwise, that forbids us to give this recognition.

The question on which our rights hinge in this matter is a question of fact which we must decide for ourselves.

I quote from a statement of Mr. Webster, made on the 5th of April, 1842, in a paper which he addressed to Mr. Thompson:

> If citizens of the United States, enlisted in the service of an insurgent power whom the United States acknowledges as belligerent, but which is not so acknowledged by the parent State, should be treated when captured by the parent State otherwise than as prisoners of war, and their release, when demanded by the United States, should be refused, "consequences of the most serious character would certainly ensue."

Mr. Cass says on the same subject:

> I am not aware that in this country any solemn proceeding, either legislative or executive, has been adopted for the purpose of declaring the status of an insurrectionary movement abroad, and whether it is entitled to the attributes of civil war, unless, indeed, in the formal recognition of a portion of an empire seeking to establish its independence, which, in fact, does not so much admit its existence as it announces its result, at least so far as regards the nation thus proclaiming its decision. But that is the case of the admission of a new member into the family of nations.

Mr. Cass refers to "the case of the admission of a new member into the family of nations," as to which it must be observed that there is a very marked distinction. We have had three recent illustrations of the action of the Government of the United States in the admission of republican forms of government to succeed monarchies, one in France, one in Spain, and one in Brazil, in all of which, having ministers recognized by the Government which had previously existed, when the change took place from monarchy to republicanism, our Government was in haste to recognize the republics, and in the case of France, and of Spain also, authorized the recognition of the new republics by cablegram.

When, however, a country is divided asunder, some of its provinces or parts falling off from the others and claiming independence, particularly when that country is one of contiguous territory, as in the case of Texas, the recognition must be made by some other power than the President of the United States, because that fact brings a new nation into the family of nations and the political existence of that nation as one of the family of nations must be established in this country by law. Thereafter, when it is thus established and thus recognized by law, the President of the United States, as the Chief Executive, and as the constitutional conductor of our diplomatic relations, has the right to recognize the person who may preside in that Government as being entitled to exercise the functions of his office. General Cass draws, inferentially, the distinction between the two cases in the remarks that I have just read.

Mr. Fish, in a letter to Mr. Motley dated the 25th of September, 1869, says:

> The President does not deny, on the contrary he maintains, that every sovereign power decides for itself, on its responsibility, the question whether or not it will, at a given time, accord the status of belligerency to the insurgent subjects of another power, as also the larger question of the independence of such subjects and their accession to the family of sovereign states.

Thus we see that the right to recognize a foreign government as being a belligerent power is one that the Government of the United States asserts upon its own responsibility, and, I will add, with reference only to the rights and sympathies of its own people. It does not stop to consider whether or not it has a justification in the eyes of the country within whose limits an insurrection has arisen which has grown into the proportions of public war and a declaration of independence. It does not stop to consider the merits or justice of the case as between the insurgents and the mother country.

It does not stop to weigh with fine nicety of distinction what may be the appropriate moral sentiment of the mother country in refusing to give up the portion of her territory thus claiming independence. What the United States Government does and must do in a case of that kind is to follow the line of the interests and rights of her own people and the duties and obligations she owes to them.

I will admit that in acting in this way she may have very slight justification or no justification, and the motives of her action may be attributed to some jealousy of the mother country, to some ancient pique, or grudge, or revenge. If this was true, the Government of the United States could be held morally responsible in the sense of the laws of nations for having interfered without just cause or necessity in the affairs of another country. But when, as we have seen in the statements that I have brought to the attention of the Senate, commencing as far back as 1823, there is a continuous purpose on the part of the Government of the United States to see that no inhuman persecutions shall be visited upon the Cuban people because they felt the aspirations of liberty burning in their hearts, when we have pursued during all of this period of time the most guarded and conservative course toward Spain, when we have placed, as I remarked last Thursday, statutes upon our books of the severest character to prevent our people from availing themselves of the ordinary privileges of the laws of nations in cases like this, nothing can be imputed to us except that we are driven by the power of facts, for which we are not in the slightest degree responsible, to that serious attitude in which we are bound to acknowledge, in deference to the rights and feelings of our own people, that the people of Cuba are lawful belligerents under the laws of nations.

The reasons why the Government of the United States has this peculiar right under these peculiar circumstances are various and numerous. I will undertake to cite a very few of them. First, the nearness of the strife to our own borders. Mr. Fish, Secretary of State, writing to Mr. Motley, 25th of September, 1869, announces this doctrine:

> Or actual hostility might have continued to rage in the theater of insurgent war, combat after combat might have been fought for such a period of time, a mass of men may have engaged in actual war until they should have acquired the consistency of military power, to repeat the idea of Mr. Canning, so as evidently to constitute the fact of belligerency, and to justify the recognition by the neutral. Or the nearness of the seat of hostilities to the neutral may compel the latter to act; it might be his sovereign duty to act, however inconvenient such action should be to the legitimate government.

President Grant, in his annual message in 1875, says:

> The question of according or withholding rights of belligerency must be judged in every case in view of the particular attending facts. * * * This conflict must be one which will be recognized in the sense of international law as war. Belligerency, too, is a fact. The mere existence of contending armed bodies and their occasional conflicts do not constitute war in the sense referred to.
> A civil war—

said Judge Grier, giving the opinion of the Supreme Court in the Prize Cases (2 Black, 667)—

> is never solemnly declared; it becomes such by its accidents—the number, power, and organization of the persons who originate and carry it on. When the party in rebellion occupy and hold in a hostile manner a certain portion of territory; have declared their independence; have cast off their allegiance; have organized armies; have commenced hostilities against their former sovereign, the world acknowledges them as belligerents and the contest a war.

I now read from Woolsey on International Law, App. 111, note 10:

> There may be a difficulty in ascertaining when the fact of war begins, and this difficulty is the greater in cases of insurrection or revolt, where many of the antecedents and premonitory tokens of war are wanting, where an insurrection may be of little account and easily suppressed, and where war bursts out full-blown, it may be, at once. Our Government has more than once professed to govern its action by the following criteria expressed in Mr. Monroe's words relating to the Spanish South American revolts: "As soon as the movement assumes such a steady and consistent form as to make the success of the provinces probable, the rights to which they were entitled by the law of nations, as equal parties to a civil war, have been extended to them."
> But this rule breaks down in several places. The probability is a creature of the mind, something merely subjective, and ought not to enter into a definition of what a nation ought to do. Again, the success does not depend on steadiness and consistency of form only, but on relative strength of the parties. If you make probability of success the criterion of right in the case, you have to weigh other circumstances before being able to judge which is most probable, success or defeat. Would you, if you conceded belligerent rights, withdraw the concession whenever success ceased to be probable? And, still further, such provinces in revolt are not entitled by the law of nations to rights as equal parties to a civil war. They have properly no rights, and the concession of belligerency is not made on their account, but on account of considerations of policy on the part of the state itself which declares them such, or on grounds of humanity.

The writer then goes on to cite a number of instances which I will not undertake to detain the Senate by reading.

The time of this recognition is appropriate. I cite again, in support of this doctrine, Woolsey's International Law:

> The true time for issuing such a declaration, if it is best to issue it at all, is when a revolt has its organized government prepared by law for war on either element or on both, and when some act, involving the open intention and the fact of war, has been performed by one or both of the parties. Here

are two facts, the one political, the other pertaining to the acts of a political body. The fact of war is either a declaration of war or some other implying it, like a proclamation of blockade, or, it may be, actual armed contest.

In the wars that have occurred in Cuba many occasions have presented when our withholding a declaration of belligerency and neutrality has been unjust to our national character, until, indeed, our forbearance has been counted to us by other powers as proof of our weakness as a government.

Our experiences in Cuba demand that no war shall exist there without our especial supervision as to the treatment of our people who are engaged in it, or are resident there, and if it is necessary for us to treat both parties as belligerents, we must do so in order to assert against them and impose upon each the duties and obligations of civilized warfare and of respect for the rights of our people.

With insurrections occurring in Cuba frequently, and almost with a regularity proportioned to the time needed to recover from one war before another is begun, and every struggle made disastrous to the property of our people in Cuba and horrible with the sacrifice of lives and other outrages on humanity, we have the right to interpose our recognition that a state of war exists and to maintain an armed neutrality, if need be, through which we shall separate between these warring parties, and hold the Government that is guilty of wrong to our citizens to its responsibility for such conduct.

If we consent to stand by and witness these Spanish methods of dealing with our people until these long struggles are ended, and then to seek the price of their blood through the protracted delays of Spanish diplomacy, the respect we shall thus exhibit for the sensibilities of a cruel monarchy will in the end destroy our self-respect.

I prefer now, in anticipation of what is about to occur—and we know will surely occur, as it has in each of these bloody wars—to act upon the declaration of our rights made in President Jackson's seventh annual message, in 1835, from which I will read:

> Unfortunately, many of the nations of this hemisphere are still self-tortured by domestic dissensions. Revolution succeeds revolution; injuries are committed upon foreigners engaged in lawful pursuits. Much time elapses before a government sufficiently stable is erected to justify expectation of redress. Ministers are sent and received, and before the discussions of past injuries are fairly begun, fresh troubles arise; but too frequently new injuries are added to the old, to be discussed together with the existing government, after it has proved its ability to sustain the assaults made upon it, or with its successor, if overthrown. If this unhappy condition of things continue much longer, other nations will be under the painful necessity of deciding whether justice to their suffering citizens does not require a prompt redress of injuries by their own power, without waiting for the establishment of a government competent and enduring enough to discuss and make satisfaction for them.

That was a doctrine which was evoked by the fact of our being near to nations which were constantly afflicted with these spasms of turbulence and revolution. President Jackson, after his usual style, met it with a declaration that is American through and through, and just through and through, and it is upon that ground we stand to-day as firmly as we stand upon any other that affects our honor, or peace, or the safety of our people, when we demand that Spain, in the conduct of its war against Cuba, shall accord to her the attitude of a belligerent, so that if she achieves her independence we can hold her responsible for the wrongs done to our people. When Spain has succeeded in suppressing these revolts against her sovereignty in Cuba, her wars have left to us the legacy of devastated property to great amounts, for which no recompense has been made, and many lives of our people wasted without so much as an expression of regret.

It is asking too much of us in the name of courtesy or friendship that we should abstain from applying, in behalf of our people, the laws of civilized warfare, when the existence of public war is notorious and undeniable, because such a declaration may give countenance or encouragement to great bodies of people who are fighting for their liberty.

We have in many cases declared the rights in favor of our own people that are stated in the message of President Jackson from which I have quoted.

As to the occasions in the past when cruel barbarities have been perpetrated on our people in utter defiance of our treaty rights, applicable especially to Cuba, I will cite the comments of some of our eminent statesmen.

Speaking generally of the war in Cuba in 1875, Mr. Fish thus states the situation to Mr. Orth, November 15, 1875:

> You will further state that the President is of opinion that should the Government to which you are accredited find it consistent with its views to urge upon Spain the importance and necessity of either terminating or abandoning this contest, which now after a continuance of seven years has not advanced toward a prospect of success on either side, but which is characterized by cruelties, by violations of the rules of civilized modern warfare, by pillage, desolation, and wanton incendiarism, threatening the industry, capacity, and production of an extended and fertile country, the friendly expression of such views to Spain might lead that Government to a dispassionate consideration of the hopelessness of the contest, and tend to the earlier restoration of peace and prosperity to Cuba, if not to the preservation of the peace of the world.

President Hayes takes up this subject in his first annual message in 1877, and says:

> Another year has passed without bringing to a close the protracted contest between the Spanish Government and the insurrection in the Island of Cuba. While the United States have sedulously abstained from any intervention in this contest, it is impossible not to feel that it is attended with incidents affecting the rights and interests of American citizens. Apart from the effect of the hostilities upon trade between the United States and Cuba, their progress is inevitably accompanied by complaints, having more or less foundation, of searches, arrests, embargoes, and oppressive taxes upon the property of American residents, and of unprovoked interference with American vessels and commerce. It is due to the Government of Spain to say that during the past year it has promptly disavowed and offered reparation for any unauthorized acts of unduly zealous subordinates whenever such acts have been brought to its attention.

That is more than Spain has deigned to do in the present war, so far as I am informed.

Now, as to the administration of justice in Cuba in times when the civil wars were flagrant, I will read a few observations, because it is in that particular matter that our people have perhaps a deeper concern than almost any other. Mr. Fish, writing to Mr. Sickles, November 25, 1870, says:

> I inclose a copy of a decree said to have been made by a military tribunal in Cuba, and published in the Diario de la Marina on the 9th of November, current.
> This decree purports to condemn to death sundry persons named in it as the central republican junta of Cuba and Puerto Rico, established in New York, and to confiscate their property. It appears affirmatively in the decree that none of the condemned had appeared before the court.

Condemning men to death who were living at that time in New York and had never been before the court.

> This revolutionary body, known as the Cuban junta, voluntarily disbanded itself about one month before this decree was made, and announced its intention to discontinue any hostile purpose it might have entertained against Span-

ish rule in Cuba. During its previous history its acts, so far as conflicting with the laws of the United States and the international duties of this Government, were repressed by the President. This Department has also been officially informed by Mr. Roberts that the state of affairs in Cuba is regarded as a favorable one by the Spanish Government, and that in consequence of that the extraordinary powers previously vested in him had been withdrawn. This Government has therefore seen with surprise and regret the announcement of a policy in Cuba which is apparently uncalled for by any present emergencies, which is not in harmony with the ideas now entertained by the most enlightened nations as to the treatment of political offenses, and which, as it appears to us, will tend to continue the unhappy disturbances which exist in Cuba.

Very numerous controversies—one we have recently settled in the Mora case—have arisen between Spain and the United States growing out of this insurrection, and have tied to long diplomatic interchange of notes and a great deal of angry contention and disturbance between these two Governments.

In the present war we have an account from our consuls in Cuba of the arrest of twenty-seven American citizens and the expulsion of others, and of the destruction of much valuable property of our citizens. I need not dwell on these incidents as showing, by object lessons, the renewal of the horrors of former wars for the independence of Cuba.

The present war, since the more humane plans of General Campos have caused his recall to Spain, to give place to Valerian Weyler, has received an impress of cruelty in the decrees he has promulgated as commander in chief and Captain-General for its further prosecution that is more ferocious than any that any ruler has dared to avow in modern times.

It proclaims a war against the people, against the poor and the helpless, against women and children, and all movable property, trade, food supplies, and every element of personal liberty, whether of speech or action, with a cruel cunning and atrocity that has no parallel in the history of modern civil wars.

This bloody code will as surely be enforced in its terrible and discretionary penalties against our people in Cuba as that any of them are found there suspected of sympathy with the Cuban people. It violates our commercial rights and annuls the treaty stipulations for the trial of our citizens who are accused of crime in Cuba.

Summary conviction and sudden death are imposed upon those who "insult their superiors." If a fancied or affected insult to the haughty pride of the Spanish hidalgo is made by some poor victim, under the goad of imperious persecution, the courts are dispensed with and the egotistic and lordly tyrant becomes at once the judge and executioner.

If any such wicked decree is made and executed under this Weyler code against any citizen of the United States, Spain had as well understand now as later that 70,000,000 freemen will visit upon her a punishment compared with which the loss of Cuba would be as a pleasing satisfaction.

As a warning of certain redress against this dictation of a ruthless tyrant, and as plain notice to the native Cubans who may be driven into retaliation by its murderous denunciations, the least we can do is to place both parties in the national attitude of belligerents, so that we can hold each of them responsible for their conduct in dealing with citizens of the United States.

The declaration of neutrality when made by us imposes on us the duties of neutrality, and this is all that it does. I will state them very briefly.

The duties imposed upon us are that we are bound to restrain enlistment by belligerents; we must restrain the forming of armed expeditions; we are bound to restrain the fitting out and selling of armed cruisers to the belligerents, or the passage of belligerent troops over our soil; we are bound not to permit our territory to be made the base of belligerent operations, nor to permit belligerent naval operations in our territorial waters, nor to permit the sale of prizes in our ports; we are bound to redress damages done to belligerents by our connivance or neglect.

Now, what are the rights of our people under this declaration of belligerency, which involves, of course, the declaration of neutrality? They may trade with either belligerent and may trade with the colonies of the belligerent which are not even open to trade in times of peace. We may permit free discussion as to foreign sovereigns. We may permit our people to furnish funds or supplies to the belligerents. Our people may furnish them with munitions of war. They may enlist in the service of the belligerents, provided they do not, in contravention of our own statutes, enlist in this country or enlist in bodies formed for the purpose or actually organized into military squads. We are permitted to sell them ships or to buy ships from them. We are permitted to give an asylum to the belligerent ships or troops in our ports or on land.

Mr. President, that exhausts the list of the duties, and obligations, and the rights of persons thus involved in belligerency. It is needless to state more fully what are the rights and duties of neutrals in time of war, because this resolution is not the least indication of hostility to either of the belligerent governments in Cuba, but imposes upon us the duty of preserving a relation of friendship to both.

Whether our statutes restrain our citizens within narrower limits in their intercourse with belligerents than the laws of nations prescribe is not a material inquiry at this time, for our proposed action is based upon our sense of right and duty, and is moved by our sense of justice and our sympathy with those who are harshly treated, and not by any advantages of trade that may come to our people in their intercourse with either of the belligerents.

With peace in Cuba we have very liberal rights of trade with those people.

Spain declares that Cuba is at peace and only a faction of the people there are engaged in sedition or insurrection. But with this declaration of peace she imposes upon our trade in contraband and in supplies to places in rebellion the laws of war.

We are thus forced to declare the existence of open war that our people may enjoy the rights of neutrals in war, at the risk of capture, that are denied to them as the friends of Spain because Cuba is in a state of insurrection.

Thus peace shuts us out from trade with Cuba, and we declare that war exists there, so that we may have as much freedom of trade as a state of war will give us. As it is, our trade is virtually abolished.

Along with open war we have the right to insist that it shall be civilized warfare.

Upon this subject I could read, if I felt disposed to detain the Senate, some statements from the Cuban agents who are here, which, I think, would be highly worthy of attention; and I hope other Senators who may be disposed to engage in this debate will look up that subject, and I will furnish them with the information, if they desire to have it.

But it is a canon of universal acceptance among all Christian nations that in modern times, at least, the laws of civilized modern warfare shall be observed by all belligerents.

The next question, Mr. President, upon which I propose to make some discussion is in answer to the question put to me, I think by the Senator from Massachusetts [Mr. HOAR], or one of the Senators, as to who may declare the belligerent rights of a foreign people, whether the President or Congress, or both in conjunction. Upon this proposition, which does not really arise upon the resolution reported by the committee, I will take the opportunity of submitting some further considerations to-morrow, as it is entirely disconnected with the question of our right and our duty to recognize the belligerency of Cuba and the manner in which it shall be done, and whether this resolution, now offered in the Senate by the Committee on Foreign Relations, shall be effectual for that purpose is a question entirely aside from our right and duty to recognize the belligerency of Cuba.

I wish to say, then, Mr. President, that not one word that I have uttered on this floor, and not one word, I think, that has been or will be uttered by any other Senator, arises from any jealousy of Spain or any disposition to do her any wrong, to subject her to any humiliation or any injustice. We are speaking now only in behalf of our own people, who, innocently on their part, have been drawn into a situation where a decision must be made in their behalf as to the fact whether a war exists in Cuba or does not exist there. I have already cited and read the authorities to prove that any American citizen found in the Island of Cuba has the private right to determine for himself whether war exists there or not, and to regulate his conduct according to his intelligent decision of that proposition.

If while he is in the interior of Cuba he makes a contribution to the Cuban army, whether he does it voluntarily or under a constraint imposed upon him, he has the right, as I have proved by the authorities I have cited, to decide for himself whether the party to which he makes that contribution is engaged in public war and is the representative of a political de facto government controlling in that immediate vicinity. That decision made by him protects him, and there is not a power which belongs to the Government of the United States which will not be exerted to protect that man in making his decision, as much as it would a soldier who might muster under our flag in virtue of a concurrent or joint resolution passed this day in the two Houses of Congress and signed by the President. The fact of belligerency is the thing which determines the right—not the justification of the belligerents, not the purposes of the war; but if a public, open war exists in Cuba to-day our own private citizens may determine it, and must determine it if they are found there, as we see they have been in many cases.

The case of Mr. Atkins, to which the Senator from Massachusetts referred, is a case directly in point. What must Mr. Atkins do? he inquires. Must he pay this tribute of $8 a ton, or whatever it is, which is levied upon him by the Gomez government or the Cisneros government, the civil government and the military government of the Republic of Cuba, or shall he refuse to pay it to them? If he pays it to them voluntarily, Spain holds him accountable, and his property is within her domain and is threatened with embargo. If he does not pay it to the Cuban republicans, his property will be destroyed, or perhaps a forced levy made upon him. That man has the right to decide the question, and if he makes a payment to the Cuban rebels under such conditions and circumstances, and Spain undertakes to embargo or confiscate his property because he is giving aid and comfort to the enemy, the Government of the United States would be bound to step in and say: "Mr. Atkins was compelled to make the decision and had the right to do it; you did not have the power to extend your Government protection over him at the time, and the only protection he could gain was by his intelligent decision as to whether this was in fact a mere mob or riot or insurrection, or whether it was a public war."

So we have got to trace such questions up, in such cases, beginning with our people whose persons and property are upon that island, and we have got to follow them through all of its stages, so as to see that men who have even gone contrary to our own laws and enlisted in the Cuban service, or, if you please, in the Spanish service, are protected by the laws of civilized warfare.

There is no public reason, there is no reason founded in justice, there is nothing which animates the heart of an honest American which furnishes to us, in my judgment, on this serious occasion the slightest justification for refusing to recognize a fact which the whole world is bound to acknowledge. If we make that recognition now, it may have some impression upon this war to carry it in favor of one party or the other. If it does, that is not our intention. What we intend to do is to declare a state of public war as existing there, because that is the fact, because that is the truth. It is our duty to our own people to recognize it, and only to them.

More than that. If we make this recognition now, and if this rebellion be put down, if this insurrection is quelled, the next one which comes, or the next—for come they will, come they must, and we know it—will come under the premonition of a decided policy of the United States of America. When these people in search of their liberties and in demand of their natural rights again flare out into open public war, though it may be done in an hour, though it may not be done in a month or a year, Spain will have notice that she can not consider them and our people who may be there and who may be obedient to the authority of the de facto government in the light of mere criminals and culprits, liable to be shot to death when she captures them with arms in their hands, or without; she must hereafter treat them according to the fact, and when the fact becomes obvious, and is known the world over, and there is none who can honestly dispute it, she must recognize that fact and extend to the belligerents the rights of civilized warfare.

I desire to retain the floor for a few moments to-morrow on the pending resolution.

Mr. DUBOIS. Mr. President——

Mr. WHITE. Will the Senator from Idaho yield to me for the purpose of allowing me to offer a substitute for the pending resolution, simply that it may be printed before to-morrow, and for no other purpose? I do not wish now to offer any remarks about it.

Mr. DUBOIS. I yield for that purpose.

Mr. MORGAN. Let the proposed substitute be read, Mr. President.

2777

The VICE-PRESIDENT. The proposed substitute will be read. The Secretary read as follows:

Resolved, That the Senate contemplates with solicitude and profound regret the sufferings and destruction accompanying the civil conflict now in progress in Cuba. While the United States have not interfered and will not, unless their vital interests so demand, interfere with existing colonies and dependencies of any European Government on this hemisphere, nevertheless our people have never disguised and do not now conceal their sympathy for all those who struggle patriotically, as do the Cubans now in revolt, to exercise, maintain, and preserve the right of self-government. Nor can we ignore our exceptional and close relations to Cuba by reason of geographical proximity and our consequent grave interest in all questions affecting the control or well-being of that island. We trust that the executive department, to whose investigation and care our diplomatic relations have been committed, will, at as early a date as the facts will warrant, recognize the belligerency of those who are maintaining themselves in Cuba in armed opposition to Spain, and that the influence and offices of the United States may be prudently, peacefully, and effectively exerted to the end that Cuba may be enabled to establish a permanent government of her own choice.

The VICE-PRESIDENT. The amendment will be printed.

* * * * * * *

February 25, 1896.

The Senate resumed the consideration of the concurrent resolution reported by Mr. MORGAN on the 5th instant from the Committee on Foreign Relations.

Mr. MORGAN. Mr. President, I had reserved to myself, with the consent of the Senator from Delaware, who will succeed me in this debate, the opportunity to present to the Senate the documents that I spoke of yesterday; and being very desirous to get before the country and the Senate, as far as it is possible to do so, an authentic statement of all the facts that are necessary to be considered in discussing this resolution and in coming to a vote upon it, I will present the civil organization of the Republic of Cuba, of which Mr. Salvador Cisneros Betancourt is the President, and which was adopted at Mangus de Baragua on the 16th of October, 1895. I will not undertake to read this document, but I will ask that it be appended to my remarks as it is printed from page 30 to page 35, both inclusive. (See Appendix A.)

There are a number of other regulations affecting the military and also laws ordained to govern the civil relations of the people of the Republic of Cuba which would be very interesting for examination; and I hope that those who choose to debate this question and those who wish to give it a very thorough consideration will refer to those laws, some of them relating to civil marriage and to other civil institutions, laws for the service of communications and the postal system, laws to regulate the public treasury, and laws of the government council of the nation, all of which are very admirably prepared and embody a most excellent system of government as it is adapted to the situation in Cuba at this time.

My purpose in presenting this paper is to show that there is a civil foundation for that government. Cisneros Betancourt is the president of that republic. He was the president of the republic at the time of the surrender in 1878. That fact is stated in the papers sent in by the President of the United States in his message May 14, 1878, which I will also print as an appendix to my remarks, in which will be found two letters written by the then minister of Spain at this capital, Antonio Mantilla, which relate to the terms of the capitulation that were entered into by the Republic of Cuba in 1878. I will read from one of the dispatches announcing the result of that reconciliation. It is from Flores, and was dated at Santa Cruz on the 12th of February, 1878. It is addressed to Director del "Diario de la Marina," Habana, and is as follows:

> The peace of the island is now a fact about to be realized. The president of the Cuban Republic, Maximo Gomez, chamber and government in accord with the force of the Camaguey, are at work to realize peace. Also, in the Villas and Oriental departments. For those two departments commissions of important chiefs have left with that object. Hostilities suspended in all the island.
>
> FLORES.

An examination of these papers shows a distinct recognition of the existence of the Republic of Cuba at the time this capitulation took place, and it shows that Maximo Gomez, who is the commander-in-chief of the armies of the Cuban Republic as it now exists, was busily engaged in an effort, which was applauded by the Spaniards, an honorable effort, to secure peace upon the terms of the capitulation that was entered into at that time between the Spaniards and the Cubans. That capitulation contains various stipulations, some of them added to the original article by after agreement.

In order to get the history of that transaction clearly before the Senate and the people of the United States, I will ask leave to print as an appendix to my remarks each of these letters. I would not encumber the RECORD with these extensive publications but that it is necessary in order to get at an exact statement of the political situation in the Island of Cuba at the time this capitulation took place. I also wish to emphasize the fact that the constitution and plan of organization of Cisneros, who was then president of the republic, and is now again president of the republic as it is at present declared, is in substance the same government that is now restored and is in operation, as is set forth in the document which I now present. (See Appendix B.)

These papers show the existence in 1878, and for more than ten years before that time, of a republic in the Island of Cuba, which was recognized as such in the capitulation itself, not in the very language of the capitulation, but in all of the attendant information and facts which were given out to the public by the minister of Spain at this capital in order to justify the conduct of the Spanish Government and also to satisfy this country that permanent peace had ensued.

I mentioned on yesterday that the Cubans who now comprise this government, including of course the army that is now in existence, insist that their present action is justified entirely, and by subsequent abuses which took place after that capitulation, which involve violations of the agreement entered into between Spain and Cuba, on various occasions, some of which acts, as charged by the Cubans, are very outrageous, if they be true. Perhaps it is not necessary for me to express an opinion on the question as to whether their allegations are true or not, except as a justification of the course that the committee have taken and that I am now advocating on the floor of the Senate. I do believe in their truth; I have nowhere seen them disputed. They stand forth as facts which have been published to the world now for more than a year without any contradiction that I have ever seen.

The war which has ensued for the purpose of the redress of those grievances and for the reclamation of those rights that were thus betrayed into the hands of the Spanish Crown by a breach of their solemn obligation has progressed to the degree and condition of open, public war, which I undertook yesterday to establish both from the accounts of the Cubans and from the accounts given by our own consuls in their communications sent to this Government.

Martinez Campos is everywhere spoken of in the papers to which I have just referred as a man of broad patriotism, great ability and benevolence; as a man who, when he was fighting the men against whom he was arrayed from 1867 to 1878, always regarded them as if they were brethren in arms opposed to him, and his conciliatory spirit, his desire to reconcile the people of Cuba to further submission to the Spanish monarchy, is everywhere complimented and referred to with applause as being the cause of the composure which took place at the end of that civil war. When Martinez Campos was recently removed from his command of the army of Spain that occupied the Island of Cuba, apprehensions were entertained and expressions on all sides were heard that no one could succeed him who could conduct that war in such a way as to heal up the wounds between the Cubans and the Spanish people, nearly all of whom are descended from the same stock, and when he was recalled to Spain after the failure of his campaign there, and after the resources of Spain had been almost exhausted, there was one general expression of regret by the people of the civilized world that so great and so noble a character had been withdrawn from the arena of war and had been retired into private life.

I do not hesitate, Mr. President, on my part, to express my regret at that occurrence, because while Campos was in the field I still had a hope that the Government of Spain would see that in order to keep her hold upon the affections of the people of Cuba and to command their honest allegiance she would be compelled to accord to them a form of government corresponding to that which is exercised in Canada as a province of the Crown of Great Britain; but the Spanish Government seems to be infatuated with the idea that absolute submission must take place in that island to every demand which is urged against those people, and when anything that is demanded is refused,'extermination is to be the result.

When General Weyler was sent there as Captain-General he assumed to himself the double function of a supreme-court judge and Captain-General, and announced in the proclamation (which I will print in my remarks) that he assumed at one and the same time the functions of generalissimo and commander-in-chief of the army and the office of supreme judge of that country. Thereupon he issued a manifesto consisting of three proclamations, which I will place in the RECORD, which show, without any possibility of misunderstanding, his determination to sacrifice private life and all the liberties of the people whenever he chose to do so for the purpose of extending, consolidating, and enforcing his decrees and his power. By that judgment he placed every inhabitant of Cuba, without reference to nationality, in a position of absolute subjection to his individual and unrestrained will. Then he goes into various details which affect the people of Cuba, the people who live out in the forests and in the country, to such an extent that life itself would be an intolerable burden when it has to be lived under such circumstances. These are the papers which I desire to put in the RECORD. (See Appendix B.)

A gentleman has sent me this morning a newspaper printed in the city of Washington, The Evening Times, a very respectable paper, containing in its telegraphic columns a statement from Dr. Guiteras, in which he makes reply to a recent statement made by

General Weyler in the matter of his execution of this decree. It seems that General Weyler had denied that since he had been in command of the island a single execution had been made. Dr. Guiteras scarcely credited the reports of these executions which came from the island, but yesterday a batch of letters in cipher was received by him, and after translating them he said:

> I have been loath to believe the reports of the killing of prisoners in the field and in the prisons since the arrival of Governor Weyler. These reports have been specially denied by General Weyler himself. I have received today letters from Habana that confirm the report. I am now firmly convinced that prisoners are quietly disposed of by some officer in the field, and that some prisoners have been brought to the forts in Habana and Matanzas who have subsequently disappeared without their friends knowing what has become of them.
> I have in one of these letters the names of three prisoners, but can not give them at this time, as it would disclose the source of my information. I would add that this question has been referred to me especially by friends in Cuba with an appeal that I should exert whatever influence I may have to bring about a termination of this frightful state of affairs. I can do nothing better than appeal to the American press. The section in a letter from Habana which treats of the matter is as follows:
> "It happens every day that prisoners are brought to this city. Some are sent to jail, and others to the fortifications. These last, if they belong to the lower classes, are made to disappear. A reason assigned is that there is not money enough to keep them. That is, you will understand, frightful. I am absolutely sure of what I am telling you, and you must make an effort to put a stop to it by appealing to the press of America.
> "I have heard of similar stories for some time, but I could find no responsible person to repeat them to me, and I thought them too horrible to believe, though I know the man we are dealing with, but no doubt is left in my mind. It is known that the procedure is common in the field, but is not so frequently employed in the city."

I have an apprehension, which I can not repress, that if General Weyler remains in the command of the army of Spain in Cuba, there will be destruction of life at his will and pleasure, perhaps in such a manner as not to be disclosed to the world for two or three or four years to come; but it seems that it is already apparent, in the case of three prisoners, that they have been killed after being captured.

I do not care, Mr. President, to enter more fully into a recital of these horrible incidents, because this is not in the slightest degree necessary to justify the position of the Government of the United States that war exists in Cuba, open, public civil war, and that it is to the interest and welfare of our own people, regardless of our sympathies for the Cubans, regardless of the effect it may have upon the Spaniards or the Cubans, that we should give a recognition, justified by the fact of the belligerency of those two powers in Cuba, and that is as far as we need to go.

Something has been said in this debate on the subject of the proper method of making this declaration. The resolution before the Senate declares that, in the opinion of Congress, a state of public war exists in Cuba, and that it is the duty of the United States to recognize the belligerency of the hostile parties.

What is the effect of such a declaration of opinion on the part of the Congress of the United States? If the effect should be to cause some contrary attitude to be imputed, as existing between the President and the two Houses of Congress, it would be indeed very unfortunate. If Congress should pass a resolution of this kind and the President of the United States, conceiving that our action was only advisory and was not mandatory, should withhold the declaration or should not predicate any Executive act upon it, it would leave the Government of the United States in a position to be severely criticised by our people and by the other powers of the world.

I do not anticipate any such difficulty between the President and Congress. I have no right to do so, from the message which the President sent us at the beginning of this session of Congress, for he recognized the fact of the existence of open and bloody war in Cuba; and I must suppose—I do suppose, and I believe also—that when the President of the United States becomes satisfied that it is to the best interests of the people of the United States that there should be a recognition of that belligerency he will concur in the opinion that is expressed in this resolution, and will exert whatever of authority he has as the Chief Executive of this nation to sanction and enforce that resolution. But if he should decline to do so, then the attitude of Congress would be such that we should be regarded as intermeddling with matters with which we have no constitutional concern, and we should be amenable to such a criticism in the event that I have supposed, because the President of the United States can not refuse to respect the will of Congress when it is expressed in a constitutional method upon any subject.

If it is a matter of legislation to which his veto power applies, and if he shall exercise his veto, he is bound to respect the act; he is bound to consider the measure; he is bound either to return it to the House in which it originated, or else he may let it pass over for ten days, in which case it becomes a law and an effectual expression of the legislative will. But to put ourselves in an attitude in reference to a great question of this kind, where the President is at liberty to act or not to act, as he sees proper, and where it is to be imputed to his action that it is to give validity and effect to what we do or to the opinion which we express here, it becomes a very serious matter whether we should pass this resolution in the form in which it is now presented.

The question of the power of the President of the United States in respect of the declaration of belligerency between two foreign powers has never undergone conclusive judicial investigation, nor has the Congress of the United States ever given to this subject a decided expression of their opinion upon it. It may therefore be styled a new question. In the consideration of this question the Constitution of the United States alone can rule. There is no other law to which we can appeal to arrive at a decision as between the Executive and the Congress of the United States upon this matter.

Suppose, for instance, that some one should propose to amend this resolution and strike out the words "in the opinion of Congress," and leave it as a clear, emphatic, unequivocal declaration on the part of the two Houses that a public war exists in Cuba and that the Government of the United States recognizes the belligerency of those parties in order that the Government and the people may be put in an attitude where the duties of neutrality would attach to us under the international law, then we should have a declaration here which would assume upon the face of it that this concurrent action on the part of the two Houses of Congress would of itself be a recognition of the existence of the public war, the belligerency of the two parties, and our consequent international neutrality.

Mr. FRYE. Will the Senator allow me?

The PRESIDING OFFICER (Mr. WHITE in the chair). Does the Senator from Alabama yield to the Senator from Maine?

Mr. MORGAN. Certainly.

Mr. FRYE. Suppose some one, in addition to the amendment of striking out the words "in the opinion," should add "and Congress hereby recognizes the belligerent rights," etc., what does the Senator have to say as to that?

Mr. MORGAN. That would only make the resolution a little more impressive or a little more emphatic in the definition of the attitude of Congress, because if we should strike out the words "in the opinion of Congress," that would then leave this as the declaration on the part of the two Houses of Congress that a public war does exist in Cuba and that we recognize neutrality.

Mr. FRYE. But suppose the words "it is the duty" were left out of the resolution, what then?

Mr. MORGAN. Perhaps those words ought to be left out to make the declaration as emphatic as the Senator from Maine now suggests.

Mr. PEFFER. While the Senator is on that point, will it not also involve concurrent action on the part of the Executive? Because, as the Senator very properly stated the other day, this question involves the right of seizure and involves certain Executive acts that might amount to watching and guarding and sometimes affirmative action on the part of the Executive. Would not such a declaration as the Senator from Maine suggests to that extent also involve the Executive; and if so, suppose the Executive should differ with Congress?

Mr. MORGAN. Mr. President, the committee of course have endeavored to avoid raising a question of this kind. They have not anticipated that any action of the Executive would make it necessary that they should raise it, or that the question would arise, or that it should be settled by any vote to be taken here. I will repeat that I do not anticipate that a question of that kind will occur; yet it might; and in shaping our resolution here we must be careful that we keep ourselves within the line of our constitutional powers and duties, and also careful that we do not surrender to any other department of this Government a portion of the power that the Constitution lodges in Congress.

Mr. FRYE. That is just what I should like to hear the Senator upon, whether or not, in his judgment, the Congress itself has the power to recognize belligerent rights without any intervention of the President of the United States.

Mr. MORGAN. Mr. President, in section 8 of Article I of the Constitution there is an enumeration of the powers of Congress. Several powers are mentioned, such as to coin money, etc., establish post-offices, promote the progress of science, to define and punish piracies and felonies committed on the high seas, to declare war, grant letters of marque and reprisal, and make rules concerning captures on land and water.

This power to declare war is associated with all those other powers in the same section, which affect and relate only to the civil administration of the Government, to the Government in a state and condition of peace, and for that reason some very able gentlemen have concluded that, being thus associated with this general delegation of powers to Congress, it must take its class with them, and be subject to all of the incidents that belong to the exercise of these general powers in other cases.

I am not prepared to subscribe to that construction of this instrument. I believe that the power to declare war and grant letters of marque and reprisal, and more especially the power to declare war, is a power which, from the very nature of it, when taken in connection with the other provisions of the Constitution relating to war and the conduct of war, stands by itself, and it must be exercised by Congress without the aid, or assistance, or participation of the Executive. It is the nature of the power to be thus exercised that I rely upon as separating it in its incidents and consequences from the other general powers which Congress has conferred upon it under the eighth section of the first article of the Constitution, from which I have just been reading. The power to declare war is not a legislative power.

The framers of the Constitution understood perhaps as well as or better than any of us to-day—because they were in the midst of war and the Government which they were founding had just passed through a great struggle with the greatest monarchy then in the world—they understood particularly well what were and should be the functions of the Executive of the United States and the powers of Congress in respect of the declaration of war and the conduct of war, and in respect of making provision for the support of armies and navies, so as to leave it entirely in the hands of the popular branch of Congress to make appropriations for these purposes, or to originate appropriations for these purposes, putting a limit upon the power of the House in making the appropriations that they should be renewed once every two years; thus showing that, in the consideration of the war powers of the Government of the United States, they dissociated these powers from the general mass of powers that are conferred upon the Congress of the United States and placed them in a peculiar light; and it is in that light and in consideration of the purposes that the framers of the Constitution must have had in mind when they organized this splendid system of government that we are to interpret their intentions.

We must consider this question now, and we must not forget the impressions that evidently were foremost in their minds at that time, and by neglect allow the powers of the Congress of the United States to pass into the hands of one of the coordinate departments, in whole or in part, in the extreme case, the terrible case, when this country shall be involved in war.

The war power is to be sacredly guarded, and the people who are held obedient to it and must fight its battles and suffer its devastations should have the exclusive right to declare the existence of a state of war.

The state of war as it affects the citizen, the property of the citizen, his relations to foreign countries, the treaties between this Government and the government with which we are at war, might be called a total change, a total departure, from the state of the country when it is at peace. When the country is at peace the citizen is not required, on any occasion, to give up any of his constitutional rights or protection and of resort to the ordinary tribunals of law for the redress of his wrongs or the enforcement of his rights.

When a state of war supervenes, however, his person, his property, and all that belongs to him are subjected by the laws of nations and the Constitution of the United States to the behests of the Government to answer its purposes, even though in doing so he may surrender his life and all that he has. His duty of submission to the military power of the United States, lawfully exercised in time of war, may be called almost absolute, whereas in time of peace all the guaranties of the Constitution of the United

States cluster about him to save him against any arbitrary power or the command of any individual that he shall do this or that or that he omit to do this or that. The condition of war changes almost absolutely and almost completely all the relations of this Government to its own people and to the country with which we are engaged in belligerency, and also, in a collateral way, with the people of the whole world.

So those provisions of the Constitution of the United States that were made for a state of war and adapted to a state of war must be attended with those conditions which make it possible that the Government of the United States shall act as a unit, and shall make it impossible that there should be any division of authority between the executive and the legislative branches of the Government in the recognition which is the declaration of the existence of a state of war.

If there is anything more necessary to the successful conduct of a war than all else, it is the fact that the power of the government that is engaged in a war is lodged at least in the hands of a single man, or a single tribunal. No possibility of a division of interest, a division of sentiment, a division of will between the high functionaries of a government can be admitted if the government that is bound to make this admission is engaged in a war with a foreign country, or even with its own people in insurrection. There must be unity, absolute and perfect unity, in the power that conducts a war, and any division of it that is possible is to that extent a fatal defect in the government itself.

Now. I will suppose a case. Suppose that a declaration of war by the United States Government is made under a joint resolution, which would go to the President of the United States, and that he, for reasons of public policy or reasons of private interest or affection, should veto the resolution, what would be the situation of this country under those circumstances? The Government would perish in the effort to defend its rights or vindicate its honor; perish upon a division of opinion between the Congress of the United States and the President of the United States. So in regard to making peace; so in regard to every other incident attending the conduct of war, such as the issue of letters of marque and reprisal, etc.

Mr. FRYE. How about raising supplies? Suppose the President should veto a resolution raising supplies?

Mr. MORGAN. He could veto a resolution to raise supplies. I think there is no doubt about that.

Mr. FRYE. And he could defeat——

Mr. MORGAN. But that is not the actual conduct of war. It is a provision for the conduct of war, and he might constrain us to agree to a peace after we had been at war, or perhaps he might prevent us from getting into a war by the veto of a resolution or bill to raise supplies for the purpose of carrying on the war. But I am not now speaking of that legislative power which might attend the conduct of a war or provision for its support. I am speaking now of those matters which concern the inauguration of war and which relate to the power of the President and the Congress to change the attitude of the Government of the United States and the duties of all the people in it from a state of peace to a state of war. These acts are entirely distinguishable.

Perhaps no argument could be made upon this point which would be entirely consistent with itself in any direction in which you might choose to trace it, unless, indeed, we should admit that the President of the United States, when Congress passes a declaration by a joint resolution, I will say, in proper form, to the effect that the United States is at war with some foreign power, has the right to bring his veto to bear upon it and to deny the fact. While there are no actual decisions conclusive of the point I am now debating, there are various utterances and some official acts on the part of the early Presidents of the United States to which I desire to call attention, and also on the part of some of our wisest constitutional lawyers. I will read several extracts from the opinions of those lawyers and those Presidents which I think support very clearly the proposition that Congress, and Congress alone, has the power to declare war.

But before reading them, Mr. President, I should like to say (and I will cite the authorities in support of that proposition when I come to them) that the power of Congress, as it is expressed in the Constitution, is not to wage war. not to create war; it is the right to recognize its existence. The existence of war in the United States, between this and a foreign country, or the existence of a war in some foreign country, is simply a fact, and when a recognition is made by the Congress of the United States or by the lawful authority of this country of the existence of war, it amounts to a declaration of war. A declaration of war is not a pronunciamento against some other nation as to which Congress demands that war shall be waged, but it is a declaration that a state of war actually exists at the time when the declaration is pronounced. This is not a legislative act.

Mr. FRYE. Actually exists anywhere.

Mr. MORGAN. That a state of war actually exists anywhere at the time the declaration is made; and the declaration is nothing more than a recognition of the fact, a statement of the fact that a state of war actually exists. It places that declaration in legal form. It is not a legislative act; it may be a political act.

Mr. HOAR. Mr. President——

The PRESIDING OFFICER. Does the Senator from Alabama yield to the Senator from Massachusetts?

Mr. MORGAN. Certainly.

Mr. HOAR. I should like to get instruction from the Senator from Alabama, who is so competent to give it on this question, by asking him a question and perhaps putting an illustration.

In regard to our relations with France shortly after the close of the Revolutionary war, some very principal authorities, including, I believe, my honorable friend from Ohio, maintained as a reason for not paying the French war claims that that was a war, not an act of international oppression of individuals. Suppose a citizen were proceeded against for corresponding with the enemy, giving aid and comfort to France at that time, on the ground that she was an enemy of the United States. Does the Senator claim that a resolution like this, passing both Houses of Congress, the President withholding his signature, would be accepted in court as having any validity or virtue whatever in regard to settling that question?

Mr. MORGAN. The illustration used by the Senator from Massachusetts furnishes me an opportunity to make what I conceive to be a just distinction between the duty and obligations of citizenship and the duties and rights of Congress in dealing with a question of this kind. A citizen must submit himself to the laws of his country as they are declared by the highest legislative authority, and until the laws of his country are changed or altered they impose upon him as a citizen the duties that belong to him in time of war, and he can neither appeal from that declaration as to those duties or those rights nor can he avoid them when the Government of the United States has placed him in that situation by declaring that his country is engaged in war.

When I said a moment ago that the existence of war is a fact, I meant to say that the existence of hostilities which have progressed to that degree where a private person coming in contact with the armies engaged in those hostilities would have the right to decide that a war existed would be what is called a state of war, although it is not the state of war that is made obligatory upon the citizenship of a country. It is a state of hostilities that has become so general and the parties to which have become so organized that the citizen himself when brought in contact with the question could decide for himself that it is an open and public war. But his decision bears upon no person except himself.

Now, it requires the act of a government to put the people at large, the nationality, into a condition of recognizing the existence of war.

Mr. HOAR. Including the President?

Mr. MORGAN. Including the President.

Mr. HOAR. I do not like to interfere with the Senator from Alabama, but perhaps he will not mind my asking him another question. I thought his argument was that the phrase in the Constitution "to declare war," where the power is given to Congress to declare war, has a different meaning, a different scope and effect, from the other similar enumerations of the powers given to Congress, to establish a uniform system of bankruptcy, for instance; that in that particular instance Congress is referred to as the two Houses, without the consent of the President. That is the reason why I put the question.

Mr. MORGAN. That is the position I take, and I believe it is the correct one.

Mr. HOAR. Then, if it be true that under the Constitution the two Houses of Congress, without the consent of the President, have the power to declare war, does it not follow that, the two Houses of Congress, without the President, having declared war, a citizen of this country is bound so to treat the citizens of the country which is declared to be an enemy, and is liable to the charge of treason for giving them aid and comfort?

Mr. MORGAN. Whenever a declaration of war is made by any competent authority of the United States, without now touching upon the question as to what is the competent authority, a citizen of the United States is put in the attitude of a citizen of a country which is at war, and he must obey and respect it, because that declaration defines who is the public enemy, and the citizen is bound to give respect to the declaration.

On December 6, 1805, Mr. Jefferson, discussing Spanish depredations on our territory, said:

Considering that Congress alone is constitutionally invested with the power of changing our conditions from peace to war, I have thought it my duty to await their authority for using force in any degree that could be avoided. I have barely instructed the officers stationed in the neighborhood of the aggressions to protect our citizens from violence, to patrol within the borders actually delivered to us, and not to go out of them but when necessary to repel an inroad or to rescue a citizen or his property.

This act of Mr. Jefferson in refusing to recognize the existence of war, as a legal status, until Congress had made the declaration is very impressive. It proves his regard for the limitations of the powers of the coordinate departments of our Government.

Mr. Webster, as Secretary of State, writing to Mr. Severance on the 14th of July, 1851, states:

> In the first place, I have to say that the war-making power in this Government rests entirely with Congress; and that the President can authorize belligerent operations only in the cases expressly provided for by the Constitution and the laws. By these no power is given to the Executive to oppose an attack by one independent nation on the possessions of another. We are bound to regard both France and Hawaii—
>
> There was a controversy between France and Hawaii—
>
> as independent States, and equally independent, and though the general policy of the Government might lead it to take part with either in a controversy with the other, still, if this interference be an act of hostile force, it is not within the constitutional power of the President; and still less is it within the power of any subordinate agent of Government, civil or military.

Those words are very closely measured by that great statesman and jurist, and they state an opinion to which I am bound to yield my acquiescence.

Mr. Cass, following, in 1857, on the subject of the power of Congress, said:

> This proposition, looking to a participation by the United States in the existing hostilities against China, makes it proper to remind your lordship that, under the Constitution of the United States, the executive branch of this Government is not the war-making power. The exercise of that great attribute of sovereignty is vested in Congress, and the President has no authority to order aggressive hostilities to be undertaken.
>
> Our naval officers have the right—it is their duty, indeed—to employ the forces under their command not only in self-defense but for the protection of the persons and property of our citizens when exposed to acts of lawless outrage, and this they have done both in China and elsewhere, and will do again when necessary. But military expeditions into the Chinese territory can not be undertaken without the authority of the National Legislature.

In the third annual message of President Buchanan, in 1859, when he was contemplating, doubtless, that war that might take place in the United States and a war that was then flagrant in Nicaragua, he said:

> I deem it my duty once more earnestly to recommend to Congress the passage of a law authorizing the President to employ the naval force at his command for the purpose of protecting the lives and property of American citizens passing in transit across the Panama, Nicaragua, and Tehuantepec routes against sudden and lawless outbreaks and depredations. I shall not repeat the arguments employed in former messages in support of this measure. Suffice it to say that the lives of many of our people, and the security of vast amounts of treasure passing and repassing over one or more of these routes between the Atlantic and Pacific, may be deeply involved in the action of Congress on this subject.
>
> I would also again recommend to Congress that authority be given to the President to employ the naval force to protect American merchant vessels, their crews and cargoes, against violent and lawless seizure and confiscation in the ports of Mexico and the Spanish American States, when these countries may be in a disturbed and revolutionary condition. The mere knowledge that such an authority had been conferred, as I have already stated, would of itself, in a great degree, prevent the evil. Neither would this require any additional appropriation for the naval service.
>
> The chief objection urged against the grant of this authority is that Congress, by conferring it, would violate the Constitution—that it would be a transfer of the war-making or, strictly speaking, the war-declaring power to the Executive. If this were well founded, it would, of course, be conclusive. A very brief examination, however, will place this objection at rest.
>
> Congress possess the sole and exclusive power under the Constitution "to declare war." They alone can "raise and support armies" and "provide and maintain a navy." But after Congress shall have declared war and provided the force necessary to carry it on, the President, as Commander-in-Chief of the Army and Navy, can alone employ this force in making war against the enemy. This is the plain language, and history proves that it was the well-known intention of the framers of the Constitution.

Now I will read an extract from the opinion of Judge Grier in the prize cases, 2 Black, where the court found it necessary to make an emphatic declaration on this subject in order to sustain its jurisdiction of a cause that arose during the Confederate war:

> By the Constitution Congress alone has the power to declare a national or foreign war. It can not declare war against a State, or any number of States, by virtue of any clause in the Constitution. The Constitution confers on the President the whole executive power. He is bound to take care that the laws be faithfully executed. He is Commander-in-Chief of the Army and Navy of the United States and of the militia of the several States when called into the actual service of the United States. He has no power to initiate or declare a war either against a foreign nation or a domestic State, but by the acts of Congress of February 28, 1795, and March 3, 1807, he is authorized to call out the militia and use the military and naval forces of the United States in case of invasion by foreign nations, and to suppress insurrections against the government of a State or of the United States.

It will be observed here that the court makes a distinction between the power of the President of the United States to declare war, to recognize the existence of a state of war and to make it obligatory upon the Government by his declaration, and his power under a statute of the United States, without declaring the existence of a state of war, to do certain things—that is to say, to resist enemies who may be invading the country and to suppress insurrection or rebellion in the States. There the court makes the manifest distinction which established the proposition by our highest judicial tribunal that whenever it becomes necessary that the attitude of the Government of the United States should be changed from peace to war, either wholly or in part, that action by the Constitution is intrusted entirely to Congress and that the President can not assume it to himself.

Mr. GRAY. From what has the Senator been reading?

Mr. MORGAN. From Judge Grier's opinion in the prize cases.

Mr. GRAY. I have read the cases which the Senator has in his hand, and I read the opinion differently, if the Senator draws the conclusion from those cases or from the opinion of the court that Congress without the consent of the President can declare war. All that Judge Grier says in that opinion, as I understand, is what the Constitution says, that it belongs to Congress and not to the Executive to declare war; but when it belongs to Congress it belongs as one of the enumerated powers which he must exert in the way prescribed by the Constitution.

Mr. MORGAN. It goes to the extent of denying to the President the power even to conduct war except in cases where he is empowered to do so by statute. It does not go to the extent of saying that Congress, in making a declaration of war, can act independently of the President. That point was not up. But I think it necessarily follows from the decision in this case that if the President can not declare war he has nothing to do with a declaration of war. If Congress must act, and the President must act conjointly with Congress in a declaration of war, then of course war can not exist until both departments of the Government have determined it—I mean legally exist, for it may exist in hostilities, but not in the form of war legally declared.

But here we find that the President of the United States, by the decision of the Supreme Court, is excluded from the power on his part of making this declaration. Then the question remains, and it is the only question, whether or not the Congress of the United States can make a declaration of war without the concurrence and consent of the President. That brings the question down to a single point upon this adjudication, as I understand it. I will read the balance of what is furnished here as the argument upon which the Supreme Court sustained that proposition:

> If a war be made by invasion of a foreign nation, the President is not only authorized but bound to resist force by force. He does not initiate the war, but is bound to accept the challenge without waiting for any special legislative authority; and whether the hostile party be a foreign invader or States organized in rebellion it is none the less a war, although the declaration of it be "unilateral." Lord Stowell (1 Dodson, 247) observes: "It is not the less a war on that account, for war may exist without a declaration on either side." It is so laid down by the best writers on the law of nations. A declaration of war by one country only is not a mere challenge to be accepted or refused at pleasure by the other.
>
> "The battles of Palo Alto and Resaca de la Palma had been fought before the passage of the act of Congress of May 13, 1846, which recognized 'a state of war as existing by the act of the Republic of Mexico.' This act not only provided for the future prosecution of the war, but was itself a vindication and ratification of the act of the President in accepting the challenge without a previous formal declaration of war by Congress."

So we went on and provided by statute various cases in which the President might command the Army and the Navy for the suppression of insurrection and rebellion, and also in the case of a foreign invasion that might be made against this country.

But we now have the question down to a single inquiry—admitting that that question is authority to rule our action in any sense—and that is, Must the President act conjointly with Congress in a declaration of war in recognizing the fact—in other words, that a state of war exists—and making that state of war and the attitude of war obligatory upon the people of the Government of the United States?

Now, I believe that the power to declare war and the power to conduct all matters in connection with its immediate prosecution was separated from the other powers in the Constitution of the United States, and, as stated by Mr. Webster, placed solely within the control of the two Houses of Congress, either acting in concert or acting contemporaneously without actual concurrence.

The strongest argument that suggests itself to my mind is the fact that the President of the United States, by the Constitution, has two distinct functions. One is political and the other is military, exclusively so. Wherever the President of the United States has to exercise his political functions, those that belong to legislation or to appointments to office, or in the special case of the negotiation of treaties and the exchange of ratifications, he either acts upon the peculiar powers and in the peculiar way assigned to him by the Constitution of the United States or else he acts by a general participation, in the legislative sense, with the two Houses of Congress.

The veto, backed by the sword, is not given to the President in our Constitution.

The President in negotiating a treaty is a diplomat, and yet he is the Chief Executive; he is the representative of this Government in its sovereignty so far as it touches the relations between this Government and foreign countries. When he performs this act of diplomacy and brings a treaty into shape, the two governments have got into agreement about it through the powers delegated to another body, distinct and separate from all other bodies in the United States, which rises up under the Constitution for the purpose of determining upon the validity of that treaty. That body is required to act almost as a unit. It requires two-thirds of the vote of the Senate of the United States to confirm a treaty.

Mr. DAVIS. Two-thirds of a quorum.

Mr. MORGAN. It requires two-thirds of the Senators forming a quorum of the Senate of the United States to confirm a treaty. That is not a legislative act, and yet it is legislative in its results, because the treaty when thus confirmed and when ratifications have been exchanged becomes, by the express declaration of the Constitution, a part of the supreme law of the land. So, in our constitutional system of government, various functions are given to different persons who discharge at the same time other functions which are just as separate as if they were exercised by two different persons. If we had had, like the Indians have, a war king and a civil king, questions of war would have been referred entirely to the war king and questions of legislation and national polity entirely to the civil ruler; as they had at one time in Japan when the Shogun was the absolute imperial ruler of the army and navy of Japan and the Mikado was the spiritual and political ruler of the same Empire.

But we made no such division of power into the hands of two men. We divide and separate the power in the hands of one man. We give the military power to the President of the United States to a certain extent, and to the extent that it was not given to him it remains in Congress. To what extent was it given to him? He is the Commander-in-Chief of the Army and Navy. He is a military officer by the Constitution, holding his commission under that instrument. He is the highest military officer in the United States, and every other military officer in the United States is subordinate to his command. But in that function he is just as separate from his other capacity to participate in the legislation of the country as he is when he negotiates a treaty. The functions are quite as different and quite as separate.

Now, I maintain that there was a reason for this, and it was to prevent the possibility of any conflict between the supreme departments of this Government in that most serious matter of declaring the existence of war. If there is any chance for us by a proper construction of this instrument to have the war-making power or the war-declaring power in the hands of a single department of the Government instead of having it oscillating between two, then it is due to the strength and future safety and power of our Government that we should so declare, and we should say that the Congress of the United States is empowered to declare war and the President is forbidden to participate in that declaration, because the war affects him in his office as General-in-Chief of the Army; that he must take his orders from the Congress of the United States, and must be thereby compelled to recognize that the occasion has arisen in which the functions of his military office come into full play, and he must exercise them.

There is no difficulty in this attitude, because we are not taking from the President anything that is useful in connection with his administration of the affairs of this Government, but if we concede to him the power to declare war, or by the application of his veto to defeat war, when he holds the commission of Commander-in-Chief of the Army of the United States, we acknowledge the principle that the military is superior to the civil power; that is all of it. Right there more than anywhere else in our constitutional system that maxim obtains, which is as strong as any feature of the written Constitution in this country, that the civil power is superior to the military.

The President of the United States ought not to be permitted, and I am glad to believe that by the Constitution of the United

States he is not permitted, in the exercise of his military powers, to place himself as Commander-in-Chief of the Army and Navy above the civil power of this country. Being such Commander-in-Chief and having his commission from the Constitution, which therefore is irrevocable on the part of Congress, when the Congress of the United States chooses to declare that the attitude of the Government of the United States toward any foreign country is not war but peace, or is not peace but war, the President of the United States ought not to have the power, in connection with this supreme military command, of saying whether or not the condition has arisen. As Commander-in-Chief, he must obey the civil power, under which he is bound to take the field under the command of Congress and lead its armies. The disassociation of the veto power, if that is what it means, from the control of the President of the United States in reference to war, is to take from him the power, after we have put the sword into his hands, to refuse to exert its authority over belligerent nations that are at war with the United States.

If we are to make an error in this respect, let us make it on the side of maintaining the supremacy of the civil power of this Government over the military power of the President. I admit that this argument would not hold good if the President was not the Commander-in-Chief of the Army and Navy, but being such, and his commission being irrevocable, Congress not having the power to put him out of office even if he were to sign any joint resolution to that effect, being beyond the reach of any power in this world except his own resignation, and he being the supreme head of the Army of the United States to whom all others are subordinates, let us not make the error of enabling him to use the veto power, which he can use upon any bill that we pass here of a legislative or political sort, to defeat the will of the people of the United States unless two-thirds of each House shall concur in passing the bill over his veto.

The time may never arise when this will become a grave and serious question, but I venture that if Napoleon Bonaparte had found such a power as that in the French constitution, construed as it seems we are likely to construe it, he would not have failed to have seized upon it to carry out his great ambitions, against which I have never made a complaint; they have my full admiration.

Mr. GRAY. Will the Senator from Alabama permit me?

Mr. MORGAN. Certainly.

Mr. GRAY. Now, do the arguments that support the exclusive power of Congress to declare war independently of the President not apply also to the other power contained in the Constitution giving Congress the power to raise and support armies?

Mr. MORGAN. Even that power is very limited, showing that the framers of the Constitution, when they were considering the war powers of this Government, were very guarded. Bills of that kind to raise and support armies must originate in the House of Representatives, as I understand. That has always been conceded; but there is another restriction (and, as I mentioned a moment ago, that is very important) to show that the framers of the Constitution were putting restraints upon the hands even of the legislative power, by requiring that appropriations for the Army should be renewed once every two years. In every direction that we regard this question we find that the framers of that Constitution were extremely cautious in hedging about the war-making and war-declaring and war-executing power, so that when it fell into the hands, perhaps, of some ambitious man who wanted to perpetuate his rule he would find himself confronted with a power in the Constitution of our country which would defeat his ambitious schemes.

Following that train of thought, which evidently possessed the minds of the framers of this instrument, it seems to me that in making a declaration, if we are going to make a declaration, if we are forced at any time to make a declaration upon this subject, it ought to be in favor of the power of Congress as it is declared in the Constitution and is supported by the great men from whose writings I have had the honor to quote.

This is as far, Mr. President, as I care to go now in the statement of this question or in the argument of it. I have no doubt that it will engage the attention of Senators in this debate; but whether the question is brought up or not it is very apt to be debated, for it has been suggested on all sides and evidently is a subject of very anxious inquiry on the part of the Senate, as it should be. I will therefore leave the further discussion of this branch of the subject until the debate has progressed further and I have heard from some other Senators upon the subject.

APPENDIX A.
MANGOS DE BARAGUA.

The national council, in a meeting held on the 10th of October, 1895, resolved that the publication in book form in an edition of 500 copies of all the laws, rules, decrees, and other orders passed by it be printed after being previously approved by the council and sanctioned by its president.

JOSÉ CLEMENTE VIVANCO,
The Secretary of the Council.

CONSTITUENT ASSEMBLY, REPUBLIC OF CUBA.

I, José Clemente Vivanco, secretary of the national council and chancellor of the Republic of Cuba, certify that the representatives of the different army corps into which the army of liberation is divided met in constituent assembly on the 13th day of September, 1895, at Jimaguayu, and agreed to have a preliminary session, where the character of each representative would be accredited by the respective credential of his appointment. There resulted, after the proper examination by the chairman and the secretaries, who were temporarily citizens, Salvador Cisneros Betancourt and secretaries José Clemente Vivanco and Orencio Nodarse, the following distribution:

Representatives of the First Army Corps, Citizens Dr. Joaquin Castillo Duany, Mariano Sanchez Vaillant, Rafael M. Portuondo, and Pedro Aguillera.

For the Second, Citizens Licentiate Rafael Manduley, Enrique Cespedes, Rafael Perez Morales, and Marcos Padilla.

For the Third, Citizens Salvador Cisneros Betancourt, Lopez Recio Loinaz, Enrique Loinaz del Castillo, and Dr. Ferminin Valdes Dominguez.

For the Fourth, Licentiate Severo Pina, Dr. Santiago Garcia Canizares, Raimundo Sanchez Valdivia, and Francisco Lopez Leiba.

For the Fifth, Dr. Pedro Pinan de Villegas, Licentiate José Clemente Vivanco, Francisco Diaz Silveria, and Orencio Nodarse.

They proceeded to the election of officers for the following session, and the following appointments were made: Salvador Cisneros Betancourt, president; Rafael Manduley, vice-president; secretaries, Licentiate José Clemente Vivanco, Francisco Lopez Leiba, Licentiate Rafael M. Portuondo, and Orencio Nodarse.

The assembly having been organized as above, and in the presence of the above representatives, they proceeded to hold the sessions to discuss the constitution which is to rule the destinies of the republic. These sessions took place on September 13, 14, 15, and 16, instant, and all the articles which were to form the said constitutional charta were discussed. Every article of the projected constitution presented to the assembly by the representatives Licentiate, Rafael M. Portuondo, Dr. Joaquin Castillo Duany, Mariano Sanchez Vaillant, and Pedro Aguilera, was well discussed, and, together with amendments, reforms, and additions, were also discussed by the proposers. On deliberation, in conformity with the opinion of the assembly, it was unanimously resolved to refer the said constitution, with the resolutions of the said assembly, to a committee of revision of the text, composed of the secretaries and of the representatives, Dr. Santiago Garcia Canizares and Enrique Loynaz del Castillo, who, after complying with their mission, returned the final draft of the constitution on the 16th. It was then read, and the signature of each and every representative subscribed.

The president and other members of the assembly, with due solemnity, then swore upon their honor to loyally and strictly observe the fundamental code of the Republic of Cuba, which was greeted by the spontaneous and enthusiastic acclamations of all present; in testimony of which are the minutes in the general archive of the government.

In compliance with the resolution passed by this council in a meeting held to-day, and for its publication, I issue the following copy, in the Mangos de Baragua on the 18th of October, 1895.

JOSÉ CLEMENTE VIVANCO,
Secretary of the Council.

CONSTITUTION OF THE PROVISIONAL GOVERNMENT OF CUBA.

The revolution for the independence and creation in Cuba of a democratic republic in its new period of war, initiated on February 24 last, solemnly declares the separation of Cuba from the Spanish monarchy, and its constitution as a free and independent state, with its own government and supreme authority under the name of the Republic of Cuba, and confirms its existence among the political divisions of the world.

The elected representatives of the revolution, in convention assembled, acting in its name and by the delegation which for that purpose has been conferred upon them by the Cubans in arms, and previously declaring before the country the purity of their thoughts, their freedom from violence, anger, or prejudice, and inspired only by the desire of interpreting the popular voice in favor of Cuba, have now formed a compact between Cuba and the world, pledging their honor for the fulfillment of said compact in the following articles of the constitution:

ARTICLE I. The supreme powers of the republic shall be vested in a government council composed of a president, vice-president, and four secretaries of state, for the dispatch of the business of war, of the interior, of foreign affairs, and of the treasury.

ART. II. Every secretary shall have a subsecretary of state, in order to supply any vacancies.

ART. III. The government council shall have the following powers:

1. To dictate all measures relative to the civil and political life of the revolution.

2. To impose and collect taxes, to contract public loans, to issue paper money, to invest the funds collected in the island, from whatever source, and also those which may be raised abroad by loan.

3. To arm vessels, to raise and maintain troops, to declare reprisals with respect to the enemy, and to ratify treaties.

4. To grant authority, when it is deemed convenient, to order the trial by the judicial power of the president or other members of the council, if he be accused.

5. To decide all matters, of whatsoever description, which may be brought before them by any citizen, except those judicial in character.

6. To approve the law of military organization and the ordinances of the army, which may be proposed by the general-in-chief.

7. To grant military commissions from that of colonel upward, previously hearing and considering the reports of the immediate superior officer and of the general-in-chief, and to designate the appointment of the latter and of the lieutenant-general in case of the vacancy of either.

8. To order the election of four representatives for each army corps whenever in conformity with this constitution it may be necessary to convene an assembly.

ART. IV. The government council shall intervene in the direction of military operations only when in their judgment it shall be absolutely necessary to do so to realize high political ends.

ART. V. As a requisite for the validity of the decrees of the council, at least two-thirds of the members of the same must have taken part in the deliberations of the council, and the decrees must have been voted by the majority of those present.

ART. VI. The office of councilor is incompatible with any other of the republic, and requires the age of 25 years.

ART. VII. The executive power is vested in the president, and, in case of disability, in the vice-president.

ART. VIII. The resolutions of the government council shall be sanctioned and promulgated by the president, who shall take all necessary steps for their execution within ten days.

ART. IX. The president may enter into treaties with the ratification of the government council.

ART. X. The president shall receive all diplomatic representatives and issue the respective commissions to the public functionaries.

ART. XI. The treaty of peace with Spain, which must necessarily have for its basis the absolute independence of the Island of Cuba, must be ratified by the government council and by an assembly of representatives convened expressly for this purpose.

ART. XII. The vice-president shall substitute the president in the case of a vacancy.

ART. XIII. In case of the vacancy in the offices of both president and vice-president on account of resignation, deposition, or death of both, or from any other cause, an assembly of representatives for the election to the vacant offices shall be convened, the senior secretaries in the meanwhile occupying the positions.

ART. XIV. The secretaries shall have voice and vote in deliberations of resolutions of whatever nature.

ART. XV. The secretaries shall have the right to appoint all the employees of their respective offices.

ART. XVI. The subsecretaries in cases of vacancy shall substitute the secretaries of state and shall then have voice and vote in the deliberations.

ART. XVII. All the armed forces of the republic and the direction of the military operations shall be under the control of the general in chief, who shall have under his orders as second in command a lieutenant-general, who will substitute him in case of vacancy.

ART. XVIII. All public functionaries of whatever class shall aid one another in the execution of the resolutions of the government council.

ART. XIX. All Cubans are bound to serve the revolution with their persons and interests, each one according to his ability.

ART. XX. The plantations and property of whatever description belonging to foreigners are subject to the payment of taxes for the revolution while their respective governments do not recognize the rights of belligerency of Cuba.

ART. XXI. All debts and obligations contracted since the beginning of the present period of war until the promulgation of this constitution by the chiefs of the army corps, for the benefit of the revolution, shall be valid, as well as those which henceforth the government council may contract.

ART. XXII. A government council may depose any of its members for cause justifiable in the judgment of two-thirds of the councilors and shall report to the first assembly convening.

ART. XXIII. The judicial power shall act with entire independence of all the others. Its organization and regulation will be provided for by the government council.

ART. XXIV. The present constitution shall be in force in Cuba for two years from the date of its promulgation, unless the war for independence shall terminate before. After the expiration of the two years, an assembly of representatives shall be convened which may modify it, and will proceed to the election of a new government council, and which will pass upon the last council. So it has been agreed upon and resolved, in the name of the republic, by the constituent assembly, in Jimaguayu, on the 18th day of September, 1895, and in witness thereof we, the representatives delegated by the Cuban people in arms, signed the present instrument. Salvador Cisneros, president; Rafael Manduley, vice-president; Pedro Pinan de Villegas, Lope Recio, Fermin Valdes Dominguez, Francisco Diaz Silveira, Dr. Santiago Garcia, Rafael Perez, F. Lopez Leyva, Enrique Cespedes, Marcos Padilla, Raimundo Sanchez, J. D. Castillo, Mariano Sanchez, Pedro Aguilera, Rafael M. Portuondo, Orencio Nodarse, José Clemente Vivanco, Enrique Loynaz Del Castillo, Severo Pina.

ELECTION OF GOVERNMENT.

The constituent assembly met again on the 18th of the said month and year, all the said representatives being present. They proceeded to the election of members who are to occupy the offices of the government council, the general-in-chief of the army of liberation, the lieutenant-general, and the diplomatic agent abroad. The secret voting commenced, each representative depositing his ballot in the urn placed on the chairman's table, after which the count was proceeded with, the following being the result:

President: Salvador Cisneros, 12; Bartolome Maso, 8.

Vice-President: Bartolome Maso, 12; Salvador Cisneros, 8.

Secretary of war: Carlos Roloff, 18; Lope Recio Loinaz, 1; Rafael Manduley, 1.

Secretary of the treasury: Severa Pina, 19; Rafael Manduley, 1.

Secretary of the interior: Dr. Santiago Garcia Canizares, 19; Carlos Dubois, 1.

Secretary of the foreign relations: Rafael Portuondo, 18; Armando Menocal, 1; blank, 1.

Subsecretary of war: Mario Menocal, 18; Francisco Diaz Silveira, 1; blank, 1.

Subsecretary of the treasury: Dr. Joaquin Castillo, 7; Francisco Diaz Silveira, 5; José C. Vivanco, 3; Armando Menocal, 3; Carlos Dubois, 1; blank, 1.

Subsecretary of the interior: Carlos Dubois, 13; Orencio Nodarse, 5; Armando Menocal, 1; blank, 1.

Subsecretary of foreign relations: Fermin Valdes Dominguez, 18; Rafael Manduley, 1; blank, 1.

Therefore, the following were elected by a majority of votes:

President, Salvador Cisneros; vice-president, Bartolome Maso; secretary of war, Carlos Roloff; secretary of the treasury, Severa Pina; secretary of the interior, Dr. Santiago Garcia Canizares; secretary of foreign relations, Rafael M. Portuondo; subsecretary of war, Mario Menocal; subsecretary of the treasury, Dr. Joaquin Castillo; subsecretary of the interior, Carlos Dubois; subsecretary of foreign relations, Dr. Fermin Valdes Dominguez.

The vice-president of the assembly immediately installed the president in the office of the government council that had been conferred upon him; the latter in turn installed those of the other members elected who were present, all entering on the full exercise of their functions after previously taking the oath.

On proceeding to the election of those who were to occupy the positions of general-in-chief of the army, lieutenant-general, and diplomatic agent abroad, the following citizens were unanimously elected by the assembly for the respective places: Maj. Gen. Maximo Gomez, Maj. Gen. Antonio Maceo, and Citizen Tomas Estrada Palma, all these appointments being recognized from that moment.

LAWS FOR THE CIVIL GOVERNMENT AND ADMINISTRATION OF THE REPUBLIC.

CHAPTER I.—*Territorial Division.*

ARTICLE I. The Republic of Cuba comprises the territory occupied by the Island of Cuba from Cape San Antonio to Point Maisi and the adjacent islands and keys.

ART. II. This territory shall be divided into four portions, or States, which will be called Oriente, Camaguey, Las Villas or Cabanacan, and Occidente.

ART. III. The State of Oriente includes the territory from the Point Maisi to Port Manati and the River Jobabo in all its course.

ART. IV. The State of Camaguey includes all the territory from the boundary of Oriente to the line which starts in the north from Laguna Blanca through the Esteros to Moron, passing by Ciego de Avila, follows the military trocha to El Jucaro in the southern coast, it being understood that the towns of Moron and Ciego de Avila belong to this state.

ART. V. The State of Las Villas has for boundary on the east Camaguey, on the west the River Palmas, Palmillas, Santa Rosa, Rodas, the Hannabana River, and the Bay of Cochrinos.

ART. VI. The State of Occidente is bordered on the Las Villas, extending to the west to Cape San Antonio.

ART. VII. The islands and adjacent keys will form part of the states to which they geographically belong.

ART. VIII. The State of Oriente will be divided into ten districts, which shall be as follows: Baracoa, Guantanamo, Sagua de Tanamo, Mayari, Santiago, Jiguani, Manzanillo, Bayamo, and Tunas.

Camaguey comprises two—the eastern district and the western district.

Las Villas comprises seven—Sancti-Espiritus, Trinidad, Remedios, Santa Clara, Sagua, Cienfuegos, and Colon.

That of Occidente comprises sixteen—Cardenas, Matanzas, Union, Jaruco, Guines, Santa Maria del Rosario, Guanabacoa, Habana, Santiago de las Vegas, Bejucal, San Antonio, Bahia Honda, Pina del Rio, and Mantua.

ART. IX. Each of these districts will be divided into prefectures, and these in their turn into as many subprefectures as may be considered necessary.

ART. X. For the vigilance of the coasts there will be inspectors and watchmen appointed in each state according to the extent of the coasts and the number of ports, bays, gulfs, and salt works that there may be.

ART. XI. On establishing the limits of the districts and perfectures, the direction of the coast, rivers, and other natural boundaries shall be kept in mind.

CHAPTER II.—*Of the government and its administration.*

ART. XII. The civil government, the administration, and the service of communications devolve upon the department of the interior.

ART. XIII. The secretary of the interior is the head of the department; he will appoint the employees and will remove them whenever there will be justifiable cause, and will have a department chief to aid him in the work of the department.

ART. XIV. The department chief will keep the books of the department, take care of the archives, will be the manager of the office, and will furnish certifications when requested to do so.

ART. XV. The department of the interior will compile from the data collected by the civil governors the general statistics of the republic.

ART. XVI. The civil governor will inform the department of the interior as to the necessities of his state, will order the measures and instructions necessary for compliance with the general laws of the republic and the orders given by that department, will distribute to the lieutenant-governors the articles of prime necessity which will be delivered to them for that purpose, will communicate to his subordinates the necessary instructions for the compilation of statistics, and will have a subsecretary who will help him in the discharge of his functions.

ART. XVII. The lieutenant-governor will see that the orders of the governors are obeyed in the district, and will have the powers incident to his position as intermediary between the civil governors and the prefects. In case of absolute breach of communication with the civil governors, they will have the same powers as the latter.

ART. XVIII. The prefect shall see that the laws and regulations communicated to him by his superior authorities are complied with. All residents and travelers are under his authority, and, being the highest official in his territory, he in his turn is bound to prevent all abuses and crimes which may be committed.

He will inform the lieutenant-governor as to the necessities of the prefecture; will divide these into as many subprefectures as he may consider necessary for the good conduct of his administration; he will watch the conduct of the subprefects; he will distribute among them with equity the articles delivered to him, and he will have all the other powers incident to him in his character of intermediary between the lieutenant-governor and the subprefects.

ART. XIX. The prefect will also have the following duties: He will harass the enemy whenever possible for him to do so; will hear the preliminary information as to crimes and misdemeanors which may be committed in his territory, passing the said information to the nearest military chief, together with the accused and all that is necessary for the better understanding of the hearing. He will not proceed thus with spies, guides, couriers, and others who are declared by our laws as traitors and considered as such, for these, on account of the difficulty of confining them or conducting them with security, shall be tried as soon as captured by a court, consisting of three persons, the most capable in his judgment in the prefecture, one acting as president and the others as members of the court. He will also appoint a prosecuting officer, and the accused may appoint some one to defend him at his pleasure.

After the court is assembled in this form, and after all the formalities are complied with, it will in private judge and give its sentence, which will be final and without appeal; but those who form the said court and who do not proceed according to our laws and to natural reason will be held responsible by the superior government. Nevertheless, if in the immediate territory there be any armed force, the accused shall be sent to it, with the facts, in order that they shall be properly tried.

The prefect will take the statistics of his prefecture, setting down every person who is found therein, noting if he is the head of a family, the number of the same, his age, his nationality and occupation, if he is a farmer, the nature of his farm, and if he has no occupation the prefect will indicate in what he should be employed. He will also keep a book of civil register, in which he will set down the births, deaths, and marriages which may occur.

He will establish in the prefecture all the factories that he can or may consider necessary in order to well provide the army, as it is the primary obligation of all employees of the Republic to do all possible so that the hides shall not be lost, and organizing in the best manner, and as quickly as may be, tanneries, factories of shoes, rope, blankets, and carpenter and blacksmith shops.

He will not permit any individual of his district to be without occupation. He will see that everyone works, having the instruments of labor at hand in proportion to the inhabitants of his territory. He will protect and raise bees, he will take care of abandoned farms, and will extend as far as possible the zones of agriculture.

As soon as the prefect learns that the secretary of the interior or any delegate of this authority is in his district he will place himself under the latter's orders. This he will also do on the arrival of armed forces, presenting himself to their chief in order to facilitate the needed supplies and to serve him in every possible manner. He will have a bugle to warn the inhabitants of the enemy's approach; he will inform the nearest armed force when his territory is invaded. He will collect all horses and other animals suitable for the war and lead them to a secure place, so that when the army may need them or they may be required by the civil authorities to whom they may appertain.

He will provide the forces that may be, or pass through his territory with whatever they may need, which may be within his power, and especially shall he provide guides and beeves and vegetables which the chief may require to maintain the said forces. He will also deliver the articles manufactured in the shops under his immediate inspection, demanding always the proper receipts therefor.

He will also provide the necessary means for the maintenance of all the families of the territory, especially those of the soldiers of the army of liberation.

Until otherwise decreed, he will celebrate civil marriages and other contracts entered into by the residents of his prefecture; he will act in cases of ordinary complaints and in the execution of powers and wills, registering the same in a clear and definite manner, and issuing to the interested parties the certificates which they may require.

ART. XX. The subprefect will see that the laws and orders communicated to him by his superior authorities are obeyed in territory under his command; he will inform the prefect as to the necessities of the subprefecture and will see to the security and order of the public; arresting and sending to the prefects those who may travel without safe-conduct, seeing that no violation of law whatsoever is perpetrated, and will demand the signed authority of the civil or military chief who has ordered a commission to be executed.

ART. XXI. The subprefect will compile a census in which the number of inhabitants of a subprefecture will be stated and their personal description; he will keep a book of the births and deaths which will occur in his territory, and of all this he will give account at the end of the year. He will invest the means provided by the prefect to pay the public charges, and if the said resources are insufficient he will collect the deficit from the inhabitants; he will not authorize the destruction of abandoned farms, whether they belong to friends or enemies of the republic, and he will inform the prefect of the farms which are thus abandoned.

ART. XXII. For the organization and better operation of the State's manufactories a chief of factories shall be appointed in each district, who will be authorized to establish such factories which he may deem convenient, employing all citizens who, on account of their abilities, can serve, and collecting in the prefectures of his district all the instruments he can utilize in his work. These chiefs will be careful to frequently inspect the factories, to report any defects which they may notice, and to provide the superintendents with whatever they may need, that the work may not be interrupted.

Together with the prefect he will send to the department of the interior the names of the individuals he considers most adapted to open new shops, and on the first day of each month he will send to that department a statement of the objects manufactured in each shop of his district, indicating the place of manufacture, what remains on deposit, what has been delivered, with the names of commanders of forces, civil authorities, or individuals to whom they were delivered.

ART. XXIII. The coast inspectors will have under their immediate orders an inspector, who will be his secretary, who will occupy his place in his absence or sickness, and as many auxiliaries as he may deem convenient. He may demand the aid of the prefects and armed forces whenever he may consider it necessary for the better exercise of his functions. The duties of the inspectors will be to watch the coasts and prevent the landing of the enemy, to be always ready to receive disembarkments and place in safety the expeditions which may come from abroad, to establish all the salt works possible, to capture the Spanish vessels which frequent the coasts on his guard, and to attend with special care to the punctual service of communications between his coast and foreign countries.

ART. XXIV. The coast guards will acknowledge the inspector as their superior, will watch the places designated to them, and will execute the orders given.

ART. XXV. The lieutenant-governors, as well as the inspectors of whatever class, will have their residence, wherever the necessity of their office does not prohibit it, in the general headquarters, so that they can move easily, furnish the necessary aid to the army, and carry out the orders of the military chief.

Country and liberty.
OCTOBER 17, 1895.

The secretary of the interior, Dr. Santiago Garcia Canizares, being satisfied with the preceding law, I sanction it in all respects.
Let it be promulgated in the legal form.
SALVADOR CISNEROS BETANCOURT.
The President.

OCTOBER 18, 1895.

APPENDIX B.

PROCLAMATIONS OF GENERAL WEYLER.

HABANA, *February 18.*

The following is a verbatim copy of translations made of proclamations published to-day:

"Proclamation—Don Valeriano Weyler y Nicolau, marquis of Teneriffe, governor and captain-general of the Island of Cuba, general-in-chief of the army, etc., desirous of warning the honest inhabitants of Cuba and those loyal to the Spanish cause, and in conformity to the laws, does order and command:

"ARTICLE 1. All inhabitants of the District of Sancti Spiritus and the Provinces of Puerto Principe and Santiago de Cuba will have to concentrate in places which are the headquarters of a division, a brigade, a column, or a troop, and will have to be provided with documentary proof of identity within eight days of the publication of this proclamation in the municipalities.

"ART. 2. To travel in the country in the radius covered by the columns in operation, it is absolutely indispensable to have a pass from the mayor, military commandants, or chiefs of detachments. Anyone lacking this will be detained and sent to headquarters of divisions or brigades, and thence to Habana, at my disposition, by the first possible means. Even if a pass is exhibited which is suspected to be inauthentic or granted by authority to persons with known sympathy toward the rebellion, or who show favor thereto, rigorous measures will result to those responsible.

"ART. 3. All owners of commercial establishments in the country districts will vacate them, and the chiefs of columns will take such measures as the success of their operations dictates regarding such places which, while useless for the country's wealth, serve the enemy as hiding places in the woods and in the interior.

"ART. 4. All passes hitherto issued hereby become null and void.

"ART. 5. The military authorities will see to the immediate publication of this proclamation.

"VALERIANO WEYLER."

"HABANA, *February 16, 1896.*"

MILITARY AND JUDICIAL PROCESSES.

The second proclamation is as follows:

"PROCLAMATION.

"Don Valeriano Weyler y Nicolau, marquis of Teneriffe, governor and captain-general of the Island of Cuba, general-in-chief of the army, etc.:

"In order to avoid suffering and delay other than that essential in time of war, and the summary proceedings initiated by the forces in operation, I dictate the following proclamation:

"ARTICLE 1. In accordance with the faculties conceded to me by rule 2, article 81, of the military code of justice, I assume, as general-in-chief of the army operating in this island, the judicial attributes of H. E. captain-general.

"ART. 2. In virtue of rule 2 of said article, I delegate from this date these judicial attributes to the commanders-in-chief of the first and second army corps and to the general commanding the third division—that is, in Puerto Principe.

"ART. 3. Prisoners caught in action will be subjected to the most summary trial without any other investigation except that indispensable for the objects of the trial.

"ART. 4. When the inquiry is finished, subject to consultation with the judicial authorities, the proceedings will continue during the course of operations, and in the presence of the judicial authority, with an auditor, the sentence may be carried out. When said authority is not present, the process will be remitted to him and the culpable parties detained at the locality where the division or brigade headquarters is situated.

"ART. 5. The military juridic functionary of whatever rank who accompanies in the operations the judicial authorities, when the latter thus decides, will act as auditor, dispensing with the assessors' assistance at court-martial during operations, in cases where no other member of the juridic body is at hand.

"SENTENCE IN CERTAIN CASES.

"ART. 6. When the sentence is pronounced, if the sentence be deprivation of liberty, the culprit will be brought to Habana with the papers in the case, so that the testimony can be issued as to the penalty and the sentence be carried into effect.

"ART. 7. The said authorities will be acquainted with all cases initiated against the accused in war.

"ART. 8. I reserve the right of promoting and sustaining all questions of competence, with other jurisdictions, as also with the military, and to determine inhibitions in all kinds of military processes in the territory of the island.

"ART. 9. I reserve likewise the faculty of assuming an inquiry into all cases when it is deemed convenient.

"ART. 10. No sentence of death shall be effected without the acknowledgment by my authority of the testimony of the judgment, which must be sent to me immediately, except when no means of communication exists or when it is a case of insult to superiors or of military sedition, in which case sentence will be carried out and the information furnished to me afterwards.

"ART. 11. All previous proclamations or orders conflicting with this on the question of the delegation of jurisdiction in this island are hereby rendered null and void.

"VALERIANO WEYLER.

"HABANA, *February 16, 1896.*"

The third proclamation is as follows:

"PROCLAMATION.

"Don Valeriano Weyler y Nicolau, marquis of Teneriffe, governor and captain-general of the Island of Cuba, general in chief of the army, etc.:

"I make known that, taking advantage of the temporary insecurity of communication between the district capitals and the rest of the provinces, notices which convey uneasiness and alarm are invented and propagated, and some persons, more daring still, have taken advantage of this to draw the deluded and the ignorant to the rebel ranks. I am determined to have the laws obeyed and to make known by special means the dispositions ruling and frequently applied during such times as the present, through which the island is now passing, and to make clear how far certain points go in adapting them to the exigencies of war and in use of the faculties conceded to me by No. 12, article 7, of the code of military justice, and by the law of public order of April 23, 1870. And I make known, order, and command that the following cases are subject to military law among others specified by the law:

"Clause 1. Those who invent or propagate by any means notices or assertions favorable to the rebellion shall be considered as being guilty of offenses against the integrity of the nation and comprised in article 223, class 6, of the military code, whenever such notices facilitate the enemy's operations.

"Clause 2. Those who destroy or damage railroad lines, telegraph or telephone wires, or apparatus connected therewith, or those who interrupt communications by opening bridges or destroying highways.

"Clause 3. Incendiaries in town or country, or those who cause damage as shown in caption 8, article 13, volume 2, of the penal code ruling in Cuba.

"AID AND COMFORT OF THE ENEMY.

"Clause 4. Those who sell, facilitate, convey, or deliver arms or ammunition to the enemy, or who supply such by any other means, or those who keep such in their power or tolerate or deal in such through the customs and employees of customs, who fail to confiscate such importations, will be held responsible.

"Clause 5. Telegraphists who divulge telegrams referring to the war, or who send them to persons who should not be cognizant of them.

"Clause 6. Those who through the press or otherwise revile the prestige of Spain, her army, the volunteers or firemen, or any other force that cooperates with the army.

"Clause 7. Those who by the same means endeavor to extol the enemy.

"Clause 8. Those who supply the enemy with horses, cattle, or any other war resources.

"Clause 9. Those who act as spies; and to these the utmost rigor of the law will be applied.

"Clause 10. Those who serve as guides, unless surrendering at once and showing the proof of force majeure, and giving the troops evidence at once of loyalty.

"Clause 11. Those who adulterate army food or conspire to alter the prices of provisions.

"Clause 12. Those who by means of explosives commit the offenses referred to in the law of June 10, 1894, made to extend to this island by the royal order of October 17, 1895, seeing that these offenses affect the public peace, and the law of April 23, 1870, grants me power to leave to the civil authorities the proceedings in such cases as are comprised in captions 4 and 5, and treatise 3 of volume 2 of the common penal code, when the culprits are not military or when the importance of the offense renders such action advisable.

"Clause 13. Those who by messenger pigeons, fireworks, or other signals communicate news to the enemy.

"Clause 14. The offenses enumerated, when the law prescribes the death penalty or life imprisonment, will be dealt with most summarily.

"Clause 15. All other proclamations and orders previously issued in conflict with this are annulled by this.

"VALERIANO WEYLER.

"HABANA, *February 16, 1896.*"

✻ ✻ ✻ ✻ ✻ ✻ ✻

2777

March 16, 1896.

The Senate resumed the consideration of the report of the committee of conference on the disagreeing votes of the two Houses upon the resolutions relative to the war in Cuba.

The PRESIDING OFFICER. The Senator from Alabama [Mr. MORGAN] is recognized as being entitled to the floor upon the pending question, which is on concurring in the report of the committee of conference.

Mr. MORGAN. Mr. President, I had supposed that my colleague [Mr. PUGH] would proceed with his argument until it was closed, but it appears that he is not physically able to go further with it to-day; and as is customary with myself I will come in now for the purpose of filling up the time until some one who is more interesting is ready to proceed, or some subject that is better entitled to public attention has been called in the Senate.

I supposed when we entered upon the investigation of this matter in regard to Cuba it would be very becoming in us to go slowly and deliberately, but at the same time that when we had set our faces in a certain direction—the direction indicated by the resolutions passed by both Houses—we would persist in our action until we came to some final conclusion, because it is scarcely fair to ourselves, to Cuba, to Spain, or to the people of the United States that we should keep a subject in anxious agitation before the Senate for any considerable length of time, particularly one that attracts such grave attention and is in itself so very important as this subject must be admitted to be.

The resolutions of the Senate and of the House, adopted by an almost unanimous vote, with the exception perhaps of a mere verbal criticism, mean exactly the same thing; and there is, therefore, no substantial ground for any controversy between the two Houses as to the wording of the resolutions that we shall adopt. Personally I am entirely satisfied with either form of expression, believing that there is no substantial difference between the resolutions of the House and the Senate upon this subject.

I am more particularly of that view because neither the House nor the Senate has undertaken to reach any conclusion which in its effect upon the Government of the United States would be in the slightest degree mandatory. We have halted deliberately and purposely and wisely within the domain of opinion, without reaching the domain of mandate or enactment, in this matter. We have thought that it was our right and our duty to respond to the voice of the American people as it has been presented here in various memorials and petitions from State legislatures and from communities and from societies, some of them political, some religious, some commercial, and from the very large number of people of the United States, who, being perfectly aware of the situation of affairs in Cuba—being perhaps as well (or even better) advised on that subject as the Senate and the House—have thought that it was their privilege to present their views to the Congress of the United States in the form of petitions and memorials.

When the people of the United States unite, as has been done here very largely in the presentation of their opinions formulated in memorials and resolutions and petitions, we have the right to believe that they have taken a sincere and a sedate view of the question; that they know what they are talking about; and that the views and wishes they express in regard to Cuban independence and Cuban belligerency and the conduct of the war in Cuba are justified by their own examination into the facts.

2777

Amongst the memorials which have been sent to the Committee on Foreign Relations of the Senate I find one from the general assembly of the State of New York, which, for the moment, I can not lay my hand upon. I can, however, state the substance of it. It is that the general assembly of the State of New York memorialize Congress that we shall recognize the existence of belligerency in the Island of Cuba. Another memorial I am informed has come from the State of Mississippi. The precise form of it I am not able to recall—I do not think that I have even heard it read. I will ask the Senator from Mississippi [Mr. WALTHALL] if I am mistaken in regard to a memorial having come from the legislature of his State on the subject of Cuba?

Mr. WALTHALL. There was such a memorial presented last Friday.

Mr. MORGAN. Coming from the legislature of Mississippi?

Mr. WALTHALL. From the legislature.

Mr. MORGAN. What was the purport of it, if the Senator will tell me?

Mr. WALTHALL. I can turn to it in a moment. Here it is, in the RECORD of Friday's proceedings.

Mr. MORGAN. It is as follows:

Concurrent resolution memoralizing the President and the Congress of the United States to grant belligerent rights to the Cuban Republic, and asking our Representatives and Senators in the Congress to vote for securing the same.

Be it resolved by the senate and house of representatives of Mississippi, That we extend our sympathy to the Cuban people in their struggle for freedom and independence, and we call on the Congress and the President of these United States and request them to grant belligerent rights to the Cuban Republic, and ask our Representatives and Senators in the Congress to vote for securing the same, and that the secretary of state be instructed to transmit a copy of the resolution to the President and Congress.

Passed the house January 29, 1896.

JAMES F. McCOOL,
Speaker of the House.

Passed the senate February 10, 1896.

J. H. JONES,
President of the Senate.

Approved February 24, 1896.

A. J. McLAURIN, *Governor.*
J. L. POWER, *Secretary of State.*

There is a memorial coming from an extreme Southern State, a very close neighbor to Cuba. That memorial has been well considered. That is no claptrap. That is no suddenly formed opinion. That is not an opinion which is without foundation in justice and in fact. It comes from a great State that is entirely willing to make its contribution of whatever may be needed for the purpose of sustaining the attitude of the Government of the United States whenever it is taken upon this question. You will observe that in the resolutions of the Senate and of the House and in the report that is now the subject of discussion we have not gone anywhere near the extent that has been gone by the general assembly of Mississippi. Now, here is the memorial of the general assembly of New York:

STATE OF NEW YORK, IN ASSEMBLY,
Albany, January 13, 1896.

On motion of Mr. Warner:

Whereas a condition of civil war exists between the Government of Spain and the Government proclaimed and for some time maintained by force of arms by the people of Cuba; and

Whereas the struggle for independence and for republican institutions by the Cubans has awakened in the people of the United States a deep sympathy for their cause and a hope that they may succeed in their momentous contest.

Resolved (if the senate concur), That we participate in the deep interest which is felt for the success of the people of Cuba in their struggle to establish their liberty and independence.

Resolved, That the President and Congress of the United States be, and they are hereby, petitioned to extend to the insurgents of Cuba a formal recognition of their rights as belligerents.

Resolved, That copies of this resolution be duly certified by the clerk and forwarded to the President and presiding officer of the United States Senate and House of Representatives.

By order of the assembly.

A. E. BAXTER, *Clerk.*

Mr. HILL. Did the senate concur?

Mr. MORGAN. I do not know.

Mr. HILL. It does not seem to have done so.

Mr. MORGAN. It reads, "By order of the assembly."

Mr. HILL. I will state that the legislature is composed of the assembly and the senate. The senate does not seem to have concurred.

Mr. MORGAN. This is a memorial of the house of representatives.

Mr. HILL. Of the assembly.

Mr. MORGAN. That means the house of representatives.

Mr. HILL. It would be analogous to the house of representatives; but there is a senate and an assembly.

Mr. MORGAN. They are the direct representatives of the people.

Mr. HILL. Both are elected at the same time.

Mr. MORGAN. Both are elected at the same time and comprise one general body of legislative authority. The people, therefore, of the great State of New York, which has the control—I might say the domination—of the commercial and financial power of the whole United States in a certain sense, and perhaps of the whole Western Hemisphere in a pretty large sense, have disrobed themselves of their fears and apprehensions. They have stepped forward in answer to this plea of the people of Cuba for independence and for recognition and for justice, and have expressed themselves in that State through at least one of the houses—through the popular house—in favor of the attitude that a great many gentlemen in the House and the Senate of the Congress of the United States think ought to be taken—that is to say, direct, immediate recognition of the independence of Cuba.

Following that come some memorials from a mass meeting of citizens of Pawtucket, R. I., favoring the recognition of the belligerency of Cuba; a memorial from a public meeting held in Delaware, without any indication of the number of persons who were assembled, to the same effect; a letter from the secretary of the St. Louis Merchants' Exchange, favoring Cuba's belligerency; a memorial from the American Protective Association, favoring the acknowledgment of the independence of Cuba; a memorial from Joe Hooker Post, No. 21, Grand Army of the Republic, Mount Vernon, Ohio, in favor of granting belligerent rights to Cuba; resolutions of the Merchants' Exchange of St. Louis, Mo., asking Congress to grant belligerent rights to the people of Cuba, now struggling for their freedom; a petition of the Trades and Labor Assembly of Colorado, in favor of the Cuban insurgents; a resolution of the Board of Trade of La Crosse, Wis., urging the recognition of Cuban belligerency; a resolution of the Rutland Board of Trade, of Vermont, urging Congress to recognize the belligerency of Cuba; a resolution of the Board of Trade of Kansas City, Mo., favoring the recognition by

Congress of Cuba; a resolution from the Board of Trade of Kansas City, favoring the granting of belligerent rights to the people of Cuba; another resolution from the Board of Trade of Kansas City, requesting Congress to grant belligerent rights to the people of Cuba, largely signed; a resolution of the Board of Trade of Indianapolis, in favor of Cuban independence; a resolution favoring the recognition of Cuban insurgents, which was offered in the Senate by the Senator from Nebraska; a memorial from the A. P. A. of Nebraska, favoring the granting of belligerent rights to the Cuban patriots; resolutions indorsing the cause of Cuba passed by the Ministerial Association of Harrisburg, Pa. I shall read that for the purpose of getting before the Senate some idea of the sentiment of the religionists of this country on this subject. It is as follows:

Resolutions indorsing the Cuban cause, passed by the Ministerial Association of Harrisburg, Pa., Monday, October 28, 1895.

Whereas life, liberty, and the pursuit of happiness are the essentials for the maintenance of all that appertains to man; and

Whereas the monarchical tendencies of European powers have always tended to persecute and enslave America and Americans; and

Whereas, for the complete emancipation of American institutions guaranteeing the freedom and permanent establishment of a government "for the people, of the people, and by the people," our fathers were forced to have recourse to arms to break the yoke of British tyranny; and

Whereas the Monroe doctrine proclaims an edict dear to every American heart, "America for Americans;" and

Whereas the patriotic sons of Cuba find themselves to-day in the identical position which actuated our forefathers to strike for liberty; and

Whereas the despotism, the oppression, and the excessive burdens forced upon Cuba by Spain to maintain an oligarchy in Europe and an extravagant, expensive, and unnecessary retinue in Cuba, to the detriment and political enslavement of a liberty-loving people, we find the stroke for liberty by the Cuban people to be patriotic and praiseworthy in every way; and

Whereas the Spanish authorities have not been able to crush out what was called a band of robbers, but have been taxed to their utmost ability by placing thousands of troops in the field and marshaling the aid of all other countries to deprive the Cuban patriots of the necessary resources to contend successfully with them; and

Whereas in the face of all these difficulties the patriots have been able to increase their armies, organize and maintain a provisional government, and defeat the enemy upon many battlefields, they are entitled to belligerent rights under the usage and customs of international courtesies: Therefore,

Be it resolved, That this ministerial association indorse and extend our sympathies to the Cuban cause, and hereby petition to the President and Congress of the United States to grant to Cuba belligerent rights and the recognition of her provisional government, thereby emphasizing the spirit and the letter of the Monroe doctrine, and that every American be allowed, without let or hindrance, to have commercial intercourse with the Cuban patriots, furnishing commodities or munitions of war without being subjected to the espionage and arrest by our officials or the military or naval despotism on the part of Spain.

Resolved, That a copy of these resolutions be sent to the President of the United States, the President of the Senate, and the Speaker of the House of Representatives as our prayer in behalf of the independence of Cuba.

Further be it resolved, That a copy be sent to the Cuban junta of New York, to be forwarded to the pesident of the provisional government, showing our appreciation and support in behalf of their noble cause.

H. C. C. ASTWOOD, *Chairman.*
W. H. MARSHALL.
WM. P. LAWRENCE.

In that memorial, which comes from that body of ministers of the Christian gospel, there is presented in a condensed form nearly all that can be said on this subject so far as our rights, duties, and sympathies coincide in moving us to action. It contains also a statement in concise form of those facts which are undeniable to the whole American intelligence, a denial of which would shame any man who seeks to make it.

Resolutions were presented also from the city council of St. Augustine, Fla., favoring a recognition of Cuba; resolutions in the nature of a memorial of the city council of West Tampa, Fla., favoring recognition of the independence of Cuba; resolutions of sympathy with Cuba adopted by citizens of Quincy, Ill.; memorial from the city council of Tampa, Fla., favoring the recognition of Cuba; resolutions of a mass meeting of citizens of the city of Des Moines, Iowa, praying Congress to recognize the freedom of the people of Cuba; resolutions of George A. McCall Post, No. 31, Grand Army of the Republic, of West Chester, Pa., favoring the recognition by this country of belligerent rights to Cuba; resolutions adopted by the city council of Jacksonville, Fla., in favor of the recognition of the Cuban revolutionists as belligerents; resolutions of Nassau Camp, No. 104, United Confederate Veterans, of Fernandina, Fla., favoring the recognition by the United States of the Cuban revolutionists as belligerents; resolutions of the Ohio Normal University, expressing sympathy for the Cuban insurgents; resolutions of the students and teachers of the Normal University of Ada, Ohio—the same place, I suppose—in favor of Cuba, and signed by other persons; resolutions of the Board of Trade of Kansas City, Mo., requesting Congress to recognize the belligerent rights of Cuba; resolutions of 149 citizens of Fairfield, Iowa, praying for the recognition of the Cuban revolutionists; resolutions of citizens of Newark, N. J., expressing for Cubans who are struggling for independence their sympathy. These resolutions were passed by a mass meeting assembled in Newark on the 13th of December, 1895.

Then follows a memorial of citizens of Pueblo, Colo., expressing sympathy for the Cuban insurgents. A large mass meeting seems to have been held for the purpose of getting up that expression. Then follow a petition of citizens of Fremont, Nebr., asking recognition of Cuban belligerents; resolutions adopted at Providence, R. I., December 20, 1895, asking Congress to recognize now the belligerent rights of the Cuban revolutionists; resolutions of citizens of Akron, Ohio, in favor of the recognition of Cuban belligerents; resolutions adopted at a mass meeting held at Kansas City November 20, 1895, favoring recognition of Cuban belligerents; petition of the Houston Typographical Union, No. 87, favoring recognition of Cuban insurgents; memorial of the students and teachers of the Ohio Normal University, at Ada, Ohio—an additional one; resolutions of the National Grange of Patrons of Husbandry, favoring the acknowledgment of Cuban belligerency and extending sympathy to the Cuban cause; petitions of citizens of Madison, S. Dak., praying the Congress of the United States to grant to the Cubans belligerent rights; resolutions of a mass meeting of the people of Newark, N. J., recommending that belligerent rights be accorded to Cuba; petition from the Twenty-eighth Ward of the city of Philadelphia, praying for a speedy recognition as belligerents of the Cuban patriots in their struggle for freedom; resolutions of sympathy with Cuban insurgents from the Federation of Labor.

Here are petitions from the people of Florida demanding belligerent rights to Cuba, largely signed; here is a petition from citizens of Minerva, Ohio, to the same effect, largely signed, headed by the question, "Shall Cuba be free?"; here are memorials from citizens of Florida, urging the Government of the United States to grant the Cuban combatants the rights of belligerents; a petition of citizens of Ashland County, Ohio, in favor of the recognition of Cuban independence; a petition praying for a speedy recognition of belligerency in favor of the Cuban patriots in their struggle for freedom by the citizens of Hobart, N. Y.; a petition of the citizens of Oregon, favoring the recognition of the independence of Cuba, extensively signed; a petition of citizens of Chicago, Ill., praying for the speedy recognition as belligerents of the Cuban patriots in their struggle for liberty, largely signed; a petition of sundry citizens of Akron, Ohio, in addition to those heretofore submitted; the petition of Amethyst Council, No. 40, of Amethyst, Colo., A. P. A., for the recognition of the Cubans as belligerents.

Mr. President, I also hold here a mass of petitions signed by 1,688 individual citizens from all over the United States. It would seem that almost every county in the United States is represented in this wide reach and range of petitions.

Mr. SHERMAN. If the Senator will allow me, I am authorized to say that in the House of Representatives petitions and memorials from various parts of the United States to the same effect were presented, sufficient to fill a large box. There had been presented there many times the number that have been presented in the Senate.

Mr. HALE. We are all of us familiar with the methods by which a great many of these petitions come to us and are gotten up in all parts of the country. I do not know whether it is so in this case, but I presume it will be found by anybody who looks at these petitions that they are all upon printed headings sent out from a single source and signed and returned. The spontaneity of petitions of this kind comes not from the country at large, but from New York or Washington.

I do not suppose that the Senator from Ohio had strictly the right to refer to anything that occurred in the House of Representatives, but I have no doubt that what he states is true; that this deliberate plan, this whole proceeding prepense, has gone on and that petitions have gone to the other House just as they have come here.

Mr. MORGAN. In reply to what the Senator from Maine assumes or presumes in regard to these petitions, I will hand him this package of petitions, memorials, and resolutions and let him see how many of them are written in that way.

Mr. HALE. If the Senator will send them to my desk, I shall be very glad to look at them.

Mr. MORGAN. The Senator can investigate to see whether or not anybody has been putting up a fraud on the Senate and House of Representatives of the United States in this matter.

Mr. FRYE. It is just exactly as easy to get remonstrances signed as it is to get petitions signed, and they are ordinarily obtained in the same way. I should like to inquire of my colleague if he has ever heard of a remonstrance being presented to Congress against the recognition of Cuban belligerent rights?

Mr. HALE. Yes. I will tell my colleague that I have had hundreds of letters from business men all over the country——

Mr. FRYE. I am not talking about letters.

Mr. HALE. They are to me of much more force and effect than these cut and dried petitions. I have had—and I am glad my colleague has brought me out on that point—hundreds of letters from business men all over the country, which I did not think it worth while to put before the Senate, protesting against this whole crusade.

Mr. FRYE. But there never has been presented a remonstrance on the subject to either House of Congress by anybody.

Mr. HALE. Letters are the best form of remonstrances that can be brought before Congress—earnest expressions of opinion of business and conservative men all over the country.

Mr. MORGAN. Mr. President, it has got to be the habit, and I think it is a very evil one, too, of men who are called business men—men who own estates and property—setting themselves against Congress and against the public sentiment of the people of the United States, widely, universally, and sincerely expressed, in private communications to Congress for the purpose of keeping down any legislation that might cost them a little money or a little disturbance of their peace or their business relations. I know we are in the presence of such difficulties as that; but men who thus seek privately to influence Senatorial action and are not willing to come out with their public protests and memorials and avow what they propose to have us do and to act upon are not much in the way of an enemy, when the American people happen to have one.

What chance, Mr. President, have the few representatives of these Cuban insurgents, who are denounced as robbers, as pirates, as mulattoes, as negroes, as Spaniards and dagos, and as a contemptible, low crowd, by the high authorities, the ministerial authorities of Spain present in this Government, to manufacture sentiment to influence the people of the United States or the Senate or the House of Representatives? None whatever. They have neither the money nor the means with which to do it. There is no indication in that mass of petitions of any false presentation of sentiment. I doubt not that every man who signed those petitions—and they are signed with pen and with pencil, and some of them signed with a cross mark—honestly expressed to the people of the United States what his convictions were. The Senator from Maine probably does not think that the legislature of New York or the legislature of Mississippi have gotten up any bogus representations here to us or have been operated upon by some spasm of indignation or patriotism to cause them to lay before us an earnest admonition and request to grant belligerent rights and also independence to the Island of Cuba.

The Committee on Foreign Relations had not supposed until this very moment that they were being dealt with improperly in the presentation of this great mass of petitions, and in all sincerity they have acted upon them as if they came voluntarily from the American people and expressed their honest views.

I brought these forward merely to show the amount of pressure that had been brought upon the Committee on Foreign Relations in the Senate, and in connection with that, to show how conservative and careful had been the action of that committee. Notwithstanding this very great pressure, and notwithstanding the gratification we could have given to hundreds and thousands, if not millions, of the people of the United States by being prompt and urgent in our response to their demands, we have gone as slowly and as patiently as it was possible for us, with a decent respect for the opinions of mankind, to the step in this direction which we have taken at last.

Not only that, but we were told in the debate the other day that the Spanish minister here had sent a paper or a memorandum of some kind before the Committee on Foreign Relations of the Senate which had not appeared anywhere in the papers in this case.

There was such a paper sent to us, and it has not appeared. It was a memorandum sent by the Spanish minister through our Secretary of State, for the purpose of advising us of the situation of affairs in Cuba, with a view to get us to delay our action upon assurances from that minister that the steps which had already been taken in Cuba for the suppression of the rebellion were about to become successful. Any Senator who desires to do so is entirely at liberty to read it. So it is a matter of no consequence at all, except that, notwithstanding this great pressure of petitions and memorials to which I have just referred, the Senate Committee on Foreign Relations hesitated, stopped in their movements for a month or more, to see whether or not the Spanish minister was correct in his view of the progress of the efforts in Cuba to suppress this insurrection and rebellion. Therefore we have not come before the Senate of the United States or before the country without opinions deliberately formed, and without a careful investigation of every fact within our reach connected with this very delicate and very important subject. We have neither been asleep nor have we been too hasty.

We have tried to control our action by a profound regard for the rights of Spain and the rights of the Government and the people of the United States, and a profound respect for the Senate of the United States. So that when we should come in here with our final action we should be able to present some scheme or project of action upon which both Houses could unite and which would present the views of the American people at this moment of time upon this great question, saying nothing about what progress we might make in our views upon further developments in either direction—either in favor of the revolutionists there or in favor of the Government of Spain—but confining ourselves, as we thought it our duty to do, to the situation as it appeared to be presented in the facts at the moment of our report.

Now, I trust that after this, Mr. President, there will not be anything more said or even thought in respect of the action of the committee to the effect that it has either been inconsiderate, or that it has been hasty, or that it has been too slow. I believe we have acted as dutifully as it was possible for a committee to do.

Mr. HALE. Will the Senator allow me?

The PRESIDING OFFICER. Does the Senator from Alabama yield?

Mr. MORGAN. I do.

Mr. HALE. I have not been present during the entire time of the Senator's remarks, and I do not know whether or not he has referred to the statement of the Spanish minister, which, to the surprise of some of the Senate, was brought before the body on Friday. If he has not, before he closes I hope he will explain to us what in some respects was a mystery.

The Senator from Ohio [Mr. SHERMAN], the chairman of the Committee on Foreign Relations, on Thursday referred to the Spanish case, which nobody outside of the committee before that had heard of, and stated that the committee did not have it before them; that the junior Senator from Massachusetts [Mr. LODGE] had communicated with the State Department and had learned the Spanish case from some statement of the Spanish minister, and had told the committee what it was. On the next morning the junior Senator from Massachusetts corrected the Senator from Ohio, and stated that he had had no personal communication with the Department, but that the case as made out for the

Spanish Government by the Spanish minister had been presented to the committee, and had been read to them by my colleague [Mr. FRYE], upon which the Senator from Indiana [Mr. TURPIE], the third member of the committee, who appeared upon the scene, rose in his place and stated that the resolutions which had been reported from the conference committee had never been before the Committee on Foreign Relations and had never been approved by them.

Now, the Senator from Alabama [Mr. MORGAN], the fourth member of the committee, has arisen to more explanations. Before he sits down I hope he will state to the Senate whether the Committee on Foreign Relations, which the Senate trusts as a conservative committee to present this whole case to this body, did have the statement of the Spanish minister, because members of the committee complained bitterly that the Spanish minister had appeared and appealed to the country through the newspapers, but had not approached the committee through the proper channels. I hope the Senator will not leave the floor before stating, if the Spanish minister did through the State Department send a statement to the committee, why it was that in some way or other the committee did not report that fact to the Senate.

Mr. MORGAN. Mr. President, the notes of the Reporter will show that it has not been ten minutes since I stated that whole thing to the Senate.

Mr. HALE. I have just stated to the Senator that I was not present here all the time, and did not hear all he had said.

Mr. MORGAN. I can not keep the Senator from Maine in his seat, of course, but I suppose I must go back and repeat what I have said for his satisfaction.

Mr. HALE. Then I will ask the Senator to explain—for I do not think he has done that to the satisfaction of the Senate, although I was not here—why it was, if the committee had that document, had that statement, and had that case, it did not at some time, before it was unwarily disclosed to us by the Senator from Ohio, report it to the Senate, and give us the benefit of it?

Mr. MORGAN. The Senator from Maine is a lawyer, and he knows it is very seldom that an affidavit or a statement made on a motion for a continuance is offered in evidence on a final trial.

Mr. HALE. But this is not the case of a new trial. The Senate has never decided this case, and Congress has never decided it.

Mr. SHERMAN. I simply wish to say that what the Senator from Maine has said is not a correct statement of what I either said or did.

Mr. HALE. Did not the Senator say——

Mr. SHERMAN. I will not engage in any wrangle about it. I will refer to the RECORD.

Mr. HALE. Certainly we understood the Senator from Ohio, the chairman of the Committee on Foreign Relations, to state that the Spanish case had been brought out by the Senator from Massachusetts [Mr. LODGE], who had been in communication with the State Department, and who had told the committee what it was. The next day the Senator from Massachusetts himself rose in his place and corrected the Senator from Ohio and stated that the case of the Spanish minister was brought to the entire committee. I listened in vain, Mr. President——

Mr. MORGAN. If I can get the floor long enough to make an answer to a question that is a good deal longer than my speech, I will try to do it, and try to satisfy the Senator from Maine about this business before I get through.

Spain was anxious to delay action in the Senate of the United States. Spain was afraid, I suppose, that this grave body would get into a tantrum, and finding an opportunity, would launch forth some very belligerent declarations in regard to Cuba. And so the minister from Spain sent a memorandum to the Secretary of State, Mr. Olney, setting forth, according to what he thought, a proper view of the situation in Cuba as well as in Spain. Mr. Olney, so far as I know (I know nothing about it; the chairman of the committee can correct me if I am mistaken about it), concluded that it was his duty to send that paper to the Senate committee. I do not know whether it was called for or not. But, at all events, the paper came to the Senate committee. It was not sent in in any official form. The original paper which was submitted by the Spanish minister to the Secretary of State was sent to the committee. I was not there when the paper arrived, nor was I there when it was being read, being detained from the committee by some fortuitous matter. I came in just about the time of the close of the session, and the chairman called my attention to the fact that a paper from the Spanish minister had been read, and it being in the hands of the clerk of the committee, I asked leave to glance over it, as it was going right back to the State Department; and I looked it over. The only impression it made upon me at the time was that it was a plea for continuance, for postponement, on the part of Spain.

Mr. HALE. Let me ask the Senator——

Mr. MORGAN. I have it here.

Mr. HALE. I am not going to ask the Senator about the text of the memorandum; but was any indication ever given to the Senate by the Committee on Foreign Relations that that committee had had any such paper——

Mr. MORGAN. There was no occasion for it.

Mr. HALE. Or that there was any case on the other side until it was unwarily brought out by the Senator from Ohio?

Mr. MORGAN. Ah, there is no use for the Senator from Maine to attempt to cast suspicion upon the integrity of the Committee on Foreign Relations in a matter of this kind.

Mr. HALE. I do not attempt to cast suspicion upon the integrity of the committee, but I do say that there is a general feeling that the committee itself has not communicated to the Senate any information whatever upon which it has based its action, and it never was more illustrated than it was on Friday, when the Senator from Indiana [Mr. TURPIE], in his seat, said that the resolutions reported by the committee of conference had never been approved by the Committee on Foreign Relations.

Mr. MORGAN. I have the floor on this question, and I am going to keep it until I get through with it.

Mr. HALE. The Senator can prevent me from asking a question——

Mr. MORGAN. The Senator from Maine is endeavoring to raise a case of surmise and suspicion against the Committee on Foreign Relations, that they have concealed from this body some fact that bears upon the condition of the case as stated by Spain. I will read the paper and comment on it as I go along, for the purpose of showing that nothing has been withheld here that Spain contended for at all. Nothing has been attributed to Spain that she does not admit, except perhaps in some casual remark by a Senator— But nothing in the way of facts has been presented on this floor in behalf of the committee that Spain does not admit.

Mr. HALE. I am very glad at this late day to have the Senator bring in the paper he has.

Mr. MORGAN. It is not a late day. The paper was sent back to the State Department because the Secretary of State required it to be done. He did not communicate to us a copy of it, as I think he should have done. He should have left it with the committee instead of keeping it as a state paper which he would not communicate. So on last Saturday I wrote to the Secretary of State and asked him for a copy of the paper. His reply to me was that he would consult the Spanish minister, and if he consented to it, I might have a copy.

Mr. HALE. Did he consent?

Mr. MORGAN. Yes. Mr. Olney says:

MY DEAR SIR: The Spanish minister says he has no objection to your reading the inclosed as part of your speech to the Senate on the Cuban resolutions. I accordingly send it to you.

There Spain, through her minister, seems to have some closer relation to the Secretary of State than has the Committee on Foreign Relations. He can send a paper up through the Secretary of State to be read in our committee room and withdrawn and carried back to the files of the State Department and kept there, not communicated; and when I asked that the paper might be sent here the Secretary says, "I will confer with the Spanish minister, and if he consents to it, I will let you have a copy."

The committee did not keep a copy of the paper, as perhaps they might have done and as perhaps they ought to have done, because they regarded it precisely in the light in which it was intended to be considered, as a petition on the part of Spain for further time, that we would delay action until Spain got ready to have some very favorable report made by the Senate of the United States in her behalf. There is added to this a paper dated the 11th of January, 1896, marked "Confidential." I do not believe that paper was before the committee, but I am not certain of it:

SIR: In reply to a telegram addressed to the governor-general of Cuba, in which I asked Gen. Martinez Campos some questions whose answers I have not been able to inclose in my memorandum of yesterday for the short time I had at my command, I have received the following answer:

"The so-called insurgent government has no fixed residence. They came to the Villas and have returned to Camaguey. One hardly knows where they wander about as soon as a column of the army goes in their persecution. They do not live nor reside in any inhabited place, and do not exercise any act of civil government."

That is all true, no doubt—all true. How many places of habitation did the government of the confederacy have during the Revolutionary war in the United States? Nine different places to which they resorted, escaping from the British in one quarter to find protection in another.

Mr. SHERMAN. The Continental Congress moved back and forth from place to place.

Mr. MORGAN. Not merely the executive government, but the whole Congress moved backward and forward until they had nine habitations in the United States. The British Government could not chase them down sufficiently to capture them. Where was our Government when this Capitol was set afire and burned to the ground by the British who came across the Atlantic Ocean?

A fugitive in Virginia. What was its local habitation then? Does this gentleman expect to make a point upon the people of Cuba because they are compelled in the exigency of their situation to change their government from place to place? Yet the truth is, as is shown by reports made and published in the Evening Star from Captain Mannix, who visited the place on two occasions, that there has been from the outbreak of the revolution a permanent capital in Cuba, at Cubitas, on the top of the mountains at the eastern end of the island. It has never been changed, it has never been attacked, and it has never been approached by the Spaniards. It is the place from which justice is administered and the civil law is executed in its protection of the rights of property, life, and liberty.

So the complaint of Martinez Campos, which is contained in the telegram that he sent to Mr. Dupuy de Lôme, is merely that the insurgent government has no fixed residence. "They came to the villas and have returned to Camaguey." What does he mean by "returned to Camaguey"? He means they came to the villas for the purpose of executing their orders and administering justice, as Mr. Mannix explains, through the prefects and subprefects of the different districts of Cuba. When they had gotten through with the establishment of civil government and their inspection of the offices of civil government there, they returned to Camaguey. Camaguey is the capital province of Cuba, and Cubitas is the town, the village, if you please, in which that government is established, and has been from the beginning. The Spaniards have never dared even to attempt to attack it.

That seems to have been a necessary part of the programme which Mr. Dupuy de Lôme wants to lay before the Government of the United States in order to satisfy us that it would never do for us to recognize the belligerency of a government which is scattered about as that is from place to place.

If the establishment of a government as a civil government depends upon the place where it is obliged to be in order to escape from capture, then, of course, those men can never establish civil government until they have first conquered and driven the Spaniards out.

Mr. HALE. Will the Senator from Alabama allow me to ask him a question?

Mr. MORGAN. Yes, sir.

Mr. HALE. Has the Senator read that most interesting account of the peregrination and wanderings of the correspondent of the Evening Star in trying to find this nebulous capital, in which he entirely failed?

Mr. MORGAN. Captain Mannix?

Mr. HALE. Yes.

Mr. MORGAN. Is that the name—Captain Mannix?

Mr. HALE. Does the Senator believe that there exists at the place which he has named anything that is in the form of a representative government?

Mr. MORGAN. I do.

Mr. HALE. Does he believe that at this place, at this small village which the correspondent either did not find or barely found, there exists any such legislative body, any such judicial tribunal, any such head of the army and the navy as existed at Montgomery, and afterwards at Richmond, in the Confederacy, or as existed all through the war of the Revolution, at the time of the rebellion, if you call it so—the war against Great Britain? Does the Senator believe that any such condition exists in Cuba to-day, or has existed for the last year?

Mr. MORGAN. I supposed I had the floor for the purpose of explaining this paper and making some remarks upon it. But I find I am here only for the purpose of answering questions like a school child at a kindergarten.

Mr. HALE. It is not my fault if the Senator appears like a school child who ought to be questioned. It is not my fault——

Mr. MORGAN. No; I will come at the Senator about that and put him on his answer to questions. When he got up here he asked me if I had read an article published in the Evening Star, in which its correspondent had wandered all through Cuba and had failed to find the capital.

Mr. HALE. Or barely found it.

Mr. MORGAN. No, sir. In the first question the Senator put to me he said Captain Mannix had failed to find it. Then, when he found that Captain Mannix, whose story he read just as well as I have, did find it, and not only found it, but afterwards returned to it and was treated with great hospitality and kindness while he was there, and had to march for miles on foot, meeting with many guards, in order to get there—when he found that he says perhaps Captain Mannix found it, and if he did it was some miserable little village or place, one, perhaps, that a decent government had not any right to be at.

Mr. HALE. I took the Senator's words about a village. It is a very small place. There is no doubt about that.

Mr. MORGAN. It is a small place.

Mr. HALE. With that interruption, I am not going to worry the Senator any longer.

Mr. MORGAN. The Senator does not worry me. He is worrying——

Mr. HALE. I had the honor to address the Senate on the subject a few days ago, and I welcomed interruption. I was interrupted by several Senators.

Mr. MORGAN. I do not care about discussing that matter. If the Senator will just let me have a little breath of time to say a word or two together, it will be all right.

Mr. HALE. I do not think that any Senator can prevent the Senator from Alabama from occupying——

Mr. MORGAN. I will prevent interruption by refusing to let the Senator interrupt me.

Mr. HALE. I will not interrupt the Senator again.

Mr. MORGAN. Do not do it any more. If the Senator does, I will call him to order.

Mr. CHANDLER. While the Senator from Alabama takes a breath, will he allow me to make a statement about Cubitas?

Mr. MORGAN. Yes.

Mr. CHANDLER. Not only is the statement of the Senator from Alabama correct, but it is to be borne in mind that Captain Mannix described fully, when he went to Cubitas, exactly how he went, what train he took; that he went to Matanzas. He describes the whole physical conformation of the country after he reached the interior village, where is the capital. He describes his return from it, and he afterwards described another visit which he made there.

Mr. MORGAN. Yes, a second visit.

Mr. CHANDLER. And that the Spanish Government, with that information in their hands, have not taken the capital and never have dared to try to take the capital is very good evidence that the insurgents, whether or not they need to have a capital to entitle them to recognition as belligerents, have a capital, and that even all the Spanish troops in Cuba can not reach and capture it.

Mr. MORGAN. Gomez and Maceo have come nearer to capturing Habana than the Spanish Crown has ever come to capturing Cubitas.

Mr. CHANDLER. The insurgents have been within a half dozen miles of Habana, and there is no evidence that the Spanish troops have been within 50 miles of Cubitas.

Mr. SHERMAN. The insurgents have been within 10 miles of Habana within a few days.

Mr. MORGAN. That so great a man and so great a general as Campos, in reply to the telegram of the minister, could state no better reason than that for discarding the existence of a civil government in Cuba is something which to me is very surprising. Why did he not say a Cuban Government does exist; it has its prefects and subprefects, its collectors of taxes, its judicial organization? Why did he not say that it is supreme over the military, and that Gomez and Maceo hold their commissions to-day signed by Cisneros and countersigned by the secretary of war, combining together the civil and military authority, all of the elements of a republic except a navy? They have not any navy because they have no money to buy ships and no chance to build them. The mere fact that Gen. Martinez Campos should say no more against the Government of Cuba than he has said in this dispatch is enough to convince any sincere man, it seems to me, of the actual existence of that Government in Cuba.

More than that, that Government is not a stranger to Cuba. It is the same Government, headed by the same men, Cisneros as president, Gomez as commander of the army, which capitulated in 1878, hauled down the flag of the lone star of Cuba upon terms and conditions made with Spain which recognized, expressly recognized, their existence at that time as a republic. When they went out as a republic they yielded up their sovereign authority, as they claimed it, into the hands of the monarchy of Spain. When it is found, as will be demonstrated even more fully than it has been, and beyond the power of all denial, that Spain has broken every covenant in that capitulation, when Cisneros comes back to the head of the civil government, and Gomez comes back to the head of the war establishment, and they hold a convention for the purpose of establishing a constitution which is now printed in the records of Congress, sent to us by the Secretary of State—when that has been done, it is too late for General Campos or any person else to say that a government does not exist in the Island of Cuba on the part of the revolutionists which has power over life, liberty, and property; and to-day when any private citizen of the United States, of Spain, of Cuba, or of any other Government comes within the purview of its power he is bound to yield his obedience, because it is at least a government de facto.

If an American citizen in the heart of the Province of Camaguey should lend or give a thousand dollars to this provisional government, or this government de facto, for the purpose of carrying on the war, and the Spanish monarchy after the war was over should arrest him on the island and try him for that as an act of treason or as a breach of their laws against the insurrection, the Government of the United States would be bound to thrust its arm in and say, "Stop; you can not try this citizen and condemn him for obedience to a government de facto established in Cuba which you did not have the power at the time to overthrow." That is the situation, stated in a very brief way, but in a concise and perspicuous one, I trust, so that there can be no doubt left about it. That government is powerful enough to protect any man who is within reach of its influence, even though he enters its armies and takes the oath of allegiance to it, because he can not refuse to do it if he is conscripted or if enlistment is demanded of him.

The Spanish minister then goes on to state his reasons why we should not recognize the belligerency of the Cubans. He lays them out in extenso at an early day in the month of January; I do not recall the date. What does he say about it?

Sugar does not pay direct taxes. The especial tax on manufacture was abolished. The only tax now paid by sugar is 75 cents per ton on exports, with the name of "load permit."
If the crop could be entirely lost, and the average exportation of 600,000 tons were absolutely impossible, the loss for the treasury would be $450,000. This is less than 1 per cent of the war expenses.
The insurgents do not occupy any part of the country permanently.

That means the men in arms, of course—the insurgents. They "do not occupy any part of the country permanently." General Washington's army did not occupy any part of this country permanently while the Revolutionary war was going on. His army was operating from Quebec down to Savannah, back and forth, oftener chased than chasing. The people, however, who lived in the country were some of them hostile to the Government of Great Britain and some were friends to it. They were divided up into parties that were called Whig and Tory, in some communities about equally divided, and in some the Tories had the ascendency. They were not called the insurgents. It was the army led by General Washington that was called the army of the rebellion, the insurgent army. They moved about, of course, as military necessity required, from place to place. They had no great forts that they could fortify and remain in, and the Cubans would not take Morro Castle and agree to hold it as against a fleet, because they have not the powder and ammunition to do it with. They could not do it. That is not their style of fighting. Their campaign is not suited to any such exigency. He says:

The insurgents do not occupy any part of the country permanently. If they would occupy a well-known one, the army would be there immediately.

That is to say, they will not sit down and let the Spaniards come up and cut their throats, and that is a very bad thing to do.

As they are all mounted and are continually changing horses, it is easy for them to outmarch the troops.

We know that is so.

Their tactics have always been not to engage in a fight, and to destroy all the cultures and to attack the small towns garrisoned only by a very small force of militia.

Legitimate warfare—proper, good tactics.

If there are more than 20 soldiers, they never approach the blockhouses. Only when their forces greatly outnumber those of the army a part of them stands to fight to better allow the others to follow their usual tactics.

That is from General Campos, an extract from that same dispatch. That is a serious complaint for General Campos to make against the Cubans, but the Cubans were whipping him with those tactics all the time. They drove him off the island, and they sent him 15 miles with his chief of staff at nighttime on foot through the morasses of Cuba, after they had whipped the army and driven it until he could not find it. I do not wonder that he complained at it. But, Mr. President, the complaints have been getting louder and louder from that day to this, and these Cuban tactics, it seems, are too much for the power of the Spanish army. He says:

> Please consider this letter as a complement of my memorandum, and accept the assurance of my highest consideration.
>
> E. DUPUY DE LÔME.

Now, here comes the memorandum:

> The situation in the Island of Cuba, considered on a military point of view, is unchanged, and probably, taking only in consideration the final result of the war, has been bettered by the raid of the two Cuban leaders, Maximo Gomez and Maceo.
>
> The advance of the command of those two men to the Province of Matanzas and Habana and to the limits of Pinar del Rio has been prepared with the intention of producing a theatrical effect and to impress the public opinion in the United States.

Mr. President, that is tragedy; they have been slain, and it has not been played with puppets either. That theatrical effect about which Mr. Dupuy De Lôme speaks has been a very severe effect upon the military situation of Spain in Cuba. He says:

> It is probable also that (has been planned—and in this they have utterly failed—with the desire of producing an uprising in some of the larger towns of the most thickly populated part of that island.

A month's time has revealed that they did not fail in that. Maceo went down in Pinar del Rio and came back with an army at present estimated at an increase of 10,000 soldiers, more than half of them following Maceo in the hope of getting guns from the hands of the Spaniards or their dead comrades when they were killed in battle.

> The reports of the press and of interested persons have presented the insurgents as a victorious army marching toward the capital of the island, and they have even considered the possibility of the investment of Habana.

They might well have done so. Circumstances have been strongly tending in that direction.

> Nothing further from the truth—

Says the minister, and yet we hear by every mail that comes from Habana of the burning of railroad stations, the breaking up of the trains, and the destruction of the railroad lines within 7, 8, 10, and 15 miles all around Habana.

> To understand the war in Cuba it is necessary to bear in mind the nature of the soil—

Now, mark this—

> the nature of the soil and the kind of warfare that is only possible there. The commander-in-chief of the Spanish forces had to comply with the moral duty of every government to protect as much as possible the private property. The army has been scattered to garrison the sugar estates, and has been successful to a great extent in preventing the burning of the buildings and the destruction of the machinery. The rest of the forces have been in constant persecution of the insurgents, preventing them to remain in a place, obliging them to wander about, and succeeding in having engagements, which have never been decisive, because the policy of the enemy has been to disband at the approach of the forces of the army.
>
> The war against the insurgents in Cuba can only be compared with irregular guerrilla wars and Indian wars, in which only by mere chance it is possible to deal a severe and decisive blow.

The same war, with the same guerrilla bands, that drove Napoleon out of Spain; the same tactics—Spanish tactics—applied to the Spanish army by these poor vagrant Cubans of whom he speaks.

> The peace can only be attained by the constant persecution of the bands, by preventing them from establishing themselves in a part of the country, by lessening their number by constant engagements, and by discouraging them, diminishing their resources, and proving them that—

"To them" I suppose he meant—
that they can not succeed, because the greater and better part of the country not only is not with them, but against them.

That is a dolorous outlook for a man who is going to conquer that country in a few short months. How long are we to wait here until Spanish tactics and Spanish power can provide for Spanish authority in Cuba, against this declaration that "peace can only be attained by the constant persecution of the bands, by preventing them from establishing themselves in a part of the country, by lessening their number, by constant engagements," etc.? If that is the only chance to get peace in Cuba, good-bye to peace in that island; it will never be realized except when the Spanish power has consented to the independence of the people.

This fact—
He says—
has been completely demonstrated in the actual campaign. The insurgents, it is true, have gone from one place to another, and have traversed a large part of the island, but in doing so they have not been gaining ground, but changing the field of their operations.

The two principal leaders of the Cuban rebels, the Dominican Maximo Gomez and the mulatto Antonio Maceo, are now in the province of Habana, but, although to follow them it has been deemed necessary to withdraw an important number of troops from Puerto Principe, Santa Clara, and the western province of Santiago de Cuba, nothing has occurred there, showing not only that they have no means at their disposal, but also that the country at large is not in their favor.

And yet no single public meeting has ever been held in the Island of Cuba during this revolution outside of Habana to indicate that the people, as they call them, of Cuba are in favor of the monarchy and against the republic.

It seems that this ought to be the moment to show sympathy and give support when the attention of the Spanish commander-in-chief has been called near the political and business capital of the island.

What does this mean? It is a suit to us, a petition to us, not merely that we should delay the action demanded of us by the people of the United States in their petitions and memorials and by these legislatures, but it is a moment that ought "to show sympathy and give support when the attention of the Spanish commander-in-chief has been called near the political and business capital of the island." That is to say, it is a confession that Gomez has been driven into Habana, and that is the critical moment at which the Government of the United States ought to give its support and express its sympathy for Spain as against the Cubans. They become the petitioners, they become the solicitors of our interference, and Spain to-day is angry with the people of the United States only because we have not expressed for them outward and open sympathy and issued proclamations and done all else to drive them from our coasts when they applied here for shelter against Spanish persecution. No words could more plainly express what is demanded of us than is contained in that paper. He proceeds:

The present advance is not difficult to explain. Maximo Gomez and Maceo had an engagement, if I well remember, on the end of November, in the State of La Reforma, near the line dividing the Province of Puerto Principe from the Province of Santa Clara. The commander of the Spanish troops defeated what he thought was the main body of the enemy, and went in the persecution of him in the region known as Camaguey; then Maceo and Maximo Gomez, taking advantage of the nature of the soil, pushed in two bodies to the west, leaving the Spanish columns and lines to their rear guard. It was the beginning of the raid that has brought so much destruction to property and that has so greatly influenced the public opinion and the press.

2777

There he confesses that Gen. Martinez Campos was outwitted and defeated, in fact, in his purpose by Maceo and Gomez, and he laments that that is the cause of the destruction of the large amount of property in the Habana district and also down in Pinar del Rio.

Nothing is easier, although unfortunate, than what has been done by the two Cuban leaders. They are at the head of a few thousand men, in their great majority negroes, mounted, without commissary department to delay their movements. They meet or disband, according to the necessities of the occasion, marching continually, stealing and changing horses, avoiding the regular army, running and disbanding when the soldiers reach them, exchanging only a few shots, to reform again, sending marauding parties to destroy the cane fields.

A new description, a new history, of Francis Marion, of the American Revolution. We did not find any fault with Francis Marion's tactics. We looked at the splendid results achieved by that gallant and devoted man, and his name will go down to history among the most splendid lights of the American military family.

It is well to say that nothing is easier than to burn the sugar cane. It has always been in Cuba a current proverb that a negro with a box of matches can prevent the gathering of the total sugar crop. The destruction has been confined, with very few sad exceptions, to the cane fields, a thing that has been impossible to prevent, as everybody familiar with the condition of the island well knows. They have not dared to approach the buildings and plantations that were protected by detachments of the army or volunteers, nor have they, in all the time that the revolution has lasted, tried to attack or hold any town of medium importance. Not a single town or village has risen in their favor, raising the rebel flag, although the bulk of the bands has passed sometimes at a near distance.

As it has been said above, the military situation of the island has not changed. The insurgents have not gained ground.

At the beginning of the military operations, after the arrival, late in December, of the third army corps of 25,000 men to the Island of Cuba, and when the dry season was well settled, the insurgent chiefs have made a bold raid, with the intention, that has not been concealed, of influencing public opinion abroad. That is all. They know that they can not succeed, and their only hope is founded, directed by the Junta of New York, in what they most desire—in the possibility of bringing difficulties in the relations of Spain and the United States. The Junta has not succeeded, although it has tried to; they have not been able, although engaged continually in it, to violate the neutrality laws that they have never obeyed, and now they look for an indirect intervention to help them in a fight that they can not win because they are a small minority.

The insurgents have ridden through the provinces of Matanzas—

Listen to this—

The insurgents have ridden through the provinces of Matanzas and Santa Clara and nothing else—

That was in January—

destroying a great deal of property of noncombatants, not only of the supporters of the Government, but also of foreigners. The excuse for such acts of unnecessary vandalism is that they want to cut the resources of the Spanish Government. This reason is too preposterous. The tax derived from sugar in the Island of Cuba can sustain an army of over 100,000 men in campaign only for a comparatively short time.

Therefore it is preposterous. That is all they had—their sugar and tobacco—for exportation, to get money with, and I have always understood that any belligerent power not only would, but that it had the right to destroy the resources of the enemy by burning up his crop or whatever else he had that would contribute to his strength.

Mr. SHERMAN. It was done on both sides in our civil war.

Mr. MORGAN. Of course it was.

The real reason of the destruction is to punish the landowners for their loyal support to the Spanish Government, which represents peace, freedom, and civilization in the island—

Well, I really enjoy reading such words coming from the pen of a Spaniard. "Peace, freedom, and civilization in the island"— and at the same time to drive to their ranks the many laborers that will be left without the means of subsistence, and to prevent the desertions in their ranks that were anticipated the moment that many thousands of men that have been driven to their ranks by the crisis brought about by the low prices of sugar in the last years would be offered honorable means of gaining a salary.

The rebel bands that have been presented to the American public as an army have been near Habana. They have not been able to attack or even to surround the city, and it seems absurd even to consider it, remembering that to the present moment they have not even tried to hold a place where to establish what they call their government. They have destroyed the railroads in Matanzas, but these have been immediately repaired and are running, and have brought part of the troops by which they have immediately been surrounded. They are so now, and by enough forces to give us the hope that they will be compelled to fight, and that their retreat to a more favorable field for the operations of guerrilla bands will be prevented—

I suppose that the Senator from Maine [Mr. HALE] would be delighted with a resolution passed by the Senate of the United States that the Cuban forces should stop and fight and should not run any more into the swamps, like Marion did. That would suit exactly. That is the sort of support we could give to Spain down there that would be of material assistance—

If the military situation has not changed, and to a certain point is better, the political also is not changed. The rebels, to answer the request of their sympathizers abroad, have formed what they name a government, and have written a constitution for the only purpose of printing it in the New York papers. But that government has no place where to reside; it has been wandering from one place to another in the fastnesses of the mountain of Najasa. They have no regular functions; there is no civil government; they do not exercise any jurisdiction in fact. The only one is that exercised by the rebel bands that wander about without a place where to rest. The direction of the rebellion is on the field and chiefly by the organization that with the name of "Junta" resides in New York, and is composed of individuals who have adopted the American nationality and sworn allegiance to the American flag.

It is said in Cuba that the actual war has been imported against the will of a large majority of the country. Everything has been planned abroad; for years political clubs established in the United States and in some countries of South America have collected funds and prepared the uprising, and when a law giving a large measure of self-government to the island, accepted and voted even by the Cuban deputies of the Home Rule party, was passed, when they were losing all hopes of having followers in Cuba, the war was imported by leaders that are mostly foreigners or colored men, and that were nearly all of them abroad.

The insurrection has spread, and it is not a wonder, taking into consideration the class of men that form its ranks. Out of a few young and enthusiastic men who have joined the ranks of the rebels, only what would be called in all countries old demagogues are at the head of the revolution. Not only they have not established a government, but they will not be able to form one, even if it were possible that the Island of Cuba would be separated from Spain.

The advance of the bands of Gomez and Maceo has brought close together all the political parties of the island deciding to support the Spanish Government, because even the most liberal and radical in the Home Rule party know that order and law are impossible in the present condition of the island without Spain.

In this revolution the negro element has the most important part. Not only the principle leaders are colored men, but at least eight-tenths of their supporters. The black population of the island forms a little more than one-third of the 1,600,000 Cubans, but they are strong and numerous in the eastern part, and the result of the war, if the island could be declared independent, will be a secession of the black element and a black republic on that part of the island.

The revolutionary organization that from New York has directed the present uprising has been mistaken in its appreciation of the forces of Spain. They did not imagine that Spain could send in a short time a large army with such facility and in Spanish bottoms. At the same time they have not been able to suppose that Spain could have, as she has and will have, the necessary money to sustain what she is bound to sustain, the integrity of her territory. They could not understand the unanimous and staunch determination of the

2777

political parties and of everybody in Spain to sacrifice the last man and the last dollar to prevent a bad minority of people without standing in the island to oblige the large majority to accept, against their will, a change of government that will bring the total destruction of an island that is to-day the richest territory of the Spanish-speaking nations in America.

In all what is said—

I suppose "that" is meant—

in favor of a few thousand rebels; all is forgotten about the large majority of Cubans loyal to Spain and ruined by the revolution; nothing is said of the hundreds of thousands of citizens born in Spain but who have lived since childhood in Cuba, and by their economy and thrift have built the foundation of the riches of the island; nothing of the foreigners that want to be protected against their deliverers.

The insurgents have not shown that they can succeed; they have not established a government and will not be able to establish one. It is the opinion of everybody that in a very short time the main body of the insurgents, which is in a critical position, will be dealt with; but if the chances of war should make necessary the increasing of the Spanish forces, it is not idle to state that, according to the latest orders of the war department of Spain, the 1st of January, 1896, the roll call of the standing army in Spain was over 89,000 men; and, at the same time, that in the system of mobilization that has brought to Cuba three army corps of 25,000 men each, 43 battalions of 1,000 men have not been touched, and can be sent at a moment's notice.

The Cuban insurgents are, and represent, a small minority of the people of the island; they do not occupy permanently any town or part of the territory; the principal feature of the revolution is a radical war; they have not a civil government established, and no civil and judicial jurisdiction is exercised; the revolution has been started from abroad, is maintained by foreign aid, and its last and only hope is to be supported by foreign intervention, obtained by a systematic misrepresentation of facts.

Now I have read the whole of that miraculous and mysterious paper, and I have shown that it is what I claimed it to be, a mere petition for delay. And the Senate granted it by giving the delay, by waiting to see whether or not the conjectures of the minister from Spain would be realized in the near future or how the tide would turn.

Very soon after this was handed in, the Spanish Government, despairing of any conquest of the insurrectionists of Cuba through the powers of Martinez Campos, who was the greatest man, both in a military sense and in the sense of being a great statesman, that Spain has produced perhaps in a century, finding that he could not accomplish the result of the conquest of Cuba, recalled him and sent Weyler in his place. They threw the sword of extermination into the scale by sending Weyler to Cuba, and they determined that Cuba should feel the blade that leaves nothing to grow after it has struck.

Mr. SHERMAN. Will it be convenient for the Senator from Alabama to go on now, or does he desire that the Senate shall adjourn so that he may finish his argument to-morrow?

Mr. MORGAN. I will yield as soon as I mention one more fact which I wish to go into the RECORD this evening.

Mr. SHERMAN. All right.

Mr. MORGAN. The senior Senator from Maine [Mr. HALE], in his speech in opposition to this resolution and in opposition to the independence and the belligerent rights of Cuba, delivered in the Senate last week, relied almost entirely and based his argument upon an alleged dispatch that was received from the premier of the Spanish Government. He read it at large with an attentive, respectful, almost religious presentation, and after he had gotten it upon record he based his argument upon it to show the magnanimity of the Spanish Government, to show the grounds of their action in Cuba, and to show their relations with the Government of the United States.

Now comes out the declaration of Mr. Castillo that he wrote no such dispatch and was not responsible for it. The Senator from Maine was overreached; he mistook the Spaniard; the Spaniard, it appears, had neither mercy nor consideration in his heart for the poor people of Cuba. These poor mulattoes, negroes, vagabonds, described by the Spanish minister, Dupuy de Lôme, have no recognition at the court of Spain; never have had and never will have; and they quarrel with any American citizen, particularly with any Southern man who was raised in a negro community, who has been the owner of slaves, because he stands up on the floor of the Senate of the United States and demands for them all the rights of men. The Senator from Maine, when he presents these questions to the Senate of the United States, negatives that demand. He is not willing that they should be free men in Cuba, and I take it for granted that he is not willing they should be free men here, unless by some hook or by some crook they can be made to vote the Republican ticket.

I will close, Mr. President, at this place, retaining the floor.

Mr. SHERMAN. I move that the Senate adjourn.

Mr. NELSON. I ask the Senator from Ohio to yield to me a moment to obtain the consideration of a bill for the benefit of a private soldier.

Mr. SHERMAN. I yield to the Senator from Minnesota.

*   *   *   *   *   *   *

March 17, 1896.

Mr. MORGAN. I ask that the conference report upon the disagreeing votes of the two Houses upon the resolutions relative to the war in Cuba be laid before the Senate.

The PRESIDING OFFICER (Mr. BACON in the chair). The Senator from Alabama calls up the conference report indicated by him. The question is upon concurring in the report, upon which he is entitled to the floor.

Mr. MORGAN. Mr. President, I have on several occasions since I have been in this body experienced the disadvantage of being compelled to break an argument upon a question in half and proceed on some later day to complete it. I never felt this disadvantage more seriously than I do to-day. It seems to me that this is a case that deserves consecutive argument and treatment, because it involves principles of law which are intricate and undecided in the United States, and it involves also our relations with a foreign government, which are delicate at this moment of time, are the subject of considerable irritation, an irritation not provoked by anything that has been done either by the people or the Government of the United States, but provoked, as I understand it, by the supersensitiveness of Spain, because she feels that the sand is crumbling from under her feet. and that she is about to lose the beautiful gem of the Antilles, to which she attaches such a vast importance, and always has, and justly. This gem of the Antilles is an orange that Spain and her feudal lords have been sucking now for nearly four centuries. While it is true that they have very nearly gotten all the substance, all of the juice and sweetness, out of it, it still remains as the only territory that they seem to have a particular fondness for, and it seems to gratify all the tastes of Spain for dominion and power, accompanied with the control of men and things in the sense of the severest despotism.

2777

The paper that I last read and commented upon yesterday was the best statement that the Spanish minister could then make, on the 11th of January, as to the prospects of Spain in her efforts to suppress the rebellion in Cuba. It was hastily withdrawn from the committee, no copy being left with us, and no one on the committee has seen it, I think, or has scarcely remembered its existence, until I presented it to the Senate yesterday, after it had been made the subject of animadversion of a somewhat severe character by the Senator from Maine [Mr. HALE] against the Committee on Foreign Relations. His animadversions, if they are due to anybody, are due to the Secretary of State and the Spanish minister, his particular friend, and I dislike to become a sort of scapegoat for what the Senator now finds upon looking into the subject is the fault, if fault of any person, of Mr. Olney and Mr. Dupuy de Lôme.

That is a very weak statement, if it was then, or is now, all that Spain has to say about the Cubans and the war they are waging, and about her power to suppress the rebellion. I do not know why it has been held in seclusion, but I suppose, rationally I think, that this forecast of Spanish success and this prophecy of the suppression of the rebellion have been so utterly disproved by subsequent events that the reproduction of this paper would discredit Spain's capacity as a diviner of the future, and would increase into a wail of despair the note of anxious apprehension which pervades that statement.

Never was a demand for liberty met with a feebler protest; never was the success of an enemy disparaged by so weak a refutation; never did a victor have to recount so many defeats, such artful strategy, and so many narrow escapes as the story of this war reveals as it is told in the letter of General Campos and the comments of the Spanish minister upon this semitragic warfare.

The plea of the Cubans for liberty is answered by the assertion that negroes are fighting those fierce yet sacred battles. The plea for independence is answered by the assertion that Gomez is a Dominican and Maceo a mulatto, and they could not conduct civil government if they had independence. The plea for humanity is answered by the fact the supplicants are mere subjects, not citizens with a voice that can even utter a prayer—poor, dejected outcasts, without the right to human benevolence.

The PRESIDING OFFICER. The Senator from Alabama will suspend. The hour of 2 o'clock having arrived, the Chair lays before the Senate the unfinished business, which will be stated.

The SECRETARY. A bill (S. 502) to approve a compromise and settlement between the United States and the State of Arkansas.

Mr. BERRY. I ask that the unfinished business be temporarily laid aside, without losing its place.

The PRESIDING OFFICER. The Senator from Arkansas asks that the unfinished business be temporarily laid aside. Is there objection? The Chair hears none. The Senator from Alabama will proceed.

Mr. MORGAN. The plea set up by the Spanish minister for a further exercise of our long-suffering patience is that these miserable wretches are exceedingly hard to whip, because they will not stand up in line and be shot down. That, having few arms, little ammunition, and no artillery, after they have delivered a single blow they seek shelter in the thick woods, after the example of that fox, Francis Marion, whose headquarters were in the islets of the Dismal Swamp, in our Revolution. They are accused of discarding the strategy and high etiquette of chivalric warfare, knowing that the Spaniards who will kill them when they are captured, though they are left wounded on the field of battle, will receive honors, badges, and promotions for such service. Yet they turn their prisoners free, because they can not feed them and have no prisons like the Isle of Pines, Fernando Po, or Ceuta in Africa, to which they can condemn them, in chain gangs, to perpetual imprisonment.

These lawless rebels are charged with being naked and barefooted, without commissary trains, and in such bad plight and of such fierce and daring nature that the senior Senator from Maine [Mr. HALE] exhibits the deepest abhorrence when denouncing them as "guerrillas" and "savages."

For more than two centuries we have fought savages, in guerrilla warfare, savages compared with whom the worst of the Cubans and some of the Spaniards are preux chevaliers—very angels of light; yet our history in these five hundred wars has been humane, and we have never refused belligerent rights, as to the humanities of warfare, to any Indian tribe engaged in open hostilities. It is otherwise in Cuba, where the barbarities practiced by the monarchy, in former wars, of old, and of late, and at present, have provoked retaliation until human life, like that of serpents and noxious worms and beasts of prey, is considered as being fit only for extinction.

Spain has made this bad record so distinctly a part of her history that her wars with Cubans blush with the crimson hue of murder and are blackened with rapine as a universal assumption of fact. When the Spanish minister was sending his "memorandum" to the Senate committee as a plea for delay, we had the right to recur to the facts of the history of the last war of Cuba for independence, and to the outcry of the world against their repetition in the present war, and to ask ourselves if we could afford to give our silent acquiescence to the Spanish assertion that a million people are rebel traitors and deserve death in any form that Spanish ferocity or vengeance shall choose to inflict. We dared not to give such an answer to the petitions of our people, yet we were constrained into longer silence by our duty and our reverence toward our own country. We were compelled to answer that there is no reasonable ground for the expectation of any change for the better in the character of the present war.

The furtive allusion to sugar in the memorandum of the Spanish minister which I read yesterday, and to the burned plantations of our citizens in Cuba, intended to sweeten the invocation of our sympathy and for our aid in crushing the rebellion, did not serve to convince us that Spain, without our aid, could again subjugate these people in their war for justice, liberty, and life. That covert plea was almost a conclusive proof that Spain had despaired of success.

That memorandum treats of Cuba as a mere feudatory of Spain, whose people are incapable of self-government and do not deserve the treatment even that is due to coolies or serfs. This is the true relation between Spain and Cuba that has been established by the cruelties of that Monarchy. This is the blot on the escutcheon of Spain that will not out. It is not provincial or colonial; it is only feudal. What voice Cuba has in the Spanish Cortes is the voice of rulers selected for them and seduced into tyrannical exactions upon them by divisions of the spoils gained from their robbery.

The feudalists of Spain have their friends and supporters among the feudalists in Europe and America. Of late that new rank has had a great accession of strength, even in this plain Republic, notably among the nouveau richesse. Their power seems to brood over this Senate and to check the earnest movement of the people in the direction that their noble ancestry have never refused to march, whatever the peril or the cost. Facts that prove the existence of open war in Cuba are admitted in the memorandum of the Spanish minister, sent to the committee through the Secretary of State, which I read yesterday. And yet the feudalists demand further proof. The existence of an organized civil government among the insurrectionists, that they at least obey, is distinctly admitted by the Spanish minister. But its efficacy is denied, and it is alleged that it has no permanent capital.

It is the existence of war and not its atrocities, Mr. President, or its prospects of ultimate success, that gives to us the right to assert our neutrality as between these belligerents.

If open war exists in Cuba, we can not afford to call it peace. As it is a war for the liberty of nearly 2,000,000 people, we are not unjust or inimical to Spain if our sympathies go out to the Cubans who put their existence in the scale, finding that life is intolerable under Spanish persecution.

It is not the location of the civil government, it is not its capacity to command the allegiance, the support, or the obedience of the people outside of the domain of its military command, but inside that territory, that fixes its right to recognition as a belligerent power. A de facto civil government, having power to command obedience to its decrees, within its military command, whether that power is civil or military, is a government that can conduct lawful warfare under the laws of nations. It needs no capital or seaport or garrisoned fortresses to prove its right to fight for the liberties of its supporters.

We did not hold permanently a single seaport during our war for independence, and our Congress, like a hunted hare, had its seat wherever it found temporary shelter.

The next open appearance of the Spanish minister, as he seems to be working a crusade for political influence and power against the Congress of the United States, is his appeal from an indulgent Congress, acting within the limits of its duty and without injustice to Spain, over its head to the people of the United States.

When the people of the United S ates, who are our constituents, impeach us and become our judges on the demand of a supercilious foreign minister, it will be high time for the Senate and the House to close their doors and go into retirement, for then it will become true, as it never has yet been true in America, that a foreign representative of a monarchy can call in question the House and the Senate, and members of the House and members of the Senate, for words uttered in debate on these floors, against which our Constitution protects us.

Before proceeding to discuss this matter, I will first ask the Secretary to read that appeal and the answer of the agent of the Cuban Republic to it, and I will then remark upon both papers as coming from men who are equally reliable. I can not assume when dealing with Spaniards who speak unofficially that the office they may hold enhances their authority or that a Cuban is not entitled to credit because his credentials are not signed with the royal signet of Spain. I will ask the Secretary to read from the remarks of the Senator from Maine [Mr. HALE], which I will send to the desk, what the Spanish minister had to say in his celebrated diatribe against the Senate and against Senators particularly, commencing on page 2941 of the CONGRESSIONAL RECORD.

The Secretary read as follows:

Senator SHERMAN, in the sitting of February 28, quoted freely, among other things, from an article published in a New York morning paper of Sunday, February 23. He said, giving in very strong language his opinion of the present commander-in-chief of the Spanish army in Cuba, the following: "A book was published in Spanish, which I am very sorry I can not get from the library, written by a Spaniard by the name of Enrique Donderio, who came over from Spain with the Spanish troops to see the war of 1872, and who was so horror-stricken with the high crimes that he saw committed that he flew to the United States and there published his manuscript. Telling is this evidence, and it shows General Weyler," etc.

I have made an investigation about that book, and I have found that the name of the author is not Enrique Donderio, as originally printed, but Enrique Donderis. For this reason probably the Senator was unable to find the book in the Congressional Library. Should he have found it, he would have seen that in the book, which is a small pamphlet of 43 pages, not a single time the name of General Weyler is mentioned.

I have carefully read, and have had the pamphlet read by other persons, and I see in it that many horrors are described attributed both to the Spaniards and to the rebels, but in it, as I said before, and as I most emphatically affirm again, the name of General Weyler is not mentioned one single time. I have the book at the disposal of anybody who would like to controvert my statement.

I have been told that that person, Enrique Donderis, was a Spanish officer who fought in Spain against the Government, and was sent to Cuba. He fought there in the Spanish side, then deserted, and afterwards fought in the rebel ranks. But, although this fact has been stated by a Cuban sympathizer, it can not be vouched by me, and it is of no consequence.

What is important is that the honorable Senator from Ohio said in good faith that all the crimes that he related were attributed by Spanish authorities to General Weyler, and that his good faith has been imposed upon. General Weyler went to Cuba as a lieutenant-colonel in 1869, and returned to Spain as a brigadier-general in 1873. A part of the campaign he held the position of staff officer, he being one of the general staff, and some time later he held the position of colonel of a regiment of volunteers, which was made up and paid by the merchants of Habana. He defended the town of Holguin, being commander-general of that jurisdiction, but he has never had in Cuba other position than that of a subordinate officer.

In my investigations I have read many pamphlets written by Cubans during the war from 1868 to 1878, with all the natural bias when a contest is standing, and have failed to see the name of General Weyler recorded as responsible for the horrors that now, when he is at the head of the army against the rebels, are attributed to him.

MR. MORGAN AND HIS AUTHORITY.

Senator MORGAN, in the sitting of February 24, said that, according to official reports forwarded from Madrid by the United States minister, "13,000 Cubans had been killed in battle up to August, 1872, besides 43,500 prisoners, whom the Spanish minister admitted to have been put to death."

Senator MORGAN said that his authority was the American Cyclopedia. A friend of mine addressed Messrs. D. Appleton & Co., publishers of the cyclopedia, inquiring as to the authority of the book quoted by Senator MORGAN. In reply to his inquiry, Mr. Rossiter Johnson, associate editor of the American Cyclopedia, says that the article was written by Mr. Antonio Bachillery Morales, a Cuban, who was a decided and partial enemy of Spain, and that he presumes that it will be easy to get access to the official reports in the Department of State at Washington. I have accepted the advice, and in the State Department the following answer has been given me: "The minister of the United States to Spain, on the date of August 16, 1872, quoted from the Imparcial, described as a semiofficial journal of Madrid, of which the colony minister was the director until he entered the present cabinet, the following: 'From the beginning of the hostilities in Cuba 13,000 insurgents have been killed in battle, and 43,500 taken prisoners,' the minister adds, 'as it is believed that all prisoners of war taken are shot or garroted.'"

It is plain that the American minister, who was General Sickles, read the statement in a paper. The paper (El Imparcial) was owned by a cabinet minister (Señor Casset y Artime). General Sickles said, in a general way, that it was believed that the prisoners were all shot or garroted. Of course, that is not true; that simply is a belief, an opinion. From the expression of a belief an official report is made; from the statement in a newspaper that the prisoners were taken the conclusion that they were executed is derived, and because the Imparcial was the property of a minister of the cabinet the assertion is advanced that a cabinet officer admitted that they had been put to death. That has been said in the United States Senate and indorsed by a vote of that high body.

MR. LODGE AND A GARBLED INTERVIEW.

Senator CABOT LODGE, in a speech made on the 25th of February, quoted from the Liberal, of Madrid, an interview sent by telegraph from Cadiz in the moment in which General Weyler embarked for Cuba. The translation which has been given to the Senator from Massachusetts is a fraud. My attention was called to it by a telegram from Mr. Taltavull, correspondent in the United States of the Liberal, from Madrid, and a former member of the Cortes. This distinguished gentleman wired to me: "General Weyler never said, in any interview or conversation published in the Liberal, that he would exterminate the filibusters. What he said was that he would clean out the western provinces of Cuba of filibusters, and that he would exterminate the small bands of bandits." I have now before me the text of that interview. I will not stop to discuss the historical importance of a nonauthorized interview. But, even taking as granted that General Weyler said what is printed, the words that the person who has furnished documents to Senator CABOT LODGE have made him pronounce are not exact. The exact translation of what General Weyler said is: "On my arrival to Cuba I propose in the first place to clean out of filibusters the provinces of Habana, Pinar del Rio, and Las Villas; be it well understood that I refer for the moment to the large bands which have invaded them. Then will remain the small bands of bandits, which I will exterminate gradually."

Nobody can believe that General Weyler in the word "exterminate" meant to put to death; but even if that sense is applied to his words, it is necessary to understand what those bands of bandits in Cuba are and have been. I would like to know the opinion that the American planters, respectable, law-abiding citizens, who are working for their own interests and for the prosperity of Cuba, have in that respect; what would be done in this country with the people who have been kidnaping and blackmailing the honest toilers living out in the country. What treatment do they think deserve people like Manuel Garcia, Mirabal, Matagas, Perico Delgado, and others? The paper to which I refer is at the disposition of the Senator from Massachusetts, and of anybody who wants to see it.

CRUELTIES OF WAR.

I can not understand how all rules of war that have been given by all civilized nations are so criminal, so cruel, and so tyrannical when they are applied to Cuba. I have before my eyes a summary of charges of inhumanity in connection with the war of the rebellion in the United States to both sides, taken from American history. I am sure that many of them are false, most of them exaggerated, some necessary, and others unavoidable. But, taking only as an illustration and for the sake of argument what I see in that list, I can not understand how people who are familiar with those necessary evils of war have been able to use such harsh, unjust, and offensive language against Spain.

Mr. HALE. The Secretary may read the extracts which are cited there from contemporaneous literature about the struggle in America, which show how unreliable these are.

The VICE-PRESIDENT. The Secretary will read as indicated.

The Secretary read as follows:

"In an English paper of those days I read the following opinion of the American civil war: 'Stripped of its trappings, it is a mere quarrel for territory. The antagonists are acting like Delawares and Pawnees. War to the knife, pushed to absolute extermination, is what they have resolved on, and people breathe a language of massacre and extermination.'

*　　　*　　　*　　　*　　　*　　　*　　　*

"This charge was no more justified than the charges which are brought now against Spain. I said nothing when that language was used in the press, but I believe it is my duty, although against the conventionalities of my position, to appeal, as I have said, to the honest common sense of the American people when those words are uttered from the Capitol of the United States.

"Nothing has now done in Cuba that has not been done and has not been deemed necessary in other countries when at war. It would be possible and easy for me to quote many facts not different from those which now arouse public sentiment against Spain. I will only ask persons wanting an impartial and honest opinion to read what the commanders-in-chief of the American armies on both sides and what those of the armies of France and Germany have deemed necessary for the protection of their soldiers and the carrying out of the war.

"General Weyler has, in my opinion, been grossly traduced. I should add I feel confident that it is owing to misinformation, to an erroneous prejudice, to systematic attacks on him personally by interested enemies, that the people of the United States and their public representatives have formed a monstrously erroneous opinion about the governor-general. The question of loyal politics does not enter into the subject. No matter whether a man is an ultra-Spanish Monarchist, a Liberal, a Home Ruler, or a Separatist rebel, there is no occasion to speak untruly about an individual who is in opposition to his views.

"Campos spoke kindly of Gomez personally, and I have yet to hear that General Weyler does otherwise. I see that the American newspapers publish charges that prisoners are ill treated and killed by summary execution. Here again is an incorrect representation of facts. I have been striving for autonomy for many years. I have ardently labored in the Cortes to secure all possible reforms and benefits that could ameliorate the condition of Cuba. I love my country, Cuba, and I will do all in my power to advance her interest. When I speak as I do I think I do so disinterestedly and fairly.

"I am astonished to perceive how unacquainted with the true conditions are the public men in Washington. When Cuba lies so close to the borders of the United States it would be supposed a much wider intelligence concerning the internal affairs of the island would exist. If the book said to have been quoted in Congress against General Weyler was by Enrique Donderis, I never heard of its author. I fancy it is a nom de plume.
"WILLIAM SHAW BOWEN."

Mr. MORGAN. Mr. President, the surprise of the Spanish minister that we get no better information from Cuba would certainly indicate that he knew that the channels of information were all open; when, on the contrary, there is a strict, rigid censorship on the cable between the island and the American coast; and I was informed yesterday by a Catholic priest, who knows perfectly well Cuba and Spain, that the mails between Cuba and the United States are constantly opened and their contents examined. He is a gentleman of veracity, and evidently of impartiality, because he was very strict in his expressions and careful not to offend either against Cuba or against Spain.

We know perfectly well that the information that comes to the United States from Cuba is doctored when it comes on the telegraph lines unless it happens to be favorable to the Spanish cause. We find, however, that the Spanish Government has access over the cable lines that run through Europe and across the Atlantic Ocean to the bosom of the Senate here for the purpose of informing Senators as to all that relates to the opinions, the decrees, the judgments, the forecasts, the prognostics, and the sentiments of the Spanish Crown as expressed through its premier. One side of this question seems to have full access to all the information that is favorable, while it is entirely shut off from the other side. The Committee on Foreign Relations have felt this embarrassment very much as the people of the United States have, and they have been compelled to rely upon that suspected source of information, which, after all, when it is sifted out, is the best and truest source of information—the American press.

The minister from Spain, however, did not have any difficulty in ascertaining what I had said in debate in the Senate, for the RECORD discloses exactly what I did say, and it was very presumptuous on his part to misquote me as I was reported in that RECORD and to undertake to palm that off—a false quotation—on the people of the United States as being true. I must say that I have little respect for a minister or any gentleman who will misquote a Senator on this floor when he has the RECORD before his eyes and evidently was making up his statement from that RECORD.

In answer to this arraignment of myself, along with my colleagues on the committee, the Senator from Ohio [Mr. SHERMAN] and the junior Senator from Massachusetts [Mr. LODGE], before the bar of the American people, by the Spanish minister, I will take occasion to answer what he says as to the misquotation, or as to the affirmation which he says I made, by reading from the

2777

RECORD extracts to fully display the context of what I said on that subject.

The question was asked me by the Senator from Maine [Mr. FRYE]:

Has the Captain-General ever been a Cuban?

I said:

Oh, no; that was never within the contemplation of the Government of Spain, so far as I have ever heard.

I do not know whether I am accurate about that or not, but I think I am. I had stated, as follows, a part of Spanish history in Cuba:

In 1851 fifty men of the Lopez expedition were shot in Habana. These are not referred to by General Grant except in general terms. In 1854 Pinto and his associates to the number of 100 men were shot or deported. Then followed the ten years' war from 1867 to 1878, during the progress of which these enormities occurred to which General Grant refers. Spain had more than 90,000 troops in the field in that war. In 1869 the Spanish troops committed atrocities that shocked the civilized world in the wholesale slaughter of men, women, and children in Habana at the Villa Nueva Theater, at the Louvre, and in the sacking of the house of Aldama.

The number of these cruelties is almost beyond comprehension, and the loss of life is appalling. Spain marched into the war 80,000 troops and brought out 12,000. It is stated—

Here is the particular part of it—

It is stated on high authority that—

Now, quoting from the book—

according to official reports forwarded from Madrid by the United States minister, 13,600 Cubans had been killed in battle up to August, 1872, besides 43,500 prisoners whom the Spanish minister admitted to have been put to death.

Then I say:

I confess that when I came across that statement in an authentic history to which we give credit I read it over and over to ascertain whether it could have been possible that such a multitude of humanity had been slaughtered within 90 miles of the coast of the United States during that ten years' war; and I inquired of myself, What has Christianity been doing in the world if in this age, the nineteenth century, it has been possible that such things could be done in an island like Cuba, and that this great and free Republic could stand indifferently by, knowing the facts, and not unsheath its sword and strike the brutal monarch to death who inflicted them?

Then the junior Senator from Maine addressed the following question to me:

Mr. FRYE. I failed to catch the name of the authority for the wonderful, the horrible statement which the Senator from Alabama has just made in relation to the slaughter of prisoners to the number of over 40,000.

Mr. MORGAN. I am sorry that for the moment I can not recall his name. I will hand it to the Senator.

Mr. FRYE. It is from history?

Mr. MORGAN. Yes; deliberately written, and written by a Spaniard.

The point is made there that he was a Cuban, but I suppose he is a Spaniard notwithstanding he is a Cuban, and his name shows that he is a Spaniard—

Mr. FRYE. Does the Senator credit it?

Mr. MORGAN. For a long time I hesitated to credit it, but I had to credit it or else deny the evidence of a deliberate statement made by a historian in a book of universal acceptance, one of reliable authority.

Mr. GRAY. Will the Senator from Alabama state the name of the historian or the book?

Mr. MORGAN. It is the American Encyclopedia, under the title of Cuba.

Then the Senator from Florida [Mr. CALL] interposed to read an extract from a newspaper, for which, of course, I had no responsibility, but which, I have no doubt, presented an exact statement of facts.

The country will see, when what I have read from the RECORD appears, together with the Spanish minister's arraignment of me, that he has misquoted that RECORD and has put me as stating that it had been officially communicated to the Government of the United States that 43,500 prisoners had been shot by the Spanish Government in August, 1872. The Spanish minister, in casting his eye over all of the statement I made, could find no error in it, except as to the question whether I had stated that this statement had been made as an official communication to the United States Government. He does not deny the fact that here was the series of bloody murders which I referred to—the statement of them spread before his eyes—and he does not deny any of them, but quibbles, in his arraignment of me, upon the point whether I had asserted that that was an official document or an official report. Why did he not, when he was vindicating his country and arraigning me, come out and deny what I put upon that RECORD, and which he has not denied and can not deny in the light of truth? No, sir; the facts stand confessed against Spain through the lips of her own minister, because, having full opportunity to make denial, he evades it and leaves it unanswered and tries to force a controversy with me upon a misquotation of the RECORD of this body.

I should leave that subject just there, but I think that in justice to General Sickles I ought to call the attention of the Senate, if I have the document here—I supposed I had it, but can not at the moment lay my hands on it, and I shall cite it at some other time. It is a letter written by General Sickles on that occasion to his Government, in which he made the statement, not affirming that the 43,500 people had been actually slain, but giving the evidence upon which the statement was made, it being drawn from a newspaper that was then owned and conducted by a member of the imperial cabinet. I regret that the paper has been mislaid for the moment, because I wanted to give General Sickles the benefit of the full statement of all he said, and I shall place it in the RECORD later.

Mr. President, that letter of the Spanish minister found its way into the newspapers upon an alleged right of his to go into the public prints, provided he did not sign his official name to his communication, and arraign the Senate for words uttered in debate here. Some Senators have thought that it was a light matter that he should do this, and some have brought his accusations into the Senate with a spirit almost of hilarity, and have repeated them here upon his authority against Senators. I take occasion here totally to dissent from any opinion expressed, it makes no difference by whom, to the effect that a foreign minister in this country has the right to resort to the press for the purpose of affecting any measure or matter which is then pending before the Houses of Congress, or has been recently pending, or in regard to any policy of the United States which he may consider to be offensive or injurious to his country. I may be considered a little old-fashioned in referring to authorities which have been some time forgotten, at least by members of this body, upon a question like that.

Nevertheless, I think it is well worth our while on this occasion, when this flagrant abuse of our privileges has been entered upon, that we should record our opinions upon this question even at the expense of a little public time, for it certainly is time that the diplomatic affairs of this country were withdrawn from public tinkering and tampering by foreign ministers in the newspapers, and that they were confined to official statements between the Governments concerned. If the Senate is to be continually put in an uproar and confusion by telegrams coming from the premier of the Spanish Government to some newspaper editor in the United States, to be read here as authoritative statements of the attitude of Spain in regard to this question and of its feelings and purposes, then, sir, we had as well dismiss our Secretary of State, disband the whole of the State Department, and rely upon these men who have acquired eminence in one way and another in newspaperdom for the knowledge of what is transpiring in foreign governments with reference to our affairs and official information as to the designs and purposes of foreign governments toward the United States.

A country that addresses the American people on diplomatic questions or situations through the newspaper press so far violates all recognized rules of courtesy as to forfeit its right to any representation at this capital. Whether it is Congress, or either of the Houses, or the members thereof that is criticised by a foreign government, or whether it is the President or the Supreme Court that is assailed for official conduct, the offense is the same, and is inexcusable.

I will remark here that so far as my privileges as a Senator are concerned they are, equally with those of my colleagues on this floor and the members of the House of Representatives, very sacredly guarded by the Constitution of the United States. We have the right here, in the presence and under the eye of Almighty God, to state anything that we think it proper to state relating to matters pending in Congress, and the Constitution of the United States gives us a guaranty that we shall not be called in question for it in any other place. If I, in my place, were to make a statement about a citizen of the United States who has some supposed or actual connection with public affairs which would calumniate him, and which would be actionable or indictable for libel if uttered by a private person, the Constitution of the United States, in deference to the exalted position which my State has conferred upon me and the oath which I have taken, protects me and would stand as a shield between me and that citizen, and would give to me free liberty of speech, under my own control, under my own judgment, subject only to the ruling of the Senate as to whether it was appropriate and whether it was in order.

Mr. GRAY. The citizen's freedom of speech would not be curtailed.

Mr. MORGAN. The citizen's freedom of speech would not be curtailed, I very freely grant you, but the minister from Spain is not a citizen; and he is protected by the law of nations against any suit or proceeding on my part to hold him accountable for any calumny he may utter against me as a Senator or as a man. There the rule comes in that seals his mouth in respect of all communications and all utterances that affect the affairs of the Government of the United States, or that call in question the statements of any Senator made on this floor in regard to him or his Government.

The law of nations forbids a Senator or a member of the House of Representatives, and equally forbids any citizen of the United States, from bringing an action or a criminal proceeding against a foreign minister who is enjoying our hospitality, it makes no difference how outrageous his action may have been, if it is not dangerous to the public peace. He can stand here, if he chooses to do it, and fulminate libelous accusations against members of the Senate or either of these bodies, and he will go entirely free and unwhipped of justice, unless the President of the United States sees proper to dismiss him and send him back to his country. There is where he has that advantage. He enjoys a hospitality in the United States that is absolutely sacred so far as his protection is concerned, and while he does that he makes accusations against Senators connected with the conduct of affairs in which his Government has a vital interest, and he does it under circumstances which disable us from doing anything else except to take this floor and vindicate and defend ourselves against his accusations. Perfectly ensconced in the provisions of international law, which protect him against liability in our courts, he violates that law of our own Constitution which throws around us the ægis of its protection and declares that we are not responsible elsewhere for words uttered in debate.

Now, let us see whether or not that agrees with the teachings of our fathers upon this question. I will first read the minutes of a conversation between Mr. Jefferson, Secretary of State, and M. Genet, on July 10, 1793. First Genet asks Jefferson a question, to which he replied as follows:

* * * He asked if they (Congress) were not the sovereign. I told him no, they were sovereign in making laws only, the Executive was sovereign in executing them, and the judiciary in construing them where they related to their department. "But," said he, "at least Congress are bound to see that the treaties are observed." I told him no, there were very few cases indeed, arising out of treaties, which they could take notice of; that the President is to see that treaties are observed. "If he decides against the treaty, to whom is a nation to appeal?" I told him the Constitution had made the President the last appeal. He made me a bow and said that indeed he would not make me his compliments on such a Constitution, expressed the utmost astonishment at it, and seemed never before to have had such an idea.

Mr. Jefferson proceeds:

He was now come into perfect good humor and coolness, in which state he may with the greatest freedom be spoken with. I observed to him the impropriety of his conduct in persevering in measures contrary to the will of the Government, and that, too, within its limits, wherein unquestionably they had a right to be obeyed. "But," said he, "I have a right to expound the treaty on our side." "Certainly," said I, "each party has an equal right to expound their treaties. You, as the agent of your nation, have a right to bring forward your exposition, to support it by reasons, to insist on it, to be answered with the reasons for our exposition where it is contrary; but when, after hearing and considering your reasons, the highest authority in the nation has decided, it is your duty to say you think the decision wrong, that you can not take upon yourself to admit it, and will represent it to your Government to do as they think proper; but in the meantime you ought to acquiesce in it, and to do nothing within our limits contrary to it."

I will presently call attention to a further declaration of Mr. Jefferson upon that subject, for I think the extract I have been reading is not the full statement of his entire views upon that occasion or upon some other, in which he was in conversation with M. Genet. Mr. Jefferson again said to the same person, November 22, 1793:

He (the President) being the only channel of communication between the country and foreign nations, it is from him alone that foreign nations or their agents are to learn what is or has been the will of the nation, and whatever he communicates as such they have a right and are bound to consider as the expression of the nation, and no foreign nation can be allowed to question it, (nor) to interpose between him and any branch of Government, under the pretense of either's transgressing their functions, nor to make himself the umpire and final judge between them.

Again, Mr. Jefferson, in a letter to M. Genet, dated December 31, 1793, writes as follows:

PHILADELPHIA, *December 31, 1793.*

To M. GENET.

SIR: I have laid before the President of the United States your letter of the 20th instant, accompanying translations of the instructions given you by the Executive Council of France to be distributed among the members of Congress, desiring that the President will lay them officially before both Houses, and proposing to transmit successively other papers to be laid before them in like manner, and I have it in charge to observe that your functions as the missionary of a foreign nation here are confined to the transactions of the affairs of your nation with the Executive of the United States, that the communications which are to pass between the executive and legislative branches can not be a subject for your interference, and that the President must be left to judge for himself what matters his duty or the public good may require him to propose to the deliberations of Congress.

Mr. Randolph, Secretary of State, said to Mr. Fauchet, June 13, 1795:

A foreign minister has a right to remonstrate with the Executive to whom he is accredited upon any of those measures affecting his country. But it will ever be denied as a right of a foreign minister that he should endeavor, by an address to the people, oral or written, to forestall a depending measure, or to defeat one which has been decided.

Here is a case which is a little closer, perhaps, in its application to the facts in this case than those that I have been quoting. It is in a letter of Mr. Livingston, Secretary of State, to Mr. Buchanan, on the 2d of January, 1833, in which he says:

Even though the Globe, as published during the Administration of President Jackson, should be regarded as a Government paper, the Government "is and can be, from the nature of our institutions, only answerable for official articles; on all the rest the Globe is as independent of the Executive as any other gazette." Hence, the Government, as such, can not be properly called on by Russia to explain the insertion of articles in the Globe injurious to Russia in relation to Poland, or the publication of what Russia may consider inaccurate and unjust report from France or England of Russian affairs.

That was a correspondence directly between our Government and the Russian minister. Then, again, Mr. Forsyth, in a letter to Mr. Livingston, March 5, 1835, after making some discussions of some preliminary matter, says this:

As one of its branches, the Chief Magistrate, in his messages, commits the Government to foreign nations no more than the two Houses of Congress can by their separate action, and it would be a most extraordinary movement of the foreign power to discuss the resolutions of either House of Congress, or of both, if passed by less than two-thirds, and not approved by the President, as if those resolutions were causes of complaint against the United States, to be subjects of discussion with the Executive. The President corresponds with foreign governments, through their diplomatic agents, as the organ of the nation. As such he speaks for the nation. In his messages to Congress he speaks only for the Executive to the Legislature. He recommends, and his recommendations are powerless unless followed by legislative action. No discussion of them can be permitted. All allusions to them, made with a design to mark an anticipated or actual difference of opinion between the Executive and Legislature, are indelicate in themselves, and if made to prejudice public opinion, will immediately recoil upon those who are so indiscreet as to indulge them. If they contain anything injurious to foreign nations, the means of self-justification are in their own power without interposing between the different branches of this Government—an interposition which can never be made, even by those who do not comprehend the true character of the Government and the people of the United States, without forfeiting the respect of both.

Again, he says:

Were any foreign powers permitted to scan the communications of the Executive, their complaints, whether real or affected, would involve the country in continual controversies; for, the right being acknowledged, it would be a duty to exercise it by demanding a disavowal of every phrase they might deem offensive, and an explanation of every word to which an improper interpretation could be given. The principle, therefore, has been adopted, that no foreign power has a right to ask for explanations of anything that the

President, in the exercise of his functions, thinks proper to communicate to Congress, or of any course he may advise them to pursue. This rule is not applicable to the Government of the United States alone, but, in common with it, to all those in which the constitutional powers are distributed into different branches. No such nation, desirous of avoiding foreign influence or foreign interference in its councils—no such nation possessing a due sense of its dignity and independence, can long submit to the consequences of this interference. * * * If the principle is correct, every communication which the President makes in relation to our foreign affairs, either to the Congress or to the public, ought in prudence to be previously submitted to those ministers, in order to avoid disputes and troublesome and humiliating explanations.

Then Mr. Buchanan, while Secretary of State, in a letter to Mr. Rosa in 1845, says:

Communications of the President to Congress and the debates of Congress are domestic matters, concerning which this Department will not entertain the criticisms or answer the questions of foreign sovereigns.

Would that we had somebody here now who had a just conception of the constitutional rights of the different departments of this Government.

There are various authorities following in the same line, but I shall not detain the Senate by reading them. I will cite, however, Mr. Lawrence's Wheaton, edition of 1863, page 385, for the information of any gentlemen who may desire to prosecute the study of this question further.

Mr. Webster, Secretary of State, said to Mr. Hülsemann:

The President's communications to Congress are matters of domestic concern which are not within the range of the official notice of foreign sovereigns.

Then Mr. Marcy says:

The President's annual message is a communication from the Executive to the legislative branch of the Government; an internal transaction, with which it is not deemed proper or respectful for foreign powers or their representatives to interfere, or even to resort to it as the basis of a diplomatic correspondence. It is not a document addressed to foreign governments.

Mr. Seward, on the 2d of January, 1868, said:

It is neither convenient nor customary with the executive-department to discuss or give explanations concerning the expressions of opinions which are made in incidental debates and resolutions from time to time in either or both of the legislative bodies, at least until they assume the practical form of law. When they assume that form, they are constitutionally submitted to the President for his consideration, and he is not only entitled, but he is obliged to announce his concurrence or nonconcurrence with the will of the Legislature.

It would not be becoming for me to entertain correspondence with a foreign state concerning incidental debates and resolutions in regard to the treaty for the two Danish islands while it is undergoing constitutional consideration in the Senate and in Congress.

Mr. Fish, in 1878, said:

Correspondence by a foreign minister with the press in this country on subjects connected with his mission, such correspondence involving an appeal to the people on diplomatic issues, is ground for his dismissal.

A case could scarcely be more perfectly in point than that which falls within the denunciation of that great Secretary, Mr. Fish. I have not asked any dismissal of this minister; I do not expect to do so, and I regret this serious breach of privilege on his part. Let him stay if he wants to, or if his Government is satisfied. But I have a right as a member of this House to claim the protection of the Constitution of my country against any attack that may be made upon my vote or my speeches on this floor by one who holds a commission as a minister from a foreign government, and who, under that commission, enjoys our hospitalities and is protected against any liability to legal redress. Under the eye and in the presence of the American people, as an

American Senator, I feel perfectly protected against those assaults, and I am quite sure the Senator from Ohio [Mr. SHERMAN] and the junior Senator from Massachusetts [Mr. LODGE] feel in like manner protected against them.

Attorney-General Lee has given us a proper view of this question, and I will read what he says. It is an opinion delivered at a time when the United States was a weak infant as compared with its present strength, but in the hearts of those great and noble men who won the liberties of these people and established this Republic upon eternal foundations there was a regard for national honor and duty and a protection of the different departments of this Government which, I am sorry to say, has disappeared, if the expression of some Senators and their conduct in bringing in the Spanish minister's accusation against us as an arraignment is to be the criterion. This letter is addressed to the Secretary of State, and is in response, doubtless, to a demand from the Secretary of State as to what was the state of the law upon a certain proposition.

PHILADELPHIA, *July 27, 1797.*

You will observe—

He says—

that my letter of this date contains an answer to yours of the 24th instant upon one of the subjects which you submitted to my consideration; and I shall now give my opinion on the other.

The Chevalier de Yrujo, in sending a translation of his letter to you of the 11th instant to Benjamin Franklin Bache and William Cobbett, and directing it to be printed, deviated from propriety. A foreign minister here is to correspond with the Secretary of State on matters which interest his nation, and ought not to be permitted to do it through the press in our country. He has no authority to communicate his sentiments to the people of the United States by publications, either in manuscript or print, which he shall write and circulate while resident among us; but his intercourse is to be with the Executive of the United States only, upon matters that concern his mission or trust. His conduct in this instance I deem a contempt of the Government, for which he is reprehensible by the President.

I can not discover that this letter is libelous on the Government or any public officer, though it may be charged with a degree of indecency and insolence.

The publication of it by Mr. Bache first, and Mr. Cobbett afterwards, can not be considered as criminal, unless in the light of a contempt to the Government of the United States, for they ought not to have joined the minister in the act. I am of opinion, therefore, that no prosecution of either of the editors can be maintained for a libel in this instance, and that no legal prosecution of either of them is advisable.

Why not? Why could it not be done? Because they had acted in concert with a foreign minister, and the law of nations protected him against a suit for libel.

Mr. President, I have gone into this subject for the purpose simply of giving the authority upon which I make the emphatic denunciation of any right of a Senator of this body to take the public prints of this country in which he finds accusations written and signed by a foreign minister which are in any way derogatory to any member of this body, or which in any way might affect his vote or action upon any question, and repeat them, approvingly, to the Senate. I claim the privilege to deny this right as against my brother Senator, as well as against a foreign minister. Whoever may treat the subject lightly, I can not do so, not because I am wounded in spirit, for I have a perfect indifference to what Mr. Dupuy de Lôme may say about me and my conduct upon the floor of the Senate, but I have a regard for my privileges and rights and my duties and the honor of the position which I hold in the Senate, which I am not going to subordinate quietly and without a word of protest to any man who lives, and more especially to a foreign minister whose country is now being made the subject of serious examination in the councils of the Senate.

Sir, we have brought no accusations like this at any time against any other country. The accusations of the kind that we have been forced to bring into this record were produced in justice to the history of the occasion and in justification of the attitude of the Senate committee in reporting this very mild resolution, expressing only our opinions. We had the right to resort to the history of Spain and Cuba, recorded in books of authority recognized on all sides, for the facts that have hitherto formed a part of their conduct in their dealings with each other. It was not expected of the committee, I hope, that they should write up the history of all that Spain has done and of all the blood she has shed since the times of the wars of Pizzaro and Cortez down through those of the Netherlands and through the civil turmoils that have agitated Spain from year to year during the whole of this century. It was not requisite that we should form a compendium of history when the facts are open to the access of every mind and the scrutiny of every eye, and bring it here to inform Senators as to what the history of Spain has been, or that it has impressed upon her warfare in Cuba a type of ferocity which is utterly inconsistent with the civilized methods of conducting war in modern times.

Mr. HALE. Before the Senator departs from his strictures upon the Spanish minister for the writing of the letter which he has characterized in so strong terms, I call his attention to the statement which the chairman of the Committee on Foreign Relations, the Senator from Ohio [Mr. SHERMAN], made upon this subject when he last addressed the Senate, showing that he, although chairman of the committee, has not this feeling about that communication which the distinguished Senator from Alabama has. For he says, if the Senator will allow me to read three or four lines:

As I said before, I do not complain that the Spanish minister wrote his letter. I think he had a right to defend his country and his countrymen whether here or anywhere, before the people or in the Department of State. I do not believe in the narrow idea that a man may not defend his Government and people anywhere wherever he goes and in any community.

Mr. MORGAN. The Senator from Maine is very apt in quoting the Senator from Ohio when he happens to make an expression, perhaps thoughtlessly or in the heat of debate, out of which he can get some possible comfort for the peculiar attitude that he holds toward us. But when it comes to following the Senator from Ohio in the facts that he states, that Senator is put upon excruciating interrogatory all through the debate. When it comes to expressing differences of opinion upon questions of law with the Senator from Ohio, the chairman of the committee, the Senator from Maine experiences no difficulty in finding in the midst of his own great researches of law a full and complete answer, to his own satisfaction, to all that the Senator from Ohio had to say. When it comes to speaking of the presidency by the Senator from Ohio of the great Committee on Foreign Relations the Senator from Maine has no sort of compunction about insinuating, I will not say accusing, that the Senator from Ohio has been guilty of suppressing papers that ought to have come before the Senate in the course of the investigation of this case.

Mr. HALE. The Senator I think will allow me——

Mr. MORGAN. Wait until I get through my answer.

Mr. HALE. Very well.

Mr. MORGAN. When the Senator from Maine is able to quote upon me an expression of the Senator from Ohio that he is indifferent to what the Spanish minister did, the Senator from Maine does it with great unction. But the Senator from Ohio is no higher authority for me upon questions of my Senatorial rights and propriety than he is to the Senator from Maine upon questions of fact and his demeanor in office in connection with this business.

I do not agree with the Senator from Ohio upon that subject, though I did not intend to take occasion to say so until I have been called in question and compelled to do it.

Mr. HALE. I made the citation for the purpose of showing that the two eminent Senators do not agree upon this subject. But the Senator from Alabama must not charge that I insinuate, in any form or by any suggestion, that the Senator from Ohio has deliberately suppressed facts. I did not need to do that. There would have been no justification for it. I simply took the ground and, I think, showed pretty conclusively that the Senator from Ohio had been imposed upon, and that he had honestly and seriously and in good faith read from what he thought was good authority, but which, it was discovered afterwards, was no authority whatever. All that the Senator from Ohio said was that the paper that he read from, not the original authority, had General Weyler's name in it. He did not claim or assert that the original book, which he thought he was representing to us from the paper, contained any allegation against General Weyler.

I wish to say now here that the Senator from Alabama has no right to use the words that he has used when he charged me with insinuating that the Senator from Ohio undertook to delude the Senate or to deceive it. I never thought of it; I never harbored that idea; and I was careful, very careful, sir, entirely to exclude it from what I said.

Mr. MORGAN. Mr. President, the Senator from Maine called the Committee on Foreign Relations in question time and again, yesterday and previously, upon the proposition that a paper had been before the committee which they had not produced here and of which they had made no mention. He dwelt upon it as a circumstance to convey the idea of a suspicious and clandestine movement on the part of the committee to keep from the Senate the possession of facts in regard to the case of Spain. That is patent. The Senator, with an art which of course is creditable to his tact and talent, in his statement made a moment ago has evaded the question. He has tried to turn the issue between him and me upon the question whether or not an accusation was made against the Senator from Ohio in regard to his quotation from some Spanish book that he found. No, sir. My remarks were addressed to this proposition.

The Senator from Maine, as I understood him, distinctly attempted to cast reproach upon the Committee on Foreign Relations because a paper came before the committee which had not been mentioned in debate, and which, as he characterized it at the time—I do not quote his words, but I have the idea—was inadvertently brought into this debate by some remark of the junior Senator from Massachusetts [Mr. LODGE].

I do not care to wrangle about personal matters in this debate, so far as I am concerned. I have no feeling about the question between the Senate or Senators and the minister from Spain, but I want this business to stop. Senators time and again have been arraigned on this same kind of appeal because of expressions and facts that they have stated here. Personally I have suffered egregiously in that matter, and I stood with mute astonishment when compelled to feel and to know that I had a Government that was entirely indifferent to my rights as a Senator.

There is no man in the United States—there is no man in the world—who can make an accusation against the President of the United States on this floor which treats him with injustice or can make a statement of fact which does him wrong without calling me to my feet for the purpose of vindicating that high representative of the sovereignty of the American people. And so the Department of State and the President of the United States owe it to Senators and Members of the other House, owe it to the legislative department as much as they owe it to the department of the judiciary, that when those who are enjoying the hospitality of this country and have official connection with it make accusations against us or criticisms of what we do or how we vote here, to call them to order and tell them that that thing must be corrected or they must cease to enjoy our hospitality. When we place the government back upon the line of conduct such as I have read to-day from these eminent American statesmen and jurists, then we will have a government that we can respect and love, and until we do it we will have a government that will receive only our silent, unspoken contempt.

Now, having gone through with this matter, there is an answer to what the minister from Spain has said, coming from an authority that is quite as respectable as his in point of personal character. I refer to the letter written by Mr. Quesada, which, I believe, is his name, who is the representative of the Cuban Government at this capital, and who when he had a case to make in favor of Cuba sent his communication to the Department of State. Although he had no ministerial or official recognition, the Secretary of State thought enough of it to communicate it to a committee of the Senate, and it has now become one of the published documents of this controversy. Strip Mr. Dupuy de Lôme of his royal commission and put him upon his Spanish blood and his Spanish character and his history, of which I know nothing—I do not even know the gentleman personally—and bring Mr. Quesada here upon his history and his Spanish blood and his character, of which I know nothing, for I do not know the man—confront them as they are confronted through the newspapers, and let both speak.

Sir, if the letter of the Spanish minister arraigning the Senate of the United States and appealing from this body to the people had not been introduced here by a member of this body, no one could ever have induced me to go to a newspaper to find Mr. Quesada's answer to it. But it has been invited and it must go into the RECORD, with the permission of the Senate. Will the Secretary please read the letter of Quesada?

The VICE-PRESIDENT. The Secretary will read as indicated.

The Secretary read as follows:

HIS REPLY TO DE LÔME—HORRORS OF SPANISH WARFARE RECALLED BY A CUBAN—CRIME CHARGED TO GENERAL WEYLER—SECRETARY GONZALO DE QUESADA, OF THE CUBAN DELEGATION, SAYS SENATORS SHERMAN, MORGAN, AND LODGE SPOKE THE TRUTH, AND THAT THEIR STATEMENTS CAN BE SUBSTANTIATED, DESPITE THE SPANISH MINISTER'S ASSERTIONS TO THE CONTRARY.

Editor Post:

Minister Dupuy de Lôme, against all propriety and precedent, has turned from his unsuccessful work in diplomatic circles to the newspaper arena. The Cubans are glad to see him discuss this burning question of the revolution in the public press, which he has so often condemned, but we will not allow him to distort facts, as he has to his Government, if the reported cable be true in which he said that the President of this great country had taken him into the confidence of the Administration and declared that during Mr. Cleveland's term of office the Cubans would not be recognized as belligerents.

Mr. Dupuy de Lôme will find that we are prepared to meet him here, none the less, as our gallant armies in Cuba meet the thousands of unfortunate recruits who fight to maintain oppression and the power of Spain in the island which so liberally pays a Spanish minister in Washington to insult the land from which comes his salary.

The newspapers of this country need no defenders. In every one of them the minister sees an enemy, because he does not want the truth to be known. Why have the correspondents been denied entrance into the ranks of the Cubans? Why have they all had to leave the island? To-day an American reporter—Michelson—tells of his experiences in the Morro for trying to expose the fruits of Gen. Valeriano Weyler's recent brutal proclamations—"a massacre of unarmed, peaceful country people at the town of Guatao, a dozen miles from Habana, by Spanish volunteers," and describes the tortures to which Walter Grant Dygart, an innocent American, is subjected.

Sylvester Scovell, another reporter, was thrown into jail as soon as he arrived in Cuba, and yet Dupuy de Lôme cynically says that statesmen do not know the real situation in Cuba.

HORRORS OF 1871 RECALLED.

But let us refute the minister's statements. The book of Donderis exists, and if the name of Weyler does not specifically occur it is because Valmaceda and other superiors of his take the credit for his atrocities. Will Minister Dupuy de Lôme deny that eight students were butchered in Habana in November, 1871? Will he deny the assassination committed by Burriel in the *Virginius* affair, where Americans and Cubans were murdered and afterwards their private parts desecrated, as was done with the brave Crittenden and his 50 Kentuckians, from whose skulls Spanish beasts drank Spanish wine?' Is the crime of the Mora family of the 6th of January, 1871, forgotten by Spain, when two of Cuba's most beautiful women and their children were violated?

Mr. CHANDLER. I suggest that the reading of the remainder of the extract be omitted. The Senator from Alabama has no objection.

Mr. MORGAN. Let it be inserted in the RECORD. I am sorry to have it to do, Mr. President, but at the same time——

Mr. HALE. I should be very glad indeed to have it read.

Mr. CHANDLER. If the Senator from Maine insists on having it read, all right.

Mr. MORGAN. All right; let the Secretary go ahead.

Mr. HALE. I have read it myself. I should like to have it read, and I should like to have the whole tone of it regarded by Senators, so that it may be taken for what it is worth.

Mr. CHANDLER. The Senator from Alabama asks not to have it read, and the Senator from Maine insists on having it read.

Mr. HALE. Yes; I should be very glad to have it read.

Mr. MORGAN. I make no indorsement of the truth of what is stated in the paper. What I mean to say is that, so far as I know and believe, the author of this paper is quite as good a character as Mr. Dupuy de Lôme.

The VICE-PRESIDENT. The Secretary will continue the reading.

The Secretary read as follows:

Is the crime of the Mora family of the 6th of January, 1871, forgotten by Spain, when two of Cuba's most beautiful women and their children were violated, insulted, and burned alive to conceal the horrible crime? And did not Hamilton Fish, the Secretary of State of the United States, himself take cognizance of the barbarities committed by Spain's officers, among whom was Weyler?

Can Mr. Dupuy de Lôme deny this crime of Weyler committed under his command on the farm of Lavado, in the territory of Las Tunas? There are witnesses to this occurrence, and it is no excuse for Weyler to say that he only obeyed orders, or for De Lôme to argue that he was a subordinate.

Two young men, Eugenio and Lorenzo Odoardo, brothers, and relatives of Aguilera, the vice-president of the Cuban Republic, were sick on their farm.

They were cared for by a lady, who was accompanied by her daughter 8 years old. The troops of Weyler surprised the place, captured the men and the woman and child, and took them to the camp of Weyler. Weyler ordered the men to be killed with machetes in the presence of the lady. He formed the soldiers in a circle, placed in the center the poor woman and the child, despoiled the woman of her clothes, and, naked, forced her to dance by whipping her before the drunken and passionate soldiery. All the efforts of the virtuous woman to cover herself with the child were unavailing; the troops laughed and jeered; the unfortunate victim was given up to the lust of the troops; she died the next day. Weyler was the executioner of the French family of Rigoteau, for which Spain had to pay a large indemnity.

DIARY OF IGNACIO MORA.

Let Dupuy de Lôme read the diary of "Ignacio Mora," a copy of which is in my possession, dated the 27th of May, 1872, the very epoch in which Weyler was in command of the Spanish forces in that province. "The details," he declares, "which the postillira, Juan Lorres, gives me of the operations of the enemy are horrible. They assault the families; they rob them.

"They killed Mercedes Hernandez and the wife of Lieutenant-Colonel Sanchez. They also assassinated the children of that unfortunate woman. They committed other assassinations. On the 1st of June, 1872," he says in the Migian, "they killed Juana Gregoria Torres, after violating her, and her child, a few months old. The total number of murders committed in Canto from the 8th to the 28th of May was 28, of which 13 were women and 11 children. In Estancia Grande they killed 3 women and a child of 8 years."

Weyler branded the Cuban women in the bosom, as if they were cattle. He killed the prisoners in the jails by suffocating them with charcoal. It was this man of whom Martinez Campos said once that if he came to Cuba the very dead would rise against Spain.

The French papers of a year ago tell how he crushed anarchism in Barcelona. He arrested by wholesale innocents and suspects in the darkness of night. He tortured them most inhumanly. If Minister De Lôme wants to know how, he can read the press of that time. I dare not repeat, for decency's sake, the torments to which he submitted the prisoners. He gave them salt codfish as their only food and tantalized them by offering them water which he did not allow them to touch. He applied the inquisition. He killed 200 people, among them women and children.

I have asked for the terrible exposure of his acts published in a Parisian paper, and when it comes I shall send a copy to the minister who defends the man who is to-day sending hundreds of men to Africa and the Isle of Pines, and who is, in fact, clearing the prisons by killing the captives. Of course Mr. De Lôme would like names of persons who have seen these horrors. They dare not speak. They know what happens to those who disobey the decrees of the autocrat; but the book of blood will ere long be published, similar to the one which was published in the last war, a copy of which Minister De Lôme can obtain in New York, and in which he will see the thousands of defenseless Cubans executed by his Government, by his nation, which lost Italy by her crimes, the Low Countries by her murders, and the entire American Continent as a punishment for her extermination of the Indian, for her treachery and ingratitude to the native races. The data used by Senator MORGAN "were from the official reports forwarded from Madrid by the United States minister," were revised by Mr. John D. Champlin, and are incontrovertible, and as to the translation of Senator LODGE, in which the word "exterminate" is used for "clean out," there is no essential difference; it is a mere quibble of the casuistic mind of Philip II.

PROPERTY OF THE SLAIN.

And as to the conduct of the war, when in the history of any civilized nation has the property of the slain gone to the general and officers of the victorious army? Gen. José Marti was killed at Don Rios; instead of his watch and valuables being given to his widow and only child, the watch was given to the minister of war in Spain, the ring was kept by an officer of the noble Spanish army, who took it from the dead hero's finger, and the rest of his things were distributed among the gallant representatives of the chivalric mother country.

Of the horrors committed in this revolution by the Spanish commander the American press have daily reports. It is indeed worthy of note that the Cubans have not been the authors of those reports, and it would be too much for Minister De Lôme to declare that either the great American press has sold itself to the Cubans or that all the American newspaper men send "exaggerated reports to cater to the American taste."

I will very soon publish as many of General Weyler's innumerable crimes as possible. I am now getting such accurate facts together as will identify Weyler as the author of similar if not the same crimes exposed by Donderis in his book, and by citing year and place prove to the world that Tourquemada, Alva, Morillo, and Bores, Spanish angels, renowned in history for their humane methods, are all incarnate in the Captain-General of Cuba, Valeriano Weyler, "the Butcher."

GONZALO DE QUESADA,
Secretary of the Cuban Delegation.

WASHINGTON, *March 8.*

Mr. HALE. I desire that this recital by this man, as horrible as it is, should be read to the Senate that Senators may have time to reflect that it is not the fashion in this country to make charges of that horrible kind which are past human belief without furnishing testimony. The American people and the American Senate will not believe those things of any man unless facts are given, unless there is something more than a promise to give facts, but will demand that they shall be supported by evidence. I do not credit those recitals as against this Spanish general in the least. I believe they are figments of the brain and could not have been true.

Mr. MORGAN. In his statement the Spanish minister goes on to open up the war of 1868-1878—the ten years' war—and undertakes to refute some statements made in regard to that war. The statement which I had the honor to submit upon the authority of General Sickles, which is found to be sustained in his letter to the Secretary of State, when that gets into the RECORD—I have misplaced it for the moment—related entirely to the conduct of the war during the former ten years. I have here statements from General Grant and Mr. Fish, made directly to the Spanish minister, which themselves show that much of what is stated there by these Cubans is true. I rely upon that authority. I do not rely upon this authority, and yet I know of no reason why Mr. Quesada is not a man of as good reputation as Mr. Dupuy de Lôme. The mere horror of the transactions which are there recited will not do as a disapproval of their existence. If we were to tell all we know of the Duke of Alva in the Netherlands before we could believe that in regard to Spain——

Mr. HALE. It certainly throws the burden upon those alleging such atrocities. The Senator is an old lawyer, and he must admit that.

Mr. MORGAN. It is rather impossible now to prove by living witnesses all that was done in that war, and yet I have some evidence before me of men who participated in it, and whose character is vouched for on the floor of the Senate, which I shall presently proceed to read. This is a very disagreeable thing to me, extremely so, in fact; it is a very disgusting thing; but it must be remembered that both of the controversialists bear the Spanish name and are of Spanish blood, and doubtless both of them have worn Spanish titles of honor among the old families of Spain.

If I were reciting the horrors of warfare that have existed in the United States on the part of the Ute Indians, the Apaches, the Arapahoes, the Cheyennes, the Comanches, etc., I would perhaps have to go into the details of greater horrors than have been detailed here. At the same time we know how very true are the awful recitals of our own American history in respect of those savage tribes. Men who can accuse each other and their Government of having been particeps criminis in horrible iniquities of this kind and go into the public prints and present them are men who on both sides are to be regarded with caution, I will grant you, in accepting their statements; but when they are at war so near our coast and war on the property of our own people, and when they take our own men captive in their armies, and the like of that, it becomes us to look at both pictures and see what is possible among such people.

I do not deal with Spain, I must say, in this matter as I would deal with Canada at all. I would deal with both Canada and Spain upon their historical record. We can not be expected to go back and hunt up the evidence to prove all these transactions, the onus of which the Senator from Maine would cast upon us. But before I get through with my remarks I will cast upon him the onus of denying what Mr. Fish said to Admiral Polo in a communication which he sent to him, which involves not all the details, but horrors equivalent to those that are presented in the statement made by Mr. Quesada.

Now, inasmuch as we must have evidence brought here, under the requirements of the Senator from Maine, I will send to the desk an article taken from the New York Tribune of recent date upon the subject that I referred to in the speech I had the honor to make in this case when trying to present it on behalf of the committee in the first instance. I believe the New York Tribune is accredited as high authority in its anti-Cuban sentiments.

The VICE-PRESIDENT. The Secretary will read as indicated.

The Secretary read as follows:

[New York Tribune, March 16, 1896.]

INNOCENT MEN SHOT DOWN—A STORY OF A SPANISH OUTRAGE IN THE TEN YEARS' WAR—THEY WERE CUBAN MEDICAL STUDENTS AND THEIR CRIME WAS VISITING A CEMETERY, WHEREIN A BURIAL PLACE WAS FOUND TO HAVE BEEN DISTURBED.

"Whenever you read accounts of Spanish atrocities in Cuba do not make the mistake of believing that they are in any way exaggerations. I have lived in Habana, and while not personally familiar with this present war, I was there during the ten years' war, and I know whereof I speak." This statement was made in Brooklyn yesterday by a medical student of one of the colleges in New York, who is an American, born in Habana. His father is at present in Cuba and a well-known man there, but in order to save his family in Cuba from annoyance and persecution the student stipulated that in the story he was about to tell his name should not be mentioned.

"I want," he continued, "to tell you a tale of a Spanish outrage which happened in Habana in 1878, almost at the close of the ten years' struggle, which I witnessed. In all the terrible history of Spanish misrule and butchery in that island, the killing of seven innocent medical students by the order of the Captain-General, at the instigation of a mob, is about the most heartless and inhuman act that I ever heard of, and I tell it simply to illustrate Spanish methods, and to show that in the present war similar cruelties are being onacted which the world will never hear of. In Habana there is an old cemetery surrounded by four stone walls, built with niches in tiers, and thick enough to hold a coffin lengthwise. The fronts of these niches are covered by a panel of thick glass, so that the coffin may be seen inside. In the latter part of 1878 one of the Spanish generals died and his coffin was placed in one of the niches. The Habana Medical College at that time was situated near the cemetery.

"One day fourteen students, having nothing else to do, visited the cemetery. That night one of the cemetery attendants noticed that the glass in the Spanish general's niche was scratched. He told the parish priest of the 'outrage,' and the priest in turn sent word to the authorities. Next day a number of policemen visited the college and arrested every student—to the number of about fifty—who had been at the college on that day. They were taken to the Spanish jail, and at once a report spread through the city that a Spanish grave had been desecrated by young Cubans. The volunteers, who, let it be understood, consisted of Spaniards living in the island and of some of the lower classes, were aroused. Within an hour the jail was surrounded by a howling, frenzied mob. Balmaceda was absent in the eastern part of the island at that time, and the segundo cabo, or lieutenant-general, was in command. He assembled his troops in front of the palace and told them he would investigate the case and punish where punishment was due.

"NO EVIDENCE AGAINST THEM.

"A commission of Spanish officers was immediately assembled and the case was tried then and there. Not a single well-known Cuban was called into the case. The gardener of the cemetery, who had been called as a witness, said that he had noticed some scratches on the glass and had also seen that a few flowers were missing. Further testimony on the part of the assistant gardener showed to the commission that the students were in no wise guilty of any wrongdoing whatsoever. The assistant gardener said that the scratches had been on the glass several days before. Upon hearing this the Spanish commission shut him up and practically threw him out of the room.

"Then, out of the whole commission arose one Spanish officer, Captain Capdevilla, and said that there was nothing upon which to hold the students. He advised their release and the dispersion of the mob, and said if those students were harmed it would be an act of inhumanity. The captain was immediately put out of the room, and next day was arrested for treason for daring to voice such sentiments in a high military court of Spain. The mob was every minute growing larger and more vociferous for the lives of the students. A great uproar was heard without the palace, and the segundo cabo appeared on the balcony and made a speech, saying there was really no evidence against the students. The volunteers and their supporters would not have it this way and demanded the lives of some of the accused men. There was a further conference of the commission, and the additional fact was brought out that of the 14 students who visited the cemetery only 7 were in that part of the inclosure where the grave was located, and only one youth among this number possessed a diamond ring with which it might have been possible to scratch the glass. With this flimsy accusation and in order to appease the volunteers, the commission decided that 7 of the boys, whose ages ranged from 14 to 20 years, should be killed and the other 7 transported to an African dungeon.

"The parents of the unfortunate prisoners became frenzied when they heard of the sentences. They offered the weight of the prisoners in gold to the Spaniards if they would free them. The commission was obdurate. The volunteers must be appeased. The prisoners had to be killed.

"SHOT DOWN BY A REGIMENT.

"Next day was a fête day. Early in the morning, as the seven young fellows were lined up in front of a blank wall surrounding the Carcel, a brother of the youngest prisoner offered to stand up for him and be shot, but this was not allowed. Instead of having a file of soldiers, as is usually the case, the lieutenant-general called out an entire regiment to perform the massacre. The order to fire was given and the seven were literally shot to pieces.

"I know of similar atrocities committed in that war of which General Weyler is guilty, and while he had nothing to do with that particular massacre, he is inhuman enough for anything. The strict censorship now prevailing prevents the world from hearing of crimes equally as bad which are committed every day. If the Cubans can hold out for another summer, or if, by chance, the war should be prolonged for two summers, fever would reduce the present number of 150,000 Spanish troops on the island to about 13,500. In the end Cuba will be free."

Mr. HALE. Read the name. A statement of that kind ought not to be given to the Senate without giving the name.

The PRESIDING OFFICER. (Mr. CHILTON in the chair). There is no name attached, the Chair is informed.

The SECRETARY. New York Tribune, March 16, 1896; not signed.

Mr. HALE. This purports to give the personal narration of somebody, and is there no name signed to it?

The PRESIDING OFFICER. There is no name, the Secretary informs the Chair.

Mr. HALE. It does not seem to me that that is a very good piece of evidence. If that is a case of mob violence and a lieutenant-general protesting against it——

Mr. MORGAN. The Senator can comment on the evidence when it gets into the RECORD.

Mr. HALE. I certainly supposed it was going to be followed by giving the name.

Mr. MORGAN. I had stated that I got it from the New York Tribune, which has been an anti-Cuban paper, I understand. I supposed the New York Tribune would not without some excuse publish those facts. I referred to that same incident in the first speech I made on this subject in the Senate, that to which Mr. Dupuy de Lôme replied. He made no reference to my statements on that subject which I extracted from history and not giving the details. He had a safe opportunity to reply to it and deny it if it was not true. I suppose whoever reads about such things at all knows about that massacre of students in Habana.

If the Senator from Maine requires witnesses to be brought and names to be stated, as a matter of course they ought to be brought here to the bar of the Senate, and in such a case I would ask that the Spanish minister and Mr. Quesada be summoned to the bar of the Senate in order that we might examine them, if we are going into that sort of detail. What I am trying to do is to get a general and I trust a just view of what is the situation in Spain as respects the feeling of those people and of that Government against the Cubans. I have here——

Mr. HALE. If the Senator will allow me a moment, I shall not then interrupt him again.

Mr. MORGAN. I do not like to be replied to as I go along. The Senator from Maine will have plenty of time. I did not interrupt him to any extent, and such a course diverts me from my ideas and keeps me on my feet until after a while I shall get so weary that I can not say anything.

Mr. HALE. I thought in a case of that kind some authority should be given for such a statement.

Mr. MORGAN. I think not.

Mr. HALE. I do not agree with the Senator.

Mr. MORGAN. I do not agree that any more authority should be given to that than to an extract taken from the public history of an important event. This paper is a historian; it professes to be. It selects its extracts with a view of informing the people of the United States. The Tribune certainly would not put an article of that kind into its paper that was not well authenticated in history.

A letter was written on the 6th of March, 1896, from Virginia, to a member of this body. The gentleman who wrote the letter is known to some Senators on this floor, and he is known to be a man of good reputation.

Mr. HALE. Who is he?

Mr. MORGAN. I will not give his name, but I will show you the letter. I will myself read the letter.

MARCH 6, 1896.

DEAR SIR: Noting that certain cowardly sheets, always opposed to everything American, are trying to break the force of your statements of Spanish atrocities in Cuba by alleging them to be vague, general assertions, made on hearsay, and incapable of proof, permit me to offer this testimony as to what I have myself seen and heard in that island.

In 1869, 1870, and 1871 I served as captain of cavalry in the liberating army of Cuba under General Ryan and General Federico Cavada, my observations extending from the north coast to the south, and from Las Tunas in the east to Cienfugos in the west, embracing some 300 miles of the center of the island.

The Spaniards held the cities, towns, and some of the plantations in the sugar-producing part of Santa Clara, with forts and strong garrisons; the Cubans held all of the country beyond gunshot from the Spanish forts.

There was fighting somewhere almost every day. The Spanish operated by marching strong columns through the country, gathering up all they could carry off, and burning houses and whatever else they could not carry. The Cubans operated by ambuscading the columns, making sudden attacks on the forts, blockading them, cutting off detachments, convoys, etc. The Spaniards could beat us in a pitched battle, from their superiority in equipment; but they lost in action or by death and desertion at least five men to our one.

We were compelled to adopt this system by the nature of the country, which does not admit of the maintenance of large armies in the field, and by the want of arms. We had plenty of men, but not more than one gun to four men. Hundreds were camped, unarmed, in different places, waiting for arms to come from the States. We could not reduce the Spanish forts for lack of artillery, but sometimes carried them by surprise or assault. In these cases they were dismantled and destroyed, as it was not our policy to stand a siege in them.

The whole country was laid waste. The Spanish burned every house they came to. They killed every man and boy they found, whether armed or unarmed. Sometimes they killed the women and girls; sometimes they * * * sometimes they carried them on with the column; and sometimes after killing the men they left the women crying over the corpses and the ashes of their homes.

The population of the country and the refugees from the cities had taken to the woods, and lived in palm-leaf huts and wigwams in the depths of the forests and swamps and in caves in the mountains; but when these hiding places became well known from the numbers resorting to them, they were noted by Spanish spies, who often carried the enemy there and surprised the women and children, the old, and the sick and wounded before they could get away into the woods.

Neither side gave quarter to prisoners, and every victory ended in a massacre, except that Spanish prisoners who elected to join the liberating army were released and received into full fellowship. Most of our drillmasters and many of the officers and men were Spaniards.

This violation of the laws of war was forced upon us by the Spanish Government. The Cubans wanted to save all prisoners and exchange them, and the Spanish in the field would have agreed to it; but the administration required all prisoners to be put to death, and we were obliged to retaliate in self-defense. It would have been suicidal madness to send hundreds of men back to the Spaniards to fight us again and carry them information as to our positions, numbers, etc.; and we had nowhere to keep them until the war ended. The course of the Spanish Government in Cuba is exactly the same as was the course of Philip II in the Netherlands. Three centuries have not changed it in one iota. Valmaseda, Weyler, and Pando are just Alva, Vargas, and Tel Rio over again——

Mr. HALE. My attention was called away for the moment. What is the date of these occurrences? I did not catch that.

Mr. MORGAN. 1869, 1870, and 1871—

For specific allegations I mention these:

In May, 1870, an American named Coyneo, who wished to leave the island, surrendered to the Spanish in the neighborhood of Najasa. He was murdered, and we found his body, fearfully mutilated, in the road where they left it.

In May, 1870, in Las Temas, on a forced march, we had to leave one of our men who was wounded. Three days afterwards we found him in the same place, where the Spanish had overtaken him. He had a large chunk cut out of his throat by what they call "dos puñalados," and was dead.

About the same time, between Najasa and Yara, six unarmed men who were gathering bananas for their families were surrounded by the Spanish and murdered. Our men found them lying dead. Each one had a banana rammed down his throat by way of a joke.

Two days before the action at La Gloria, in June, 1870, while scouting with General Ryan, we found the body of an old, unarmed man who had been surprised and murdered by the Spanish while he was getting honey out of his beehives.

Brig. Gen. Edwardo Del Marmol, chief of staff to General Cavada, was shot through the body in the action at Altamira, in July, 1870, and was carried to a potrero in western Camaguey to be nursed. The Spanish came suddenly and butchered him in his bed.

At the Caridad of Curana, in August, 1870, Capt. Ramon de Varona, of the staff of General Ryan, was on sick leave at a retreat where were his lovely young wife and several other ladies and girls belonging to the leading families of Camaguey. The Spanish surprised them, killed Captain Varona, unarmed and sick, in the presence of the ladies, stripped his corpse, mutilated it in the most atrocious manner before them, and dragged it about with a rope around the neck. The Spanish commander (name unknown to me) then pointed to the terrified and sobbing ladies, and told his men that they "could take their choice of those rebel bitches;" and the ladies were treated in a manner not fit to be described.

Two days afterwards I saw two of these ladies and a colored woman who had been present, and heard them relate what had happened.

In August, 1870, in the vicinity of Rio Seco, while looking for the chief of ordnance, I came to a house in the woods occupied by others of the Varona family. The ladies were in tears, and told me that their brother, a young boy, had been shot down by the Spanish the day before. He was unarmed, and, as I understood, not over 11 years old.

In August, 1870, near Rio Seco, I was told by several families living there in the woods that the Spanish had come to a house near by a few days before, and finding no one but women spared their lives, but burned their house and carried off one of the daughters, who was a beauty, behind an officer. They tore the girl from her mother's and sister's arms, and swore they would kill her and the whole family if she did not go. These Spanish were a part of the force of Colonel Monteneo, then commanding at Santa Cruz del Sur. The poor girl's name was told to me, but I do not remember it now after so many years.

In June, 1870, near La Glorico, I heard General Ryan examine a Spanish prisoner. This man gave a detailed account of the state of certain Spanish camps, and named certain Cuban ladies whom he had seen kept there by certain Spanish officers, describing their wretched condition, their appearance, and their actions very minutely. His statements had every appearance of truth. The Cuban officers who were present said that they knew the ladies named, and that they were at that time prisoners in the hands of the Spanish.

Capt. Henry Earl, of Brooklyn, who won great distinction in the patriot service before his death, showed me the marks of the wounds given him by the Spanish after the action in Holguin in 1869. They found him lying on the field after the fight, shot him and bayoneted him several times, and left him for dead. General Jordan had gathered up some of his wounded and left them in a house to be cared for. The Spanish surrounded the house, set it on fire, and burned up the wounded men. One of these was a young New Yorker, a sort of clerk to General Jordan. I have heard, but do not remember, his name.

Gen. Ignacio Agramonte, General Ryan, General Cavada, and many other officers and men whom I knew personally were at different times taken by the Spanish. They were in every instance murdered. I never head of any one escaping death.

I knew a family named Mola, prominent people, living in the western part of Camaguey. The mother and three young daughters were refined, cultivated ladies, famous for kindness and courtesy to everyone, and much beloved. Major Mercer, of Boston, our chief of artillery, and I had especial cause, as strangers, to thank them for hospitality and kindness. Some time after we went westward into the Villas with Cavada these four ladies and one of the sons, a boy of about 10, were murdered by the Spanish. A captain and his men came to their house one night, seized them, * * * murdered them and their mother and brother, and burned their house down over their bodies. The only one who escaped was the youngest boy, aged about 7. In the confusion and darkness he slipped into the bushes near the house and saw and heard what was done. I did not see this, but it is matter of common notoriety.

I have seen hundreds of burned houses, bones, and graves, and have heard many circumstantial and undoubtedly true narratives of Spanish atrocities, but prefer to give these specimen cases which came under my own observation, and when I can give the time and place. This sort of war was waged all over Cuba. The present war is just the same as the last; the same men, Weyler, etc., are in command. The Cuban question is just this: Are 1,500,000 people to be massacred that Spain may hold the island a few years longer, or is it to be stopped? The only way to keep the Cubans down is to kill them all; and if all these were killed and the island repeopled from Spain, a new war for independence would come as soon as a native-born generation grew up. All the Cubans are for independence. Those in the Spanish cities are forced into the so-called volunteer battalions to save their lives, families, and property; but the Spanish do not dare to trust them where they would have any chance to desert, knowing they would go over to the patriots by whole battalions.

As for the objection that the Cubans wage only guerrilla war, it is the sort of war that gives them the advantage, and they would be fools to give it up to wage grand guerre.

Maximo Gomez is a great captain, who understands how to handle his men so as to neutralize the many advantages enjoyed by the Spanish. His vigorous offensive obliges them to divide their forces and guard a hundred points at the same time, while he selects his point of attack and is as successful as a man with a knife can hope to be in fighting a man with a gun.

It is the sort of war by which Robert Bruce freed Scotland, with which Spain opposed the great Napoleon, and by which her other colonies obtained their independence.

It is the sort of war which General Washington proposed to adopt in our own Revolution when he expected to be driven out of Pennsylvania to his last stand in Virginia's mountains. It is the war which Nathaniel Green, Daniel Morgan, Henry Lee, William Campbell, Isaac Shelby, John Sevier, Thomas Sumter, and Francis Marion adopted for the recovery of the Carolinas and Georgia after the Continental armies had been destroyed at Charleston and Camden.

Why, then, should any American denounce the Cubans as guerrillas? Are not these good examples to follow?

There is only one way to settle the Cuban question. Every generation that grows up is going to fight for independence. Millions of people may be butchered, and the struggle may go on for centuries, but in the end the Cubans will be free.

The writer of that letter is a graduate of the Military Institute of Virginia and also of the University of Virginia.

Mr. THURSTON. Mr. President, I desire to give notice that on to-morrow morning, during the morning hour and after the dispatch of the ordinary routine business, I shall ask unanimous consent to present an argument, by request of the chairman of the Committee on Privileges and Elections, in favor of the seating of Henry A. Du Pont as Senator from Delaware.

Mr. MILLS. I want to say to the Senator that I have the floor for to-morrow by common consent, and have had it given to me for three or four days on this question. I understand that we are to have this question concluded before we take up the Du Pont case, and I must object to yielding the floor now and further giving way, as I have given way for three or four days.

Mr. CHANDLER. I will say that there is no such understanding as that the Du Pont case is not to be taken up until the Cuban question is disposed of.

Mr. MILLS. I understood from the Senator from Oregon [Mr. MITCHELL] that he intended to give way, and let the Cuban question go on.

Mr. CHANDLER. There will be no difficulty in having the Senator from Nebraska and also the Senator from Texas speak to-morrow; but the reservation was distinctly made that, as the Senator from Nebraska [Mr. THURSTON] was obliged to go away at the end of the week, he should be permitted to speak on the Du Pont case.

Mr. THURSTON. I am perfectly willing, if it be agreeable, to have my announcement take effect on Thursday morning just the same. I only wish an opportunity to speak before I leave.

Mr. MILLS. All right. There is no objection to that.

Mr. CHANDLER. Do I understand the Senator from Texas to claim the whole day to-morrow?

Mr. MILLS. Oh, no; but I wish to follow my friend from Alabama [Mr. MORGAN].

Mr. MORGAN. Mr. President, I have an interview of General Sickles, which he did me the honor to send me with his card. Of course it is a correct and authentic interview, and I will ask the Secretary to read it.

Mr. PLATT. What is the date of the interview?

Mr. MORGAN. It is a very recent date. I believe I have General Sickles's note here transmitting the interview to me.

The PRESIDING OFFICER. The Secretary will read as requested, in the absence of objection.

The Secretary read as follows:

Gen. Daniel E. Sickles, who was United States minister to Spain during a part of the ten-year Cuban rebellion, and whose dispatches from Madrid while minister were mentioned in the recent debate in the Senate over the Cuban resolutions, was interviewed by a Sun reporter yesterday at his home in Fifth avenue.

"While you were minister to Spain," asked the reporter, "did you have occasion to consider the question of the shipment of arms and ammunition to Cuba?"

"Yes, I did," said the General, "and I must say that there seems to be a great deal of misapprehension about the rules of international law, and our own law as well, on that subject at the present time. In the absence of a recognized state of war it is no offense for sailing vessels or steamers sailing from this port or any other American port to carry arms and ammunition for whomsoever it may concern. No government can, by the law of nations, be held responsible for the shipments of arms, munitions, or material of war made by private individuals at their own risk and peril. These views have been repeatedly declared by our Government.

"During the former insurrection in Cuba, Captain-General de Rodas issued a decree in contravention of this principle. He closed a number of ports, interdicting trade with them of any kind, and threatened the summary execution of the officers and crews and passengers of vessels transporting arms or passengers suspected to be in the interest of the insurgents, affecting to treat them as pirates. This extraordinary decree caused a profound sensation in the United States, and our Secretary of State, Mr. Fish, addressed the Spanish minister under date of July 16, 1869, a strong protest, in which he said:

"'The transport on the high seas in time of peace, by outsiders, of what is commonly known as contraband of war is a legitimate traffic and commerce which can not be interfered with or denounced unless by a power at war with a third party in the admitted exercise of the recognized rights of a belligerent. The freedom of the ocean can nowhere and under no circumstances be yielded by the United States. While Spain disclaims a state of belligerency, or until the United States may find it necessary to recognize her as a belligerent, the United States can not fail to look with solicitude upon a decree which, if enforced against any vessel of the United States, can not but be regarded as a violation of their rights that may lead to serious complications.'

"Again, in a note to the Spanish Government, written by Secretary Fish on the 18th of April, 1874, he makes this declaration:

"'A friendly government violates no duty of good neighborhood in allowing the free sale of arms and munitions of war to all persons, to insurgents as well as to the regularly constituted authorities; and such arms and munitions, by whichever party purchased, may be carried in the vessels on the high seas without liability to question from any other party. In like manner the vessels may freely carry unarmed passengers, even though known to be insurgents, without thereby rendering the government which permits it liable to a charge of violating its international duties. But if such passengers should be armed and proceed to the scene of the insurrection as an organized body which might be capable of levying war, they constitute a hostile expedition, which may not be knowingly permitted without a violation of international obligations.'"

These extracts from the notes of Secretary Fish, as they were quoted by General Sickles, are particularly interesting when considered in connection with the recent seizure of the steamship *Bermuda* off Liberty Island. More interesting still is this statement, which the General went on to make:

"I have satisfactory reasons for believing and knowing that our Government to-day accepts and enunciates the same views of international law and of our own laws expressed by the Administration of President Grant. I have it from the best authority that this Government can not and will not stop the shipment of arms and ammunition from any of our ports; nor will it stop the departure of passengers on a vessel bound for any foreign port. What it must stop is 'any military expedition or enterprise' intended to make war on a nation with which we are at peace. That is to say, if some ammunition and men are sent off together under circumstances such as show an intent to do hostile acts on foreign territory or on the seas against a friendly nation, our neutrality laws and our international obligations are violated.

"Surely ample room may be found between these several lines of procedure for the friends of the Cuban patriots to supply them with arms and ammunition, and even with men, if men were necessary, without violating our laws. If passengers embark, let them do so in the usual way. Their destination concerns nobody but themselves. They are free to go where they choose to go. If arms and ammunition are shipped, as may be rightfully and lawfully done, do not send men with them in the same vessel. If men are sent, let them go by themselves, unarmed. Such shipments of arms or such embarkation of passengers may be made, and should be made, in open day without concealment or secrecy, because no law is violated and no interference would be lawful. I am persuaded if the course thus outlined should be followed, our Cuban friends could supply their people with all they need without any other risk than capture by the Spanish land and naval forces within Spanish jurisdiction; that is to say, in Cuba or within a marine league of the shore of the island."

"General, have you noticed in the recent Senate debates a reference to some of your dispatches, in which you speak of the shooting of prisoners of war in Cuba during the former insurrection? If so, the Sun would like to have a reference to them and know something of their purport," said the reporter.

"Yes," replied the General, "my instructions from Washington frequently directed me to invite the attention of the Spanish Government to the barbarous and inhuman manner in which prisoners of war and noncombatants suspected of sympathy with the insurgents were put to death. The dispatch referred to in the Senate debate is my No. 426, dated August 16, 1873, and appears in the red book for that year on page 563. I referred to the hostilities in Cuba as 'four years of war without quarter.' This was notorious. These campaigns had been conducted mainly under the direction of Count Valmaceda. His campaigns were as conspicuous for cruelty as for incapacity. His decree of April, 1869, indicated his character and temper. He waged a war of extermination without quarter, against which our Government made repeated remonstrances. The decree to which I refer declared:

"'That any man from the age of 15 years upward found away from his habitation, and not proving a sufficient motive therefor, would be shot.

"'That every habitation unoccupied would be burned.

"'That every house not flying a white flag should be reduced to ashes.'

"Repeated reclamations were made by the Government of the United States for indemnity for the lives of American citizens shot pursuant to that decree. In Madrid no one doubted or denied, so far as ever I heard, that prisoners of war were shot. In the dispatch referred to I quoted statements from the Imparcial, a semiofficial journal in Madrid, of which the colonial minister at that time had been the director until he entered the cabinet, showing the captures of prisoners and war material in Cuba up to August, 1872, and the number of insurgents killed in battle.

"I was justified from the notoriety of the facts undisputed in adding to the number of slain in battle 13,600, as alleged, the number of 43,500 claimed to have been taken prisoners. This statement was made in these words:

"'As it is believed that all prisoners of war taken are shot or garroted, it would appear, taking the total of age of killed in battle and prisoners captured, that more than 57,000 insurgents have fallen since the war began.'

"I may remark, however, that this computation was based upon the assumption that the figures given in the semiofficial organ of the Government were accurate. It must be said that as a rule no dependence could be placed upon such figures. It was customary to amuse the Spanish public then, as now, with frequent reports of battles won and captures made of prisoners and war material. Indeed, scarcely a month passed during the long years the war continued in which statements were not published in the Madrid journals, claimed to be gotten from official sources, that the rebellion in Cuba was practically ended, that only a few roving bands of insurgents kept the field so long as they could hide in the mountains inaccessible to Spanish troops.

"Mr. Fish stated in his dispatch No. 432, dated October 20, 1872, page 532 of the red book of that year, that 'the insurrection in Cuba has now lasted four years. Attempts to suppress it, so far futile, have been made, probably at a sacrifice of more than 100,000 lives and an incalculable amount of property.' In my dispatch No. 374, dated May 30, 1871, page 71 of the red book of that year, I stated that 'reports of the most cruel severities against prisoners of war and against noncombatants perpetrated by both parties continue to reach Madrid.' Mr. Fish wrote to Mr. Cushing, my successor, on February 6, 1874, that 'our people are horrified and agitated by the spectacle at our very doors of war, not only with all its ordinary attendance of devastation and carnage, but with accompaniments of barbarous shooting of prisoners of war or the summary execution by military commissions, to the scandal and disgrace of the age.' Of course, all our people are familiar with the slaughter of the prisoners of war taken on the *Virginius* in 1873, the horrors of which I need not repeat.

"Our people, who are accustomed to regard the Spanish nation at home as chivalrous and cultivated, of course find it difficult to reconcile a belief in such atrocities as take place in Cuba with their high conceptions of Spaniards at home. The solution is to be found in the peculiar situation of things in Cuba.

"Mr. Fish points out in the dispatch to which I have just referred 'that the struggle is continued in Cuba with incidents of desperate tenacity on the part of the Cubans, and of angry fierceness on the part of the Spaniards unparalleled in the annals of modern warfare.' Again he says that 'by the slaveholders' resolutions of January, 1869, in Habana, General Dulce, whose generous intentions have been feelingly referred to by Admiral Polo, was driven out of the island, and the substance of political power passed into the hands of the Casino Español, where it has since remained.' This Casino Español is the governing power in Cuba to-day, as it was in 1874, when Mr. Fish wrote the passage quoted.

"If the Spanish governor of Cuba disobeys the wishes of the Casino, his position is made inestimable. If he conducts war in a civilized way, the volunteer guard, organized by the Casino and inspired by it, menace the Captain-General with their vengeance, and he is forced to succumb or quit his post. This has recently happened to Captain-General Martinez Campos, as it happened to General Dulce in the former insurrection. Dulce was succeeded by De Rodas and Lamacida and Jobellas, and Campos is now succeeded by Weyler. The volunteers rule the Spanish authorities of the island at the instigation of the Casino.

"The truth is that the authority of the Spanish Government is not recognized in Cuba unless it is agreeable to this dominating class, incorporated in the Casino Español and its instruments known as the volunteers. We are, therefore, confronted not with the question how far we should respect the sovereign rights of Spain in Cuba, but rather how far we are expected to tolerate a condition of things existing on the island which prevails in spite of

Spanish authority, in a great degree, and for which an irresponsible body, such as I have described, is essentially accountable.

"The responsibility of the Spanish Government for the atrocities and outrages committed in Cuba, as well upon the persons and property of American citizens as upon the insurgents, is found in the fact that since 1825 the Captain-General of Cuba is endowed by the Government with plenary powers to suspend the execution in Cuba of any law of Spain or any decree of its executive government at his pleasure. Whenever, therefore, the Madrid Government may attempt to mitigate the horrors of war or to introduce into the struggle any of the amenities of civilized hostilities, the Casino Español, with its branch of volunteers, creates a situation in Habana compelling the Captain-General to yield to its demands and to execute its will regardless of the instructions or wish of the Spanish Government."

Mr. MORGAN. If I had chosen I could have rested this whole matter upon that interview and statement of General Sickles, which he did me the honor to send me in a letter postmarked, I think, the 14th of this month, March. Everyone who knows anything of General Sickles, not merely in regard to his ability, but his Americanism and his truthfulness and uprightness and honor, knows that he has no motive in bringing these facts to the attention of the American people except to keep his own Government, which he loves very dearly and in whose service he has made sacrifices, on proper ground in regard to this transaction between Spain and the United States respecting Cuba.

Now, I have here a letter from a native American, dated Philadelphia, February 13, 1896. He sent his card along with the letter. He resides in Philadelphia. His card is open to the inspection of any Senator who deires to see it. I do not feel authorized, however, to put his name in the RECORD. I will read what he says to show what were his personal experiences in the Island of Cuba during the previous ten-years war:

BELLIGERENT RIGHTS—WHY THEY SHOULD BE ACCORDED TO THE STRUGGLING CUBAN REVOLUTIONISTS.

To the Editor of the Press:

SIR: The New York Herald published an editorial on the 10th instant entitled "The Government should go slow in the matter of belligerent rights." This article evidently emanated from the brain of an overzealous Spanish sympathizer. He says first, "Government action is quite different from popular sympathy." If this is, as I understand it, a government of the people, by the people, and for the people, therefore the will of the sovereign people should prevail. Then why go slow in recognizing the belligerency of Cuba? Did Spain go slow when she recognized the Southern Confederacy? We have nothing to lose by recognizing the Cubans; on the contrary, we would have considerable to gain; they would owe us a debt of gratitude and all their imports would come out of this country, while most of their products would seek our markets, being the nearest of access. If we do not recognize them, we lose their friendship and gain nothing; for, granting that Spain is responsible for damage done to American properties up to the present time, what does that responsibility amount to if she will not pay—in fact, does not pay the numerous claims our citizens have against her? Outside of the Mora claim, which took twenty-seven years to collect, can anyone tell me of any other claim paid by her to citizens of this country in the last thirty-five years?

The comparison made between the insurrection of 1868 and the present insurrection is not a fair one. In the former the Cubans never had in the field more than 7,000 men, and they were confined to the eastern district and never came as far as Colon, yet it lasted ten years. In the present revolution the Cubans have marched at will from Cape Maisi to Cape San Antonio, the full length of the island. They now have in the field nearly 60,000 men, well organized; they also have an established government, which virtually occupies the whole island, excepting the seaports, which are occupied by the Spaniards, backed up by a strong navy. It would be folly for the Cubans to capture a seaport, that they could only hold a few hours, with great sacrifice of human lives.

Give them recognition and they will soon have afloat enough cruisers to wipe out Spain's navy. By recognition it will shorten the struggle and save thousands of lives, as Spain would soon be obliged to give up the contest. If not recognized, the war will last as long as there is a Cuban living, for Spain is doomed to lose the last jewel of her tyrannical crown. The Herald states that Spain would board our vessels on the high seas. What of that? If the vessel's papers are in order and her cargo legitimate and lawful merchandise, it would be allowed to proceed; if she has contraband of war, let them capture her if they can; these are the chances of war. As far as recognition interfering with our commerce with the Island of Cuba, this is erroneous, as we have none now; therefore, if Spain blockaded the ports of Cuba, it would be no loss to this country, for you can not lose what you do not possess.

The Cubans are not fighting for autonomy; they want independence the same as we fought for when we seceded from England, and when recognized by other nations; let us then reciprocate and give them the same chance that we had. Blaine was in favor of reciprocity, and it worked well while it lasted. General Campos tried to reciprocate with the Cubans by being humane with prisoners, as the Cubans were with his soldiers; because he was humane, tyrannical Spain recalled him and sent to Cuba in his place General Weyler, commonly known as the butcher, and she says with instructions to be humane. How can you make a lamb out of a hyena? This is an impossibility. Time will tell, and a very short time at that, how he carries out his instructions. Let this Government act—not slowly, as the Herald suggests, but swiftly; it can not be too swift—and Spain will understand that the United States are not going to tolerate or allow her to murder innocent and inoffensive old men, women, and children.

From my own personal observation, during the years 1863-1870, at which time I resided in Cuba, I know that if a race of people ought to have their independence they are the Cubans. Under the Spanish rule they are not allowed to have any voice in the government of the island, and are taxed to such an extent that if any city in the United States should try to collect an equal amount per capita it would refuse to pay and revolt in a short time and not stand it as the Cubans have for years.

Why should the United States recognize them? Because they have suffered so much through Spanish misrule and are only trying to be recognized as human beings and of some value to this world. We not only ought to recognize them, but to help to drive the Spanish from this part of the world. We have not to go to Armenia to find work for the Red Cross Society, for in Cuba I have seen men torn from their homes at night, taken on board of a Spanish man-of-war, condemned to exile to the Isle of Fernando Po, and not even allowed to say good-bye to their families. Men taken from trains and shot. Prisoners would be condemned without being allowed any defense, and sent to Habana, but never reach there—shot on the way by the guards, who said they tried to escape.

In February, 1893, I was in Habana; heard some of the shots that sent some of the Cubans to their final resting place. They came from the country under promise of full pardon if they would leave the island; they came under this promise to Habana, went on board the royal mail steamer, and were shot down by the harbor police, acting under the orders of the Government, while talking to their wives and children in their staterooms. These men had come under a flag of truce, supposed to be respected by all nations of the world, but not by the Spanish Government. Under such state of affairs as this a halt should be called and the Spanish rule in America should be made a thing of the past. The nation that should do this is the United States. Instead of going slow in giving the Cubans belligerent rights they should go fast to help them to their independence. These are the ideas of

A NATIVE AMERICAN.

PHILADELPHIA, *February 13, 1896.*

Those are the ideas of a native American, whose name is here. If the Senator from Maine wants to know it, I will give it to him, but I will not put it in the RECORD. That is only a part of the recitals I could bring upon authentic statements of personal knowledge in regard to the ten years' war.

Here is a man, J. Frank Clark, who is the correspondent of the Richmond (Va.) Times, and who writes from Habana under date of March 7, 1896. He goes on to say:

Arrests of civilians under the sweeping provisions of General Weyler's proclamations of February 16 have been made at such a rate and in many cases with so little evidence of guilt that General Weyler was compelled a week ago to issue instructions to his officers to be more careful, as he required more proof than verbal denunciation. Yesterday he issued a circular in which he stated that absolute proof must be furnished by other than interested parties before accused prisoners will be deported, and warning commanders that they will be held responsible for false arrests. Without doubt General Weyler has in view the effect of this order abroad as well as here, for the manner in which Cubans who have never borne arms against Spain have been dragged from their homes, from their families, the stores, or their farms and thrown into prisons with felons and after a few days' delay placed on board ship for what is probably the vilest penal colony on the face of the earth has become a shame that cries aloud for redress.

General Weyler upon his arrival set at liberty a number of these civilian prisoners whom General Pando had taken from their daily occupation in the eastern end of the island. I saw twenty of them at the palace one day. They were white, intelligent looking, and bore the appearance of being shopkeepers or clerks. They were not bronzed by exposure to the weather, as all who are in the field are. The only evidence against these men was a paper purporting to be a list of the people who were aiding and communicating with the enemy. It was made up by a Spaniard. Since that time General Weyler has released others captured in the same way. Hundreds have, however, been sent to Ceuta, Africa, and to the Isle of Pines, and the arrests are increasing in number.

DOES WEYLER APPROVE?

General Weyler has removed the alcaldes of all towns in whom he had not absolute confidence, and has appointed the ranking military officers of regular troops or volunteers alcalde or mayor. These men are usually of the grade of lieutenant or major. They possess arbitrary powers. Under the proclamation the life or death of every man, woman, or child in their zone is in their hands. A large proportion of these commanders believe Weyler to be a man of severe measures, a man who will quietly approve any extreme act on their part. They look upon his circulars as intended for effect in the United States. They look for no punishment for summary executions of Cubans who sympathize with the insurgents. They expect praise and promotion for shooting war prisoners as soon as taken. In their reports they are careful to have the prisoners or the peaceful citizens killed found in the field after an engagement, but between the lines the manner in which the victims met their death is not difficult to decipher.

He then gives a number of other cases, which I will not stop to read, but will insert in my remarks:

OTHER MASSACRES.

Dozens of reports of affairs similar in that unarmed citizens are killed by Spanish troops have been received here, but the authorities have placed such obstacles in the way of correspondents that it is impossible to visit the localities and establish the facts. In a dozen cases refugees from towns where fights have occurred state that after the rebels are driven away citizens who took no part were shot down and counted in the official reports as dead insurgents. The Government officials deny these stories, and while it is common talk in Habana that certain affairs were butcheries the correspondents are in most cases obliged to accept the Government version.

I have visited towns where nearly every family had fled in terror, leaving dishes standing upon the tables and everything in disorder, showing the haste in which homes were abandoned. I talked with the few who remained, and was told that the people did not dread the insurgents, but fled from fear of the excesses of the Spanish troops. On the other hand, in some sections where towns have been used by the Spanish, the insurgents have burned the whole town, and the people were left homeless. Other towns which have harbored rebels have been destroyed by the Spanish troops, and the wreck and ruin which is being visited upon the fair Island of Cuba is pitiful to contemplate.

NATURE ALONE IS KIND.

But for the warmth of the climate and the ease with which life is sustained in the Tropics thousands would have perished ere this, and the island would be a charnel house before the end is reached. In many towns there have been no provisions for weeks. People have lived by sucking sugar cane and eating plantains. Families have camped for days upon the ruins of their homes in burned districts, sleeping upon the ground nights and crawling under a thatch during the heat of the sun. Those who could have sought refuge in the cities, and the few in proportion who had the means have escaped to the United States, Mexico, or some other country where peaceable citizens are not liable to summary execution.

There is a great deal more of it, but I do not choose to encumber the RECORD with these statements on either side further than to show that a state of open, horrid war exists in Cuba, and it is a war which involves the peace, the property, the rights, the liberties, and the lives of American citizens who happen to be there.

Our treaty of 1795 and all our treaties since that time, though none has really changed the attitude of the Governments toward each other since that date on this question, guarantees to our citizens the right to go into Cuba and reside there and carry on business and the like of that, and gives the same right to Spanish people who come here. It is as much our duty to protect the Spaniards in this country as it is theirs to protect our people in Cuba.

Are they able to do it? Can they do it? The Spanish Government and the Spanish minister, in his memorandum which he sent to the Committee on Foreign Relations, show their utter inability to do it. War is flagrant in that country, without the ability of either side to protect American property and citizens against the other. I merely want to establish that proposition; and it is not a matter of concern to me whether one Spaniard who is called a Cuban is more ferocious than another who is called a Spaniard proper.

That is not a question for us to decide. We are not weighing our sympathies in the balance. Neither our sympathy nor our indignation ought to enter into this case at all. Yet we can not of course avoid it in giving our votes. But the line of action for us to take is to declare that a state of open, public war exists in Cuba and that the laws of war shall apply to it. We can not protect our citizens otherwise. Are we to stand still when we know that our people and their property are being sacrificed in Cuba, and to wait, how long we do not know, ten years or twenty years, for a termination of a guerrilla warfare that exists there, which may amount to the extermination of the native population and almost the entire Spanish army as well? Are we to wait for that result before we can interpose for the purpose of taking care of our people?

These resolutions, as has often been observed, are matters of opinion. We go no farther than the boundary and domain of opinion. The other House put in the opinion that in certain contingencies and events the Government of the United States ought to be prepared to intervene. I like the resolution of the House better than that of the Senate merely because it takes that ground, for if this matter is to continue, and the outrages and the horrors of the ten-years war is to be repeated, as they are being repeated, by the very same people and under the same circumstances, then I say that it becomes our duty to do that which General Grant was so anxious to do—intervene and stop it. Yet we do not undertake on our part to declare for intervention, except that on certain conditions and under certain circumstances it should become a matter of duty on the part of the Government of the United States. That is our opinion, and is only expressed as our opinion.

I expected when I rose to speak on this case, now for the fourth time, that I would have an opportunity of answering some of the flings which have been thrown at the Committee on Foreign Relations, such as that it is a sleepy committee and the like of that, by the senior Senator from Massachusetts [Mr. HOAR] and the Senator from Maine [Mr. HALE]. But I believe, sir, that the occasion is one of too great solemnity and too great importance to permit me to thrust myself into this debate personally or as a member of the Committee on Foreign Relations. I can only say that we have most carefully, attentively, faithfully examined into all of the great mass of petitions and of opinions expressed by thousands of American citizens in legislative assemblies and elsewhere, and we have undertaken in forming our opinions, and only to that extent, to conform them to what we believe to be the truth as it has been ascertained and expressed by the great body of American citizens. There is where we stand, in perfect line with the American people in the expression of their candid, honest, sincere and well-sustained opinion.

Now, it will not do for the purpose of overturning those opinions for anyone to say that that committee must have summoned before it those who were personal eye observers of all these things. American opinion is formed justly and honestly upon the broad facts of the case as they are known to the American people. They have sought for information through the best and most sincere and candid sources of information, for the purpose of informing themselves as to the opinions that they ought to entertain. These are not new to us. They are old opinions. They are opinions that have been crystallized in respect to Cuba and her relations to Spain now for more than forty years—yes, through the whole of this century.

The House resolution now before us and the Senate resolution differ only as a strong expression of opinion differs from one that is stronger and a wide field of consideration differs from one that is wider.

In both resolutions the two Houses have confined themselves to the mere expression of opinions, neither of them having taken any action that is intended to define the legal attitude of the Government or the people of the United States toward Spain or Cuba.

Our attitude toward Spain is that of peace. Our relation to Cuba is that of peace and sympathy.

We have opinions as to the conduct of Spain, in peace and war, toward her "gem of the Antilles" that are disagreeable to that monarchy that we feel at liberty to express; that our people, almost with one accord, have expressed; that we are compelled to express, as they relate to the condition of a people who are so near to our borders, and so intimately associated with our people, socially and commercially; opinions that we would express if Cuba were as distant from us as Armenia is. A decent regard for the liberty that is sustained and encouraged by our own free institutions requires us, at least, to disavow our open or tacit approval of the conduct of Spain toward Cuba for the last thirty years.

In doing this in proper language, which conveys no censure, if we offend against Spain, we disclaim such a purpose, but we will not on that account violate or conceal the truth. The expression of our opinion on this subject has given grave offense to Spaniards, and probably to Spain, which we would deeply regret if they were unjust, as they are not.

These opinions have given serious offense to some cidevant Americans who edit newspapers, and others who write anonymous threats in letters and on postal cards to members of Congress.

That interesting body of emigrés in the great cities of Europe, new pupils in the old schools of feudalism, who, to escape taxation and the duties of American citizenship, and to enjoy the good society to which our coupon bonds admit them and the hospitalities they would otherwise seek for in vain in the kitchens and servants' halls of London, Paris, and Berlin, are very much offended at the American opinion about Cuban affairs that is expressed in the votes of the two Houses on these resolutions.

The newspapers they own and control in New York, London, and Paris flare up in fervid abuse of Congress for responding to the uttered voice of the American people and for daring to utter a word of sympathy for Cuba.

Yet they are not bold enough to attack the 262 votes to 17 in the House and the 64 votes to 6 in the Senate who voted these **opinions**.

The story of "Johnny Hook," read by the Senator from New York on last Thursday, and the resolutions of the general assembly of that great State, and of Mississippi, which I have read, seem to convince them that they are a little overmatched by the people and the two Houses of Congress, and in their anger they turn upon individuals of the Senate Committee on Foreign Relations and rend us.

I have never had a very high respect for those foreign princes and prime ministers whose personal familiarity with our refugees from social coventry is sold for money or whose recognition is won by their mean and slavish contributions to their vainglory.

The most degrading phase of contraband diplomacy is the recent travesty of informing our Government, through certain newspaper owners, of the views of European royalty as to American affairs and politics.

Next to that is the meanness of that species of cowardice that selects a single friend of a great movement of the people, voiced in the resolutions of Congress, and assails that movement by making a personal assault on him.

I would not make a personal matter in the Senate of anything that such persons choose to say about me in their newspapers, but the effort to disparage a great public measure by attributing to me a purpose in its advocacy that has no place in my thoughts, and never had, is a wrong against the public welfare.

If I were asked, as I may have been, and as has often been asked on the floor of the Senate in this session of Congress, where we are to get the money to meet the expenses of war, if we should have to meet its horrors, I would answer that we would not find it necessary to borrow it, as our mines would furnish all we might need for that purpose. This is true; but it is no more a reason for going to war than would be the increased value of iron, or coal, or wool, or cotton, or sugar, or copper that would result from war.

The production of both gold and silver would be increased by any foreign war in which we might engage.

I saw the Confederacy arm its soldiery, while the war was flagrant, by digging the iron ore and the coal from the earth to fashion into guns and swords, and the saltpeter from the caves to manufacture gunpowder.

Since that development of the genius of our people I have never feared that the mighty resources of our people will not be equal to any war that may befall us.

Such fears only beset those feudalists who are rich enough to dread the taxes of warfare and the cost of hiring substitutes. If the liberties and rights of our people rested alone upon the shoulders of gamblers in stocks and men who make corners on the food and raiment of the patriotic soldiers who must fight our battles, the bulls and the bears of the great exchanges would crucify the Republic and cast lots for its raiment, in the presence, even, of the thick darkness that would enshroud its death.

No; I would not sacrifice any honest American citizen, however poor, in a cause that is not holier than life and sweeter than all its hopes. Yet I would not sacrifice his liberties or the true honor of his country to secure the comfort or increase the wealth of every heartless monopolist and nabob in Europe and America.

I abhor the man who would sacrifice human life in any cause save that of justice and liberty. It is this that excites my utmost resentment, when I see men, women, and children starved by feudal monopoly in any of its hideous forms. It is this that compels me to despise the minions of monopoly—the craven feudatories—when, for hire, they sell their influence to increase poverty and breed despair, and seek the shelter of our flag to betray our people by vile assaults upon true Americans who would defend them with their lives.

The Senate, that stands in perpetual organization as the bulwark of the Republic—an eternal rock of defense—is the body that these hired traitors assail with unceasing warfare. That they find support in high feudal quarters, and sometimes in the membership of this body, is as true of us as it was in other times when the foundations of government sank and disappeared in anarchy. But our Senate is an everlasting rock of defense to the Republic, and the powers of death will not prevail against it.

Some Senators have done me the injustice, through a total misunderstanding of my position on these resolutions when they were pending in the committee, to charge me with the motive and purpose of fomenting a war with Spain.

I state without hesitancy that the cry of Cuba for justice, humanity, and mercy, in which there thrills a plea for liberty to which we have listened for a half century, has the full right of appeal to all that I am and all that I feel as a citizen of the United States. It has not fallen upon dull ears or a listless and hardened heart. But for the restraints imposed upon me by the solemn responsibilities of my duty as a Senator I would be abreast with the foremost of those tens of thousands of Americans who urge us to decisive intervention in the name of humanity.

But every member of the Committee on Foreign Relations and its records and the records of the Senate will bear me witness that I have moved slowly and with extreme caution in the course of our progress in this matter.

I have not the honor of the acquaintance of the Spanish minister or of any Cuban agents, and I have even been rude in my refusal to receive or communicate with the Cuban agents while this matter was pending in the committee. Above all else I desired to reach impartial conclusions upon the best evidence that was available as to our rights of neutrality by recognizing that open, general war that now exists in Cuba between the people and the Crown. My vote was for delay until we could be reasonably sure of our ground, although I felt that patriots were dying for the cause of liberty while we deliberated about our giving a wound to the pride of the Spanish monarchy. I knew from the past history of Spanish wars, beginning with the conquests of Cortez and Pizarro, and in the Netherlands, and the civil war in Spain at the close of the last century, and in the wars of the Mexican revolution and those of Central and South America, and especially in the great ten-years war for emancipation and civil liberty in Cuba, and the wars for the republic in Spain, that Spanish enemies were all treated as rebels and traitors, and that submission or extermination was the sole alternative of Spanish ferocity.

Extermination is the established penalty for resistance to any demand of Spain when made upon Spanish subjects. If we must support their dominion against alleged insurrectionists, we must also support the utter ruin and destruction of those who rebel against Spanish authority for whatever cause. It is a dear price for an American to pay for the forms and ceremonies of international comity and for the good will of a tyrannical despotism.

Yet such seemed to be the demand of our own Government in

its long and oft-repeated vigilant watch and guard against our own people which has converted every great harbor on our eastern and southern coasts into a Spanish picket post, on which we have mounted guard with police and soldiers and warships, with their guns pointed at our own shores.

On my part, I have followed these movements of our Government "afar off," but with faithful obedience.

So I waited in silent discontent while the tide of blood still flowed and the fires of desolation swept the beautiful island.

At last the time for action came; the time when threadbare patience could no longer conceal the demand of duty, and the committee took up its responsible task.

I had offered no resolution in the Senate or in the committee, and had the whole field to select from. They were all intense in expression and decisive in their proposed action.

Any one of them would have provoked Spain to war as certainly as a torpedo in the neck of a Spanish bull would excite him to deadly war against the matador.

And yet not one of them that related to belligerent rights was, in law or by intention, in the least degree hostile to Spain.

No decent, law-abiding, or self-respecting nation in Christendom would have treated such resolutions as derogatory to its pride, insulting to its honor, or unfriendly in purpose.

Yet I had read enough of Spanish history in Cuba from authentic statements of our own Government, made directly in the teeth of Spain, to know that any movement, even to lessen the horrid barbarities of Spanish warfare, would cause her to charge upon us as a Spanish bull would charge a red flag in their national sport.

When we took up this mass of petitions lying before me, which is growing daily, I presented a declaration and resolutions that were the mildest possible plea for humanity in the mere conduct of the war. I will ask the Secretary to read them.

The PRESIDING OFFICER. The Secretary will read as indicated.

The Secretary read as follows:

Resolved by the Senate (the House of Representatives concurring), That the present deplorable war in the Island of Cuba has reached a magnitude that concerns all civilized nations to the extent that it should be conducted, if unhappily it is longer to continue, on those principles and laws of warfare that are acknowledged to be obligatory upon civilized nations when engaged in open hostilities, including the treatment of captives who are enlisted in either army; due respect to cartels for exchange of prisoners and for other military purposes: truces and flags of truce; the provision of proper hospitals and hospital supplies and services to the sick and wounded of either army.

Resolved further, That this representation of the views and opinions of Congress be sent to the President, and if he concurs therein that he will, in a friendly spirit, use the good offices of this Government to the end that Spain shall be requested to accord to the armies with which it is engaged in war the rights of belligerents as the same are recognized under the laws of nations.

Mr. MORGAN. I will have the declaration preceding the resolutions and forming the report of the committee inserted in my remarks without stopping to read it. The Senate is familiar with it.

The PRESIDING OFFICER. Without objection, it is so ordered.

The report submitted by Mr. MORGAN from the Committee on Foreign Relations January 29, 1896, is as follows:

The Congress of the United States, deeply regretting the unhappy state of hostilities existing in Cuba, which has again been the result of the demand of a large number of the native population of that island for its independence, in a spirit of respect and regard for the welfare of both countries, earnestly desires that the security of life and property and the establishment of permanent peace and of a government that is satisfactory to the people of Cuba should be accomplished.

And to the extent that the people of Cuba are seeking the rights of local self-government for domestic purposes, the Congress of the United States expresses its earnest sympathy with them. The Congress would also welcome with satisfaction the concession, by Spain, of complete sovereignty to the people of that island, and would cheerfully give to such a voluntary concession the cordial support of the United States. The near proximity of Cuba to the frontier of the United States, and the fact that it is universally regarded as a part of the continental system of America, identifies that island so closely with the political and commercial welfare of our people that Congress can not be indifferent to the fact that civil war is flagrant among the people of Cuba.

Nor can we longer overlook the fact that the destructive character of this war is doing serious harm to the rights and interests of our people on the island, and to our lawful commerce, the protection and freedom of which are safeguarded by treaty obligations. In the recent past and in former years, when internal wars have been waged for long periods and with results that were disastrous to Cuba and injurious to Spain, the Government of the United States has always observed with perfect faith all of its duties toward the belligerents.

It was a difficult task thus forced upon the United States, but it was performed with vigor, impartiality, and justice, in the hope that Spain would so ameliorate the condition of the Cuban people as to give them peace, contentment, and prosperity. This desirable result has not been accomplished. Its failure has not resulted from any interference on the part of our people or Government with the people or government of Cuba.

The hospitality which our treaties, the laws of nations, and the laws of Christianity have extended to Cuban refugees in the United States has caused distrust on the part of the Spanish Government as to the fidelity of our Government to its obligations of neutrality in the frequent insurrections of the people of Cuba against Spanish authority. This distrust has often become a source of serious annoyance to our people, and has led to a spirit of retaliation toward Spanish authority in Cuba, thus giving rise to frequent controversies between the two countries. The absence of responsible government in Cuba, with powers adequate to deal directly with questions between the people of the United States and the people and political authorities of the island, has been a frequently recurring cause of delay, protracted imprisonment, confiscations of property, and the detention of our people and their ships, often upon groundless charges, which has been a serious grievance.

When insurrections have occurred on the Island of Cuba, the temptation to unlawful invasion by reckless persons has given to our Government anxiety, trouble, and much expense in the enforcement of our laws and treaty obligations of neutrality, and these occasions have been so frequent as to make these duties unreasonably onerous upon the Government of the United States.

The devastation of Cuba in the war that is now being waged, both with fire and sword, is an anxious and disturbing cause of unrest among the people of the United States, which creates strong grounds of protest against the continuance of the struggle for power between Cuba and Spain, which is rapidly changing the issue to one of existence on the part of a great number of the native population.

It is neither just to the relations that exist between Cuba and the United States nor is it in keeping with the spirit of the age or the rights of humanity that this struggle should be protracted until one party or the other should become exhausted in the resources of men and money, thereby weakening both until they may fall a prey to some stronger power, or until the stress of human sympathy or the resentments engendered by long and bloody conflict should draw into the strife the unruly elements of neighboring countries.

This civil war, though it is great in its proportions and is conducted by armies that are in complete organization and directed and controlled by supreme military authority, has not the safeguard of a cartel for the treatment of wounded soldiers or prisoners of war.

In this feature of the warfare it becomes a duty of humanity that the civilized powers should insist upon the application of the laws of war recognized among civilized nations to both armies. As our own people are drawn into this struggle on both sides, and enter either army without the consent of our Government and in violation of our laws, their treatment when they may be wounded or captured, although it is not regulated by treaty and ceases to be a positive care of our Government, should not be left to the revengeful retaliations which expose them to the fate of pirates or other felons.

The inability of Spain to subdue the revolutionists by the measures and within the time that would be reasonable when applied to occasions of ordinary civil disturbance is a misfortune that can not be justly visited upon citizens of the United States, nor can it be considered that a state of open civil war does not exist, but that the movement is a mere insurrection and its supporters a mob of criminal violators of the law, when it is seen that it requires an army of 100,000 men and all the naval and military power of a great kingdom even to hold the alleged rebellion in check.

It is due to the situation of affairs in Cuba that Spain should recognize the existence of a state of war in the island, and should voluntarily accord to the armies opposed to her authority the rights of belligerents under the laws of nations.

The Congress of the United States, recognizing the fact that the matters herein referred to are properly within the control of the Chief Executive until, within the principles of our Constitution, it becomes the duty of Congress to define the final attitude of the Government of the United States toward Spain, presents these considerations to the President in support of the following resolution:

"*Resolved by the Senate (the House of Representatives concurring)*, That the present deplorable war in the Island of Cuba has reached a magnitude that concerns all civilized nations to the extent that it should be conducted, if unhappily it is longer to continue, on those principles and laws of warfare that are acknowledged to be obligatory upon civilized nations when engaged in open hostilities, including the treatment of captives who are enlisted in either army; due respect to cartels for exchange of prisoners and for other military purposes; truces and flags of truce; the provision of proper hospitals and hospital supplies and services to the sick and wounded of either army.

"*Resolved further*, That this representation of the views and opinions of Congress be sent to the President; and if he concurs therein that he will, in a friendly spirit, use the good offices of this Government to the end that Spain shall be requested to accord to the armies with which it is engaged in war the rights of belligerents, as the same are recognized under the laws of nations."

FEBRUARY 5, 1896.—Mr. MORGAN, from the Committee on Foreign Relations, reported the following concurrent resolution as a substitute for concurrent resolution No. 19, reported January 29, 1896:

Resolved by the Senate (the House of Representatives concurring), That, in the opinion of Congress, a condition of public war exists between the Government of Spain and the Government proclaimed and for some time maintained by force of arms by the people of Cuba; and that the United States of America should maintain a strict neutrality between the contending powers, according to each all the rights of belligerents in the ports and territory of the United States.

Mr. MORGAN. I felt that I owed an explanation to the committee for the mildness of such a response to the demand of our people for a more cogent expression.

I said to the committee in substance:

"I offer this declaration because it places the United States on ground that no civilized nation can possibly criticise. I do this in the firm conviction that when we listen to the petitions of our indignant people and turn our faces in the direction they are moving, the first step we take, however short, whether it is an inch or an ell, will result in a war with Spain. I keep my eyes fixed steadfastly on that result without reference to its justice, wisdom, or necessity. Spain can not conquer Cuba with her burden of debt and the political dissensions that lurk about the Spanish throne. Spain knows this, and her pride will force her to prefer to lose Cuba in conflict with some great power rather than surrender it as she has done her other American possessions, to a body of insurrectionists whom she despises and denounces in the most opprobrious terms. So far as I am concerned I am convinced that war with Spain is inevitable as the outgrowth of this Cuban affair. It will come at an early day, and nothing but our denunciation of the Cubans can delay the conflict. In voting for this mild declaration I feel that I am in the act of drawing the sword and laying it upon this table, and am saying to Spain, 'Take it up if you will.'"

The committee laid aside my resolutions and adopted, provisionally, a much stronger one than those which I proposed.

At the next meeting the committee adopted my declaration and resolutions and ordered me to report them to the Senate, which I did.

Within twenty-four hours the cable brought us accounts that this overture excited anger in Madrid for its insolence, contempt for its weakness, and derision for its singularity, and with it there came a storm of blustering gasconade.

Campos was recalled, and the temper of Spain was heated to the degree that only Weyler could keep pace with. Weyler was ordered to Cuba. The committee met again and concluded, after anxious discussion, to set aside the resolutions they had ordered me to report, and directed me to report the resolution that passed the Senate, after being amended with the addition of the resolution for Cuban independence offered by the Senator from Pennsylvania.

Now, what excuse can there be for the attack made upon me in the Senate, followed by some newspapers in New York, charging me with drawing the sword and challenging Spain to take it up, and that I had said to some person whose name is not mentioned that I desired a war with Spain because it would result in the remonetization of silver?

Why did they not charge that motive to me for the earnest support I gave to Mr. Olney's noble avowal and definition of the Monroe doctrine? Men from the North send me postal cards warning me that Maceo is a negro, a very black one, they say, and advising me to quit the country and consort with him in the Cuban cabinet.

This thrust deserves at least a parry. The freedom of the slaves was a prime factor in the ten-years war in Cuba, which began at the close of our civil war. In both wars negro troops were used, and with nearly equal savagery. In Cuba, as in our Southern States, the mass of the negro population adhered to their masters. In Cuba the masters took sides with the Government; in the United States the Government was at war with the slaveholders.

General Grant and Mr. Fish, his Secretary of State, desired above all things else connected with Spanish troubles the emancipation of the slaves. The republicans in Spain adopted the American demand for emancipation, and upon these ideas they dethroned Amadeus and established a republic. In the time of the Republic an ordinance of gradual emancipation was proclaimed. But the Spanish sugar planters and the New York sugar merchants and refiners found it to their interest to crush out Gomez and Cisneros, who were fighting for the full emancipation of the negroes and for the independence of the island, and General Grant and Mr. Fish came to believe that, the Republic in Spain having been abandoned in favor of the Crown, it was better for the Cubans that they should surrender on pledges guaranteeing important liberties to them, and that a republic was then impossible in the island.

General Grant, acting against his personal convictions and the humane sympathies of his nature, sent in his message of June, 1870, refusing to recommend the recognition of belligerent rights for the Cubans. That refusal virtually ended the war, and Gomez became the active promoter of the general capitulation. The terms of that capitulation were in letter and spirit violated by Spain, and Gomez and Maceo returned to take up arms and Cisneros to resume the civil presidency, and the emancipated slaves, one-fifth of the population, united with them to raise again the flag of Cuban independence.

The negro population in Cuba is about in the same proportion that exists in the United States. This added element of military strength accounts, in a large degree, for the great increase of the forces at war with Spain.

Those men of the North mistake me when they assume that I could have any prejudice toward the negro race that would cause me to deny to them good government, safety in life and property, and every personal liberty that I enjoy in our free Republic.

I do not believe, any more than Congress or the people of the District of Columbia believe, that the negro race is a useful or necessary factor in the government of a great republic. We place the Indian tribes and the Chinese on even a lower scale in political government, while we give them full measure of liberty. But the negro has the same right as the white man to escape from the tyrannical despotism of Spain and to have a fair opportunity to enjoy the true and full value of independence. That blessing, like the air of the heavens, the sweet waters that flow from the green hills, and the safe shelter of the roof tree of home, should be the heritage of every freeman.

I would rather be in the cabinet of a republic with Gomez and Maceo than in the cabinet of the Spanish Monarchy with Valmaseda and Weyler.

I gather my impression of the war policy and methods of the Spanish Monarchy from the records of impartial history, without any prejudice against these people. The progress of civilization seems to have no effect or tendency to mitigate the stern rule of extermination applied by Spain to all who are found in rebellion against her authority. No country in Europe, and probably none in the world, has suffered more revolutionary changes in government than Spain has had during the present century.

In the previous growth of the Spanish monarchy both hemispheres were watered with innocent blood and dotted with graves of innocent people of all ages and conditions, to extend the dominion of avarice and pride through the destruction of all opposing political or religious parties and sects that Spain had the power to crush. After Protestant Netherlands had fought for her liberties and had lost a full generation in the struggle, Spain's period of decline set in rapidly. Since the year 1800 scarcely a period of three years, on the average, has elapsed without a change of government in the mother country or in the colonies that involved war, attended with great sacrifice of life.

In the transitions of the colonies into independent republics under our great example, this young and then unproved Republic, the near neighbor and sympathetic exemplar of free constitutional government, by a course of honorable justice and firm assertion of our rights and the careful observance of duty, maintained its neutrality during the prevalence of wars for independence in the great colonies of Spain.

We did not withhold our expressions of sympathy for the colonies in revolt, or refuse to recognize their rights as belligerents, or their independence when that was won or appeared to be certain of realization; yet we took no part in these wars, and had no thought of taking advantage of them for territorial aggrandizement. These facts should impress Spain with our sense of justice and duty, when, to save our people from suffering the losses and hardships of the present war in Cuba, we seek only to apply the laws of civilized warfare to an open, confessed, and universally admitted state of civil war in that island.

We do not seek to change our relations to Cuba upon any claim of right to interfere in the domestic affairs of Spain in that island any more than we do in Puerto Rico, where war does not exist. Our duty is to our own people, and it is a duty that Spain can not prevent us from performing. We have, in a spirit of forbearance, omitted to demand our rights in the chronic state of war that has afflicted Spain during all this nineteenth century, and have gone no further than to protest against the losses of liberty, life, and property that have been entailed on our people in these Cuban insurrections. We have stood by while our people were being murdered in Cuba and their property confiscated without law or a trial, and only in a few cases have we been able, after long delay, to collect the price of this blood in money. We find now that our forbearance is reckoned with as if it were weakness, and our neutrality is abused by Spain.

I prefer, and our people demand, that Spain shall not destroy our citizens or their property on a credit, but she must hereafter pay as she goes. We no longer choose to permit our people to be persecuted and slain by either party in Cuba under the pretext that neither of them has the power to prevent such wrongs, and if it must be, we will intervene to prevent it, even at the risk of shocking the keen sense of propriety that some Senators are troubled with.

In the midst of the last ten years' war in Cuba Spain, on the 11th of February, 1873, discarded the monarchy and established the republic under Fiqueras. It had been three years in process of full development, but the tendency was all the time toward the republic. Isabella fled to France in 1868, and a triumvirate under Serrano formed a provisional government. Cuba was immediately involved in revolution. Much blood was shed in Spain to promote the republic, and many lives were destroyed in Cuba to sustain the same cause.

The emancipation of the slaves was the avowed task of the Republic of Spain, and in this Government General Grant felt that Cuban independence would ultimately find its greatest ally and friend.

No one could have been more determined than General Grant was that the republican movements in Spain and Cuba should result in the abolition of slavery. This great purpose inspired and strengthened every hope of good that he expected from that revolution both in Spain and Cuba. Spain was striving to put down monarchy at home and to put down the republic in Cuba. Spain, whether it was monarchic or republican, clung to slavery in Cuba, and a large body of Cubans demanded the abolition of slavery and the republic, with national independence.

General Grant was convinced that the success of the republic in Spain would result in the abolition of slavery in Cuba, and that the people of Cuba would not be able, against the opposition of both parties in Spain, to abolish slavery. His policy then became clear and definite. It was to encourage the republic in Spain on the condition that the republic would abolish slavery in Cuba. This condition was accepted by the republic in Spain and was ultimately accomplished.

The people of the United States were restive under the horrors of the Spanish methods of warfare in Cuba, and in 1870 General Grant sent his message to Congress to inform them of the grounds upon which he discouraged their demand for belligerent rights for the Cubans in arms. This was when the insurrection had progressed only a single year.

Had the United States then recognized the rights of belligerency in favor of the Cubans, it would have united all parties in Spain against the emancipation of the slaves. The great and inspiring hope of a voluntary act of emancipation would have perished and the antislavery men in the United States would have been driven to the alternative of liberating the slaves in Cuba by force, and to the odium of encouraging a servile insurrection in order to promote anarchy for the sake of emancipation. The other alternative, of procuring the freedom of the slaves in Cuba through the creation of the republic in Spain, was free from any strain on American sentiment and was joyfully accepted by the President.

But General Grant would not intervene to repress the people of Cuba in their struggle for independence. All he could do, until emancipation of the slaves was secured, was to await results without interference. His good offices were constantly pressed upon the Republic of Spain for a settlement that would add to their decree of emancipation of the slaves a guaranty of equal rights and liberties to the native white Cubans. This pledge was obtained from Spain, and Gomez and Cisneros laid down their arms and, accepting this pledge, became most active and efficient in persuading the Cuban people to desist from further warfare. The treaty was made and broken by the Spaniards, cruelly broken, and the emancipated slaves are united with the native white people in a renewed demand for the republic, for liberty, for justice, and for the safety of life.

General Grant could not openly declare this great line of policy. That would have been fatal to his success. If our people could have seen it, they would have been more patient during the eight years of cruel warfare that followed after the repressive message of 1870. But they felt that their Government was looking with indifference upon the horrible saturnalia of blood and fire which President Grant mentioned, as a warning to Spain, in the message of 1870, and they went alone and in small bands to the devastated islands to help the patriot people in their war for existence.

General Grant was far from viewing those atrocities with indifference. I will read a letter of Mr. Fish to Admiral Polo after a while that will clear that point, and will show the grounds on which I rest our present action. That letter would sustain a line of action far more decisive and effectual than is now proposed. I have not chosen to adopt it, on my part, because I do not wish to give Spain any pretext for any result that her conduct has invited which would seem to cast the blame on the United States.

Let the attitude of Spain toward the native people of Cuba, black and white, find its justification or its excuse in her own policies and counsels, and not in anything short of a positive duty that we shall do.

In my studies of the situation in Cuba and of the duties of Congress connected with it I have taken the message of 1870 as my guide, although I believe it is far too narrow in its limitations upon our rights, and I have found that the facts of the war in Cuba and the law as it is stated in that message bring the case entirely within the most restricted requirements of that paper.

We have never settled the powers of Congress, acting independently of the President, as to mandatory action with reference to the recognition of a state of belligerency or a declaration of war. We do not know what is or will be the policy of the President in the Cuban imbroglio. Acting, then, as representatives of States that memorialize Congress and the people who shower petitions upon us, it is wiser that our response to them should indicate clearly the opinions of Congress rather than some decisive act to which the Executive might dissent. When the people and Congress have expressed their opinions in a way that is practically unanimous, if the President does not concur, he will assume the responsibility.

The letter to which I referred, Mr. President, is that of Mr. Fish to Admiral Polo de Bernabé, who was at that time the minister of Spain to this country. Mr. Fish says, in some of the places which I will quote, what I will read. I will put the entire part of the letter referring to this matter in the RECORD as an appendix to my speech. On the 10th of September, 1869, the minister of transmarine affairs at Madrid, in an official paper, said:

> A deplorable and pertinacious tradition of despotism, which, if it could ever be justified, is without a shadow of reason at the present time, intrusted the direction and management of our colonial establishment to the agents of the metropolis, destroying, by their dominant and exclusive authority, the vital energies of the country and the creative and productive activity of free individuals. And although the system may now have improved in some of its details, the domineering action of the authorities being less felt, it still appears full of the original error, which is upheld by the force of tradition, and the necessary influence of interests created under their protection, which, doubtless, are deserving of respect so far as they are reconcilable with the requirements of justice, with the common welfare, and with the principles on which every liberal system should be founded. A change of system, political as well as administrative, is therefore imperatively demanded.

Mr. Fish says, after quoting this remark:

> But while admitting the existence of the injuries which had provoked the outbreak at Yara, the government of the revolution of 1868 refused to remedy them until the armed insurrection should be suppressed. "Spain would already have given all constitutional liberties to Cuba," said Mr. Silvela to General Sickles, "if the unfortunate insurrection of Yara, and the cry of 'Death to Spain,' uttered by some Cubans, had not alienated the sympathies of the nation, and obliged the government to accept the impolitic contest to which it was provoked. The government considers that it can come to no definite decision in regard to the political situation and future government of the Island of Cuba until the insurgents lay down their arms and cease the struggle."

That is the quotation. Then Mr. Fish says:

> This would indicate that it is the resistance to admitted wrongs, and not the wrongfulness of resistance, which Spain is endeavoring to repress.

I pass on to some few other extracts. Mr. Fish says:

> It must be frankly confessed that there were many persons in the United States who shared the theoretical opinions of the Spanish statesmen, but who could not agree in the diametrically opposite policy which Spain pursued toward Cuba under their directions.
> It was natural for the people of the United States to feel an interest in the prosperity of Cuba. This and the reasons for it were well understood at Madrid. Mr. Martos, in the presence of his colleagues, Mr. Becerra and Mr. Rivero, had officially spoken to General Sickles of "the common interests shared by the United States and Spain in Cuba." He said "that whatever retarded the prosperity of the island was injurious alike to both countries; that the welfare of Cuba was of more commercial importance to the United States than to the mother country."

Mr. Fish says upon this quotation:

> This wise statesman might have added that the interest of the United States in Cuba was heightened by a desire that the deadly struggle on the island might end in the acquisition of self-government (whether under or free from Spanish rule was, of course, immaterial to an American) and in the abolition of slavery. Such was undoubtedly the fact. The undersigned feels convinced that these views were shared by the mass of the liberal statesmen

of Spain, modified probably by the patriotic wish that the island should retain its political connection with Spain. But it could not be expected that foreigners would share in the full warmth of this wish of Spanish statesmen. The mass of the people of the United States certainly gave little heed to the matter beyond the natural preference that a disturbing element of European politics should be removed from the American system.

I must pass on, because the time is drawing near when I must take my seat.

On the 24th of March, 1869—

Said Mr. Fish—

the Captain-General of Cuba issued a decree, which is referred to by Admiral Polo, and from which the following is an extract:

"Vessels which may be captured in Spanish waters, or on the high seas near to the island, having on board men, arms, and munitions, or effects that can in any manner contribute, promote, or foment the insurrection in this province, whatsoever their derivation and destination, after examination of their papers and register, shall be de facto considered as enemies of the integrity of our territory, and treated as pirates, in accordance with the ordinances of the navy.

"All persons captured in such vessels, without regard to their number, will be immediately executed."

A copy of this decree was received at this Department on the 2d of April, 1869, and the undersigned, although but then just entered upon the duties of his office, and greatly pressed with other public matters requiring immediate attention, put everything aside, by direction of the President, and on the next date wrote as follows to the minister of Spain at Washington:

I will only quote from that one paragraph:

"This Government certainly can not assent to the punishment by Spanish authorities of any citizen of the United States for the exercise of a privilege to which he may be entitled under public law and treaties."

Mr. President, that is the law of Spain to-day in this war. Mr. Fish says further:

The order to indiscriminately slaughter "all persons captured in such vessels, without regard to their number," could not but shock the sensibilities of all humane persons. The undersigned felt, however, unwilling to object to the execution of the order except when proposed to be enforced against citizens of the United States.

I am sorry he was unwilling to do that, but he had a great motive, or the President had, which held him in check.

In regard to the second point thus stated by Admiral Polo's esteemed predecessor, the undersigned was constrained by a due regard to universally recognized principles of international rights and duties to declare that, in the absence of a recognized state of war, it was no offense in the sailing vessels and steamers of the United States to carry arms and munitions of war for whomsoever it might concern.

I am sorry that the Senator from Massachusetts [Mr. HOAR] is not present to hear this overturning of the sedate and sage enunciation of the law made by the chairman of the Judiciary Committee two or three times in this debate.

The undersigned has uniformly said that no government can by the law of nations be held responsible for shipments of arms, munitions, or materials of war, made by private individuals at their own risk and peril. If a state of war should exist, if Spain should be entitled to the rights of a belligerent, parties concerned in the shipment of arms and military supplies for her enemy would incur the risk of confiscation by her of their goods; but their act would involve no ground of reclamation against their government in behalf of Spain; and consequently no right to invoke the aid of that government in preventing the perpetration of the act. Such it is believed is the established law of nations, and such the received rule even when the shipment of arms and munitions is made from the territory of the country whose citizens may be the parties engaged in the introduction of these supplies for the use of one of the belligerents.

Further on Mr. Fish says, when speaking of the decree of the 24th of March:

The objectionable decree of the 24th of March was soon followed by a proclamation of Count Valmaseda still more abhorrent to the sense of the civilized world. By this proclamation, made at Bayamo on the 4th of April, 1869, which reached the Department of State on the 9th of May, the following announcement was made to Cubans who believed, with Mr. Castelar, General Prim, Mr. Becerra, Mr. Silvela, Mr. Martos, Mr. Rivera, and other Spanish statesmen, that Cuba was suffering under oppression and wrong which ought to be remedied:

First. Every man, from the age of 15 years upward, found away from his habitation (finca), and does not prove a justified motive therefor, will be shot.

That is Weyler's decree now, with a little sugar coating:

Second. Every habitation unoccupied will be burned by the troops.

That is in full force under Weyler's decree.

Third. Every habitation from which does not float a white flag, as a signal that its occupants desire peace, will be reduced to ashes.

Women that are not living at their own homes, or at the house of their relatives, will collect in the town of Jiguani, or Bayamo, where maintenance will be provided. Those who do not present themselves will be conducted forcibly.

What will happen to them on the way God only knows. Mr. Fish further says:

The courses of trade and of social intercourse had carried many citizens of the United States into Cuba. When, therefore, this proclamation reached the undersigned, the President thought it right toward Spain that, although scarcely crediting the genuineness of the document, the undersigned should send the following notice to Mr. Lopez Roberts:

"In the interest of Christian civilization and common humanity, I hope that this document is a forgery. If it be indeed genuine, the President instructs me, in the most forcible manner, to protest against such a mode of warfare, and to ask you to request the Spanish authorities in Cuba to take such steps that no person having the right to claim the protection of the Government of the United States shall be sacrificed or injured in the conduct of hostilities upon this basis."

Mr. MILLS. Mr. President, I wish to announce to the Senate that in the morning, after the disposal of the routine business, I wish to address the Senate on the Cuban question, if there be no objection. I have been waiting for several days, and I am compelled to leave the Chamber now, or I would remain and take the floor after my friend from Alabama has concluded.

The PRESIDING OFFICER. The notice will be entered.

Mr. MORGAN. In my comments upon this matter I shall be very brief, and shall conclude in a few moments. I desire to omit everything except what is absolutely essential to my purpose to show that there exists in Cuba to-day the same condition of affairs, the same decrees, issued even by the same men, that Mr. Fish was denouncing in his letter to Admiral Polo in 1874. That was long after the message of the President of June, 1870, from which the Senator from Maine [Mr. HALE] read a brief extract:

The United States were in a state of war when the orders referred to were issued.

That is, the orders of our people.

Spain had not been slow in forcing upon them in the very incipiency of the rebellion her recognition of a state of war. She does not now recognize that she is herself at war, but appeals, as a precedent for her conduct, to rules prescribed for armies in the field. If she claims the rights, it is but logical that she accept the consequences of a state of war.

I have pointed out in the course of this debate, from the reports of our own consuls, that the Spaniards treat our exports from this country into Cuba as being contraband of war at their will and pleasure. So they claim all the rights of war, but are not willing to submit to any of its disabilities, the very case that Mr. Fish is commenting upon. Says Mr. Fish further:

The undersigned is confident that Admiral Polo will feel a sincere pleasure in thus knowing that his information respecting these instructions has been incorrect. Even had it been correct, the accomplished and generous minister from Spain and the undersigned would alike feel unwilling to contend that two wrongs could make a right.

Even in such case, however, it would be remembered that a worthy precedent might be found in the practice of the United States during a rebellion of the most mighty proportions, pending which not a prisoner was killed in cold blood; not a political crime, however grave, was visited with capital punishment. The soil of the United States remains to this day unstained by the first drop of blood taken from a political offender. Had this example been followed wherever a political insurrection had arisen, many might now be living whose blood cries aloud against the cruelty of some rulers. Christendom generally applauds the example of clemency and generosity which the United States thus exhibited.

The same spirit of generous regard for life and forgiveness marks the policy of the United States in other respects, and makes their penal codes look to the prevention more than to the punishment of crime, and often withholds the enforcement of penalties when the danger against which they are denounced is supposed to have passed. It is with much regret that it is seen from the correspondence with the representatives of Spain for the past five years, and from the frequent complaints (in the note of Admiral Polo, now acknowledged) of the omission of the United States to enforce penalties and inflict punishment, that Spain does not sympathize with the policy of clemency and forgiveness, and seems to regard punishment as the test of the sincerity with which crime is denounced and as the sole means of preventing at least political offenses. The examples of the condition of the two countries must be the criterion to determine the comparative merits of the antagonistic systems.

He then goes into an extensive discussion here of the rights of vessels on the high seas, and speaking of the restrictions imposed upon them and also of restrictions imposed upon land, he says:

In consequence of these severe measures against the persons and properties of Cubans who shared the opinions of the liberal statesmen of Spain respecting the injuries which had been inflicted upon their native country, many fled from the island to the United States. And the undersigned can not disguise from himself that these Spanish subjects, driven from their native country, have attempted to abuse the hospitality of the United States—

The very accusation that is made here now by the present minister from Spain against the refugees from Cuba—

that they have tried to make use of their safety here in order to regain what they had lost in Cuba, and that they have been restrained only by the perpetual vigilance and zeal of the officers of the United States. Alas! if the ears of the ministers of Amadeo and of the Republic could have been opened to the complaints of their Cuban friends, what criminations might have been spared us!

I believe, Mr. President, that I shall refrain from further quotations from this very remarkable and very able letter, which covers the whole subject of the present Cuban insurrection. I noticed while that war was in progress Mr. Fish called the attention of the Spanish Government in this letter to twenty-two cases of serious outrage against the property and lives of American citizens which remained to be adjusted after the war was over. I do not want to pile up a docket of that kind under these circumstances; I do not want to stand by until murder has been perpetrated, attended with extreme cruelty and outrage, and to wait until some future time when, possibly, this revolutionary movement may be crushed out, for us to demand of Spain as many even as twenty-two cases of reclamation and damages for wrongs we have suffered.

We have suffered enough; we have spent enough money in standing guard for Spain, and in keeping our people out of Cuba, and in restraining them, and in capturing their property and confiscating it when the slightest proof of conspiracy could be found to exist in regard to a purpose of invasion of Cuba—we have spent enough, and we have suffered enough, and have stood these outrages long enough; and, now that Spain is engaged in a war with Cuba that, evidently, is hopeless, I think, sir, that we may be pardoned if we express our opinion, to say the least of it, that war prevails there, and that those people ought to be entitled to the rights of belligerency, and our people ought to be entitled to the rights of neutrality, and be allowed the benefits of neutrality.

I regret, Mr. President, that I have had to spend so much time in the discussion of this question; I never went into anything with more reluctance; but I have felt compelled to take all this toil upon myself simply because, in the accident of the passage of the resolutions through the committee it devolved upon me to make the report of the action of the committee, which put me in charge virtually of these resolutions.

Sir, when we met in conference we found that the disagreement in these opinions of the two Houses related only to verbal criticisms, and nothing more. I have said before, and I repeat it, that the resolutions of either body would be entirely satisfactory to me; but in the House of Representatives, immediately after we sent our resolution to them, there was reported a resolution which involves a mere difference in stating an opinion and caused no jar upon my feelings or sensibilities. I remembered that we were attempting to do nothing but to express our opinions.

After the resolution of the Senate went over to the House it there met the resolution reported from the Committee on Foreign Affairs, to which, of course, the House of Representatives felt naturally disposed to adhere. They passed their resolution; it was brought here; we disagreed to the amendment which they proposed to the Senate resolution; and that disagreement brought us into a conference. In that conference we considered both of the resolutions, in fact, the whole programme of our previous action in both committees; and I think that we came to a patriotic conclusion when we determined that the two Houses of Congress, in taking this mild but firm action on our part, would do injustice to the will, to the honor, to the express professions and belief of the people of this country if we should recede and find that we were incapable of agreeing in the method of the expression of our opinions.

There is no preference in favor of the one over the other, except that I believe, as I said to the committee at the time the resolutions were before it, that the passage of the amendment which was offered by the Senator from Pennsylvania [Mr. CAMERON], to the effect that the President of the United States shall use his good offices with the Government of Spain to induce that Government to recognize the independence of Cuba, might be considered by that Government, and very naturally I think would be considered by that Government, as an intrusive overture on our part, irritating to their feelings. I have not any doubt that such would be the fact.

Now, I repeat what I have said on several occasions since I have been on my feet to-day. I do not wish to give to Spain or to any nation of this earth any apparent ground for criticising our action. I want us to stand on a line that includes our rights beyond dispute. That is the reason I have been willing to put up with opinions when I believed that acts ought to have been the expression of our opinions. I have never had any doubt that even the expression of an opinion unfavorable to the fanatical and deluded monarchy would be regarded as an act of hostility that would compel Spain to throw down the gage of war.

APPENDIX.

No. 21.

Mr. Fish to Admiral Polo de Bernabé.

DEPARTMENT OF STATE, *Washington, April 18, 1874.*

The undersigned, Secretary of State of the United States, has the honor to acknowledge the reception of the note of 2d of February last, which his excellency Admiral Polo de Bernabé, the envoy extraordinary and minister plenipotentiary of Spain, addressed to him respecting the *Virginius*, and the assumed relations of the United States toward the insurrection in Cuba.

The pressure of business incident to the session of Congress and a severe indisposition have prevented an earlier reply to that note.

The undersigned has observed with regret in Admiral Polo's note harsh expressions and unwarranted criticisms upon the official conduct of officers of the United States which he feels confident would not have obtained admission to the paper had they attracted the attention of the accomplished minister of Spain, whose sense of justice would not allow him to give expression to what his sensitiveness and regard for the proprieties of diplomatic correspondence would not permit him calmly to accept.

The undersigned finds in the historical part of Admiral Polo's note many misapprehensions of facts (as the facts are understood by this Government), and many errors of omission, which need to be corrected before entering upon the particular argument respecting the *Virginius*. The undersigned will endeavor to do this as briefly as possible.

The insurrection which broke out at Yara in the autumn of 1868 has had the unusual good fortune of having the justice of the complaints which it alleges in its justification recognized by those who are engaged in suppressing it. On the 10th of September, 1869, the minister of transmarine affairs at Madrid, in an official paper, said:

"A deplorable and pertinacious tradition of despotism, which, if it could ever be justified, is without a shadow of reason at the present time, intrusted the direction and management of our colonial establishment to the agents of the metropolis, destroying by their dominant and exclusive authority the vital energies of the country and the creative and productive activity of free individuals. And although the system may now have improved in some of its details, the domineering action of the authorities being less felt, it still appears full of the original error, which is upheld by the force of tradition, and the necessary influence of interests created under their protection, which, doubtless, are deserving of respect so far as they are reconcilable with the requirements of justice, with the common welfare, and with the principles on which every liberal system should be founded. A change of system, political as well as administrative, is therefore imperatively demanded."

But while admitting the existence of the injuries which had provoked the outbreak at Yara, the government of the revolution of 1868 refused to remedy them until the armed insurrection be suppressed. "Spain would already have given all constitutional liberties to Cuba," said Mr. Silvela to General Sickles, "if the unfortunate insurrection of Yara and the cry of 'Death to Spain,' uttered by some Cubans, had not alienated the sympathies of the nation and obliged the Government to accept the impolitic contest to which it was provoked. The Government considers that it can come to no definite decision in regard to the political situation and future government of the Island of Cuba until the insurgents lay down their arms and cease the struggle." This would indicate that it is the resistance to admitted wrongs, and not the wrongfulness of resistance, which Spain is endeavoring to repress.

One of the two great questions at issue between the insurgents and the authorities of Spain was understood to be the future condition of the African race in the island. The insurgents, as early as the 26th of February, 1869, decreed the abolition of slavery "in the name of liberty and the people." This act met with no response from Spain. The eloquent Mr. Castellar, when a member of the Cortes, without the responsibilities of government, said:

"I am an advocate of abolition in Cuba, with a due regard to all interests. I am an advocate of colonial reforms, and of every possible liberty to Cuba and Puerto Rico."

But when, in the turn of events, he attained to power, he was unable to do anything for Cuba, and retired with slavery untouched and with reforms still a dream.

It can not be a matter for wonder that persons in other lands sympathized with the great and liberal statesmen of Spain in their convictions that a large measure of reform was needed in Cuba, and held that one of the greatest of all was the abolition of slavery. And perhaps less surprise will be manifested that such sympathizers in other lands could not comprehend why such distinguished statesmen should insist upon subjugating the Cubans, who had taken up arms to resist oppression, before consenting to relieve them from the wrongs which they were admitted to be enduring.

It must be frankly confessed that there were many persons in the United States who shared the theoretical opinions of the Spanish statesmen, but who could not agree in the diametrically opposite policy which Spain pursued toward Cuba under their directions.

It was natural for the people of the United States to feel an interest in the prosperity of Cuba. This and the reasons for it were well understood at Madrid. Mr. Martos, in the presence of his colleagues, Mr. Becerra and Mr. Rivero, had officially spoken to General Sickles of "the common interests shared by the United States and Spain in Cuba." He said "that whatever retarded the prosperity of the island was injurious alike to both countries; that the welfare of Cuba was of more commercial importance to the United States than to the mother country."

This wise statesman might have added that the interest of the United States in Cuba was heightened by a desire that the deadly struggle on the island might end in the acquisition of self-government (whether under or free from Spanish rule was, of course, immaterial to an American) and in the abolition of slavery. Such was undoubtedly the fact. The undersigned feels convinced that these views were shared by the mass of the liberal statesmen of Spain, modified, probably, by the patriotic wish that the island should retain its political connection with Spain. But it could not be expected that foreigners would share in the full warmth of this wish of Spanish statesmen. The mass of the people of the United States certainly gave little heed to the matter beyond the natural preference that a disturbing element of European politics should be removed from the American system.

In the rapid progress of events, however, they, in common with the rest of the civilized world, were soon forced to give attention to Cuban affairs. The authorities in that island began to exercise rights of war in time of peace, and to trample out liberties which their superiors at Madrid desired to maintain and extend.

Admiral Polo expresses the opinion that the insurrection "did not find extensive sympathies in the Island of Cuba," and that "it was but a little while before its locality was limited to the eastern part of the island."

Such was not the tenor of the information received at this Department.

It is now more than five years since the uprising, and it has been announced, with apparent authority, that Spain has lost upward of 80,000 men and has expended upward of $100,000,000 in efforts to suppress it; yet the insurrection seems to-day as active and as powerful as it has ever been. And the suggestion that its locality was limited to the eastern part of the island leads one to inquire whether Villa Clara and the other of the Cinco Villas, and the railway between Nuevitas and Puerto Principe, are in that district.

Indeed, until the receipt of Admiral Polo's note, the undersigned had supposed that the extent of the disaffection in Cuba was urged as an extenuating motive for the remarkable series of measures which the undersigned will soon notice.

Soon after the outbreak of the insurrection this Government, of its own accord, without being thereto moved by the representative of Spain, caused inquiries to be made respecting "rumors of a projected expedition against Cuba" from New York, with a view, should circumstances require it, to the issue of such instructions as might be necessary for "the defeat of the schemes in question." The officer charged with the inquiry answered that he had made a thorough investigation, and added:

"It is true that a number of well-known filibusters have opened an office at 498 Broome street, in this city (New York), for the ostensible purpose of enlisting men for the invasion of the Island of Cuba, but really with a view of making money out of the resident Cubans in this city who sympathize with the cause. But I am happy to inform you that thus far they have been unsuccessful."

This fact, which exhibits the anxiety of this Government to perform its international duties, is apparently referred to by Admiral Polo with a purpose of showing a want of diligence on its part in that respect; since, in quoting the report of the officer, the passage which is underscored is omitted.

On the 24th of March, 1869, the Captain-General of Cuba issued a decree, which is referred to by Admiral Polo, and from which the following is an extract:

"Vessels which may be captured in Spanish waters, or on the high seas near to the island, having on board men, arms, and munitions, or effects that can in any manner contribute, promote, or foment the insurrection in this province, whatsoever their derivation and destination, after examination of their papers and register, shall be de facto considered as enemies of the integrity of our territory, and treated as pirates, in accordance with the ordinances of the navy.

"All persons captured in such vessels, without regard to their number, will be immediately executed."

A copy of this decree was received at this Department on the 2d of April,

2777

1869, and the undersigned, although but then just entered upon the duties of his office and greatly pressed with other public matters requiring immediate attention, put everything aside, by direction of the President, and on the next date wrote as follows to the minister of Spain at Washington:

"It is to be regretted that so high a functionary as the Captain-General of Cuba should, as this paper seems to indicate, have overlooked the obligations of his Government pursuant to the law of nations, and especially its promises in the treaty between the United States and Spain of 1795.

"Under that law and treaty the United States expect for their citizens and vessels the privilege of carrying to the enemies of Spain, whether those enemies be claimed as Spanish subjects or citizens of other countries, subject only to the requirements of a legal blockade, all merchandise not contraband of war. Articles contraband of war when destined for the enemies of Spain are liable to seizure on the high seas; but the right of seizure is limited to such articles only, and no claim for its extension to other merchandise, or to persons not in the civil, military, or naval service of the enemies of Spain, will be acquiesced in by the United States.

"This Government certainly can not assent to the punishment by Spanish authorities of any citizen of the United States for the exercise of a privilege to which he may be entitled under public law and treaties.

"It is consequently hoped that his excellency the Captain-General of Cuba will either recall the proclamation referred to or will give such instructions to the proper officers as will prevent its illegal application to citizens of the United States or their property. A contrary course might endanger those friendly and cordial relations between the two Governments which it is the hearty desire of the President should be maintained."

The order to indiscriminately slaughter "all persons captured in such vessels, without regard to their number," could not but shock the sensibilities of all humane persons. The undersigned felt, however, unwilling to object to the execution of the order except when proposed to be enforced against citizens of the United States.

Almost simultaneously with the receipt of this startling news, Mr. Lopez Roberts, on April 5, 1869, made of the undersigned the request referred to by Admiral Polo, that the President should issue a proclamation to restrain military expeditions against Cuba, accompanying the request with allegations "that piratical expeditions are in preparation against the legitimate government of Spain in Cuba," and that "arms and ammunition are sent there in sailing vessels and steamers."

In regard to the second point thus stated by Admiral Polo's esteemed predecessor, the undersigned was constrained by due regard to universally recognized principles of international rights and duties to declare that in the absence of a recognized state of war it was no offense in the sailing vessels and steamers of the United States to carry arms and munitions of war for whomsoever it might concern. The undersigned has uniformly said that no government can by the law of nations be held responsible for shipments of arms, munitions, or materials of war made by private individuals at their own risk and peril. If a state of war should exist, if Spain should be entitled to the rights of a belligerent, parties concerned in the shipment of arms and military supplies for her enemy would incur the risk of confiscation by her of their goods; but their act would involve no ground of reclamation against their government in behalf of Spain, and consequently no right to invoke the aid of that government in preventing the perpetration of the act. Such it is believed is the established law of nations, and such the received rule even when the shipment of arms and munitions is made from the territory of the country whose citizens may be the parties engaged in the introduction of these supplies for the use of one of the belligerents.

In regard to the first point thus taken by Mr. Lopez Roberts, the undersigned could not but observe that the allegations respecting alleged piratical expeditions were not only wholly unsupported by proof, but were in themselves extremely improbable.

It is quite competent for a state to apply the term of "piracy" by its municipal acts to any offenses, however trivial, and to affix to them punishments it may deem appropriate. But in thus applying the title of a crime known to international law to offenses created by municipal law, it can not invoke upon the latter penalties which international law denounces against the crimes which the nations of the world recognize as "piracy."

Within its own territorial jurisdiction the application of terms and of epithets, or even the denunciation of punishments, except so far as they may offend humanity or the civilization of the age, might not be objected to; and the undersigned does not at present feel called upon to deny that the penalties thus denounced may be enforced (without right or question by other powers) upon those who may commit the acts to which these terms are applied within the territory of the state enacting the municipal law. But it would be inappropriate to apply either such definitions of crime or penalties to matters occurring without its territorial jurisdiction or in discussions with other powers.

Piracy, as an offense against the unwritten but universally recognized law of nations, has been made the subject of many definitions. The definition by Wheaton, as explained by his commentator, Dana, would probably be recognized by the courts of all civilized powers.

Wheaton defines this crime "to be the offense of depredating on the seas without being authorized by any sovereign state, or with commission from different sovereigns at war with each other;" and Dana, in his note upon this definition, says "to constitute piracy jure gentium, it is necessary, first, that the offense be adequate in degree—for instance, robbery, destruction by fire, or other injury to persons or property—must be committed on the high seas and not within the territorial jurisdiction of any nation; and second, that the offenders, at the time of the commission of the act, should be in fact free from lawful authority, or should have made themselves so by their deed, or, as Sir L. Jenkins says, 'out of the protection of all laws and privileges,' or, in the words of Duc de Broglie, 'quin'a ni feu ni lieu;' in short, they must be in the predicament of outlaws."

It did not appear to the undersigned from any evidence that was laid before him at that time by Mr. Lopez Roberts, or from any other source, that any parties were undertaking or contemplating military expeditions from the United States against Cuba, or were proposing to make any "piratical expeditions."

The undersigned therefore felt constrained to reply, on the 17th of the same April, in the following language:

"After a careful examination of Mr. Roberts's note, the undersigned fails to perceive the necessity or the propriety at this time of a proclamation by the President of the United States such as Mr. Roberts desires.

"The publication of an instrument of the character asked by Mr. Roberts would be the exercise of a power by the President which is resorted to only on extraordinary occasions and when peculiar circumstances indicate its necessity. Such a power is not to be invoked lightly, or when the laws are in unquestioned vigor and efficiency, are respected by all persons, and are enforced by the ordinary agencies.

"At present this Government is not aware of any invasion of the Island of Cuba, or of any other possessions of Spain threatened from the United States, nor is any such believed to be in the course of preparation. Mr. Roberts has, on several occasions, intimated to the undersigned the existence of individual or private attempts in different parts of the country to violate the neutrality laws of the United States. In every such instance, as Mr. Roberts very justly admits in his note, the proper officers of the Government have been called upon immediately to vindicate the supremacy of the law, and no single instance is known or is believed to have arisen in which their interference, thus invoked, has not been efficient to prevent the apprehended violation."

The justice of these views of the undersigned on the 17th of April, 1869, have been amply vindicated by subsequent events.

Instead of resorting to the exceptionable and uncertain measure of a proclamation, this Government availed itself of the agency of special and peremptory instructions to executive officers; and by this means succeeded in preventing the formation of military expeditions in every case referred to by Admiral Polo, except in the case of the *Catharine Whiting*, and in that case it entirely broke up the proposed expedition by the use of force.

The objectionable decree of the 24th of March was soon followed by a proclamation of Count Valmaseda still more abhorrent to the sense of the civilized world. By this proclamation, made at Bayamo on the 4th of April, 1869, which reached the Department of State on the 9th of May, the following announcement was made to Cubans who believed, with Mr. Castelar, General Prim, Mr. Becerra, Mr. Silvela, Mr. Martos, Mr. Rivera, and other Spanish statesmen, that Cuba was suffering under oppression and wrong which ought to be remedied.

"First. Every man, from the age of 15 years upward, found away from his habitation (finca), and does not prove a justified motive therefor, will be shot.

"Second. Every habitation unoccupied will be burned by the troops.

"Third. Every habitation from which does not float a white flag, as a signal that its occupants desire peace, will be reduced to ashes.

"Women that are not living at their own homes, or the house of their relatives, will collect in the town of Jiguani or Bayamo, where maintenance will be provided. Those who do not present themselves will be conducted forcibly."

The courses of trade and of social intercourse had carried many citizens of the United States into Cuba. When, therefore, this proclamation reached the undersigned, the President thought it right toward Spain that, although scarcely crediting the genuineness of the document, the undersigned should send the following notice to Mr. Lopez Roberts:

"In the interest of Christian civilization and common humanity, I hope that this document is a forgery. If it be indeed genuine, the President instructs me, in the most forcible manner, to protest against such a mode of warfare, and to ask you to request the Spanish authorities in Cuba to take such steps that no person having the right to claim the protection of the Government of the United States shall be sacrificed or injured in the conduct of hostilities upon this basis."

Admiral Polo now attempts to defend these orders by saying that—

"Such rigorous measures are not confined exclusively to Spain; that the code of instruction for armies in the field published by the War Department of the United States during the civil war which terminated in 1865 authorized the destruction of every kind of property belonging to the enemy, and the penalty of death on every one who, in a section of territory occupied or subjected by one of the Federal armies, attempted to resist said army or the authorities which it had established."

The United States were in a state of war when the orders referred to were issued. Spain had not been slow in forcing upon them in the very incipiency of the rebellion her recognition of a state of war. She does not now recognize that she is herself at war, but appeals, as a precedent for her conduct, to rules prescribed for armies in the field. If she claims the rights, it is but logical that she accept the consequences of a state of war.

The instructions for the government of armies of the United States in the field referred to by Admiral Polo were promulgated on the 24th of April, 1863. The undersigned takes the liberty of quoting several passages from them, which sufficiently illustrate the humane and Christian spirit which pervades them—a spirit characterized by Dr. Bluntschli as "en corrélation avec les idées actuelles de l'humanité et la manière de faire la guerre chez les peuples civilisés:"

"Martial law is simply military authority exercised in accordance with the laws and usages of war. Military oppression is not martial law; it is the abuse of the power which that law confers. As martial law is executed by military force, it is incumbent upon those who administer it to be strictly guided by the principles of justice, honor, and humanity, virtues adorning a soldier even more than other men, for the very reason that he possesses the power of his arms against the unarmed.

"Military necessity admits of all direct destruction of life or limb of armed enemies and of other persons whose destruction is incidentally unavoidable in the armed contests of the war.

"Nevertheless, as civilization has advanced during the last centuries, so has likewise steadily advanced, especially in war on land, the distinction between the private individual belonging to a hostile country and a hostile country itself with its men in arms. The principle has been more and more acknowledged that the unarmed citizen is to be spared in person, property, and honor as much as the exigencies of the war will admit.

"The United States acknowledge and protect, in hostile countries occupied by them, religion and morality; strictly private property; the persons of the inhabitants, especially those of women, and the sacredness of domestic relations. Offenses to the contrary shall be rigorously punished.

"Modern wars are not internecine wars, in which the killing of the enemy is the object. The destruction of the enemy in modern war, and indeed modern war itself, means to obtain that object of the belligerent which lies beyond the war. Unnecessary and revengeful destruction of life is unlawful."

The undersigned is confident that Admiral Polo will feel a sincere pleasure in thus knowing that his information respecting these instructions has been incorrect. Even had it been correct, the accomplished and generous minister from Spain and the undersigned would alike feel unwilling to contend that two wrongs could make a right.

Even in such case, however, it would be remembered that a worthy precedent might be found in the practice of the United States during a rebellion of the most mighty proportions, pending which not a prisoner was killed in cold blood; not a political crime, however grave, was visited with capital punishment. The soil of the United States remains to this day unstained by the first drop of blood taken from a political offender. Had this example been followed wherever a political insurrection has arisen, many might now be living whose blood cries aloud against the cruelty of some rulers. Christendom generally applauds the example of clemency and of generosity which the United States thus exhibited.

The same spirit of generous regard for life and forgiveness marks the policy of the United States in other respects, and makes their penal codes look to the prevention more than to the punishment of crime, and often withholds the enforcement of penalties when the danger against which they are denounced is supposed to have passed. It is with much regret that it is seen from the correspondence with the representatives of Spain for the past five years, and from the frequent complaints (in the note of Admiral Polo, now acknowledged) of the omission of the United States to enforce penalties and inflict punishment, that Spain does not sympathize with the policy of clemency and forgiveness, and seems to regard punishment as the test of the sincerity with which crime is denounced, and as the sole means of preventing at least political offenses. The examples of the condition of the two countries must be the criterion to determine the comparative merits of the antagonist systems.

Prior to this time (namely, on the 12th of February, 1869), a decree, with an explanatory statement, had been issued by the Captain-General, taking from the jurisdiction of the ordinary courts a large class of crimes, and forcing American citizens charged with such crimes to be tried before a court-martial, in violation of the provisions of the treaty of 1795. When it is remembered that this decree was issued about the time when it was officially announced to the undersigned that " the rebels have no communication with each other, they occupy no place as a center of operations, nor have they in the whole island a single city, a single town, a single village or hamlet, nor even a point on the coast where they might collect their forces and date their orders and proclamations," Admiral Polo will comprehend the magnitude of this assault upon the rights secured to citizens of the United States by the treaty of 1795.

The English translation of the text of this decree is as follows:

"In use of the extraordinary faculties with which the provisional Government of the nation has invested me, I decree the following:

"ARTICLE 1. Crimes of infidencia shall be tried by ordinary court-martial.

"ART. 2. Prosecutions already commenced shall follow the legal process prescribed by the laws for the tribunals of justice.

"ART. 3. All aggressions, by act or by word, against any of the delegates of the Government, shall be considered as a crime against the authority, and will subject its author to trial by court-martial.

"DOMINGO DULCE.

"HABANA, *February 12, 1869.*"

"SUPERIOR POLITICAL GOVERNMENT OF THE EVER-FAITHFUL ISLAND OF CUBA—OFFICE OF THE SECRETARY.

"For the better understanding of the decree published yesterday (the 12th of February) it is made known that under the word infidencia, which is made use of in article 1, are understood the following crimes: Treason, or lesa nacion, rebellion, insurrection, conspiracy, sedition, harboring of rebels and criminals, intelligence with the enemy, meetings of journeymen or laborers and leagues, expressions, cries, or voices subversive or seditious, propagation of alarming news, manifestations, allegations, and all that, with a political end, tends to disturb public tranquillity and order, or that in any mode attacks the national integrity.

"It is also made known that robbery in uninhabited districts, whatever may be the number of the robbers, and in populated districts, if the number of the robbers be more than three, shall be tried by court-martial, as also the bearers of prohibited arms. And by order of his excellency the superior political governor, the same is published in the Gazette for the general knowledge."

On the 15th of April, 1869, the same policy which had prompted the authorities in Cuba to deprive citizens of the United States of personal rights guaranteed to them by treaty led to a decree of embargoes of property, which, so far as it applied to the properties of citizens of the United States, was also in direct violation of the rights secured by the treaty of 1795. The publication of this decree was followed by the publication of another decree (made on the 1st day of April), interfering with the free alienation of property on the island. And two days later another decree was published, creating an administrative council, to take charge of the embargoed estates. Under the operation of these several decrees a vast amount of the property of citizens of the United States is understood to have (illegally, and in violation of law and right) come into the possession of subjects of Spain, without having yet been accounted for or refunded.

When these decrees came to the knowledge of the undersigned, he addressed the following communication to the predecessor of Admiral Polo, under date of April 30, 1869:

"I am instructed by the President to inform you that this Department has received from the United States consulate in Cuba a decree dated the 1st day of April current, and promulgated by the Captain-General of the island on the 15th of this month, which virtually forbids the alienation of property in the island, except with the revision and assent of certain officials named in the decree, and which declares null and void all sales made without such revision and assent.

"In view of the intimate commercial relations between Cuba and the United States, and of the great amount of American property constantly invested there in commercial ventures as well as in a more permanent form, the President views with regret such sweeping interference with the rights of individuals to alienate or dispose of their property, and he hopes that steps may be speedily taken to modify this decree so that it shall not be applicable to the property of citizens of the United States, and thus prevent disputes and complaints that can not fail to arise if its execution is attempted as to such property."

2777

It is with regret that the undersigned finds himself unable to accept the declaration in Admiral Polo's note, made in connection with the seizure of private estates and the transfers of private property, that it was not without waiting for manifestations of disloyal sentiments and purposes that the decrees were made respecting the sales and embargoes. The undersigned is of opinion that a recurrence to the correspondence which he has had the honor to conduct with the Spanish legation in this capital, and through the legation of this Government at Madrid, will recall many instances of interference with the private rights and property of citizens of the United States who have had no connection with the insurrectionary movements in Cuba, and many where Spain has practically admitted the precipitancy of her officers in their haste to lay hands on private property, and has in many instances promised, and in a very few instances has granted, the restoration of property thus unlawfully seized. And in this connection the undersigned must be permitted to express the regret with which he observes the introduction into a diplomatic note of the cases of "eminent banking and commercial houses of New York and other places," which, by agreement between the two Governments, have been referred for adjudication to an international commission, and the prejudgment and denunciation of these eminent houses as having "lent their names to a pretext."

On the 7th of July, 1869, the captain-general of Cuba decreed:

"ARTICLE 1. There shall continue closed to import and export trade, as well for vessels in foreign commerce as also those in the coasting trade, all the ports situated from Cayo Bahia de Cadiz to Punta Mayso, on the north, and from Punta Mayso to Cienfuegos, on the south, with the exception of those of Sagua la Grande, Caibarien, Nuevitas, Gibara, Baracoa, Guantanamo, Santiago de Cuba, Manzanillo, Santa Cruz, Zaza, Casilda, or Trinidad, and Cienfuegos, in which there are established custom-houses or collection offices.

"Those who attempt to enter the closed ports or to hold communication with the coast shall be pursued, and, on being apprehended, prosecuted as infractors of the laws.

"ART. 2. In accordance with the same, there shall also be prosecuted vessels carrying powder, arms, or military supplies.

"ART. 3. The transportation of individuals for the services of the insurrection is much more grave than that of contraband, and will be considered as an act decidedly hostile, being proceeded against in such case as an enemy, the vessel and its crew.

"ART. 4. If the individuals to which the preceding article refers come armed, they will afford proof in fact of their intentions, and will be tried as pirates, the same as the crew of the vessel.

"ART. 5. There shall also be held to be pirates, in conformity with law, vessels which may be seized bearing a flag not recognized, whether the same be armed or not as vessels of war.

"ART. 6. On the high seas contiguous to those of this island the cruisers shall confine themselves to exercise over such vessels as may be denounced, or those that by their proceedings excite suspicion, the rights stipulated in the treaties signed by Spain with the United States in 1795, with Great Britain in 1835, and with other nations subsequently, and if in the exercise of these rights vessels should be found recognized as enemies of the integrity of the territory, they shall be brought into port for the corresponding legal investigation and trial."

This extraordinary decree caused a profound sensation in the United States, and the undersigned, as soon as it was received, addressed a note of inquiry to the predecessor of Admiral Polo, dated July 16, 1869, the material parts of which he takes the liberty of transcribing, as Admiral Polo seems to be under a misapprehension respecting it:

"The decree of the captain-general, De Rodas, assumes powers and rights over the trade and commerce of other peoples inconsistent with a state of peace, and which the United States can be expected to allow their vessels to be subjected to only when Spain avows herself to be in a state of war, or shall be manifestly exercising the rights conceded only to belligerents in the time of war.

"The first article of the decree proposes to close certain ports, embracing a large extent of the Island of Cuba, against the peaceful commerce of foreign countries. Without contesting the right of a government in time of peace to exclude from its ports the trade and commerce of a friendly people, the undersigned assumes that the exercise of this power is to be understood purely as a municipal act, to be executed and enforced wholly within the recognized exclusive jurisdiction of Spain, and only as to ports which are in the possession of the Spanish authorities. In case the success of the insurrectionary party should put any of the ports declared to be closed in their possession, the United States, as a maritime nation, will regard an effective blockade to be necessary to the exclusion of their commerce.

"The second article of the decree is vague in the absence of the limits within which it proposes to prohibit the carrying of powder, arms, or military supplies.

2777

"The transportation on the high seas, in time of peace, of articles commonly known as contraband of war is a legitimate traffic and commerce which can not be interfered with or denounced unless by a power at war with a third party in the admitted exercise of the recognized rights of a belligerent. The freedom of the ocean can nowhere and under no circumstances be yielded by the United States. The high seas contiguous to those of the Island of Cuba are a direct pathway of a large part of the purely domestic trade of the United States. Their vessels trading between their ports in the Gulf of Mexico and those of the Atlantic coast pass necessarily through these waters. The greater part of the trade between the ports of the United States on the eastern side of the continent and those on the Pacific Slope of necessity pass in sight of the Island of Cuba.

"The United States can not, then, be indifferent or silent under a decree which, by the vagueness of its terms, may be construed to allow their vessels on the high seas, whatever may be their cargo, to be embarrassed or interfered with. If Spain be at war with Cuba, the United States will submit to those rights which public law concedes to belligerents. But while Spain disclaims a state of belligerency, or until the United States may find it necessary to recognize her as a belligerent, the Government of the United States can not fail to look with solicitude upon a decree which, if enforced against any vessel of the United States on the high seas, can not but be regarded as a violation of their rights that may lead to serious complications.

"The sixth article of the decree refers to certain rights claimed to be stipulated by the treaty entered into between Spain and the United States in 1795.

"The undersigned desires to call the attention of Mr. Roberts and of the Government of Spain to the fact that the treaty of 1795 confers upon neither of the contracting parties any rights on the high seas over the vessels of the other in time of peace.

"The articles of the treaty of 1795 from I to XI, inclusive, define and regulate the reciprocal relations and obligations of the parties without reference to either party being engaged in war. The portion of the treaty from the twelfth article to the eighteenth contemplates exclusively their relations as neutrals, the duties and powers of each toward the other when one or the other may be engaged in war with a third party. The eighteenth section recognizes and regulates the right of visit or of approaching time of war, for the inspection of the passport and the identification of the nationality of a vessel of commerce by the vessels of war, or by any privateer of the nation which shall be at war. It confers no right; it limits and prescribes the manner of exercising a belligerent right when such may exist.

"The clear object and intent of this provision of the treaty is the avoidance of discussion and annoyance and the prevention of abuse or indiscretion in the exercise of a belligerent right. Its location in the treaty, the recognition of the right of a privateer (who has no existence except in war) as having the same power and right in the particular referred to with a national vessel of war, and the whole scope and aim of the eighteenth article of the treaty, established beyond possibility of question that it refers only to the rights which one of the parties may have by reason of being in a state of war.

"The treaty authorizes nothing but the inspection of the passport of the vessel of trade met with, while the sixth article of the decree of General De Rodas contemplates a search as to the character of the vessel beyond the limitation fixed by the treaty.

"If Spain be engaged in the war, it is essential to the rights, as well as to the definition of the duties, of the people of the United States that they be publicly and authoritatively advised thereof and admonished as to their obligations and liabilities in their new relation with a friendly power. And such admonition admits of no avoidable delay in view of the vast commerce that will thus be subjected to restriction, limitation, and possible detention.

"The undersigned therefore respectfully desires to be informed by Mr. Roberts, at the earliest practicable moment, whether, in the issuance of this decree, it is to be understood by the United States that Spain recognizes that she is in a state of war and claims the rights of a belligerent.

"The undersigned has the honor further to say to Mr. Roberts that the Government of the United States can not fail to regard the continuance of the decree referred to, or any exercise on the high seas near the Island of Cuba, by any vessel of war or privateer of Spain, of the right to visit or board any vessel of the United States, under color of the provisions of the treaty of 1795, as involving the logical conclusion of a recognition by Spain of a state of war with Cuba.

"Before concluding, the undersigned begs to call Mr. Roberts's attention to the very grave complication which might ensue from any interference with a vessel of the United States engaged in a lawful voyage, passing near the Island of Cuba. The United States maintain the right of their flag to cover and protect their ships on the high seas.

"In conclusion, the undersigned expresses the hope that Mr. Roberts will speedily be at liberty to announce the formal abrogation of a decree which causes so much serious apprehension to the Government of the United States, and against which this Government feels bound most earnestly to remonstrate."

In deference, as it was understood, to these views expressed by the undersigned on behalf of this Government, the decree of the Captain-General was modified as follows on the 18th of July, 1869:

"In view of the determinations adopted by the Government of the United States of America, as reported by his excellency the minister of Spain in Washington, under date of the 15th instant, and which were published in the Official Gazette of the following day, and in order at the same time to relieve legitimate commerce from all unnecessary interference, in use of the faculties which are conferred upon me by the supreme Government of the nation, I have determined to modify my decree of the 7th instant, leaving the same reduced to the first five and essential articles."

In consequence of these severe measures against the persons and properties of Cubans who shared the opinions of the liberal statesmen of Spain respecting the injuries which had been inflicted upon their native country, many fled from the island to the United States. And the undersigned can not disguise from himself that these Spanish subjects, driven from their native country, have attempted to abuse the hospitality of the United States, that they have tried to make use of their safety here in order to regain what they had lost in Cuba, and that they have been restrained only by the perpetual vigilance and zeal of the officers of the United States. Alas, if the ears of the ministers of Amadeo and of the republic could have opened to the complaints of their Cuban friends, what criminations might have been spared us!

Admiral Polo, in his review of the vessels which, he says, have taken or attempted to take men and arms from the United States to Cuba, speaks particularly of the *Mary Lowell*, the *Salvador*, the *Grapeshot*, the *Catherine Whiting*, the *Hornet*, the *Lillian*, the *Upton*, and the *Virginius*. He also makes reference to the *Florida*, the *Edgar Stuart*, the *Anna*, the *Fanny*, and the *Webster*.

The imperfect and in many respects erroneous manner in which Admiral Polo has referred to the vessels which he has named, and his entire neglect to notice the many proofs of the constant vigilance and of the anxious desire of the United States to perform all their international duties to Spain, make it necessary for the undersigned to give a brief review of what was actually done by the United States in respect of these matters.

It may give precision to the review to first define succinctly what the United States understand to have been their duties toward Spain as a neighbor and as a friend.

The repeated references by Admiral Polo to the doctrines laid down in the course of the discussion at Geneva induce the undersigned to say at the outset not only that the particular references and citations are from the argument of counsel, which in forensic discussions among all nations is permitted to take a wider latitude of expression than is usual in official or judicial statements, which are supposed to express settled convictions; but also that these discussions at Geneva were predicated upon the admission of a recognized state of war; and that if Spain is prepared to concede that there is a state of war in Cuba, with belligerent rights in each party to the conflict, and shall accede to the three rules set forth in the treaty of Washington, then the United States may be prepared to concede to Spain what they claimed of Great Britain at Geneva, namely, that their duties as a neutral toward Spain as a belligerent will not thereafter be fully performed by simply acting upon information which may be furnished by Spanish agents, without themselves originating any action; that, in the language of their own countercase at Geneva, "they would not thereby be relieved from the duty of an independent, diligent, and vigilant watchfulness in order to prevent evil-disposed persons from violating their neutrality."

But the undersigned is also constrained to insist that the idea of neutrality in international discussions is inseparable from the idea of a belligerency to which the neutral is not a party; and to repeat that he is unable to comprehend how propositions for the regulation of the conduct of a neutral in a state of war can be pertinently applied to the conduct of one sovereign state toward another friendly sovereign state in time of peace. Thus, when Peru, between whom and Spain a state of war existed, requested the United States to detain a large number of vessels of war which certain contractors were constructing within the territories of the United States for Spain, it became the duty of the United States to detain the vessels; but, when the assent to their release was given by Peru, it was not regarded by Spain or by the United States as any violation of international duty to permit the vessels to be constructed and delivered and dispatched, notwithstanding the existence of an armed insurrection against Spain in Cuba. Nor can it be claimed that the United States have been guilty of any neglect or want of duty in allowing Spain on more than one occasion to make use of their public dockyards for the preparation of vessels of war.

So far as relates to the past, Spain has never been willing to concede that a state of war exists in Cuba. The rights and duties of the United States toward Spain, therefore, from the commencement of the insurrection, are to be measured by the rights and duties of one nation toward another in case an insurrection exists which does not rise to the dignity of recognized war.

What one power in such case may not knowingly permit to be done toward another power, without violating its international duties, is defined with sufficient accuracy in the statute of 1818, known as the neutrality law of the United States.

It may not consent to the enlistment within its territorial jurisdiction of naval and military forces intended for the service of the insurrection.

It may not knowingly permit the fitting out and arming or the increasing or augmenting the force of any ship or vessel within its territorial jurisdiction, with intent that such ship or vessel shall be employed in the service of the insurrection.

It may not knowingly permit the setting on foot of military expeditions or enterprises to be carried on from its territory against the power with which the insurrection is contending.

The learned and accomplished minister of Spain, toward the close of his able discussion of this subject, cites the authority of Lord Palmerston to establish that a sovereign power "should not permit its territory to be made use of as a place of shelter from which communication should be carried on for the purpose of disturbing the tranquillity of the neighboring states."

These duties of good neighborhood were recognized by this Government more than a quarter of a century before Lord Palmerston made the speech referred to by Admiral Polo; and the neutrality law of 1818 was then enacted for the purpose of defining the acts of disturbance which should be prevented, and of providing a punishment for such persons as might be found to be guilty of them.

But a friendly government violates no duty of good neighborhood in allowing the free sale of arms and munitions of war to all persons, to insurgents as well as to the regularly constituted authorities; and such arms and munitions, by whichever party purchased, may be carried in its vessels on the high seas, without liability to question by any other party. In like manner its vessels may freely carry unarmed passengers, even though known to be insurgents, without thereby rendering the government which permits it liable to a charge of violating its international duties. But if such passengers, on the contrary, should be armed and proceed to the scene of the insurrection as an organized body, which might be capable of levying war, they constitute a hostile expedition which may not be knowingly permitted without a violation of international obligation.

During the late Franco-German war each party was free to purchase arms and munitions of war in this country, and did so, and Frenchmen whose hearts were with their struggling countrymen at home, or Germans who wished to join the invading armies of Germany, were free to leave the shores of the United States for that purpose, so long as they left as private citizens, unarmed, and without engagement made in this country to enter the service of a belligerent. They did thus leave, in vessels of several different nationalities. Neither this Government nor any other neutral government which may have allowed its merchant marine to transport the arms and munitions of war or the passengers to Europe was guilty of a violation of its duties as a neutral.

Even recognized war, therefore, can not oblige neutral nations to contract the right of their citizens to engage in such commerce which is lawful in time of peace, or to abridge the liberties of persons enjoying the protection of their flag to such a point as to render illegal either of these proceedings, although in time of actual war the transportation on the high seas of articles known as contraband of war is to be made subject to the right of capture. But in time of peace no vessel of war has the right to capture, or even to interfere with, molest, or detain upon the high seas, a regularly documented vessel of another power.

This doctrine is not new in the intercourse of nations.

On the 10th day of April, 1858, Mr. Cass, then Secretary of State of the United States, wrote to Lord Napier, the envoy of Great Britain:

"Undoubtedly a right vested in the armed cruisers of one state to stop and examine the merchant vessels of another might be so exercised as to contribute toward the suppression of crimes upon the ocean. But this power of armed intervention might also be exerted at the expense of the maritime rights of the world. Such an exercise of force, so liable to be abused, will never meet the concurrence of the United States, whose history abounds with admonitions warning them against its injuries and dangers. They have no disposition to surrender the police of the ocean to any other power, and they will never falter in their determination to enforce their own laws in their own vessels and by their own power, and to oppose the pretensions of every other nation to board them by force in times of peace. * * *

"To permit a foreign officer to board the vessel of another power, to assume command in her, to call for and examine her papers, to pass judgment upon her character, to decide the broad inquiry whether she is navigated according to law, and to send her in at pleasure for trial, can not be submitted to by any independent nation without injury and dishonor. The United States deny the right of the cruisers of any other power whatever, for any purpose whatever, to enter their vessels by force in time of peace. No such right is recognized by the law of nations. As Lord Stowell truly said, 'I can find no authority that gives the right of interruption to the navigation of states upon the high seas except that which tho right of war gives to belligerents against neutrals. No nation can exercise a right of visitation and search upon the common and unappropriated parts of the ocean except upon the belligerent claim.'"

On the 8th of June, 1858, Mr. Dallas, the minister of the United States in London, had an interview with Lord Malmesbury at the foreign office on the subject of the detention and visitation of documented vessels of the United States by British cruisers on the high seas. Lord Malmesbury furnished Mr. Dallas with a written minute of the conversation which then took place:

"Her Majesty's Government are not prepared to justify or excuse such acts on the part of their officers as have been complained of by the United States Government, if they are truly reported. Her Majesty's Government recognize the principles of international law as laid down by General Cass in his note of the 10th of April, and that nothing of the treaty of 1842 supersedes that law. Her Majesty's Government, however, think it most indispensable in the interest of civilization and the police of the seas that there should be a power of verifying the nationality of a vessel suspected, on good grounds, of carrying false colors.

"Her Majesty's Government would wish to learn from the United States Government their views in detail on this point, in the hope that some mutual arrangement, by way of proceedings to be executed by our respective officers, may be found effective without being offensive. The French have lately proposed and laid down this one, viz, that a boat may be sent alongside of a suspected ship, and may ask for papers, but not, unless invited, board the vessel. Such is our arrangement with France. Lord Malmesbury has given Mr. Dallas a copy of our instructions to our officers. Pending our negotiation on the above point, orders will be given to discontinue search of United States vessels."

On the 16th of the same June the Senate of the United States unanimously adopted a resolution—

"That American vessels on the high seas, in time of peace, bearing the American flag, remain under the jurisdiction of the country to which they belong, and therefore any visitation, molestation, or detention of such vessel, by force, or by the exhibition of force, on the part of a foreign power is in derogation of the sovereignty of the United States."

It is also understood that the enlightened Government of Spain has, in the recent case of the *Deerhound*, recognized the justice and force of the principle thus established in practice by France, Great Britain, and the United States.

That vessel was dispatched from Plymouth, England, with a cargo of arms, ammunition, and military clothing, destined for the Carlist insurgents in the north of Spain. She was captured by a Spanish cruiser on the high seas off the coast of Spain and taken into port. Lord Granville demanded her release, saying:

"Her Majesty's Government can not acquiesce in the competency of the Spanish Government to refer to a prize court the case of the *Deerhound;* neither can Her Majesty's Government admit that legal jurisdiction can be assumed by the Spanish Government over a British ship which, in time of peace, has been seized upon the high seas by a public ship of Spain."

The Government of Spain surrendered the *Deerhound*, and Mr. Carvajal informed the representative of Great Britain—

"That if her release was agreed upon, it was only because of her having been captured in neutral waters."

The learned minister of Spain seeks to maintain, by a citation from an eminent English publicist, that this right of transportation may be subordinated by the necessities of self-preservation in the government which is contending with an insurrection. It is not necessary for the undersigned to assent to or to deny the justice of this proposition in the extreme case and with the great limitations stated by Sir R. Phillimore. But the acute intelligence of Admiral Polo can not fail to perceive that the supposed act of self-preservation is none the less an act of war because alleged to be done in self-defense; and the undersigned can not permit himself to assume that Spain maintains that such an invasion of the territory of another power as Phillimore refers to would confer upon the courts or military authorities of the invading nation the right to try and condemn, for alleged crimes, persons who might be captured on neutral soil. In the case of the *Virginius*, had Spain, after her capture by the *Tornado*, restored her and her passengers and crew to the United States, to be dealt with according to their laws, the appropriateness of the citation from the British publicist would appear to be more manifest.

Admiral Polo also cites an extract from a speech by Lord Lyndhurst in the

House of Lords, in March, 1853, in which the learned jurist endeavored to convince that distinguished body that by the laws of England—

"If a number of British subjects were to combine and to conspire together to excite revolt among the inhabitants of a friendly state, and those persons, in pursuance of that conspiracy, were to issue manifestoes and proclamations for the purpose of carrying that object into effect; above all, if they were to subscribe money for the purpose of purchasing arms to give effect to that intended enterprise, such persons would be guilty of a misdemeanor, and liable to suffer punishment, and that foreigners residing in England are punishable by the common law precisely in the same manner, and to the same extent, and under the same conditions as natural-born subjects."

In view of events which have taken place since that speech was delivered, the undersigned might, were it necessary, feel disposed to doubt whether Lord Lyndhurst correctly interpreted English law, as understood by its administrators. But it is needless to dwell upon that consideration, because, as the undersigned has already pointed out, the United States have not left the character of that class of acts to be determined by unwritten common law, but have provided by statute which of them, if committed, should be regarded as criminal, and punished accordingly.

In the same connection Admiral Polo refers to a decision of a British court respecting the law of libel. It is not understood what precise bearing upon the present discussion this reference is intended to have. If it be intended to suggest the propriety or the expediency of limiting the freedom of public discussion in the United States upon the Cuban insurrection, the reply must be courteous but peremptory and distinct, that the suggestion can not be entertained. This Government tolerates the greatest freedom and latitude of discussion of public subjects. It even permits, without objection, a journal in New York, which is currently reported to receive pecuniary support from official Spanish sources, to indulge in language vulgarly abusive and libelous toward the President of the United States and the undersigned, and calculated to excite disrespect toward the Government and to destroy confidence in the institutions of the country.

The amiable and just minister of Spain will not ask a Government which permits such freedom in a foreigner to restrain its own citizens within narrower limits. And it will probably occur to him that a comparison of the tone, temper, and modes of expression of the journals of this country (where no censorship prevails) toward Spain with those of the journals of Madrid and Habana (where it is understood that the Government assumes the responsibility of controlling what shall appear) toward the United States will show that the American press is quite as temperate, wise, moderate, and just as is the Spanish.

The undersigned will now proceed to show that the United States have faithfully performed all their international duties toward Spain during the existing insurrection.

Mr. HALE. I move that the Senate adjourn.

The motion was agreed to; and (at 5 o'clock and 40 minutes p. m.) the Senate adjourned until to-morrow, Wednesday, March 18, 1896, at 12 o'clock meridian.

✧   ✧   ✧   ✧   ✧   ✧   ✧

March 23, 1896.

Mr. MORGAN. Will the Senator allow me to ask him a question?

Mr. PALMER. Certainly.

Mr. MORGAN. A paper was sent here by T. Estrada Palma, who claims to be the agent of the Republic of Cuba, to Hon. Richard Olney, Secretary of State of the United States of America, who has communicated that to Congress, first to the Committee on Foreign Relations. It has been printed, and contains a full statement of the constitution and organization of the Government of the Republic of Cuba, giving its personnel, all the provisions of law in reference to it, and several general acts passed by that government, which have been heretofore placed in the RECORD. I suppose, however, the Senator from Illinois has not observed it.

Then I hold here a letter written by Mr. Cisneros, the President of the Republic of Cuba, addressed to the people of the United States, in which he sets forth what he is doing there in the way of civil government, and also presents a very earnest appeal to the people of the United States to grant belligerent rights to the Republic of Cuba. Those papers were sent by a correspondent of the Star, and I communicated with Mr. Crosby Noyes, whom we all know—the Senator knows him perfectly well—long a resident of this city, a man of great capacity and ability and high character. I asked him whether or not those papers and the letter of Mr. Cisneros to the people of the United States were genuine, and he says as follows:

DEAR SIR: The authenticity of the Cisneros manifesto furnished to the Star by Captain Mannix is unquestionable. Had there been any manner of doubt about its authenticity it would never have appeared in the Star. All the internal evidence and all we know of our correspondent's undoubted facilities for communication with the insurgents confirm this and other important information concerning the doings and sayings of the Cuban leaders.

I would furnish these papers to the Senator from Illinois so that he could know exactly the situation there, but they were furnished to the Senate some time ago.

Mr. PALMER. To the extent that those papers are contained in the most admirable speech of the Senator from Alabama [Mr. MORGAN] I may say that I am familiar with them. I have read his speech with a great deal of interest and with the most earnest desire to concur with him not only in his argument but in his conclusions; and if I were not standing here as one of the representatives of 4,000,000 people, whose interests to this extent and in this day are in my keeping and to whom I am responsible, I would concur in much that has been said by the Senator from Alabama. In the beginning of this matter when the subject of the Cuban revolution was presented to me I sympathized with them. But I remember to-day that standing here I have no right to indulge in other sympathies than such as I may commit the people of the State of Illinois to maintain.

Mr. MORGAN. Would it suit the convenience of the Senator if I should send Cuba's appeal to the desk and have it read?

Mr. PALMER. Very well.

Mr. MORGAN. I ask the Secretary to commence with the second column.

The VICE-PRESIDENT. The Secretary will read as indicated.

The Secretary read as follows:

REPUBLIC OF CUBA, EXECUTIVE HEADQUARTERS,
Cubitas Mountain, February 1.

To the American people:

The infant and struggling Republic of Cuba appeals to the grand and powerful Union of American States.

Undoubtedly this action is most unusual in the history of nations, but because of the international standing of the Cuban Republic—more correctly because it has no recognized place among the powers of the world—are we thus compelled to appeal informally and through the medium of the press directly to the people.

Indeed, it is that international standing that we are now seeking, that we now ask the American nation to give us, and that we pray it will see fit to grant in the name of liberty and of justice.

Why do we ask the American people alone to hear us, and why do we not address this document to the entire world? The answer is well known. We call to the people who have themselves suffered oppression and felt the iron heel of the tyrant. We call to the nation of heroes who threw off the slavish yoke, and who signaled to the downtrodden of the earth that the beacon light of liberty in America would never grow dim, but would throw its rays across the oceans to strugglers for freedom in other lands. We call to the nation that has ever greeted with open arms the honest exiles from far and near; the nation that gave hope to Poland and succor to Ireland: the nation that drove monarchy from Mexico and Hawaii, and so nobly and faithfully shielded our southern sister, Venezuela.

To whom would we appeal if not to America? To what land if not to that of Washington, of Jefferson, of Monroe, of Jackson, of Grant, of Blaine, of Cleveland, and the immortal Lincoln?

CUBA'S SECOND STRUGGLE.

The present is Cuba's second struggle for liberty. From 1868 to 1878—ten long, suffering years—a little band of patriots fought gallantly on. While the wrongs then were as great as they now are, the Cuban people did not rise as they have risen in this war to throw off the Spanish yoke. The thirst for liberty which permeates the island to-day was unknown then, except to a small minority of the people, and after ten years of warfare the end came; but it did not bring success.

But even then Spain made promises to the Cuban people that she did not propose to fulfill, and from that time the island has suffered as no other section of the earth has in the same period. Spain claims she holds Cuba by divine right. Such were her pretensions with regard to all her American possessions; but a Divine hand liberated those same possessions, and to-day they are free and independent republics of the New World.

SPANISH MISREPRESENTATION.

The Spaniards have raised the cry abroad that the Cuban rebellion is merely an uprising of negroes. There is no truth in this as stated. It is not a negro uprising nor a white uprising, but a rebellion of the people of Cuba against a cruel and unrelenting despot. But even if it were a negro rebellion, would the people of the United States frown upon it?

The answer to that question is told by the firing upon Fort Sumter, the war of 1861 to 1865, the million of graves in the southland and the God-inspired proclamation of Abraham Lincoln. Was not the freedom of the black man announced in that undying language used by the martyr President? And did not the blood of a million American freemen stain grassy mounds in the now loyal and patriotic South, writing in eternal words the emancipation of the black man?

The world knows the noble yet fearful history. Spain knows it, and when her representative in the capital of the United States says the Cuban rebellion is a negro movement entirely he not only falsifies, but he insults the memory of the grand army of the dead.

We are proud to have our colored brothers with us in this glorious struggle for freedom; for Cuba, when free, will be like the land of Washington, where every man worthy of citizenship will be accorded the full rights of civil and religious liberty.

THE RIGHTS OF BELLIGERENCY.

We ask the American people to grant us, through their President and Congress, those rights of belligerency to which, according to the laws of war and of nations, we are entitled. Our armies have marched whither they might throughout the entire island, and for weeks have threatened the stronghold of Spain's power in Cuba.

Must we capture Habana and drive Spain's hirelings across the sea before we are even given the right as men to fight for that priceless gift which God destined should be universally divided among his children? Must we gain our independence before we are accorded the sanction of the world to labor for it?

THE REPUBLIC ESTABLISHED.

The Cuban republican Government of the island is a firmly established institution. Covering considerably over one-half of the area is the civil branch of our authority, with regularly appointed governors of different sections, prefectos in subdivisions, etc. Of course, Spanish formalities are still followed to a great extent in the administration of the local governments, for a complete change of method in a few months would be too radical.

Here in Cubitas are the head officers and chief departments of the republic. Here we are able and most willing to receive representatives of the United States or other nations.

On all grounds of diplomatic and international usage the Cuban Republic is entitled not alone to recognition of belligerent rights for its armies now in the field, but to actual independence. Still we do not ask that the latter be accorded us at present. All we wish now is to be looked upon by the Government of the United States as men and soldiers battling for their birthright. We do not wish to appear in the eyes of the world like bandits and rabble.

Is Spain entitled to consideration at the hands of a modern, civilized, and highly progressive nation? Does her misrule of Cuba for a century commend her to the hearts and minds of men? Are her hirelings here to lift up and educate the Cuban and make his beloved island prosperous? Under the accursed flag of Castile will not freedom's muffled shrieks still be heard on the

American hemisphere? Will not the continuance of her supremacy in Cuba mean the perpetuation of mediæval institutions, the downtrodding of right and equity, and the upholding of all that to men of the nineteenth century is debased and barbaric?

People of the free and glorious United States, Cuba appeals to you! She asks that you raise your voice in her behalf. She asks that you announce to the world that at least as against the tyrant she be given an equal chance. Cuba, the bleeding, appeals to her American sisters. She does it in the name of God, of justice, of civilization, and of America.

SALVADOR CISNEROS-BETANCOURT.

Mr. MORGAN. I hope the Senator from Illinois will allow me to say that although I have been raised from my childhood in a Southern community, among slaves and slaveholders, I applaud and approve every word in that splendid appeal of Cisneros to the American people.

*   *   *   *   *   *   *

March 24, 1896.

Mr. MORGAN. Mr. President, I wish to add a very few words to what the Senator from Texas [Mr. MILLS] has said. I want to say that I do not consider any time is wasted by the Senate of the United States in coming to a full knowledge of the situation that we are now dealing with. There is something more in this case than even the power to arouse the majestic and splendid and brilliant oratory to which we have just listened. There is a great deal of seriousness in it; there is a great deal of truth in it, of fact in it; and it seems that the Senate of the United States requires at the hands of certain gentlemen who have expressed opinions on this question, as they also have expressed opinions, that we shall continually exert ourselves to lay the evidence before the country upon which all of our proposed action is based, it makes no difference in what particular direction it may be exercised.

I desire, for a very few moments, to put into the RECORD some facts for the consideration of this body and also of the other House of Congress. I must quote from an American newspaper. It seems that in certain quarters that only source of information of which we are possessed is being continually questioned as to its truthfulness. I regret very much to find that that accusation rests upon the whole American press, as far as I have observed, for there is no dissent among the newspapers as to the facts that come from Cuba. I have yet to see a single statement in contradiction of the reports which have been made in the various newspapers of this country by the very intrepid men who have gone out there and exposed their lives and their liberties for the purpose of gaining information that we can not otherwise gain. I have a quotation here from an English paper as well as from an American paper as to the situation in London:

LONDON, *March 24.*

The Standard has a dispatch from Madrid, which says:

"The Epoca has two articles which are supposed to reflect the opinion of the cabinet and which have been much noticed. The first challenges the United States to doff its mask and display its true colors. If they want war, the Epoca says, Spain is ready to face it with becoming dignity. Otherwise, it advises the American politicians to desist from their vexatious debates and cover the hostility.

"The second article reviews Spain's chances of a European alliance.

"The other papers have similar patriotic articles. It is evident that the Government will refuse to allow an American commission to go to Cuba, because such a concession on the eve of the elections would damage Spanish prestige."

This is an extract from the London Standard.

The PRESIDING OFFICER (Mr. BLACKBURN in the chair). Will the Senator from Alabama yield? The hour of 2 o'clock having arrived, the Chair lays before the Senate the unfinished business, which will be stated.

The SECRETARY. A bill (S. 502) to approve a compromise and settlement between the United States and the State of Arkansas.

Mr. BERRY. I ask that the unfinished business be temporarily laid aside, without prejudice.

The PRESIDING OFFICER. Is there objection to the request of the Senator from Arkansas?

Mr. HALE. Mr. President, I do not object——

Mr. CULLOM. I want to say that I shall insist, as soon as the Senator from Alabama concludes his brief remarks, as I understand he desires to speak briefly, that the legislative, executive, and judicial appropriation bill shall be taken up for consideration. I hope there will be no opposition to that course.

The PRESIDING OFFICER. The Senator from Arkansas asks unanimous consent that the unfinished business which has just been laid before the Senate may be passed over without prejudice. Is there objection?

Mr. CULLOM. I have no objection to that.

Mr. HALE. I merely want to say that I do not object for the purpose of taking the Senator from Alabama off his feet; but I call attention to the fact that yesterday, at the request of the Senator from Ohio [Mr. SHERMAN], in charge of this subject-matter, it was withdrawn from the consideration of the Senate and recommitted practically to the committee of conference, with the general understanding, I suppose, that debate would be suspended until the conference committee should again report. I did not object to the Senator from Texas coming in upon his joint resolution, and I do not now, as I have said, seek to take the Senator from Alabama from the floor; but I do insist that at the end of his remarks upon the joint resolution it shall take its parliamentary course and go to the Calendar. I make the point now, so that if I am not here at the end of the Senator's remarks, the joint resolution shall take that course.

The PRESIDING OFFICER. There is no objection to the request of the Senator from Arkansas, and it is agreed to.

Mr. MORGAN. Mr. President, the Senator from Texas has brought forth a new phase of this subject, one that has not hitherto been in charge of the Senate or before the Senate. He proposes that we shall go to the Government of Spain and demand of her that she shall give autonomy to Cuba, a government corresponding, I suppose, in some of its characteristics perhaps very closely, in the contemplation of the Senator from Texas, with that of Canada on the north, and, in the event that Spain refuses to grant such autonomy to Cuba, that the American Government will use whatever force may be necessary to expel Spain from that island and take possession of it, so that the people there may have a fair opportunity to determine for themselves what form of government they will have.

That subject has not been before the Senate of the United States in that form, or in any form, up to the present moment of time. Up to the time when the Senator from Ohio asked in the Senate a disagreement to the amendment of the House, after an agreement had been suggested by the committee of conference on the resolutions, we had expressed nothing but opinion. We had confined ourselves entirely to that domain. We had proposed no measure which would be binding upon the people of the United States in any sense whatever. It was the response of Congress to the opinion of the people as expressed in the petitions sent to us that we chose to utter.

Now, for that cause, as we expected would be the case, only because the Senate and the House have concurred in the opinion that a state of public war does exist in the Island of Cuba and that those people are entitled to belligerent rights—for that and for nothing more—came from the Spanish authorities in Madrid the declaration which I have just read to the Senate, showing that they regard this as an act of hostility on the part of the Government of the United States. We have disclaimed in every form that it was possible to make a disclaimer that we had any hostile intentions toward Spain, that we were acting outside of the line of our duty, even if we had progressed to the extent that I claim we shall progress, to a resolution that is now lying upon the table, of a pure recognition of belligerency and the existence of war in Cuba, and the rights of Cuba and Spain as belligerents, and our rights and our duties as neutrals in that war.

My object in taking the floor this morning is to call attention to a matter of history with which I was not familiar at the time that it was occurring. Unfortunately the people of the Southern States at that time were themselves occupying the attitude of belligerents in what was termed by the Government of the United States a treasonable insurrection against the flag and Constitution of the country, so that what transpired in the United States at that time with the Government of the United States was entirely unknown to us.

Spain came forward at an early moment, as I am informed, before a gun had been fired, or at least before any great battle had been fought, and she recognized not the independence but the belligerency of the Confederate States. She did not undertake in that recognition of belligerency to demarcate the States or the parts of States that were regarded by the United States as being in insurrection, but she took the whole area without reference to State boundaries, and wherever the Government of the United States had recognized the fact that insurrection existed Spain recognized the fact that lawful belligerency existed, thereby entirely dissipating the argument which has been made here, I believe by the Senator from Louisiana [Mr. CAFFERY], that the recognition of belligerency extended only to the area where war actually prevailed, and that we had to make a demarcation of boundary before we could recognize that the Cuban Republic was engaged in a state of belligerency.

Mr. President, what I rose for was to call the attention of Congress to the situation of the United States at the time that she was conducting war for the purpose of putting down the rebellion and after Spain had recognized the belligerency of the Confederate States. I confess when my mind was first brought to consider this question I was somewhat puzzled to understand why it was that Spain should have been so magnanimous toward the Confederacy and should have been so active in her disposition to recognize the belligerency of the Confederate States.

We had an institution in the South in common with one that existed in Cuba and Puerto Rico at that time, the institution of slavery. But, sir, Spain very soon after, if not even before, the time that she recognized the belligerency of the Confederate States had set about with a determined purpose, as it appeared, to do two things. One was to establish a republic and the other was to emancipate the slaves. So General Grant when he came into power afterwards recognized that the war that was being conducted there was really a war for the emancipation of slaves, and it was conducted by the Spanish Government with that pledge attending every act of hostility that was inflicted upon the people of Cuba.

The consultation of the authorities, the correspondence between our minister in Spain and the Government of the United States during the struggle of which I have been speaking, discloses the reasons why Spain recognized the Confederacy. She thought, first of all, that she would have an ally in the Confederacy to protect and preserve slavery, after she had consented, even in Spain, that it should be abolished, that it would be restored, for, mark you, in regard to political rights and rights of war and rights of conquest Spain acts and has always acted upon the theory that once she has been stripped of a province or of a power she has always a right to go to war to recover it.

What did she do in the case of Mexico? Thirteen years after the Republic of Mexico had been recognized, without any pretext of war at all arising in the course of her relations or transactions in Mexico, she sent her fleets and her armies there to try to recover that territory. Her declaration of war against Mexico was based entirely upon the fact that Mexico had once been her property, and having once been her property was always subject to reclamation.

But Spain went further than that, Mr. President. Very soon after our war began Spain went and took possession of San Domingo, occupied it, and held it until the war with the United States was closed or was about to close. Why did Spain invade San Domingo while our war was going on? Because she expected by establishing her power in San Domingo to check the power of the United States or the influence of the United States in Cuba, and through that instrumentality, getting on the flank of the United States and of Cuba, she expected, if the war resulted in favor of the rebellion, that everything would be straight on principle and on sentiment; if it resulted, however, in favor of the United States Government, that she would then have a military possession in San Domingo that would enable her to check any advance of the United States in that direction.

Spain was not alone among the European governments in assailing the United States on that occasion. She had a number, if not of allies, at least of sympathizers in Europe who took advantage of the struggle in the United States to come and plant themselves or attempt to plant themselves on different parts of the American Hemisphere. We find that Great Britain had already occupied, in the name of the Mosquito King, the mouth of the San Juan River to command our communications with the Pacific. We find that Austria and France and Great Britain and Spain started out together for the purpose of hunting Mexico to death and reclaiming that territory while our war was going on. After a while Spain and Great Britain dropped off. They came under the pretext of collecting interest on bonds, when everyone knew that their determination was not merely to do that, but to acquire the territory of Mexico and put it under some sovereign crown, to be ruled by a prince of the blood brought from Europe. Maximilian, having been elected, as he said, under a plebiscite in Mexico, came at last, under the auspices and protection of the Emperor of France, to occupy Mexico. But on all hands everywhere our great Secretary of State, Mr. Seward, had to wrestle with almost every important European power except Russia in trying to maintain the integrity of American soil for the government of her own people according to their own will in trying to maintain the integrity of republics on this hemisphere and to prevent them from being supplanted with monarchies.

Mr. President, I want to read a very few selections from some of the correspondence that took place at that time upon this question. The charge was made by Spain against the United States that we had negotiated a secret treaty for the purpose of acquiring the Bay of Samana, a very important piece of water, surrounded by a very important piece of land, when considered either in respect to its commercial value or its strategic value for naval war purposes. Mr. Seward, on the 23d of November, 1863, a time of very great anxiety with the Government of the United States, said, in a letter to Mr. Koerner, our minister at Madrid:

> The idle calumny that the United States have stirred up and are giving aid to the revolutionary movements now occurring in the Island of San Domingo would not be thought worthy of notice if it had not been presented to me by Mr. Tassara. I give you for your information a copy of the correspondence which has been held on that subject between him and this Department. I am further not unwilling to have an occasion to let it be known to Spain, as well as to other nations, how faithfully we practice the duties as well as assert the rights of a sovereign state. The United States neither contrive, nor aid, nor encourage, nor mix themselves up in civil or international wars of other nations. They submit their record on this matter to the examination of the world and challenge contradiction of its verity. You may express yourself to this effect, and even to this extent, if occasion should arise in your conversations with the Marquis of Miraflores.

That is dated November 23, 1863. There Mr. Seward discovered in the correspondence that was being conducted that the Government of the United States was being accused of improper interference for the purpose of acquiring some occupancy in the West India island. On the 14th of February, 1864, Mr. Koerner writes to Mr. Seward as follows:

> It is reported upon pretty good authority that a commission will be sent there to make a thorough investigation into the condition of affairs.

That is, to Santo Domingo.

> Letters from the island, freely published in the papers here, represent a thorough conquest and the restoration of lasting tranquillity there as impossible. It is easy enough for the Spanish troops to subdue the insurgent places near the coast, where such troops can be subsisted by the fleet. But the interior is said to be so thinly peopled, so little cultivated, so densely covered by primeval forests, so destitute of roads, that no armies can penetrate into the country, where bands of natives exist with ease, ready to issue forth whenever an opportunity offers to assail the Spanish ports.

That gives the state of the war between Spain and Santo Domingo while our war was progressing, February 14, 1864. What was Spain doing there making war upon Santo Domingo? That will appear a little later.

I have a number of extracts which I should like to read, but under the admonitions in regard to the waste of time here and considering other matters, I shall not do it; but I could not forbear the opportunity of laying these matters before the Senate and the country in order to show that the motive of Spain toward the United States, while our war was going on, in recognizing the belligerency of the Confederate States, was a motive connected with her determination to sieze whatever of territory she could in the time of our distress and paralysis and hold it after our struggle had ended.

On January 31, 1865, Horatio J. Perry, who was then our minister at Madrid, wrote to Mr. Seward as follows:

LEGATION OF THE UNITED STATES, *Madrid, January 31, 1865.*

SIR: The debates in the Spanish Senate, which have run over a period of about twenty days, have been unusually interesting.

On the question of the reply to the Queen's speech, senators of the opposition have taken occasion to review the whole policy of the Government.

Attacked on the questions of the abandonment of Santo Domingo and the plan for the relief of the treasury by the adherents of O'Donnell, with that leader at the head, and on the question of the encyclical letter of the Pope and general policy of ministers toward Rome and Italy by the new Catholic orators, I have rarely witnessed a debate in which there has been more vigor and persistence shown in the attack, or a cooler and more solid ability displayed in the defense. The orators of the Government have had the best of the argument on every point, but the struggle has been severe.

The name of the United States has been used as a bugbear by the orators of the opposition, who claimed that the occupation of Santo Domingo by the Spaniards was the only way of averting the annexation of Dominica to the United States and the consequent ruin of Spanish interests in the West Indies. The Duke of La Torre, the same Captain-General of Cuba who made the arrangement with the Dominican general, Santana, was the loudest in this argument.

The Marquis of Valdeterrazo, minister of Spain to London in 1860, made the declaration of which I inclose a translation.

The Marquis of the Habana (General Concha), who has been twice Captain-General of Cuba, and is now out with O'Donnell, defended the policy of abandonment, and said that the United States had long ago refused the annexation of Dominica (referring to the Cazneau treaty), and that Spain had taken them up only after they had been refused by other powers.

The Duke of La Torre (General Servaro) spoke strongly in favor of a declaration by Spain that the slave trade is piracy, and wanted steps to be immediately taken for the abolition of slavery in Cuba.

The Marquis of Habana desired the extinction of slavery, but preferred measures like those which Brazil had taken to suppress the slave trade, and which had been successful in two years.

He said that if there were anything to be apprehended from the side of the United States, or from any quarter, as a military man he must say that he thought the policy of Spain ought to be to concentrate her power as much as possible; and the possession of Santo Domingo added no strength to Spain, but was a decided source of weakness. The resources of Cuba were uselessly employed in Santo Domingo, and they might be needed in that island itself.

The debate was closed last evening, and the reply to the Queen's speech, being put to the vote, passed the Senate by a vote of 102 for and 58 against the policy of the Government.

This is not a direct vote upon the bill for the abandonment of Santo Domingo, this bill not being before the Senate, but before the lower house, to come up afterwards to the Senate; but the question is thus already debated and settled indirectly so far as the Senate is concerned, the house having done little else except to adjourn over from day to day to give the members an opportunity to be present at the Senate debates, and allow ministers also to be all present in the upper house.

This great trial of parliamentary strength over, all the interest now centers in the lower house, and the Senate adjourns over to allow ministers to be all present in the other house, as well as the Senators themselves.

But the question of Santo Domingo is already prejudged, and the bill for the abandonment is already virtually carried by the Government.

* * * * * * *

With sentiments of the highest respect, I remain, sir,
Your obedient servant,

HORATIO J. PERRY.

Hon. WILLIAM H. SEWARD,
Secretary of State, Washington.

Here is a translation, which Mr. Perry sends to his Government, of the declaration of the Marquis of Valdeterrazo:

[Translation.]

A mistake has been made in saying that the United States have made a treaty of annexation with Santo Domingo. This is not the fact.

When I was in London I was authorized by the Government of Her Majesty to occupy myself in this question, all the necessary facilities being conceded to me to engage not only the English Government but also the French to associate with the Spanish Government to carry out a demonstration to be made in the Bay of Samana.

I call attention to that, that the British Government, the French Government, and the Spanish Government, according to this statement, had made an agreement to carry out a demonstration to be made in the Bay of Samana.

Being authorized in this way, I conferred with the English Government on the serious damage which would be caused by the occupation of the Bay of Samana by the Anglo-American Government.

The English Government understood it in this light, but did not wish to bind itself unless the French Government associated itself also. I addressed myself to the latter, making a full explanation of the evils, the inconveniences, and the damage which the commerce of the three nations would receive if the United States should found an establishment or raise a fortification in that harbor. The French Government understood the gravity of the question, associated itself with the English and Spanish Governments, and the result was that the three made a demonstration toward the Bay of Samana, at the same time giving instructions to their representatives at Washington to manifest the displeasure which the three Governments would feel if the treaty of which we had advice, but whose tenor was not known, should be carried into effect.

The English Government some time after, having given the necessary orders for the uniting of the maritime forces of the three powers with the above-named object, obtained the first copy of this treaty, which it remitted to the Government of her Majesty.

In this treaty the annexation was not established. That which was alone established was the right to raise a fortification and to found a national establishment in the Bay of Samana by means of a compensation and other services to the Republic of Santo Domingo. For this reason the Duke de la Torrei said very opportunely that the occupation of Samana is highly important, and that the Spanish Government should not abandon a post of so much value not only for the Governments of England and France but much more for the interests of Spain. In this I agree with the Duke de la Torre, and I say to the ministers that the abandonment of Santo Domingo is a danger, and I also say to the ministers that they ought to consider well to what an extent the security of our provinces beyond the sea is compromised by the abandonment of Santo Domingo. The Government is still in time to avoid the evils and consequences which this measure may produce, and let it not be said that this is but an echo, for in order to defend Puerto Rico and the Island of Cuba more expense will have to be borne than is necessary to preserve Santo Domingo.

Those facts, I hope, will draw the attention of statesmen who are in this body to the situation of Spain at that time, to her purposes and why it was she was occupying the Island of Santo Domingo, while we were at war, after she had recognized the belligerency of the Confederate States. She and England and France combined to make an assault upon the United States for the purpose of displacing rights they supposed we had acquired by a secret treaty with the Government of Santo Domingo. Was her feeling toward us on that occasion friendly? Was there not a motive in her recognition of the belligerency of the Confederate States? Does she not stand before this people to-day and before the world as having been influenced in that apparently peaceful act by motives that had regard to the acquisition of power to the monarchy of Spain and in regard also to the infliction of wrong and injustice upon the people of the United States? There they had intended to violate the doctrine which the Senator from Texas [Mr. MILLS] referred to and has spoken upon so eloquently, which has been established in the expressed opinions of every statesman in America of whom I have ever heard, that we would not permit any foreign power to come and acquire dominion in these American islands. They intended taking advantage of what they supposed was the weakness or the embarrassment of the United States during a time of war to do precisely what was done by Austria and France and Maximilian afterwards—they intended to come here and intrench themselves upon this territory, and Spain came without any cause of war against Santo Domingo, a pure invasion, and took that island into her custody at the time we were engaged in belligerent operations here, in civil warfare.

Therefore, Mr. President, it will not do for us to sit by and ignore the facts of history and quietly and serenely to regard Spain as having been always our friend under all circumstances. That story has been told here until I suppose the American people were ready to believe that Spain had always been the bosom friend of the United States, and yet the very moment she found the United States in war, and before the battle of Bull Run had been fought, she recognized the belligerency of the Confederate States, and afterwards, as soon as she could marshal her ships and her armies, went and took possession of the Island of Santo Domingo, and held it until the rebel flag in the South was hauled down.

There is one other fact which I wish to put into the RECORD, and that is the proclamation of General Weyler, a circular of General Weyler's, addressed to the military officers. This is not to the people; this is to the military. He addressed another to the people, in which he prescribed specific things that they were to do, certain lines of conduct which they were to observe, on the penalty of being shot to death without trial if they undertook to violate them. He says to the military:

> I have addressed my previous proclamations at the moment of my landing to the loyal inhabitants, to the volunteers and firemen, and to the army and navy.
> I may give you a slight idea of the intentions I have and the measures I shall follow as governor general in chief, in accordance with the general desire of Spain and with the decided aim of Her Majesty's Government to furnish all the means required to control and crush this rebellion.
> Knowing this, and knowing my character—

What an appeal that was—Weyler appealing to his character—

> I may perhaps need to say no more to make you understand what is the conduct that I am to follow.

There he anchors himself to every vile precedent that he had established in the previous war and pledged himself to his officers, through his character and through the history of his conduct, that he would repeat the same enormities in this struggle.

Mr. ALLEN. He appealed to his known character as a butcher.

Mr. MORGAN. Yes; he appealed to his character as a butcher, as the Senator well says. His proclamation continues:

> But with the idea of avoiding all kinds of doubt, even keeping (as you are to keep) the circulars to be published, I deem it necessary to make some remarks.
> It is not unknown by you that the state in which the rebellion has come and the raid made by the principal leaders recently, which could not be stopped even by the active pursuit of the columns, is due to the indifference, the fear, or the disheartenment of the inhabitants.

Is that public war? Are the people so disheartened or so afraid or so indifferent as that he has now to use the torture of war for the purpose of nerving them through a greater and higher fear to stand under his colors and fight his battles? He says further:

> Since it can not be doubted that some, seeing the burning of their property without opposition, and that others who have been born in Spain should sympathize with the insurgents, it is necessary, at all hazards, to better this state of things and to brighten the spirit of the inhabitants, making them aware that I am determined to lend all my assistance to the local inhabitants.

PRAISING THE REBELS UNLAWFUL.

So I am determined to have the law fall with all its weight upon all those in any way helping the enemy, or praising them, or in any way detracting from the prestige of Spain or its army or of its volunteers. It is necessary for those by our side to show their intentions with deeds, and their behavior should leave no doubt and should prove that they are Spanish.

Since the defense of the country demands the sacrifice of her children, it is necessary that the towns should look to their defense, and that no precautions in the way of scouts should be lacking to give news concerning the enemy, and whether it is in their neighborhood, and so that it may not happen that the enemy should be better informed than we.

The energy and vigor of the enemy will be strained to trace the course of our line, and in all cases you will arrest and place at my disposal to deliver to the courts those who in any way shall show their sympathy or support for the rebels.

The public spirit being encouraged, you must not forget to enlist the volunteers and guerrillas in your districts, not preventing at the same time the organization, as opportunity offers, of a guerrilla band of 25 citizens for each battalion of the army.

I propose that you shall make the dispositions you think most proper for the carrying out of the plan I wish, but this shall not authorize you to determine anything not foreseen in the instructions, unless the urgency of some circumstances should demand it.

"Urgency of circumstances," Mr. President, is a thing that General Weyler left to his officers, and amongst the particular orders which he issued, and which I have quoted in the RECORD at another place on a former occasion, he says that persons who are captured either with arms or without arms, whether they are citizens or whether they are soldiers, shall be sent to him at his headquarters wherever they may be; but if there is any insolence toward a Spanish officer this will not be expected—I do not quote his words; I have given the idea—that is to say, if they can provoke the poor victim into any sort of expression of heat or disappointment, any insolence toward the officer who may take him, "you can take him out and have him shot, and you will do all right."

I expect that, confining yourself to these instructions, you will lend me your worthy support toward the carrying out of my plan for the good of the Spanish cause.

WEYLER.

That is all I wish to say about this business. The American people can make their own comments, and they will not be slow to do it.

*　*　*　*　*　*　*

May 6, 1896.

Mr. FRYE. I now ask that the Senate proceed to the consideration of the river and harbor bill.

Mr. MORGAN. I desire to ask the President of the Senate to lay before the Senate a joint resolution which I offered some time ago which lies upon the table, relating to a recognition of the belligerent rights of Cuba, and I ask the Senator from Maine to yield to me for a moment, as I wish to have it referred.

Mr. FRYE. I have no objection to a reference of the resolution.

Mr. MORGAN. I wish to make a motion to refer the joint resolution to the Committee on Foreign Relations, and I wish to make a statement in that connection after the joint resolution has been read.

The VICE-PRESIDENT. The Chair lays before the Senate the joint resolution referred to by the Senator from Alabama; which will be read.

The Secretary read the joint resolution (S. R. 105) declaring that a state of public war exists in the Island of Cuba, as follows:

Resolved, etc., That it is hereby declared that a state of public war exists in the Island of Cuba between the Government of Spain and the people of that island, who are supporting a separate Government under the name of the Republic of Cuba, and the state of belligerency between said Governments is hereby recognized.

Mr. MORGAN. Mr. President, I introduced that joint resolution in the Senate at the time when the conference report from the conference committee of the two Houses was pending in one of the Houses, I think in the House of Representatives, intending, if that conference report should fail, that I would immediately press the resolution upon the consideration of the Senate. Circumstances have prevented me from being here since that time, and in that way delay has occurred, and new developments have occurred in regard to the situation in Cuba which still further demonstrate the truth of the proposition upon which the Senate and the House of Representatives have voted, that a state of public war exists in the Island of Cuba. We expressed an opinion that it was proper under those circumstances that belligerent rights should be accorded to both parties in our ports and upon our territory. Having expressed an opinion of that kind, and made a declaration to the effect that public war exists there, I desire now to ask the opinion of the Committee on Foreign Relations of the Senate upon the state of facts existing which have been developed since the introduction of that resolution, which, I think, go greatly to strengthen and to confirm the proposition which the two Houses have united in voting upon, and in voting favorably upon.

I believe, Mr. President, that the time has arrived when in sheer justice to our own people, without reference to any effect it may have upon the promotion of the war in Cuba or the fortunes of either side, that it is our duty to declare that a state of public war exists there and that the laws of war as they are recognized among the nations of the earth should be applicable to that situation, and that we should not be left here in a state of doubt and uncertainty as to whether our relations to the people of Cuba or whether either the Spanish Government or the republic are to be controlled by the laws of war, or whether they are to be controlled by the laws of peace.

I can not reconcile it to myself to affirm as a matter of fact that no war exists in Cuba. The Spanish Government recognizes the existence of war there, not only in reference to the conduct that she holds toward the people that she is trying to suppress, but also in regard to our own people and our own commerce. She treats our commerce as if it were a contraband of war. No nation has a right to do that with reference to the Government of the United States when that nation is in a condition of peace. She can not hold that her relations to our own people are those of perfect peace, and at the same time that she has the right to impose upon the Government of the United States and upon its commerce or upon its people the laws of war, which they are continually doing.

I hope that some speedy action will be taken; that is to say, proper action—deliberate, of course; firm and consistent and energetic—to determine the solution of this question before this Congress adjourns. I wish to say that I do not believe that the Congress of the United States can by a final adjournment of this session afford to leave that question in the shape it is now in before the world.

The VICE-PRESIDENT. The question is on the motion of the Senator from Alabama.

Mr. CALL. Will the Senator from Maine allow me one word only?

Mr. FRYE. Yes; one word.

Mr. CALL. I introduced a resolution on the same subject some time ago, which still lies upon the table. I had hoped to obtain early action upon it, but I will ask that the same reference may be made of that resolution as that asked for by the Senator from Alabama as to his resolution.

Mr. FRYE. There is no objection to the reference of the resolutions.

The VICE-PRESIDENT. Without objection, the resolutions will be referred to the Committee on Foreign Relations.

*　*　*　*　*　*　*

April 6, 1897.

Mr. MORGAN. Mr. President——

Mr. PETTIGREW. I ask unanimous consent for the immediate consideration of——

Mr. MORGAN. I rise to a parliamentary inquiry.

The VICE-PRESIDENT. The Senator from Alabama will state his parliamentary inquiry.

Mr. MORGAN. Yesterday the Senate gave its unanimous consent that the joint resolution I introduced on the 1st instant should go over for consideration this morning. I desire to have it laid before the Senate.

The VICE-PRESIDENT. The joint resolution is in order.

The Senate, as in Committee of the Whole, proceeded to consider the joint resolution (S. R. 26) declaring that a condition of public war exists in Cuba, and that strict neutrality shall be maintained.

Mr. MORGAN. Let the joint resolution be read.

The joint resolution was read, as follows:

Resolved by the Senate and House of Representatives, etc., That a condition of public war exists between the Government of Spain and the government proclaimed and for some time maintained by force of arms by the people of Cuba, and that the United States of America shall maintain a strict neutrality between the contending powers, according to each all the rights of belligerents in the ports and territory of the United States.

Mr. MORGAN. Mr. President, this is a joint resolution. Before I proceed to discuss its merits, I wish to disclaim any purpose whatever of forcing the Executive into any attitude about this question that he may not feel entirely at liberty to take. As I view the Constitution and the history of such action in the United States, I think that the initiative properly belongs to Congress on all subjects involving a declaration of war, whether it is a declaration by our own Government or whether it is the declaration of the existence of a state of war in any other country. Therefore I think that action on such subjects ought to originate in one of the Houses. The President may not feel disposed to concur in our action, yet he may feel bound by it. He may not be disposed to exercise the veto power, if he has it, upon a joint resolution of the sort that is now before the Senate. It is a question of very grave importance, and one that ought never to occur in the history of the United States, that the Congress, being satisfied of the existence of war in Cuba, should so declare, the President not being satisfied that that state of affairs exists in the sense of requiring the Government of the United States to take part in any way in the declaration that it does exist. That ought never to be in the United States. The executive and legislative departments of the Government ought to cooperate in all declarations that relate to war, and the Congress of the United States ought never to make a declaration on that subject unless it is satisfied that the President is willing to yield obedience to the popular will, or the legislative will, as here expressed.

Mr. HALE. Mr. President, I wish that we may have order in the Chamber, because I am very desirous to hear the Senator from Alabama, and I can not hear a word that he says, there is so much confusion.

The VICE-PRESIDENT. The Senate will be in order.

Mr. MORGAN. I have not any very great amount of lung power, though I try to speak as distinctly and deliberately as I can, with a view of making the views that I have to present intelligible at least to my colleagues on the floor.

Mr. HALE. It is not the fault of the Senator from Alabama at all; it is the fault of Senators, all of us perhaps, who are in the habit of participating too much in conversation while a Senator is addressing the body. It is almost impossible for any Senator to make himself heard under such conditions, and for that reason I hope we shall be allowed to have silence, that we may hear the Senator from Alabama.

Mr. MORGAN. A question of war or peace between this country and any foreign country, or a question of the existence of a war in any foreign country, is a matter of such grave importance to all the people of the United States that its consideration should always be entered upon with the utmost degree of deliberation and solemnity, and, as far as possible, it should be free from all the exasperations of feeling that we of course have when quarrels occur between us and other powers. It is in this view, and in this sense, and with this purpose, and only this, that I approach the subject this morning.

I do not wish to create a ferment in the United States about it. It is not necessary to do that, Mr. President, if I were disposed to get up some public excitement, because the mind of the people of the United States is agitated and all their hearts are full of this subject. We are in the midst of a very trying situation that has never heretofore existed as it exists now. All the aggravations that surround us at this moment and the same sense of indignation have never heretofore existed, even in the various and frequent irritations that have occurred between Spain and the United States on the subject of her government in Cuba. We have tried so to feel, we have tried to so believe, and we have so conformed our conduct that it is a matter of indifference to us whether Spain shall persecute her own subjects in Cuba or not. I say we have tried to feel it and we have tried to believe it. At the same time the history of Spanish occupation in Cuba from the beginning of this century, and, indeed, far back of that period of time—but I will say from the beginning of this century, because our Government became concerned in it about that time—the history of Spanish occupation in Cuba has been so full of that absolute and heartless spirit of tyranny toward her own subjects as that it is not to be expected that a country organized as ours is, upon the basis of self-government and of the respect that is due from the Government to the citizen, should be free from very profound agitation, in view of the repeated and flagrant and very outrageous demonstrations of persecution that have been made by the Crown of Spain against her own subjects in the Island of Cuba.

The subject I am now about to discuss has been before the Senate for days and weeks and even months at a time, and whoever cares to read the record of those debates of a year ago will there, I think, find an exhaustive discussion of almost every proposition that could be advanced pro and con upon the subject of the duty of the Government of the United States to recognize the existence of public war in Cuba. I do not propose to go back over that record. It is made; it has been deliberately made. There is not a statement, I think, that has been made in the Senate that was not authorized by the facts; and to say the least of it, the Government of Spain has had more than a year of opportunity in which to contradict the specific facts that have been stated in the debates in this body relating to the dealing of Spain toward the people of that island. No denial has been made. They seem to be indifferent to the fact. They seem to be entirely indifferent at least to American opinion and to European opinion upon this subject.

That is not a new thing in the history of Spain. That great monarchy has never stopped to take the opinion of the civilized world upon her conduct toward any of her subjects. Whether they have been born within her home boundary or whether they have been born in colonies, or whether they have been conquered, she has never paused to ascertain what is the opinion of the world about her conduct toward her own people or toward her neighbors. That is unfortunate for us, because we have a proper regard for the neighboring countries. We feel it as well as profess it. We do not trench upon the affairs or the rights of the people of Mexico, who is a near neighbor, and who has not had a very permanent form of government until within the last fifteen years, or a very satisfactory one to us. We make no agitation in respect to the domestic policy of the Canadian Government.

In other words, Mr. President, we are in the proper sense of the word good neighbors to those whose territory adjoins ours, and we have no disposition to interfere in Cuba or in any other place for the purpose of extending our institutions or making a propaganda of any ideas that we have or of enforcing upon them the acceptance of our commercial intercourse. That is our situation. We have maintained it always.

Very early in the beginning of this century, for the purpose of making their security greater, for the purpose of cutting our people off from the temptation of making raids against Mexico, Canada, Cuba, and elsewhere, we commenced a series of legislative enactments here of a very severe character to repress all possible endeavor to give assistance to any insurrection or any war or controversy between any neighboring power or any other power and their own people or any other people. We have at great expense in money, and sometimes at an expense to ourselves of very great irritation amongst our own people, enforced those laws in a rigid way, and we are doing it to-day.

I think our desire to evince to other countries our purpose of being on friendly terms with them and of executing every purpose of government without reference to their distress or their embarrassments has involved us in some efforts to enforce our own laws that have inflicted exceeding injustice upon individuals in this country, and certainly have had a very great effect in restraining if not repressing the expressions of public sentiment which otherwise would have manifested themselves on these occasions.

That being the situation, we have for the third time within this century been drawn into unpleasant contact with a state of affairs in Cuba that has made a very profound impression upon the people of the United States, and not merely upon their sentiment and feeling, but upon their commerce and their intercourse with the people of that island. We have suffered by it on former occasions to such an extent that very large claims for damages have been piled up against the Government of Spain, and I do not remember any instance where we have received compensation for any of those wrongs, when they were established, short of twenty or perhaps thirty years after the termination of their intestinal struggle. So the delays that have been interposed in making compensation to the people of the United States for the wrongs that have been committed in that island, and which are traceable, I think, directly to the tyrannies of the Spanish Government, have been very serious upon our people, and are still very serious.

But our people have suffered in one respect a degree of mortification and humiliation as well as a degree of personal distress that it has always been within the power of our Government to prevent. If the Government of the United States had taken care of its own people in the Island of Cuba according to the full measure of its duty, many a life would have been saved in the former struggles and in the present one, much property would have been spared from destruction, great anguish of feeling would have been spared to our people, both native born and adopted. But the Government of the United States has not taken proper care of her own people in Cuba, and it is time that we begin to do so.

The object of the introduction of the joint resolution which is before the Senate to-day is to put the Government of the United States in a proper legal attitude toward the Government of Spain in Cuba, and to enable us simply to take care of our own citizens. I have always declared that this was my leading motive, and in fact my exclusive motive, as a Senator of the United States, in whatever support I have given to measures here in respect of our controversies and difficulties with Spain in the Island of Cuba. I have kept my mind fixed firmly and exclusively upon the duty of the Government of the United States to the citizens of the United States in the presence of this state of facts. I am trying to get from the Congress of the United States—and I hope the Executive will concur with us—a definition and statement of a legal status or situation which makes it possible for us, under the laws of nations, to protect the lives and property of our people in the Island of Cuba.

In accomplishing this result, Mr. President, it may turn out—and I would be very glad that it should—that assistance will be given to the people of the Island of Cuba in the establishment of their independence, in freeing themselves from an abominable yoke, which, so far as they are concerned, has never resulted in any benefit to the people there at all, but has been imposed upon them and maintained over them for the mere purpose of leeching out of them their substance and of keeping them as serfs and feudatories to the Crown of Spain and to the nobility and gentry of that country. I should be very glad that a result of that sort should follow; but whether that result shall follow, or one still more disastrous to the people of Cuba, nevertheless it is a duty that we can not abdicate to take care, so far as in us lies, of our people in that island.

In what way can we do that? That is the question which comes up here now. Can we do it by standing by and witnessing these wrongs inflicted upon them continually, aggressively, and redress them only by filing claims in the Department of State, to be urged against the Spanish Government after the war has ended and after Spain has become bankrupt? Can we accomplish this protection of our citizens by putting a price upon their blood and their sufferings, and by saying to Spain that "in the end of all of this, after the war is over, we shall charge up so many dollars and cents against you for these ruined and destroyed Americans, men, women, and children, and for their property?" In the former war we waited for ten years, and after the termination of that struggle we sent in our account, and we had a part of it allowed and a part of it disallowed, and the part that was allowed was only paid within the last two or three years. That has been nearly thirty years ago.

Now, can we afford to stand by here and see repeated, in a form that has become historic in Cuba, these wrongs and outrages against our own people, trusting to the settlement of an account for damages after the wrong has been done? Are we in that sublime state of indifference and self-denial in respect to what is going on in Cuba that we shall abstain from doing anything for our people until this struggle which is now going on has ended one way or the other? Shall we refuse to protect our people and deny to ourselves the right, the power, the opportunity, and the duty of providing for them as this struggle goes on?

Well, Mr. President, I hope that the Senate of the United States at least will not agree that it is our duty to ignore these things, to pass them by silently and quietly. I hope that the expression on the part of the Senate will be now what it has been heretofore, a year ago, and still earlier than that—that we recognize the existence of public war in Cuba, attended with all the consequences under the laws of nations that belong to that legal situation; that we will stand neutral between these parties, and that we will execute the laws of neutrality, and especially those laws of neutrality which protect our own people.

Now, as different occurrences are developed in Cuba, we might send ships of war to demand immediate indemnity, but it seems, Mr. President, that we have not got yet to the condition of following the bright British example of always sending her flag and her guns, following her people about over the earth, to demand their rescue from the hands of tyranny and wrong and injustice. We have not come to that; but perhaps after we get a little older and learn more, and have more true spirit amongst the American people, and our Government is truer to them, we will be able to send our flag and our guns about the earth and demand immediate compensation for the wrongs done to our people and their immediate surrender from the jaws of death when they are held contrary to treaties and to international law and to the laws of humanity and of mercy.

I am hopeless, Mr. President, utterly hopeless, that any Administration of the Government of the United States, particularly with the last four years of disastrous example that we have had, will get its courage to the point of sending ships of war to Habana or to any other port of Cuba, and demanding in given cases, however serious, redress for our people or liberty for them from incarceration in their prisons as the occurrences arise.

Here was the case of Dr. Ruis, who was said to have been murdered in prison at the instance and by the direction of the governor of Guanabacoa in that province, an American citizen who was a dentist, and who went back to the land of his forefathers—I do not know where he was born—for the purpose of practicing his profession, and he was said to have had no connection whatever with the strife that existed in Cuba. He was killed, and killed in prison. So it is alleged in the newspapers and so, I understand, it is alleged in the reports of our consul-general in Cuba. Now, what can we do in the case of Dr. Ruis? Of course that case must pass into the balance sheet to be added up in a sum of dollars and cents for the compensation to his widow as soon as it is ascertained in some form or other that the Government of Spain has been accessory to his murder. I understand that the reports of the consul-general indicate in no uncertain way that the Government of Spain is directly responsible through one of her military officers for this outrage.

If that is true, Mr. President, instead of hunting about for a lawyer to go down to Cuba to search out in some technical way an information such as a solicitor would find to be presented to a grand jury in secret session, the Government of the United States might very well send a ship of war to the port of Habana, with a commission upon it, and say to the government of Spain in Cuba, "We intend to have this matter investigated, and if there is evidence to prove that this man has been murdered by this governor in prison, you must have that man arrested, and you must have him shot, or you must have him disposed of in some way that the laws of war require, and you must on the spot make immediate indemnity to the family of this murdered man."

Mr. HALE. Do I understand, in a case such as the Senator has cited, and has objected to the Government sending a lawyer down there, that the Senator would object, when a case of that kind arises, to the Government sending some proper agent, be he lawyer or otherwise, in order to establish the actual facts upon which we should act afterwards? Does the Senator think that would be an improper course on the part of the Government?

Mr. MORGAN. Mr. President, as an American citizen, following the precedents and practices that have heretofore obtained in matters of this kind, I should regretfully assent to the sending of a lawyer to Habana to make an investigation; but if I were a British subject, I should expect the flag and a man-of-war to go there, for the purpose of demanding reparation on the spot and an explanation which would exculpate that governor from this charge or else would consign him to his deserved fate.

Mr. HALE. That is, the Senator would send a ship of war before he sent the lawyer to investigate the facts?

Mr. MORGAN. I would send a ship of war with a lawyer along, or without one; but I do not think that I would have very much use for the lawyer. [Laughter.]

Mr. HALE. I fancy that what the Senator is seeking is a condition of hostility and the use of ships of war and the danger incident to having them in those waters. In that case there would not be much use for a lawyer; there would be use for ships of war. There would be war there.

Mr. MORGAN. In the great and solemn duty of taking care of the lives and property of American citizens, particularly when in foreign countries, I do not think I would stop to split hairs and weigh technicalities before I undertook to enforce something in the nature of a demand for redress; and whenever the Government of the United States gets itself into that condition that it converts everything of this sort into a lawsuit, then the liberties of the American people are worth very little when they come in contact with the fury and savagery of the Spaniards in Cuba. That is my answer to the Senator from Maine. What we need, sir, is action, determination, resolution, purpose, and conclusions which shall protect our people against those outrages. One exhibition of that determined spirit in the Island of Cuba would be worth more to us than all the lawsuits that we could conduct there.

The American people, Mr. President, are a forbearing, kind-hearted, generous, forgiving people; but after all, they understand and they feel, and you can not conceal it from them, that when their rights, liberties, and lives are placed in the power of a brutal authority in a foreign country, it is the duty of this great Republic to exhibit its strength and its power early and decisively for the purpose of rectifying that wrong.

I referred to the case of Ruis as one that was perhaps more difficult of handling than any other in this diplomatic sense; but we know perfectly well, through the reports of our own consul, we know from evidence that the President of the United States has laid before this body, we know from the statements of the President of the United States in his last annual message sent to this body, not only that the property of the people of the United States is destroyed in Cuba for the mere sake of destroying it, not because it is an available resource to the enemy on either side, but we know that the jails of Cuba are stuffed, I may say, with American citizens whose names even have not been ever pronounced in this Senate, and can not be until after this war has passed and the prison doors have been opened and another "book of blood" has to be published, as was published at the close of the last Cuban war.

We are invited continually to shut our eyes to Spanish aggressions in Cuba; we are admonished whenever we speak of them that perhaps we are speaking outside of the record, and we must wait and investigate and find out what has been going on before we think of sending anyone there or a ship of war, messenger, commissioner, or anyone else for the purpose of ascertaining and determining upon the spot what is taking place and what has taken place.

I have not time to go over this record. The part of it that occurred, or a large part of it that was then capable of being discovered, was laid before this Senate more than a year ago, and, as I repeat, it has remained there uncontradicted by the Spanish Government from that day to this. A judgment by default has gone against them in the opinions of mankind for every one of those accusations which is authenticated and put upon the records of this Senate over the name of a responsible man. So I can leave the record to stand just there, and I can proceed, after these preliminary observations as to what the situation actually is and the necessity for our action, to discuss the question as to what is our duty and what are our rights as a legislative body for the United States of America in respect of this terrible involvement that has come upon us through the conduct of Spain in Cuba, for, be it remembered again, we have had nothing to do with inciting revolt in Cuba. Our people have not incited revolt in Cuba; they have cultivated the most friendly feelings and relations with Cuba, and have taken every step they could or they knew how to take to increase their commerce with that country. It has been very valuable to us, and would be again if Cuba had a chance to live.

On yesterday we passed a resolution in this body by a unanimous vote. It was not every Senator who voted for it who was present, but those who were present and did not vote for it seem not to have found it necessary or important that they should vote against it. What is that resolution passed through this body as a solemn declaration?

Whereas information has come to the Senate that Gen. Ruis Rivera, a leader of the Cuban army of independence, recently captured by the Spanish forces, is to be tried by drumhead court-martial and shot: Therefore,

Resolved, That in the judgment of the Senate it is the duty of the President of the United States, if such information is found to be true, to protest to the Spanish Government against such a violation of the rules of civilized warfare.

Mr. President, what right have we to protest against the abuse of the rules of civilized warfare in Cuba if no war exists in Cuba? What right have we to say that it is expected that a man will be tried and convicted by a drumhead court-martial and shot if there is no war existing in Cuba? What right have we to speak of a leader of the Cuban army of independence if there is no Cuban army of independence in that island? I was very gratified that the Senator from Nebraska [Mr. ALLEN] brought this resolution forward, and still more gratified at the decisive vote of the Senate, the unanimous vote, in affirmation of these various facts, to which I now appeal as a justification for the further resolution that we shall declare in a formal manner the existence of public war in Cuba and declare our neutrality between the parties to that war.

Mr. President, such a shameless and colossal falsehood has not existed in the history of this world, I believe, as that which treats and considers and speaks of and regards the situation in Cuba as being now a mere insurrection. If there is any way by which a government can commit itself openly and shamelessly to the utterance of a falsehood, that every man in this world knows to be such, it is done every time that it is declared that the situation in Cuba to-day is no more than an insurrection. We declared a year ago—more than a year ago—that public war existed in Cuba. I believe I have the resolution here before me, and I will read it to see what our declaration was. As it was passed by the concurrent vote of both Houses, it read:

Resolved, That, in the opinion of Congress, a state of public war exists in Cuba, the parties to which are entitled to belligerent rights, and the United States should observe a strict neutrality between the belligerents.

Since that time we have not cast any vote directly upon that question until yesterday. We have had votes which were incidental and showed what the mind of the Senate was since that time, one of which has occurred during the present session. We have now present in this body a number of gentlemen who were not here to participate in the debates and votes which occurred upon that resolution a year ago, and it is entirely proper that the subject should now undergo at least some degree of discussion in order that they may have the opportunity of expressing their own views upon the situation. They are fresher from the people than the balance of us, and perhaps may come inspired more directly with the feeling that the people have upon this question than we are. I presume that those Senators will not discredit the action taken by the Senate and the other House upon the facts that were presented more than a year ago, and upon which we came to the solemn resolution that I have just read. They will not, perhaps, undertake to say that public war did not then exist in Cuba, or that it does not now exist in Cuba. It is altogether proper that the Senators who have arrived in this body during the present session should have the opportunity of passing upon the question whether or not the action that we then took was justifiable upon the facts. They should also have the opportunity, as they will now have upon this resolution, of determining by their votes, so far as they are concerned, whether any change has taken place in the last year—since the adoption of that resolution—which relieves the situation in Cuba and which tends to establish the proposition that, while war existed there a year ago, it does not exist there now. So I thought it was my duty as one of the members of this body and as a member of the Committee on Foreign Relations to furnish an opportunity to Senators that they might record their votes here upon the existing situation, and perhaps by relation back to the situation as it stood at the time we adopted this very important resolution.

Does war now exist in Cuba? Mr. President, that is a proposition that is absolutely so undebatable, so far beyond the domain of discussion, that I can not see how any sensible man can take it up for consideration when the answer lies immediately before him in every act that has occurred in the Island of Cuba within the past two years, and for a period much longer than that. With the vast army that Spain has sent there, with the drain upon her resources that is now threatening to bankrupt the Kingdom, with a loss of thousands and tens of thousands of lives, with an opposing army which in the former revolution for the same causes never reached more than 10,000 men—volunteer soldiers—now reaching to the number of fifty or sixty thousand, with battle after battle fought in every part of that island, and with the occupation of that island from east to west, except in the larger, fortified towns, with the whole body of the country included within the lines of the Cuban army or within the power of their military influence—it is absolutely inadmissible, in view of those facts, to enter upon a discussion of that question. It is so palpable that no man in his senses, it seems to me, can possibly deny it.

It is true that the Senator from Maine [Mr. HALE] on yesterday, when I asked him in the course of the debate whether public war existed in Cuba, said there was a conflict there, there was guerrilla warfare, but not such war as is fought between two states in Europe. Mr. President, that is not a definition of war. The manner in which a war is conducted does not define the question of its existence at all. It is not by marshaled troops under gaudy banners and with a perfect organization and an armament cap-a-pie, and with military resources, to which you can point as being lodged within fortresses or within ports or harbors, or with ships to send abroad for the purpose of gaining new supplies—it is not with these that war is always waged. On the contrary, the most fatal and destructive wars that have existed, and those that have been best calculated to protect a country, have been just what the Senator from Maine characterizes as guerrilla warfare. When that imperial prince of all soldiers, I think, who ever lived—Napoleon—with his vast army, was occupying Spain, the Spaniards resorted to the very tactics that Maximo Gomez resorts to now, and after a few months of struggle with that unparalleled military chieftain they drove Napoleon from Spain. The Spaniards then learned a lesson in military conduct that has stood them in hand from that time to this, and the people of Cuba have been taught it, for the reason that they have not had, as Maximo Gomez has expressed it, the sympathy even of any nation in this world, except perhaps the sympathy of the people of the United States.

How was it during our civil war in this country, when Spain, taking advantage of the fact that we were engaged in fighting each other on the soil of the United States, marshaled an army and a fleet—a great one—in which she concentrated all the power at her command and went against the Island of Santo Domingo, and landed in the ports and occupied them, and took the fortresses, with a view of subjugating the Island of Santo Domingo under the Spanish Crown? How was it, when she had nobody to fight in Santo Domingo except the native negro population—for it was all negro or mulatto—Spain was driven from the Island of Santo Domingo by the impossibility of conquering those people, and she had to retire with her army back to the peninsula without having accomplished anything more than the sacrifice of a large amount of money and many lives and much property, all of which was subsequently taxed upon Cuba as a debt? They have learned, Mr. President, what war means when conducted in this guerrilla form, and there is no impeachment of that form in any sense of the word, and there is no occasion for us to demand of the Cubans as a condition of the recognition of their belligerency that they shall come out in military array and stand in the open field and be shot down by the superior artillery of the Spanish army and overwhelmed by the 150,000 troops that might be paraded against perhaps forty or fifty thousand men who are poorly armed.

No man, Mr. President, who has any respect for the rights of a people who are trying to defend themselves will criticise their methods of warfare so long as those methods are within the pale of civilized war. That argument has been heretofore made by the President of the United States; it has been made by the Secretary of State, and it is now reiterated on this floor by the Senator from Maine. It was first originated and sent into this body by some letters that Mr. Dupuy de Lôme wrote, in which he took occasion to criticise the action of Senators, and complained very bitterly that the Cubans would not fight in a way to suit the Spanish; that they would not come out into the open and be destroyed by overwhelming numbers and superior artillery. I hope that the good sense of the people of the United States will not any longer be retarded in their demand upon their representatives that they shall proceed to some definition upon the subject by the suggestion of the Senator from Maine that the Cubans are not making a fashionable fight. It makes little difference to us how that fight is conducted, I repeat, so that it is conducted within the lines and limits of civilized warfare. Here, then, is a war, flagrant and terrible, which has existed in the Island of Cuba for two years, and we want to know what are the rights of our people in that island, on the high seas, and in the United States, as they are affected by that war. We want to know what are their rights of property and their rights of commerce as they are affected by that war. We want to take some course in the Congress of the United States that will give to them every proper shelter and protection. That is what I understand we want to do, and if we do not accomplish that, we ought at least to make the effort.

The matter of the belligerency of a country foreign to us, recognized by the Government of the United States in whatever form the Government can make the recognition, seems to produce upon the minds of some people who try to comprehend it a sort of paralysis, and they imagine that there is something in it very profound and very obscure, hard to be understood, and still more difficult to be defined. Mr. President, it seems to me there is no difficulty in the matter. It is the simplest of all problems connected with our relations with foreign countries.

Now, to illustrate this I will suppose that the Government of Spain, following the example of the Government of the United States during the civil war, should declare the belligerent rights of the insurrectionists in Cuba. What would be the effect of such a declaration upon a citizen of the United States found in the Island of Cuba, attending to his own business, taking care of his own property, without attaching himself to either of the contending parties? He would have what we call the protection of the international law, and while being on one side of the line he would be in an enemy's country, and would be treated as an enemy by those on the other side of the line, still he would not be an enemy to the civil government of Spain, but an enemy simply within the meaning of the laws of nations and the laws of war. He would be technically an enemy, and it would make no difference what his feelings or his sympathies might be toward that portion of the country where his residence or his domicile happened to be or where he was found.

Now, so much for a citizen of the United States who is in that country and who is protected in that situation by the laws of war and the laws of nations. Here is Spain recognizing the belligerent rights of Cuba as the United States recognized the belligerent rights of the people of Alabama during the late civil struggle. All who were in Alabama during that time, whether they were Northern men or Southern men, whether they were Confederates or whether they were Union men, whether their sympathies were with the people on this side of the line or on the other side of the line, were technical enemies to the United States, and were so uniformly treated. In the event of their capture, what becomes of them? If they had captured a citizen from the North who had left his home and gone South, a refugee, if you please, and while in the South had contributed money, means, everything in his power, to the advancement of the Confederate cause, after the recognition of that belligerency the Government of the United States would never have thought of trying him for treason for making such a contribution to the Confederate cause. Now, why? Because that is contrary to the law of nations. Another reason is found in the universal laws of nations, municipal as well as international, that a government de facto while its power exists has the right to compel the subordination of people to its decrees who are within the range of its authority. The citizen can always shelter himself by yielding submission to governmental authority that he is not capable of resisting.

The Senator from Delaware [Mr. GRAY] calls my attention to the fact that Mr. Davis was indicted for treason—for a capital offense. I call his attention to the fact that he was never tried for it. We need not go into that, though; we need not go into Mr. Davis's case. That was perhaps considered even here as it was considered in the South, as being somewhat exceptional, because of his preeminence as the leader of the whole of the Southern hosts, as it was said. I am speaking now of an American citizen who

2777—13

is residing in Cuba. I wish to know whether, after a declaration of belligerency, the Government of Spain, coming into possession of a man's property—his house, his farm, and all that—not finding it necessary for military purposes to destroy that man's property, but for resentment's sake, would have the right under the laws of nations to destroy his property? No, sir.

Yet, without a declaration of war, if the Government of Spain finds him with arms in his hands, though he may be in his own habitation, or if the Government of Spain finds him breaking any of the numerous proclamations which are made by the Captain-General there to suit his own fancy and will, arbitrary as they may be, and puts him on trial while a state of insurrection exists, for treason, insurrection, incendiarism, or any other crime that they please so to denominate, that man, in the absence of a state of war, is amenable to the Spanish authorities, and may be tried for such political offense and may be destroyed. Why? Because, although a state of actual war exists which that man has no power to control or get away from, he is held amenable and is condemned, and the Spanish Government is protected in its authority to condemn him because the Government of the United States refuses to say that war exists in Cuba.

Now, I have described a peaceful citizen who is in Cuba with his property, who was invited to go there by the treaty of 1795, and by every treaty with Spain that has been made since that time, who is in the prosecution of those enterprises which both Governments applaud. This quiet citizen, because of the refusal of the Government of the United States to declare the truth, is thus subjected to all the horrors and ignominies that Spanish barbarism and cruelty can inflict upon him through the forms of law—even death. That is the situation as to that innocent man.

Now, I will take a soldier, a young man from the United States, who has gone there to enlist in the Cuban struggle which has been going on now for more than two years. Their acts of heroism, their glorious achievements, have adorned the characters of living and dead in such a way as to make them conspicuous in the estimation of those young men of our race who love to realize the proud prospects of an ambitious career. He is drawn there, if you please, by the mere love of humanity. He is drawn there, if you please, for the purpose of interposing his life between the machete and the torch and the body of an innocent woman or man or little child, thinking he can better serve God by staking his life there in resistance to this horrid wrong than he can in any other way. He goes there. He confers with nobody; he forms no combination or conspiracy here which is denounced by our law. He goes under a right that belongs to every human being in the world, to leave his own country, not renouncing his citizenship, and to go to assist those whom he thinks are acting justly, who are patriots in a struggle where everything sacred is at stake.

When that man goes to Cuba, he finds armies organized; officers commissioned by a civil government. He finds Gomez in command, and other generals who hold their commissions from President Cisneros and from the civil government of the Republic of Cuba. He finds armies in camp, fully equipped; thousands of soldiers—soldiers under banners, and subject to military control in the strictest sense. He enlists in that army. What does he take upon himself when he does that? Sir, he takes upon himself the character and duty of a soldier. He becomes a soldier in the Cuban army. Now, what is a soldier, and how is that character regarded in all civilized and all semicivilized, and even barbarous countries? What man fills a higher place in the estimation of his fellows, a more glorious place when he is successful, a more honorable one when he fills a soldier's honest grave, than the man who submits himself to the discipline of an army and fights under its flag according to his free will? Who stands higher in the estimation of men of this world than such a soldier? Sir, even in the church those who follow the meek and lowly Saviour of mankind find their highest encomiums in the fact that they are called soldiers of the cross. A man who becomes a soldier has an inviolable protection thrown around him by laws that are recognized throughout Christendom, and far beyond the boundaries of Christendom.

When that man is captured in battle, he is not a captured felon; he is not a stained and a dishonored man. If the nations of this earth, sir, were to decree that, they would bring to mankind a peace which no man and no nation would ever attempt to break, for if the penalty of capture of a man in open war who is an enlisted soldier means his lawful death and also disgrace, there would be no more soldiers in this world.

Now, an American goes to the Island of Cuba, whether he is native born or whether he is an adopted citizen, whether he was born in the Island of Cuba, or whether he was born in Spain or elsewhere, for the purpose of enlisting in the army under Gomez. He does enlist, and he is captured, and captured with arms in his hands. He took upon himself the whole character and all the responsibilities and duties of a soldier when he made that enlistment; but unfortunately, by some exigency of warfare, he has fallen into the hands of the enemy. Can it be said in the nineteenth century, and in the close of it, that that man is amenable, when public war exists, to the pains and penalties of felony for treason or insurrection against Spain? We can not take an American citizen who has put himself in that condition and refuse to apply to him this universal law of exemption from civil crime in rendering honorable military service. We can not say to him, "Sir, stay at home and behave yourself, and do not go down to fight for the Cubans." If he goes, we can not say to him, "You have thrown away your prestige and protection as an American citizen. You have repudiated all of your duties to the Government of the United States in going there; and now that you have been captured, all that this great Republic has to do is to stand by and see that you are duly executed—shot to death."

I maintain that the Government of the United States disgraces itself when in the face of facts like those which exist in the Island of Cuba we refuse to say that public war exists in that country, and thus protect our citizens who go there to fight as enlisted soldiers. If Spain had made the declaration of belligerency, I repeat, we would not permit them to execute soldiers taken on the field of battle who are citizens of the United States. If the United States makes the declaration of belligerency, the same result follows. If, then, the facts justify that declaration, and if the protection of human life and the safety of human reputation against dishonor is something that we have a right to care for and it is our duty to care for, let us make the declaration. It is due to the men who go there in obedience to a sense of duty, or for any other cause, and enlist in that army under Gomez. It is due to them that this Government, when the facts justify it, should so pronounce and declare that a state of public war exists in Cuba.

What else would follow, Mr. President, from an enunciation by the Government of Spain that a state of war exists in Cuba? The same thing that followed when the civil war was prevalent here. What was that? It gave to the Government of the United States, or the government of the Confederate States, if you please, the right to search Spanish vessels approaching the coast, to see whether or not they had upon them contraband of war, to see whether they were going to participate in the warfare which was declared to exist in this country. Suppose the evidence was sufficient to show that they intended so to participate. What was the penalty? The confiscation of the ship and its cargo, perhaps, and the arrest of those men and their imprisonment. How? As prisoners of war. No other consequence at all would result from it.

Sir, under our statutes we may send our revenue cutters 12 miles from shore in time of profound peace and require or authorize them to board, to detain, to make an examination of the manifests, and even the cargoes, of ships that are destined to our ports. Why so? For the purpose of discovering whether their manifests, as compared with the cargo, would show that they were engaged in some smuggling enterprise. Even in time of peace the power of search is exercised, and in time of war we have provided expressly in the treaty which we have with the Spanish Government that the right of search shall be conducted under a certain restriction of a very important character which would prevent any injury to any merchant ships of ours that might be approaching or sailing past the Island of Cuba.

You ask me if that treaty would be in force after the passage of the joint resolution which is now before the Senate. Yes, sir; beyond all question. What is the proof of it? Spain recognized the belligerency of the Confederate States, when they were fighting the United States, before the battle of Manassas was fought. Before the South had demonstrated that it had any actual strength in resistance to the magnificent Government of the United States Spain recognized the belligerency of the Confederate States. What became of our treaty of 1795 in that recognition? It was not affected by it; it was not touched by it. If now we in turn recognize the belligerency of Cuba, is the treaty affected by it? Certainly not. That ground was taken by Mr. Fish in his correspondence with the Spanish minister, Admiral Polo de Bernabé, during the former revolution in Cuba. The treaty stands unaffected, and is all the protection the United States could possibly need in respect of the right of search, and gives to us even greater rights than are accorded to most of the maritime nations of the earth. So as a matter of security the declaration which I propose that the Senate shall make would not in the slightest degree expose us to any danger from this so-called right of search.

Now, I will suppose again that Spain does what she attempted to do and what she did do for a while during the former revolution; that is, close certain of her ports to commerce—ports that have been open there for many years, some of them for more than a century. She closed them up and declared that they were blockaded, not having the naval forces with which to guard the gates of those ports. Mr. Secretary Fish, as soon as that proclamation was made, denounced it broadly, and said that the Government of the United States would respect no paper blockade of the Island of Cuba; if they chose to blockade their ports, they must have an efficient naval force there to enforce the blockade. How would it have been in the struggle with the Confederate States if the United States Government had contented itself with declaring closed all the ports from Charleston, S. C., around to the most western boundary of Texas, and had stationed no force there for the purpose of keeping out ships? Could the Government of the United States have condemned ships that came into those with supplies to the Confederates and have confiscated them when they had no force there for the purpose of keeping the ships out? Certainly not. If Spain should declare a blockade of her ports in Cuba, she must maintain it, and unless she does maintain it those ports are open to the people of the United States and to their commerce. More than that, the treaty of 1795 expressly provides that commerce with the United States shall not cease, except in contraband, during the prevalence of any war to which Spain is a party.

With all these guaranties standing perfect and unaffected by the declaration made on the part of Spain that belligerency exists in Cuba, they stand equally unaffected by a declaration made by the United States Government that belligerency exists there. The declaration of belligerency on the part of the Government of the United States is not a hostile act. We did not complain of any hostility at the time Spain recognized the belligerency of the Confederate States, nor when Great Britain recognized their belligerency, although at that time there was very strong reason to believe, especially in the case of Great Britain, that their recognition of the belligerency of the Confederate States was in response to what they believed was the sentiment of the South that we would divide the Union and put ourselves under the British flag. Yet the Government of the United States did not say to the Government of Great Britain, "That act on your part is a belligerent or an unfriendly act." By all means we did not say such a thing to Spain when she recognized the belligerency of the Confederate States. Then, if you recognize the belligerency of the Cubans, how can Spain say, in virtue of all the facts that have occurred there within the last two years and still exist, that a declaration of belligerency of the parties engaged in open war in Cuba is a hostile act toward Spain? It is impossible, Mr. President. A declaration of that sort on her part would be a mere pretext. She could not make the declaration in good faith.

Now, in the absence of a declaration of belligerency by the Government of the United States or the Government of Spain——

Mr. TURPIE. Mr. President——

The PRESIDING OFFICER (Mr. FAULKNER in the chair). Does the Senator from Alabama yield to the Senator from Indiana?

Mr. MORGAN. Certainly.

Mr. TURPIE. I wish to call the attention of the Senator from Alabama to the fact that President Monroe recognized the belligerency of Spain as he did the belligerency of the seven South American colonies in revolt one after another within two years, and that such a recognition has never been accounted an unfriendly act on the part of the United States.

Mr. MORGAN. No, Mr. President; and yet under that sweeping declaration I suppose President Monroe contributed as much as could be contributed by any public act of a foreign country, except by an actual intervention, to the release of those colonies from their dependence upon the mother country. I suppose that the independence of South America was, after all, as much promoted by that declaration of President Monroe as by any act of war almost that took place upon this hemisphere.

Mr. TURPIE. The moral effect.

Mr. MORGAN. Yes; the moral effect of it was just that; and yet neither Spain nor any other power in the world criticised the Government of the United States for protecting their own people by a declaration of belligerency.

Mr. GRAY. Does the Senator from Indiana or the Senator from Alabama recall in what form President Monroe recognized the belligerency, whether it was by an executive declaration of the President alone or whether it was by the cooperation of Congress?

Mr. TURPIE. My recollection is—and I discussed this matter to some degree in the last Congress—that he recognized it in every instance by proclamation, and he followed such proclamation by communicating the same to Congress and inviting their concurrence, and afterwards receiving the concurrence of Congress.

Mr. HALE. By asking for an appropriation.

Mr. MORGAN. That is a fact; and if the President of the United States, Mr. McKinley, to-day wanted to recognize belligerency in Cuba and perform what I conceive to be his executive duty, he would make a proclamation so far as he is concerned; he would notify foreign governments of his intention to recognize belligerency, and he would communicate the fact to Congress. Now, why would he do that? Because here, Mr. President, rests the ultimate power of making that declaration good, the declaration of war; not of war against Spain, but a declaration of a state of war existing in a province of Spain.

But, Mr. President, I am not concerning myself about forms. I am willing to take this declaration in any form that we can get it, so that we shall interpose the authority of the people of the United States through their Government to take care of our people in Cuba who are there as soldiers, or who are there as citizens, or who are there as visitors, or in any capacity at all in the presence of a great public war.

Mr. HALE. Mr. President——

The PRESIDING OFFICER. Does the Senator from Alabama yield to the Senator from Maine?

Mr. MORGAN. Certainly.

Mr. HALE. What evidence has the Senator to back up the statement he has made two or three times that prisons, places of incarceration, in Cuba are to-day filled with American citizens? I may say that I do not believe that to be the fact. I do not believe there is any evidence producible which establishes that fact, but of course I may be wrong; and I ask the Senator to state to the Senate what he has upon which to base his repeated statement that we ought to interfere now for the protection of the American citizens who lie in incarceration improperly on the Island of Cuba.

Mr. MORGAN. In answer to the question of the honorable Senator from Maine, I must resort to a method of argumentation or statement which I understand is customary in the part of the country which he represents, and that is to answer one question by asking another. I should like to know of the Senator from Maine on what ground he predicates what he says is his belief that these statements are untrue? What information has he got and from whom? Who has denied it?

Mr. HALE. I deny it.

Mr. MORGAN. Who else?
Mr. HALE. The Senator is an old——
Mr. MORGAN. No; I am not very old.
Mr. HALE. And a very good lawyer. He is a young man in vigor——
Mr. MORGAN. Oh, very.
Mr. HALE. In power, and in earnestness; and he knows, as you know, Mr. President, and everybody knows, that it is the side which propounds the proposition that has got to report testimony and give evidence. I do not believe that the prisons of the Spanish authorities in Cuba are to-day filled with American citizens who are languishing in imprisonment, and making a reason why we should interpose down there. I have seen no testimony which shows that to be the case. I am willing that the State Department, which is the organ of the Government to consider these things, shall investigate that matter. I am willing that the Senator should go to the State Department and ask if that Department has evidence to this effect. I should like him to produce from the State Department papers, documents, and proofs, if he has them, of the proposition he maintains. But it is not for me, when I am doubtful and skeptical of these statements, to be asked to furnish my proofs. The Senator must furnish proofs.

Mr. MORGAN. I accept very cheerfully indeed the onus probandi of any fact whatever that will relieve the honorable Senator from Maine from any unhappiness on account of his friends in Spain. I would hate to afflict him with any idea that a Spaniard is capable of any cruelty whatever. I would hate in his presence to refer to the transactions of the Duke of Alva, or to the Spanish Inquisition, or to the orders that are here which require the sacrifice by shooting and death and otherwise in any form—orders of General Weyler and formerly of Balmaceda—orders, Mr. President, that Secretary Fish, General Grant, and others said were a disgrace to humanity, a shock to the human sensibilities. I would dislike very much indeed to afflict the honorable Senator from Maine with any unhappiness at all in his supposition that there are perhaps no characters in the world so innocent as the Spaniards. I might prosecute that inquiry in the same direction and ask him why it is that he believes, as I know he does, that the Armenians have been sacrificed in Turkey. What evidence has the Senator that the Armenians have ever been butchered in Turkey?

Mr. HALE. I do not want the Senator to escape from my question——

The PRESIDING OFFICER. Does the Senator from Alabama yield to the Senator from Maine?

Mr. MORGAN. Oh, yes.

Mr. HALE. I do not want the Senator from Alabama to escape from my question, which relates directly to the subject-matter of this debate, by references to the Duke of Alva, or to Spanish history in the past, or to the Armenians, or the Abyssinians, or what not. I want him to give the Senate some authority for his statement that one reason why we should intervene is because the Spanish prisons in Cuba to-day are stuffed with American citizens who languish in imprisonment there. My information is just the reverse. My information and my belief is that in the last six months, notably in the last six weeks, in every case where the proper authorities of the Government to whom are intrusted and who manage our diplomatic relations have intervened for the release of American citizens in Spanish prisons in Cuba the response has been at once made in a friendly tone, and that many, and nearly all, and for aught I know all, who have been arrested have been freed. I do not say that all have. But when the Senator says that those prisons are filled with American citizens I can only say that I do not believe it. I do not believe that the Senator is making a statement that he knows to be false. I do not think that he has complete information on the subject. And my attitude of doubtfulness in this matter is not in any way caused by friendship that I have for Spain. I care nothing about that. I am only seeking to adopt the course of proceedings in this case which is in accordance with the long record of diplomacy in this country for a hundred years, which has been not inflammatory, but conservative at every point where it can be reached.

Mr. MORGAN. Now, if the honorable Senator has got done making his speech, which is all right, I will proceed and answer him as well as I can, and seriatim, too.

The Senator insists that he does not believe a word of this thing, that the Spanish prisons are stuffed with American prisoners. Perhaps the word "stuffed" grates upon the sensibilities of the Senator, and I will take that back and say "crowded," for I suppose that, according to the statements made by those who have come from there here, who are reputable people and who have made their statements to the State Department and also to the public press, as many as twenty prisoners confined in a room that is 19 feet long by 7 feet wide, without a place to lie down or a bench to sit upon, and with all of the inconveniences that it is possible to conceive of in such a situation, would be in rather a crowded state; and American citizens testify when they come out that that is true. There is sworn testimony before this body now in the form of depositions that have been given before the Committee on Foreign Relations which proves these facts. That the Senator from Maine does not believe that is not shocking to me, for I do not think the Senator is capable of believing anything that casts the slightest impeachment in the world upon a Spaniard. I repeat, he seems to have some holy idea of the Spanish character which forbids him to acknowledge that under any circumstances one of these saintly murderers could have any harm or malice in his bosom.

Mr. HALE. Now, let me say right there——

Mr. MORGAN. No; I object. I am answering you now.

The PRESIDING OFFICER. The Senator from Alabama declines to yield.

Mr. HALE. I can not, of course, interrupt the Senator except by his consent.

Mr. MORGAN. I am answering your argument now, and I object to any more interruptions on this subject.

Mr. President, we have a newspaper press in the United States, and I am very glad that we have, because through that agency we have acquired knowledge of what goes on in Cuba and elsewhere in the world, even in Armenia. In the main it turns out that the consensus of statement made by the American press in respect to a matter occurring in a foreign country is true. At all events, when they all concur in making a series of statements with one accord, it will put even the Senator from Maine upon the defensive to make some explanation or some statement on the subject. He says he has informed himself and does not believe what these papers state. When I ask him who his informant is, he declines to answer. I know who it is, and the world knows who it is. The Senator from Maine can not conceal the fact that he is in constant communication with the Spanish Government for the purpose of ascertaining the best way of defending them.

Mr. HALE. Let me ask the Senator to repeat that statement.

The PRESIDING OFFICER. Does the Senator from Alabama yield?

Mr. HALE. I was talking with the Senator from Indiana and I did not hear what the Senator said.

Mr. MORGAN. I stated that the Senator from Maine had said that he had sources of information which convinced him that these statements were untrue. Now, what are they?

Mr. HALE. Not one single item of information that I have received as to the condition in Cuba comes from the Spanish authorities or any representative of them. I have talked with man after man who has visited Cuba within the last six months. I have letters, correspondence, and statements that, if this debate continues, I shall put before the Senate, showing my authority; and they come not from Spanish authorities, but from actual American citizens, with American names, American descent, American experience, and American residence.

Mr. MORGAN. This statement that the Senator has made at last discloses where his sources of information come from. Do they contradict what the American papers say?

Mr. HALE. They do not contradict what the American people say, but they contradict very squarely what the Senator from Alabama says; and I do not recognize that the Senator from Alabama, in seeking to inflame this condition and to bring about a condition of hostilities, represents the American people, Mr. President, by a great deal.

Mr. MORGAN. It is a matter of indifference to me what the Senator thinks that I represent, Mr. President. I speak from what the American press has said here, and every man in this body knows what it is. The American press has uniformly stated that not only were there many prisoners whose names were known in the prison houses of Habana, men and women, and even little children, but that there were very many whose names were entirely unknown to the world.

* * * * * * *

April 7, 1897.

Mr. MORGAN. I move that the Senate resume the consideration of the joint resolution (S. R. 26) declaring that a condition of public war exists in Cuba, and that strict neutrality shall be maintained.

Mr. HALE. The Senator, I suppose, desires to go on with his remarks.

Mr. MORGAN. Yes.

Mr. HALE. I do not object, of course. When the hour of 2 o'clock comes——

Mr. MORGAN. Of course when the hour of 2 o'clock arrives, it will cut me off, as well as the resolution.

The PRESIDENT pro tempore. The question is on agreeing to the motion of the Senator from Alabama, that the Senate resume the consideration of the joint resolution indicated.

The motion was agreed to; and the Senate, as in Committee of the Whole, resumed the consideration of the joint resolution.

Mr. MORGAN. Mr. President, yesterday, when my observations on this subject were being somewhat systematically presented, according to a usage of the Senate which I think ought to be more honored in the breach than in the observance, there was an interruption which threw me off to a collateral question, a matter of no consequence in the consideration of the merits of the joint resolution. Leaving that matter and all that concerns it, for the present at least, I shall proceed with the argument I was endeavoring to make, to show what are the rights of citizens of the United States when a declaration of the existence of belligerency or war in Cuba shall be made either by the Government of Spain or the Government of the United States. I had proceeded with a sentence, which was broken into, stating that an announcement by Spain that such a declaration on our part was a hostile act would be a mere pretext; that she could not make the declaration in good faith.

In the absence of a declaration of belligerency by the Government of the United States or the Government of Spain we have found that all the municipal regulations, laws of Spain, whether they are specially applicable to Cuba or whether they are locally applicable to Spain, and all the edicts of the Captains-General in Cuba, who have claimed the right and have exercised it, and now exercise it, of proclaiming martial law in that island, and, under that proclamation of martial law, of defining new offenses to be punished in a military way by what we call a drumhead court-martial—all of those things have combined together for the purpose, or at least to the effect, of putting American citizenship there entirely in subordination to Spanish law, whether it is enacted by the Cortes for the peninsula or by that Government for the Island of Cuba, or whether it is Spanish law resulting from the mere edict of the Captain-General.

I can not conceive, even without reference to the Government of Spain and the enormous barbarities that have been perpetrated by that Government in the execution of its so-called laws, that any government in the world can hold toward the people of the United States a relation of that character. Not only the laws of civilized warfare but the laws of nations attend a citizen of the United States wherever he may go, and save to him at least the right of trial in the jurisdictions of that country inaugurated by the civil authority in time of peace, unless the condition of peace has been interrupted and a state of public war exists. That is rather an important statement connected with the situation of the people of the United States in the Island of Cuba.

If no government in the world has the right, under the laws of nations, to try our citizens by newly devised machinery or for offenses hitherto unknown to any civil code, and convict them and sentence them to death or to imprisonment for life without the concurrence of the Government of the United States, either expressly or by implication, it must follow that as to the Island of Cuba, where there are three situations created by law, to each of which the citizen of the United States is held responsible under different penalties and to different tribunals, there is great occasion for serious and earnest consideration whether our people in that island are being made to suffer contrary to the laws of nations. There is great and immediate occasion for requiring that the people of the United States in the Island of Cuba shall have the protection of our treaty rights. I deny utterly and absolutely that the Government of Spain can have any right at all to take up a citizen of the United States found insubordinate or inimical to her civil institutions, or raising or promoting insurrection in that island, and try him in any other mode than that prescribed in the treaty of 1795 as it has been modified by the protocol in the year 1877. It will not do for the Government of Spain to be permitted, when it has a treaty with us like that of 1795, followed as it has been since that time by modifications on several occasions, to ignore and discard the binding obligations of that treaty, and to take our citizens and try them in any form it thinks best for offenses declared by a captain-general under martial law at a time when peace is said to prevail in that island.

Now, unquestionably the evidence is plain, coming from a great many undisputed sources, that this has been done by Spanish authority. Weyler and Campos and other officials of Spain when in authority in Cuba have issued proclamations denouncing new offenses against all persons, including the people of the United States who are peaceably residing on that island—new offenses unknown to the civil code of Spain, unknown to the laws of nations, and unknown to anybody except the Captain-General who proclaims these laws—and put them in force against American citizens in a time of peace in the Island of Cuba.

That brings up the main proposition, which I state as follows: That in time of peace in the Island of Cuba the power of the Spanish Crown or any other power subordinate to the Crown can not have the right to decree new crimes, by proclamation, against citizens of the United States residing there, and put them on trial before a military court-martial for those new offenses. That is a moral and legal impossibility in the view we have always had of the rights of American people under the laws of nations, and in view of our treaties with Spain. What has been the result in Cuba? The President of the United States, in his last annual message, refers to some of these consequences and results, and without stopping to read them I will state them, because I think I can do it with accuracy and fairness. He says that the people of the United States, along with other masses of the population in Cuba, have been compelled to leave their homes and to herd themselves in the towns and villages, there to receive support from the Government of Spain through rations issued by the military authority, and a breach of those regulations is attended with a denunciation against them of penalties of such severity as would reach even to life or imprisonment for life.

Men are not allowed to pass out of those villages without passes certified by certain military authorities. That may be well enough for police purposes, but how do they get into the villages? Who brought them there? Under what authority of law were these men assembled in those villages and towns? They have been herded together like cattle and driven by the soldiery into those places, not for refuge, not for protection, but for the avowed purpose of starvation. Why do I say "for the avowed purpose of starvation?" Because they are purposely driven from their homes and are denied the privilege of drawing supplies from their own farms and gardens and are required to place themselves upon rations to be issued by the Government of Spain. This is part of a plan of general devastation. The penalty for the violation of these regulations is outlawry. That means exposure to any act that any guerrilla or any Spanish soldier may see proper to inflict upon the poor sufferer.

Having treaties with us in which Spain engages that our citizens shall live in peace upon the Island of Cuba, that when offenses are charged against them they shall be tried by certain tribunals and in a certain way, and that the offenses which are charged are described in the act of 1821, when they relate to hostility toward the Government, and not in any law to be newly enacted by the ukase or decree of the Captain-General—when these things occur, our people are protected by that treaty from all assault on the part of the military authorities of the kind that Weyler has continually waged against citizens of the United States.

The President of the United States, in his last annual message, referring to these facts, deplores them, but he offers no corrective. I believe, sir, that in that way there has occurred many of the most grievous outrages of all that have been inflicted by the Government of Spain upon the citizens of the United States. What is the pretext for this situation? The Spanish pretext is that insurrection exists in the Island of Cuba. Sir, that is no justification. The nation which declares that insurrection exists, and not war, must affirm, and does affirm, its ability to quell the insurrection by the civil authority without waging war and prosecuting military operations; and failing to do that, its responsibility for the results is confessed. When the Government of Spain admits by the attitude which she takes toward the citizens of the United States that an insurrection exists in the Island of Cuba, and that we have the right to look to her for the suppression of that insurrection, she at the same time admits that she has not any right to suspend the civil laws in the Island of Cuba and to put the island in a state of war without making a public declaration to that effect.

Now, here has been the difficulty all the time in the attitude of Spain toward the people of the United States, that while they use every measure that war justifies for controlling the Island of Cuba, for restoring the island, as they say, to peace or to pacification, they, at the same time, deny the existence of war and refuse to give to the people of the United States resident there, or who may happen to be there, the protection which belongs to a state of war. In a state of profound peace, as they assert, they not only proclaim martial law, but they enforce the proclamation by military authority and military forces, resulting almost in every instance where conviction is had in a military court in the immediate execution of the alleged convict by the guns of the soldiery. That condition of affairs plainly violates the treaty of 1795, and the President of the United States, when he sent in his annual message in December, seems to have been entirely cognizant of that fact, for he complains of it and makes his complaint a very forcible one against the Government of Spain. But no remedy comes; there is no relief.

In view of this situation, I ask the Senate of the United States how long are we to abide under the present condition of affairs? How long is this authority of the Captain-General of Cuba to continue, when he can day after day, according to his own whim and caprice, issue new orders defining new crimes, suspending civil law, and requiring our people on the island to be subjected to those orders and those offenses as he may conceive they have been perpetrated? How long are we to wait for that? When ought that to stop? What relief are our people getting from that situation? None, Mr. President, has been obtained as yet. None is promised. None is expected. Is it not necessary, therefore, that the Government of the United States should define its attitude in this matter with reference to citizens of the United States, in order that they may know what to rely upon, or that they may gather up what effects they can possibly bring away and leave the island and come home for protection?

How much property have the people of the United States in the Island of Cuba? The President of the United States says that we have $50,000,000 worth of property there. If one man is compelled to leave because of the outrages perpetrated against his property or his person, why not another? These decrees of condemnation for offenses that are defined only by the proclamations of Weyler amount not merely to outlawry against our people, but to decrees of banishment from the Island of Cuba. Sir, I maintain that no such outrage has ever been attempted to be perpetrated by one nation against another in the world as that which now holds up its haughty head and demands the submission of the United States and her people to such decrees.

I think I have sufficiently stated, yesterday and to-day, the groundwork, the basis, the principles, upon which I found this joint resolution. I could appeal to the history of the Senate, to its action of a year ago, and justify this joint resolution fully. I could appeal to its action of day before yesterday and equally well justify it in every particular. In both of these declarations we have announced the existence of a state of public war in Cuba. When that announcement is made, then there follows the necessary corollary that the laws of civilized warfare apply to the contest in the island. We can not get rid of it. Is the declaration true? Does public war exist there? If it is true, and if public war does exist there, then our citizens have the right to the shelter of the laws provided by the consent of the civilized nations of the earth for that sort of protection which is given to a people when the country they are occupying is engaged in public war. I need not go on and attempt to define all of the rights that come from this condition, but I will refer to a text-book for the purpose of showing one or two of them, and then later on I will show by evidence that I have to adduce here how far these rights have been abused in the Island of Cuba.

Yesterday I adverted to the fact that a declaration of belligerency or a declaration that war exists in a particular country places every man who is in that country in legal or technical hostility to the country with which it is engaged in war. So I will not go over that ground except merely to restate it. When a state of war exists in any country, a man who is not a spy, who is not affected by some very extraordinary aggravation of crime, either in intent or in act, and who is captured when he is engaged in waging war, is entitled to the immunities, privileges, and protection that are clearly laid down in the laws of nations for his government and the government of the powers into whose hands he may fall in time of war.

On the subject of the treatment of noncombatants when a state of war prevails this author—Col. George B. Davis—who writes very clearly and very succinctly, evidently for the purpose of making plain many things that otherwise might be obscure to any but a law student, says:

Treatment of noncombatants in the theater of war.—It has been seen that the subjects of two belligerent states become enemies at the outbreak or declaration of war. They continue in this hostile relation during its continuance. This status does not authorize them to commit acts of hostility, however, which can only be undertaken by persons having the express authorization of the belligerent governments. The rest of the population of a belligerent territory are not only forbidden to take an active part in military operations, but are entitled to personal immunity and protection so long as they refrain, in good faith, from taking part in the war. A portion of their property may be taken, with or without compensation; their houses and lands may be occupied and injured, or possibly destroyed, as a matter of military necessity, but their persons, and such of their property as is not confiscable by the laws of war, are, by the same laws, completely protected. Any offense committed against them or their property is an offense against the laws of war, and is promptly and severely punished. This exemption from the operations of war they continue to enjoy so long as they take no active part in hostile operations. If they act with the authority of their government, they become a part of its military force, and are treated accordingly. If they act without such authorization and in violation of the usages of war, they are no longer protected, but are punished according to the nature and degree of their offense.

A combatant is a person who, with the special authorization of his government, takes part, either directly or indirectly, in the operations of war. The term includes, in addition to the troops of the line, all staff officers, surgeons, and chaplains, officers and employees of the supply and transport service, all agents, contractors, and others who accompany the army in an official capacity, and who assist in its movement, equipment, or maintenance, and all retainers to the camp.

A noncombatant is a resident of a belligerent state who takes no part in the war. He is not subject to the laws of war, and is protected by them in his person and property so long as he refrains from participating in military operations.

Prisoners of war.—A prisoner of war is a combatant who, by capture or surrender, falls into the hands of an enemy. In strictness an enemy has the right to make prisoners of those persons only whom he may lawfully kill in war. In practice, however, the former class is much more numerous than the latter.

I proceed now to read from the text as to the treatment of prisoners:

So soon as an individual of the enemy ceases his armed resistance he becomes vested with all the rights of a prisoner of war. The right to injure him is at that instant changed into the duty of protecting him and of preventing his escape. The public property and arms found in the possession of a prisoner at the time of his capture become the property of the capturing state. His private property is respected and secured to him by the usages of war. Were it not so protected, every consideration of honor and humanity should deter his captor from any act of aggression toward one who, from his situation, is unable to defend himself.

* * * * * * *

Prisoners of war are not guilty of a crime in having defended their country. Their confinement, therefore, can not assume a penal character, but must consist in such measures of detention as will secure them against danger of escape. A prisoner of war in attempting to escape does not commit a crime. It is his duty to escape if a favorable opportunity presents itself. It is equally the duty of his captor to prevent his escape, and he is justified in resorting to any measures, not punitive in character, that will best secure that end. A prisoner of war may be killed in attempting to escape. If recaptured, his confinement may be made more rigorous than before.

According to the present rule of international law, the status of a prisoner of war may be terminated (1) by exchange; (2) by ransom; (3) by the treaty of peace at the end of the war.

I need not refer to that horn-book learning on the subject of the treatment of prisoners of war for the purpose of informing the Senate, but our constituents have a right to know exactly what the laws of war are in relation to a prisoner when he is captured, and what are his rights after his capture. This clear statement relieves me of the necessity of going any further into the discussion of this subject, and I turn now to the inquiry which was presented by the Senator from Maine [Mr. HALE] to ascertain whether prisoners have been made of citizens of the United States, and whether these are prisoners of war or whether they are culprits arrested under civil process and incarcerated for crimes against the municipal laws of Spain.

In every instance every prisoner who has been arrested in Cuba (I speak of American prisoners) has been held in a condition that they call "incomunicado" in prison during a number of days, varying from seven to twenty-one. What is that condition of "incomunicado?" The man is arrested without a warrant. No complaint is served upon him. He is not informed of the ground of his arrest. He does not know what accusation is brought against him. He is totally ignorant of the nature of the crime with which he may be charged. He is carried to a prison and locked in there. No human being except a military officer is allowed to have any communication with him during that period of time, and that military officer will not hold any communication with him except upon the subject of his alleged crime, using detective power most adroitly for the purpose of extracting from him statements in regard to his movements during any given period of time, afterwards getting these facts (which the officer records, perhaps, or retains in his mind) together in such form as that upon them an accusation of crime can be predicated.

That is what takes place when a man is placed in prison "incomunicado." He is not allowed to receive a letter from any human being or to read a newspaper or to gain information from any source whatsoever. He is locked up in absolute silence, and has no one to talk with him or speak in his hearing except an officer of the military force. All these arrests are military. There has not been one civil arrest made in Cuba of an American citizen during the time of the present war in that island.

Then, at a time to be fixed by this officer, usually at night—in some cases the records before us now show that these efforts to entrap the prisoners into confessions were made in the late hours of the night—at a time fixed by the officer, he enters the prison and commences to inquire of the prisoner what has taken place, what he has done and what he has said, where he has been, with whom he has communicated, and what papers or letters he has received from anyone. He is searched, as a matter of course; his house is searched; any place where he may have been is searched for the purpose of discovering testimony against him, if by possibility they can find any scrap of evidence to involve him in a crime. He makes his statement or he stands mute. If he stands mute, that is taken as a confession of guilt; therefore he is obliged to talk. He comes out and makes a statement, and a record of the statement is retained to be laid before the authorities when they formulate against him the charges upon which he is to be tried.

He remains in that condition until these secret examinations and inquisitions are entirely completed. They are the offspring of the old Spanish Inquisition. The same methods were used in the inquisitorial chambers and dungeons for the purpose of extorting by torture if necessary, by breaking on a wheel if necessary, admissions and confessions of crimes which in the majority of cases had never been committed. This offshoot from the old inquisitorial formula and practice is carried on in the Island of Cuba, and American citizens are subjected to it.

Now, I am speaking by the card, because here is the evidence, much of it sworn to, to prove that that is so. And that state of affairs has existed, and it has existed in defiance of the treaty of 1795 and the treaty of 1877 and the modifications of the treaty of 1795 that have taken place. There stands the treaty. Here are the performances of these secret inquisitions, and here is the United States, with its Senate and its House of Representatives and its President as dumb as stone statutes, standing by and looking on all this with composure, and tacitly admitting that Spain has got the right to pursue our citizens in this form and to these ends.

Now, the Senator from Maine took issue with me yesterday upon a statement as to the prisons of Cuba being crowded, or "stuffed" was the expression that I used, with Americans who had been arrested and incarcerated there since the beginning of the present hostilities in 1895.

I have here Executive Document No. 84, Fifty-fourth Congress, second session, that was sent in to us January 25, 1897, by President Cleveland. It was in response to a resolution of this body. In that paper he gives a statement of the arrest of seventy-four American prisoners who have been lodged in these jails and made "incomunicado," all put under the inquisition, some few of them discharged, others held, some condemned to death, some to perpetual imprisonment in chains, notwithstanding the provisions of the treaty of 1795 that absolutely forbid the trial of these people before the jurisdictions to which they were held responsible, and notwithstanding the laws of nations, which protect our citizens everywhere, that they shall have free and impartial trial in actions of a civil nature in the same manner that citizens of the country where they are found shall have free and impartial and open trials.

I remark again that Spain uses against the citizens of the United States only military methods for the purpose of prosecuting them for what she alleges are civil offenses committed in time of peace. No man has been arrested in Cuba upon a civil warrant. No man has had the cause of his arrest stated to him or been informed of it until he had passed through this stage of "incomunicado," and until there was extorted from him by this inquisitorial process whatever the examiner might be able to extract from him either under terror or under deception. Yet seventy-four prisoners were certified to, their names given and the offenses of which they were accused, and the place of their incarceration is stated in this paper sent by the President of the United States. And yet the Senator from Maine said that he denied the whole of it; he denied positively that there was any evidence before the country or any had been produced to show that a single American citizen, as I understood him, had been taken thus and arrested and incarcerated——

Mr. HALE. No.

Mr. MORGAN. And stuffed into a prison.

Mr. HALE. The Senator does not of course wish to make a misstatement.

Mr. MORGAN. No, I do not.

Mr. HALE. I did not by any means deny that there are cases of American citizens now in prison in Cuba, but I did deny and stated that I disbelieved the statement of the Senator that the prisons are filled. I have taken occasion since yesterday to go to the State Department, and I have found there that in all there are twelve now in prison, three or four of whom the Secretary expects will be soon released. Three were taken with arms in their hands—there is no question about them—and the others are the crew of a ship. I forget the name of it.

Mr. MORGAN. The *Competitor*.

Mr. NELSON. The *Competitor*.

Mr. HALE. The others are the crew of the *Competitor*. So, instead of the disclosure of such a situation as the prisons being filled, as the Senator stated yesterday, which I did question, there are only these cases, twelve in all, with the expectation that they will be disposed of as I have indicated. I stated yesterday that I did not know that all had been released, and I then believed that all had not been released; but I have found the condition as shown by the State Department to be precisely what I supposed it was.

Mr. MORGAN. I will not delay the Senate by reading this letter——

The PRESIDING OFFICER (Mr. CANNON in the chair). The Senator from Alabama will suspend. The hour of 2 o'clock having arrived, the Chair lays before the Senate the unfinished business, which will be stated.

The SECRETARY. A bill (S. 1035) to establish uniform laws on the subject of bankruptcies throughout the United States.

Mr. HALE. As I think it is the understanding that soon after 2 o'clock there shall be an adjournment on account of certain meetings that are to be held, and it is desirable to have a short executive session, I move that the Senate proceed to the consideration of executive business.

Mr. MORGAN. I have not yielded the floor to any gentleman for any purpose.

Mr. HALE. The Senator has not the floor after the expiration of the morning hour.

Mr. MORGAN. There is no understanding with me about anything. I am occupying the floor now, and I expect to hold it until I get ready to yield it.

Mr. HALE. I supposed it to be well understood that when the hour of 2 o'clock arrives a Senator who is speaking in the morning hour is taken off the floor by the unfinished business. He is not then on the floor. It was then that I obtained the floor and made the motion.

Mr. HOAR. You were recognized.

Mr. HALE. I was recognized by the Chair. I supposed I had the floor.

Mr. MORGAN. The Chair had not announced that the hour of 2 o'clock had arrived. I was merely desiring to put in the RECORD a part of the evidence upon which I rely. I of course recognize the fact, Mr. President, that everything must give way to a political caucus and to other matters of that kind, and therefore I must yield the floor at this moment, after putting this document into the RECORD, and there I will close my remarks for to-day.

Mr. HALE. I do not object——

The PRESIDING OFFICER. The Senator from Alabama is mistaken. The Chair had announced that the hour of 2 o'clock having arrived, the unfinished business was in order.

Mr. MORGAN. I had not heard that announcement.

The PRESIDING OFFICER. Thereupon the Chair recognized the Senator from Maine, whose motion is in order.

Mr. HALE. I do not, of course, object to the Senator putting in the RECORD the document to which he refers.

Mr. MORGAN. The Senator from Maryland [Mr. GORMAN] interrupted me just as the Chair was speaking, and therefore I did not hear what the Chair stated. That is all of it.

Mr. HALE. I supposed the Senator understood the arrangement. His side agreed to it.

Mr. MORGAN. No; I did not know anything about it. I never am cognizant of such things until drawn into the vortex of political action like a chip around the circumference of a whirlpool.

The PRESIDING OFFICER. The Chair hears no objection to the request of the Senator from Alabama, and the document referred to will be printed in the RECORD.

2777—14

The document is as follows:

[Senate Document No. 54, Fifty-fourth Congress, second session.]
LIST OF CITIZENS OF UNITED STATES ARRESTED IN CUBA

MESSAGE FROM THE PRESIDENT OF THE UNITED STATES, TRANSMITTING, IN RESPONSE TO SENATE RESOLUTION OF DECEMBER 21, 1896, A REPORT OF THE SECRETARY OF STATE COVERING A LIST OF PERSONS CLAIMING TO BE CITIZENS OF THE UNITED STATES WHO HAVE BEEN ARRESTED ON THE ISLAND OF CUBA SINCE FEBRUARY 24, 1895, TO THE PRESENT TIME.

JANUARY 25, 1897.—Referred to the Committee on Foreign Relations, and ordered to be printed.

To the Senate of the United States:

I transmit herewith, in response to the Senate resolution of December 21, 1896, addressed to the Secretary of State, a report of that officer covering a list of persons claiming to be citizens of the United States who have been arrested on the Island of Cuba since February 24, 1895, to the present time.

GROVER CLEVELAND.

EXECUTIVE MANSION,
Washington, January 25, 1897.

THE PRESIDENT:

The undersigned, Secretary of State, having received a resolution passed in the Senate of the United States on December 21, 1896, in the following words—

That the Secretary of State be, and he is hereby, directed to send to the Senate a report of all naturalized citizens of the United States of whose arrest and imprisonment, trial or conviction, or sentence, either to imprisonment at the penal colony of Centro or elsewhere, he has any information, and that he shall inform the Senate in such report of the persons now held in confinement at Centro and of the charges, briefly stated, on which they were condemned and the nature of the evidence, so far as the same appears on the files of the State Department:—

has the honor to lay before the President a list of persons claiming to be citizens of the United States who have been arrested in Cuba since February 24, 1895, to the present date, to the end that, if in the President's judgment not incompatible with the public interest, the same be transmitted to the Senate in response to the foregoing resolution.

Since the breaking out of the insurrection in Cuba, on February 24, 1895, to the present time, 74 persons citizens of the United States, or claiming to be such, have been arrested by the Spanish authorities of the island.

Passports, certificates of naturalization, registration in the consulates of this Government on the Island of Cuba, and service on ships sailing under the flag of the United States having been alike accepted by our consular officers and the Spanish authorities as prima facie evidence of citizenship establishing the rights of the claimants to the treatment secured to our citizens under our treaties and protocols with Spain, it has been deemed advisable to include in the subjoined list all persons of the classes referred to who have been arrested.

Of the 74 persons arrested, 7 have been tried, namely, Nos. 1, 69, 70, 71, 72, 73, and 74. In the cases of 2 of these (Nos. 1 and 69) appeals have been taken, and in the cases of the other 5, the *Competitor* prisoners, a new trial has been ordered.

Thirty-six persons arrested have been released after the charges against them had been investigated and found to be baseless.

Eighteen have been expelled from the island after periods of confinement lasting from a few days to nearly a year in the case of José Aguirre (No. 2); while 17 cases are still pending. The charges against 14 of the 17 are as follows:

Nos. 31 and 55, sedition and rebellion.
No. 38, rebellion.
Nos. 37, 40, 61, and 62, rebellion with arms in hand.
No. 49, purchase and concealment of arms and ammunition.
No. 53, disorderly conduct and insults to Spain.
Nos. 70, 71, 72, 73, and 74, landing arms from *Competitor* for insurgents.

In the remaining three cases (Nos. 35, 47, and 52), the nature of the charges having not yet been ascertained, demand has been made both at Habana and Madrid that they be at once formulated and communicated or that prisoners be released.

Mr. Delgado (No. 54) died in hospital at Habana on the 19th instant.

Besides the above 74 cases, 9 correspondents of various newspapers in the United States have been expelled from Cuba by the Spanish authorities, after temporary detention by the military.

No American citizen has been sentenced or is confined at Centro.

Demands have been made upon the Spanish Government in every case where trial seems to be unreasonably delayed that it go forward at once or prisoner be released.

Respectfully submitted.

RICHARD OLNEY.

DEPARTMENT OF STATE,
Washington, January 22, 1897.

List of American citizens, native and naturalized, arrested and imprisoned in Cuba since February 24, 1895, to date, stating also cause of arrest, charges, place of confinement, whether tried, released, deported, or cases pending.

1. Julio Sanguily, 49 years; native of Cuba; naturalized 1878; arrested February 24, 1895; charge of rebellion; tried November 28, 1895; found guilty and sentenced to life imprisonment; case appealed to supreme court, Madrid. Was also tried on charge of participation in the kidnaping of the sugar planter Fernandez de Castro, in 1894, by the late bandit, Manuel Garcia, and acquitted. Tried for the second time December 21, 1895, for rebellion, the case remanded from Spain, and again sentenced December 28 to life imprisonment; an appeal taken. Has been imprisoned in the Cabana fort.

2. José Maria Timoteo Aguirre, 53 years; native of Cuba; naturalized 1881; arrested February 24, 1895; charge of rebellion; confined in Cabana fort; acquitted and deported September 6, 1895; went to the United States.

3. Francisco Peraza, arrested at Sagua March 2, 1895; charge of participation in the robbery of some cattle; released March 4, 1895.

4. Francisco Carrillo, 45 years; native of Cuba; naturalized 1891; arrested at Remedios on February 24, 1895, upon a gubernative order for not having inscribed himself in the register of foreigners in any province of the island; confined in Cabana fort; released and deported to United States May 29, 1895.

5. Juan Rodriguez Valdes, native of Cuba; naturalized 1876; arrested at Puerto Principe April 5, 1895; released April 6.

6. Justo Gener, 68 years; native of Cuba; naturalized; arrested at Matanzas April 6; released April 9, 1895.

7. José Maria Caraballo, 42 years; native of Cuba; naturalized 1877; arrested at Matanzas April 6; released April 9, 1895.

8. Manuel Fuentes, 33 years; native of Cuba; naturalized 1889; correspondent New York World; arrested at Caimanera April 30, 1895; released May 4, 1895, on condition that he return to United States.

9. Manuel Vergas, arrested at Remedios July 3, 1895; released and expelled July 13, 1895; charged with being an agent of the insurgents, etc.; naturalized.

10. Domingo Gonzalez y Alfonso, 42 years; native of Cuba; naturalized 1876; arrested at Quivican July 3, 1895; expelled September 3, 1895, for the reason that his presence in the island is a source of danger to the Government.

11. Victoriano Bulit Perez, 33 years; native of Cuba, of American parents; arrested at Sagua July 12, 1895; accused of "proposing treasonable acts;" released November 9, 1895.

12. Joseph A. Ansley, 56 years; born in Habana, of American parents; arrested at Sagua August 26, 1895; charge, "presence prejudicial to peace of island;" deported to United States September 21, 1895.

13. Aurelio Ansley, 34 years; son of Joseph A. Ansley. Same as above.

14. Luis Ansley, 30 years; son of Joseph Ansley. Same as above.

15. John A. Sowers, 65 years; native of Virginia. Same as above.

16. Carlos M. Garcia y Ruiz, 28 years; born in the United States; arrested at Sagua September 7, 1895; accused of attempting to join the insurrectionists; released October 7, 1895.

17. José Martinez Gonzalez, 45 years; native of Cuba; naturalized 1873; arrested at Sagua September 12, 1895; charge of riding on railroad without paying fare; no evidence against him; released September 19, 1895.

18. Mariano Rodriguez Zayas, native of Cuba; arrested at Habana September 17; released September 19, 1895; naturalized; no charges.

19. José Martinez Mesa, 41 years; native of Cuba; naturalized 1878; arrested at Habana September 17, 1895; released September 19, 1895; no charges.

20. Eugene Pelletier, 42 years; native of Cuba; naturalized 1877; arrested at Cienfuegos December 5, 1895; charged with recruiting for the insurrection; released, under surveillance, May 17, 1896.

21. Joseph J. Trelles, native of Cuba; naturalized; arrested at Matanzas December 24, 1895; released December 26, 1895; no charges.

22. Manuel M. (or W.) Amieva, 39 years; native of Cuba; naturalized 1878; arrested at Matanzas December 24, 1895, as a suspect; released December 31, 1895; no charges.

23. Charles S. Solomon, native of the United States, arrested and released.

24. Marcos E. Rodriguez, 57 years; native of Cuba; naturalized 1873; arrested January 17, 1896, on board American steamship *Olivette;* charge, aiding the rebellion, sedition, etc.; released April 1, 1896.

25. Louis Someillan, sr., 58 years; born in Cuba; naturalized Key West 1878; arrested January 17, 1896, at Habana; released April 1, 1896; charge, aiding rebellion, sedition, etc.

26. Louis Someillan, jr., 36 years; born in Habana, son of above; arrested January 17 at Habana; released April 1, 1896; charge, aiding rebellion, sedition, etc.

27. Ladislao Quintero, born in Key West; made a prisoner of war February 22, 1896, at Guatao, where he had been wounded by Spanish troops; released April 11, 1896.

28. Walter Grant Dygert, 25 years; born in the United States; arrested February 23, 1896; imprisoned at Guines; supposed to be insurgent leader El Inglesito; finally released and sent to the United States April 24, 1896.

29. Rev. Albert J. Diaz, native of Cuba; naturalized; arrested at Habana April 16, 1896, charged with forwarding rebel correspondence; confined at police headquarters; expelled April 16, 1896; accused of abetting insurrection.

30. Alfred Diaz; brother of above; arrested, same charge; both of the Diazes were released April 22, 1896, on condition of leaving the country; went to Key West.

31. Joseph L. Cepero, native of Cuba; naturalized 1881; arrested prior to January 20, 1896, on board steamer from Cienfuegos to Batabano; case now pending before civil court Santa Clara; confined in Santa Clara prison; charge, sedition, rebellion, etc.

32. Luis Martinez, arrested about March 1, 1896; charged with treasonable correspondence; released April 13, 1896, on $400 bail; naturalized 1873.

33. William A. Glean, native of Cuba, of American parents; arrested at Sagua April, 1896; charge, rebellion; military jurisdiction inhibited in favor of civil July 28, 1896; released and returned to the United States.

34. Louis M. Glenn, brother of the above; same as above.

35. Frank J. Larrieu, native of Cuba; naturalized; arrested at Cardenas May 15, 1896; case pending; charges not made known.

36. Louis Someillan, 58 years; native of Cuba; naturalized; arrested July 7, 1896, for second time; charge, aiding rebellion; turned over to civil court; is confined in city prison; trial held January 8, 1897; sentenced January 13 to imprisonment in chains for life; appeal taken.

37. Manuel Fernandez Chaqueilo, 19 years; native of Key West; captured July 9, 1896; was the companion of Charles Govin; is in Cabaña fort; case pending, under military jurisdiction; charge, "rebellion with arms in hand."

38. George W. Aguirre, 25 years; born in the United States; captured by a Spanish gunboat July 10, 1896; case pending before civil court of Jaruco; confined in Cabaña fort; charge of rebellion.

39. Samuel T. Tolon, 45 years; native of Cuba; naturalized 1878; arrested on board American steamer *Seneca* September 3, 1896; incomunicado twenty-two days; charged with being a delegate to the Cuban Junta; released and deported September 30, 1896; went to New York.

40. Oscar Cespedes, 20 years; native of Key West; captured without arms

in insurgent hospital near Zapata swamp about September 5, 1896; imprisoned at San Severino fort, Matanzas; question of competency between military and civil jurisdiction decided in favor of military; case pending.

41. Francisco E. Cazanas, arrested as suspect at Matanzas October 14, 1896; released October 16, 1896.

42. Alfredo Hernandez, 44 years; native of Matanzas; naturalized 1876; arrested at his house at Habana September 6, 1896; suspicion of being concerned in the insurrection; expelled September 23, 1896; went to Key West.

43. Antonio Suarez del Villar, native of Cuba; naturalized; arrested at Cienfuegos September 5, 1896; charged with purchase and concealing of arms and ammunition; case sent to civil jurisdiction December 23, 1896; in prison at Cienfuegos; case pending.

44. José Curbino, native of Cuba; naturalized; arrested at Rincon September 18, 1896; surrendered to military authorities without arms; released and is residing at Santiago de las Vegas.

45. Joseph Austin Munoz, native of New Orleans; arrested at Matanzas September 18, 1896; released September 19; claimed that arrest was by mistake.

46. Ramon Rodriguez, native of Cuba; naturalized; arrested September 20, 1896, upon requisition from governor of Matanzas; had been in insurrection; surrendered and failed to report regularly; sent to Cardenas and released.

47. Esteben Venero, 22 years; native of Cuba; naturalized 1895; arrested at Los Palos (Habana Province) about September 22, 1896; charges not stated; Captain-General asked for evidence of American citizenship on December 9, which was sent him; case pending cognizance of military or civil jurisdiction.

48. Adolfo Torres, native of Cuba; naturalized; arrested October 4 at Sagua; charges not stated; release ordered November 23, 1896; question of competency not established; released November 26, officer remarking, "We have no charges against you."

49. Esteben Cespedes (colored), born in Cuba; naturalized Key West, 1891; arrested October 13, 1896, charged with naniguismo (voodoo); expelled November 7 and went to Key West.

50. Ramon Crucet, 48 years; born in Cuba; naturalized 1873; arrested in Colon November 1, 1896; charges, public censure of acts of Spanish Government; released December 18, 1896; no grounds of complaint.

51. Louis Lay, 18 years; native of Cuba, of American parents; arrested November 9, 1896, during a raid upon a social club in Regla; confined in Cabana fort; case ordered to be transferred to civil court at Guanabacoa, December 23; charges, aiding rebellion; released January 15, 1897.

52. José Gonzalez, 63 years; native of Bejucal, Cuba; naturalized 1882; arrested at Las Mangas November 10, 1896, taken to prison at Pinar del Rio; charges not yet made known to consulate-general, Habana.

53. Theodore L. Vives, native of Cienfuegos; naturalized 1801; arrested November 19, 1896; charges, first, disorderly conduct, and then insults to Spain; case pending cognizance of military or civil jurisdiction; is confined in jail.

54. Henry J. Delgado, native of the United States; captured about December 10, 1896, at an insurgent hospital in Pinar del Rio province, after having been ten weeks in a hut sick; sent to Habana to Cabana fort; removed to hospital December 28, 1896, where, our consul-general reports, he received best medical attention; died in hospital January 19, 1897.

55. Gaspar A. Betancourt, 63 years; native of Cuba; naturalized 1877; arrested December 26, 1896; confined at police headquarters incomunicado, charged with sedition.

56. Fernando Pino Hernandez, 10 years (colored); native of Key West; charged with naniguismo (voodoo); ordered to be expelled December 30, 1896; will be sent to Key West.

57. Amado Pino Hernandez, 21 years; brother of the above; same as above.

58. José Antonio Iznaga, native of Cuba; naturalized; expelled in August, 1896; no report.

59. August Bolton, naturalized 1898.

60. Gustave Richelieu, naturalized 1870; taken in a boat near Santiago de Cuba about February 23, 1896; released from prison about March 1, 1896; subsequently rearrested and recommitted for leaving Guantanamo without permission; consul considers second arrest an excuse for detention; release granted shortly after.

61. Frank Agramont, and 62, Thomas Julio Sainz, arrested with arms in their hands, May, 1895; charge, rebellion; to be tried for armed insurrection against the Government; Santiago de Cuba.

63. John D. Ferrer, no evidence against him; released March 23, 1896; naturalized at New York, 1878.

64. Pedro Duarte; 65, Jorge Calvar, and 66, Ramon Romagosa, arrested at Manzanillo for alleged conspiracy in insurrection; expelled August 11, 1896.

67. Donald B. Dodge or F. M. Boyle, arrested at Santiago de Cuba August 2, 1895; charge, rebellion (consul thinks his mind unbalanced); released August 31, 1895, and sailed for the United States; native of New York.

68. Bert S. Skiller, arrested at La Caleta, in open boat, April 28, 1896; released at Baracoa September 3, 1896.
69. Manuel Comas, arrested October 25, 1895, and released.
70. Alfred Laborde, native; arrested on steamer *Competitor* April 25, 1896; charge, landing arms for insurgents; confined in Cabana fortress; condemned to death May 8; order suspended; new trial opened May 11, 1896.
71. William Gildea, naturalized; same as above.
72. Ona Melton, native; same as above.
73. Charles Barnett, native; supposed to be one of *Competitor* crew; captured on land; same as above.
74. William Leavitt, British subject; supposed to be one of *Competitor* crew; captured on land; same as above.

List of newspaper war correspondents who have been expelled from the island.

William Mannix, native of United States; expelled as a dangerous alien, etc., February 11, 1896.

Sylvester Scovel, World, native of United States; reported that he had arrived from insurgent lines, and it was intended to deport him in January; reported January 20 that he had returned to insurgent lines.

Charles Michelson and Lorenzo Betancourt, correspondent and interpreter of New York Journal; arrested February 25; confined in Morro Castle; released February 27, 1896; charged with having communicated with insurgents by passing through Spanish lines at Marianao, etc.

Elbert Rappleye, Mail and Express; expelled March 20, 1896, for sending news to his paper which was false and disparaging to the authorities in the island.

James Creelman, World, born in Canada; expelled May 5, 1896, for sending to paper false reports touching the insurrection.

F. W. Lawrence, Journal, born in the United States; expelled May 5, 1896; same cause as above.

William G. Gay, World, native of New York; expelled June 27; went to New York.

Thomas J. Dawley, war correspondent, native of New York; arrested several times between March 24, 1895, and July 3, on suspicion; charges, "taking views of forts and conspiring to blow up same with dynamite;" confined thirteen days in Morro; released.

* * * * * * *

April 8, 1897.

Mr. MORGAN. I move that the Senate proceed to the consideration of the joint resolution (S. R. 26) declaring that a condition of public war exists in Cuba, and that strict neutrality shall be maintained.

The VICE-PRESIDENT. Is there objection to the present consideration of the joint resolution indicated by the Senator from Alabama?

There being no objection, the Senate, as in Committee of the Whole, resumed the consideration of the joint resolution.

Mr. MORGAN. Mr. President, when I left the floor yesterday, at the hour of 2 o'clock, I had asked leave to put in the RECORD the message of the President of the United States showing the number of Americans who were imprisoned in the Island of Cuba during the present war and the disposition that had been made of them. That record shows that seventy-four American citizens were imprisoned. The Senator from Maine [Mr. HALE] says that he finds on inquiry at the State Department that only twelve of those prisoners are now retained in confinement and subject to the prosecutions which have been instituted against them in Cuba.

That is an act of clemency on the part of Spain which I suppose we ought to be very grateful for, inasmuch as it has been obtained chiefly by supplication on the part of the United States. I think perhaps we ought to strengthen the future prayers of our Administration by passing some sort of recognition of the fact that we are greatly indebted to the Spanish Government for not having slain outright all of those American citizens.

Some of them were condemned to death; some of them are still on trial for alleged capital offenses; all of them are held amenable to the military laws of Spain in Cuba. More particularly amongst that oppressed class are the crew of the *Competitor*, to which I shall presently devote some attention, and I will speak with respect to those prisoners upon testimony which has been given before a committee of the Senate, on oath, by witnesses who were present at the former trial of the parties.

I notice also a list of newspaper correspondents who have been expelled from the island: William Mannix, a native of the United States; Sylvester Scovel, a native of the United States; Charles Michelson, whose nativity is not given; Lorenza Bentancourt; Elbert Rappleye, of the Mail and Express paper (his nativity is not given); James Creelman, of the World, born in Canada; F. W. Lawrence, of the Journal, born in the United States; William G. Gay, of the World, a native of New York; Thomas J. Dawley, war correspondent, a native of New York.

So bitter is the resentment of Spain toward the United States for not having come out and proclaimed an alliance with her for the purpose of crushing out her Cuban subjects that it is with the utmost degree of exasperation she regards any person who claims to be an American and goes into that island for the purpose of obtaining information.

The accusations upon which these different correspondents were removed from Cuba are that they were guilty of false statements with regard to the war and the cruelties inflicted upon private persons and upon soldiers captured in arms during the present struggle.

Mr. President, it seems very strange if among all the correspondents the papers of the United States have sent to Cuba they could find no man who has sufficient personal character and sufficient standing in the estimation of the people of the United States to be credited in respect to statements he might make for publication here, and it does seem strange that not one of them has escaped the imputation on the part of the Spanish people and Government that he was making false reports about the condition of affairs in Cuba.

We have passed through the period of three revolutions in Cuba—one twenty years ago that lasted for ten years. A more bloody, bitter, and unrelenting struggle was never waged by human hands against mortality than that. We then had correspondents there. The history of that war and of its incidents has been completed. All the civilized world has books that contain a full statement of the transactions of that war. Its truths have stained Spanish history with indelible reproach. The Spanish Government has never been able to contradict that record. So in regard to the record made by our newspaper correspondents, every one of whom has been expelled that I have heard of who went there. The Spanish Government has entered no defense in the nature of a contradiction of the specific statements that they have made, but has banished them from that country and refused them admission there again, upon the ground that they had written false reports of transactions in Cuba.

My mind continually recurs to the treaty of 1795 when I think of an American citizen and his rights in the Island of Cuba. These men have the right to go there, pushing their enterprise of gathering news and reporting it to the world. It is not only a lucrative profession, but honorable, and one to which the world is greatly indebted every day that we exist. If the daily newspaper press of the world was silent; if a band of "incomunicado" could be interposed between the people and the newspaper press, so that their utterances should not reach the people, no other cause of dissatisfaction would be more provocative of wrath than that; no privation would be considered equal to that in its distressful exactions upon human patience.

The newspaper press of the world must necessarily get some inaccurate ideas. In the vast mass of information that it sends over the postal lines and along the telegraph wires and across the oceans on cables it must necessarily fall into error about many things. Sometimes in their enterprise they anticipate things and conjecture things, almost undertake to prophesy about matters that are coming to the front in the future, and make mistakes. But, sir, when you look over the statements made last month or the month before in the great newspaper press of the world and get the consensus of opinion and statements that the various papers have made, you have a volume of history collected that no man will ever be able to expunge. It is history founded on the facts; it is history that reveals the truth. "What they hit is history; what they miss is mystery."

Here, then, is Spain accused by these men whom she has banished from the Island of Cuba on account of particular statements of transactions, giving names and date and locality, and no man, not even the Spanish press, has ventured to deny what these newspaper agents of the United States have published broadcast here for the last two years. I have never seen one important statement denied about them except some conjectures in regard to the manner of the death of Maceo; and yet the circumstances attending that transaction were of so peculiar a character that we could scarcely blame any man for conjecturing that Maceo had been entrapped into an ambuscade and had been slain through treachery.

Now, rated at what it is worth, rated according to its proper place in history, with all this mass of newspaper testimony piled up against Spain during the last two years, and with the great mass of information that the world possesses in regard to the same war (for it is the same war that was waged twenty years ago), it is idle for any man in this country to attempt to deny that war exists in Cuba or that it is prosecuted under circumstances, conditions, and with surroundings which violate every possible conception in the mind of a civilized man as to what war ought to be and what civilized war is.

I think, Mr. President, that there ought to be an end to the question and an end to debate upon the question as to whether war exists in Cuba. There is but one country in the world which denies it outside of Spain, and that is the United States of America. And yet in all of the correspondence of our consuls and consuls-general, in the messages which have been sent to us by the President of the United States, the confession of war is openly and frequently made. The struggle in Cuba is not spoken of by any official of the United States in any other light than that war exists in Cuba. When the pivotal point of our own action turns on that proposition and no other, when the only question the Senate has to consider in respect to the joint resolution now before it is whether war exists in Cuba, I think I should be spared the necessity of inflicting upon the Senate any debate or argument to prove a fact known to every man, woman, and child in the world who has any acquaintance at all with public affairs and general history.

When a fact so important as this, the turning point in the rights of our people, is stated upon the floor of the Senate, it is a shame that we can not get this body, the House of Representatives, and the President to come out and acknowledge the fact, proclaim the truth, and let the truth have its own logical effect and consequence.

I was reading this morning a note from Mr. Dupuy de Lôme, addressed to Miss Clara Barton. Miss Clara Barton desired to go to Cuba with the Red Cross for the purpose of relieving the distresses among the people of that island in consequence of the war. Mr. Dupuy de Lôme, in replying to that—it is a very late day at which this reply comes, however, as I can show by the records here—says:

> I duly communicated to my Government the proposition made by you to go to Cuba with a view of conveying the aid of the American people to the sufferers in consequence of the war.

The Spanish minister, with all of his diplomatic cunning and reserve, in writing to this splendid woman about the great benevolence which she is conducting, is unable to keep from the tip of his pen, or out of his mouth, or out of his thought the words which so thoroughly describe the truth of the situation in Cuba, "in consequence of the war," in which he confesses that there are "sufferers." If De Lôme can say it is a war, why can we not say so? Why do we refuse to say so? Because, Mr. President, the very moment we make that declaration, the laws of war as regulated by the laws of nations apply there, and the punishment of men for insurrection under municipal orders, decrees, and legislation at once ceases.

Mr. GALLINGER. Will the Senator permit me? Is that a recent utterance of the Spanish minister? It escaped my attention.

Mr. MORGAN. Yes, sir; it is printed in the Times of February 12 of the present year.

Mr. GALLINGER. Only a month or two ago?

Mr. MORGAN. Yes. When the consequences of the declaration of the existence of a war in Cuba are so very important, if you please, to the twelve prisoners who remain there, so important to all of the citizens of the United States who are there and who have property there, so important to our commerce and to everything connected with it, it does seem strange that in the presence of these facts we can not get our consent to make the declaration, in a form that gives to it the effect and power of a law in this country, that a state of war exists in Cuba.

Now, sir, if a state of war has existed in Cuba and the seventy-four prisoners whose names are given to us by the President had been arrested there as being persons who were in complicity with the enemy or as prisoners captured out of the armies controverting with each other upon the field of battle, instead of these men being carried before the secret, inquisitorial tribunals which I described yesterday, and instead of being tried by summary military proceedings in court-martial, they would have been confined in camps with all of the rights and privileges and guaranties of protection, of maintenance, and of the proper treatment that belongs to the character of a prisoner of war.

On yesterday I read from the elementary authors a definition of the rights and privileges of a prisoner of war. To the prisoners who are in Cuba now, and those who have been there, some of whom have suffered indescribable torture for two years in the foul prisons of Habana and other prisons in Cuba, what a great relief and happiness it would have been if a state of war had been recognized as existing in Cuba, and they, instead of being captured and confined as violators of civil duties toward Spain, had been amenable to no other confinement and no other punishment than that which is due to the character of a prisoner of war!

Mr. President, that is all in the past except as to the twelve men who are there yet, but the wound upon the honor of the United States Government is not in the past. That is an open, fresh, and bleeding wound at this moment, for the wounded honor of a nation does not heal because the occasion is past or because of the possibility of making reclamation in the form of monetary compensation or damages at some future period. The duty that the Government of the United States owes to its own citizenship is one that every American is proud to recognize and proud to claim. Would to God that the United States Government was equally proud to stand up and bestow its protection and defense! But that, it seems, is not the case.

If the individual suffering of the seventy-four men and that of their families could be laid before the Senate to-day, if the history of those men who have been incarcerated in the prisons of Cuba could be revealed to the Senate, it would perhaps show an extent of suffering which would arouse the indignation of every human being in the United States. Suppose instead of being seventy-four there had been only one. Suppose that only one American citizen had been treated in the manner these prisoners have been treated; who can say that the Government of the United States can enjoy the reasonable respect and confidence of its own citizens if it stands by and sees one man suffer at the hands of the Spanish Government, or any other government in the world, when the suffering is inflicted contrary to treaty, contrary to international law, and contrary to the sacred rights of humanity?

I hope, sir, that we are not in that miserable and low and mean condition where our citizens ought to be ashamed of us because we have not the strength of character and will to reach out the hand of justice and demand rights that belong to our people. That is all that I am claiming; but I do claim that, and will continue to do it.

In order to give a little more emphasis and make a better foundation for the remarks and characterizations that I have been compelled to employ in this debate, and that I employ reluctantly when speaking of any foreign government, let me read some statements from the last annual message of the President of the United States.

President Cleveland, in sending in his last annual message, adopted a paper which he sent in with it, a report prepared by the Secretary of State, so that the message, of course, and the report constitute but one paper. The President says, in speaking of the situation in Cuba:

> It is to the same end that in pursuance of general orders Spanish garrisons are now being withdrawn from plantations and the rural population required to concentrate itself in the towns. The sure result would seem to be that the industrial value of the island is fast diminishing, and that unless there is a speedy and radical change in existing conditions it will soon disappear altogether. That value consists very largely, of course, in its capacity to produce sugar—a capacity already much reduced by the interruptions to tillage which have taken place during the last two years. It is reliably asserted that should these interruptions continue during the current year and practically extend, as is now threatened, to the entire sugar-producing territory of the island, so much time and so much money will be required to restore the land to its normal productiveness that it is extremely doubtful if capital can be induced to even make the attempt.

We know, as I stated on yesterday, and as the President states in his message here, that the people of the United States have $50,000,000 of property in Cuba, the larger part of it invested in sugar estates. There are some railroad interests there and some iron-mining interests. Now, that single declaration made by the President of the United States would admonish any proud-spirited and honest-minded people that the time had arrived when a war conducted for the purposes declared by the President of the United States and in the manner which he states ought to be put an end to on account of the interests that we have there, which are being destroyed unnecessarily; that it ought to be put an end to if for no better reason than that, even if humanity had no voice to utter in support of the proposition.

I now turn to what the Secretary of State said on that same subject and others closely connected with it. He said:

> The nature of the struggle, however, deserves most earnest consideration. The increased scale on which it is waged brings into bolder relief all the appalling phases which often appear to mark contests for supremacy among the Latin races of the Western Hemisphere. Excesses before confined to a portion of the island become more impressive when wrought throughout its whole extent, as now. The insurgent authority, as has been seen, finds no regular administrative expression; it is asserted only by the sporadic and irresponsible force of arms. The Spanish power, outside of the larger towns and their immediate suburbs, when manifested at all, is equally forceful and arbitrary.
>
> The only apparent aim on either side is to cripple the adversary by indiscriminate destruction of all that by any chance may benefit him. The populous and wealthy districts of the center and the west, which have escaped harm in former contests, are now ravaged and laid waste by the blind fury of the respective partisans. The principles of civilized warfare, according to the code made sacred by the universal acquiescence of nations, are only too often violated with impunity by irresponsible subordinates, acting at a distance from the central authority and able to shield themselves from just censure or punishment by false or falsified versions of the facts.
>
> The killing and summary execution of noncombatants is frequently reported, and while the circumstances of the strife are such as to preclude accurate or general information in this regard, enough is known to show that the number of such cases is considerable. In some instances, happily few, American citizens have fallen victims to these savage acts.

A President of the United States and a Secretary of State who in a message to Congress can make that statement and that confession, it seems to me, could not be possibly more delinquent in their duty than to follow it up with persuasion, for that is what was done, that the people of the United States should be permitted still longer to suffer and that no relief should come to them.

In some instances, happily few—

Says the Secretary of State—

American citizens have fallen victims to these savage acts.

Now consult your memory; consult the records of Congress; consult, if you please, the archives of the State Department, and answer me, and answer the people of the United States, what has been done to correct, to demand reparation for, or to prevent the recurrence of these terrible things which are stated in the President's message?

Well, after that statement, Mr. President, it would scarcely be necessary to go into particulars about this, and yet there are particulars given to us, not only upon American newspaper authority, but upon British newspaper authority, to which we are bound to give attention, for whatever we may believe about it, or choose not to believe—for that seems to be the situation in which we are placed—the European powers understand this question thoroughly, and long ere this would have intervened there to prevent these outrages against humanity but for a declaration that we have made since the foundation of this Government, from the lips of almost every President and Secretary of State and public man that we have had, that we would not tolerate European intervention in the affairs of Cuba. We have warned off all Europe from doing anything or from even saying anything in an official way about the transactions which go on in the Island of Cuba. We seem to think that we have a sort of guardianship over Cuba, and that Europe must not intervene in any way, even for the purpose of protesting in the name of humanity against the outrages that are perpetrated in that island. Sir, our guardianship there, if we have it, is like the guardianship of the devil over a condemned soul. We are holding them in duress; we are holding them where no other power can relieve them, and where they are losing all their capacity to relieve themselves, warning the nations of the world that they must say nothing about affairs in Cuba and stand by and see the inquisitorial and savage methods of Spanish trial and Spanish warfare and Spanish dungeons visited upon the Cubans, and even our own people, without so much as a protest! Point me to the protest that has been made by the Government of the United States against these outrages.

Sir, what a firm foundation would these statements have been for a protest like this: "This transaction, thus characterized by the President of the United States in a communication to Congress, must not proceed in Cuba; we must have a guaranty from you that this persecution and wrongdoing have ceased; that this blood of innocents has stopped its flow; we must have some security from you, or otherwise we will take into our own hands that which we will not permit other nations to do—the rectification of this outrage upon the laws of humanity, the laws of nations, and the treaties of Spain with the United States." A protest like that, Mr. President, would not only have emptied the prisons of Cuba, but those Cuban people out in the hills and on the plains and in the swamps and in the dense woods of Cuba would have had their hearts lighted up with the responsive sentiment which they found aflame in the United States, and they would have stood their ground even with more fortitude and hope than they are doing to-day, and yet it can not be said of any other people in this world that they have shown more fortitude and more perseverance than the class that we call the rebels in Cuba.

Mr. President, in a field so very wide, that has now occupied so great a portion of the history of this century in Cuba, it is almost impossible to follow a consecutive and close line of argument to demonstrate exactly what the situation there is, what it has been, and what we may expect it will be, because in respect of matters of this kind we are bound to judge the future by the past. When a man or a nation has performed a series of acts which satisfy you that he or the nation has a character of certain unpleasant or dangerous complexion, humanity is bound—nations as well as individuals are bound—to take up those characteristics which have been established in the history of that man or that nation and apply them to their future conduct. In respect to Spain, there has been no proof of repentance, no change of course, no relaxation of her tyranny. Her purposes are the same arbitrary and despotic purposes which have characterized her rule of the people of Cuba from the time that that island was first occupied by her subjects. Beginning with the Indians, they destroyed them. They went to Africa and imported the negroes to take their place, and they kept them in such condition of slavery and depression as that progress amongst them, either religious, moral, or educational, was absolutely impossible. Then, when they were forced by the constraint of surrounding nations and the demand of European powers to emancipate the slaves, they now turn against them and reprobate them for struggling for the liberties enjoyed by the negroes of the United States. They want to prevent the negroes in Cuba from enjoying anything of those opportunities and privileges which seem to have been so valuable to the negro race since emancipation in the United States, and they point to the army in Cuba and tell us, as De Lôme told us in a letter read in the Senate in which he denounced Senators, that these armies in Cuba were composed of negroes, and that when the Cubans should achieve their independence we would have there, as we have in Santo Domingo and in Jamaica, negro communities in rule.

The cruelties of Spain, Mr. President, have followed the white race and the black race alike in every stage of its history. As far back as we can trace that Government there has been no sense of paternalism in Spain. They have treated their subjects as mere feudatories, who were compelled to yield them as much stipend as they could wring out of them by taxation, by the bastinado, or by the sword, and they have never regarded the common populace of Spain as being entitled to any rights except such as for the moment the military and the royal rulers of Spain chose to concede them, really for their own convenience. That has been the situation.

I wish now to advert again to the case of the twelve prisoners that the Senator from Maine [Mr. HALE] says are still retained in Cuba. Amongst those are the *Competitor* prisoners, as they are called. The little schooner *Competitor* loaded up with a few men who went down to the coast of Cuba for the purpose of landing them and sending there some arms and ammunition that they had a right to sell or to give away or to dispose of to the insurrectionists or to the Spaniards, as they saw proper. They had that right under the laws of the United States, strict as our laws are, and under the treaties that we have with Spain, and under international law. One of those young men, sir, if I remember aright, is from your own State [Mr. BERRY in the chair] and from a family of respectability; a young fellow, 19 or 20 years of age, who started out from the State of Arkansas and went to Florida, who, having some brightness and some facility for writing, engaged with the editor of a local paper in Florida that he would go to Cuba, get within the lines of the insurrectionists, and would report to his newspaper, as he might be able to do, the actual situation in Cuba.

Mr. President, I must remark for a moment upon that enterprise. This young fellow had his fortune to make, his reputation, his fame, to achieve, and he believed that he could do it, and he had the courage to step out into dangerous places for the purpose of seeking a foothold in the respect of mankind. I honor such a man. I do not regard him as a savage or a beastly intruder into other people's affairs. He had a right to go there; and if he had the courage to do so, he is to be applauded for it.

He got on a little schooner as a passenger, which appears to have had some men aboard who were going to Cuba and were taking arms there, and who doubtless intended to enlist in the Cuban army. When a Spanish gunboat came in sight, those men had landed a part of the cargo, and they deserted the vessel and went off, all but four or five. Three of those men were regular employees upon the little schooner—the captain, the mate, and perhaps the stevedore or some other sailor. Their ship had been engaged for the purpose of making this transit from the United States to Cuba—a perfectly honest and perfectly justifiable and lawful enterprise. Young Melton was captured on board the ship without any arms at all, and was taken, along with the balance of those men, carried to Habana, and incarcerated in a prison and placed incomunicado. No one was permitted to see him or talk with him, or hold any communication with him. He did not know the charges that were brought against him. After some days, and contrary to some feeble and sickly protest which the Government of the United States designed to make in respect of this poor boy, he was carried before a military tribunal—a naval court-martial—and was there condemned to death. That has been now very nearly twelve months ago. During all of this time the boy had lain in jail; his form had wasted away, his strength had disappeared, and the cloud of an early death came lowering down upon his young soul, and all the hopes of that youth, who, perhaps, might have aspired to anything that this Senate contains within its august presence—all the hopes of that boy have been utterly destroyed, and his life has been worse than destroyed by the Spanish inquisition. He was condemned to death.

Then came a protest from the Government of the United States against the manner of his trial. Not that his accusation was contrary to the laws of nations, but that he had not been tried in accordance with the act of 1821, passed by the Cortes of Spain, and the treaty of 1795 and the protocol of 1877. These require that he should have counsel, should understand the nature of the accusations brought against him, should have witnesses in his defense, and should have every advantage that could be secured under the Spanish law of 1821, and the law was named in the treaty. None of these things was done. He was taken and condemned to death. The supreme court at Madrid, however, upon the protest of this Government, or of Mr. Hannis Taylor, our minister at the court of Madrid, took the subject up and they reviewed it and reversed the decision; and instead of releasing him, as he ought to have been released, they remanded the case to the lower court for further trial, and from that day to this that boy has been in a dungeon in Habana, and is there now; no further trial has been granted to him; and he is punished for nothing else than because he is a young native-born American who had the temerity to go there and accidentally to be found in company with men whom he never knew before and had no acquaintance with. He had put his foot upon the deck of that ship to go there in company with these men who were strangers to him, one or two of whom were killed in the water, but some of them escaped and went into the Cuban army.

That is the case of Ona Melton and the crew of the *Competitor*. There were other American citizens and there was one British subject on that ship, and the consul-general at the place (I believe it was Consul-General Ramon Williams at Habana) interposed the treaty of 1795, the protocol of 1877, and the act of 1821 in behalf of that British subject and defended him. That British subject, Mr. President, was released.

Ona Melton is there now, and two other American citizens, in a loathsome dungeon. He has said that oftentimes he was incarcerated in a room that was not 20 feet long and not more than 12 feet wide, with 40 other men, for days and nights at a time, without a place to lie down or to sit down, without a blanket to put under him, and with three pails of water a day brought in to satiate the thirst of that great crowd of men after they had been fed on salted codfish the night before in order to increase the anguish of their thirst.

Am I stating romances? I am telling you now what was sworn to here by two respectable gentlemen before the Committee on Foreign Relations, one of whom I know personally, and the other I do not know. One of them is Dr. Diaz, the head of the Baptist missionary establishment in Cuba, who was sent out by the Southern Baptist Church. He had been a captain in a former revolution, and a gallant one. He had escaped from a pursuing band of soldiers just at the close of that war, along with two other men, in the nighttime. The Spaniards had chased them until they had got them out onto a sand bar or a peninsula reaching into the sea, and there, when night shut down, the Spanish soldiers were afraid to come out into the open and attack them. When night came on they built fires across the peninsula. These men found some dry cedar logs there, threw them into the sea, got upon them, and floated around, expecting the current would carry them to some hospitable point where they could land, but, instead of that, the current carried them out to sea. One of them dropped off of his raft and died in the water. The other two were picked up by an American schooner and carried to Key West, and Dr. Diaz was delivered to his friends.

He was then a captain in the Cuban army; he was a very highly educated gentleman, and was a surgeon of character at the time he enlisted in that war. He was born within 5 miles of Habana. His family, a very distinguished one, had held great titles under the Spanish Government, and great renown attached to the name of that family, running back through many generations. When he came to the United States, he engaged in manual labor as a maker of cigars, as most Cubans do who come here. Then he went to New York, but by the time he got there his health gave way. He was taken to a hospital, and there, under the ministrations of an aged lady, who was to him mother and sister and friend, his health was restored; and with the restoration of his health there came to him a blessing that Dr. Diaz esteems above all that the world contains—he became a converted man, and a Protestant. Then he went to Philadelphia, and there he was educated in theology under the tuition of an eminent Baptist divine. Then he became a reader and worker amongst the manufacturers of cigars in the city of New York; then he went to Florida upon the same mission, and then began to preach. He had become a member of the Baptist Church, and that great institution, the Southern Baptist Convention, than which no wiser and more excellent body of Christians exists in this world, put him at the head of a great mission in Cuba. He went there and established it. He established property by the contributions of the Cubans—not from the United States—in the city of Habana worth three or four hundred thousand dollars, including a splendid church edifice, with a congregation of more than twelve hundred persons in regular attendance upon his ministrations, with other missionary churches established around in different parts of Cuba, with a large hospital, with fifteen or more free schools, and with a large and beautiful cemetery.

He was there conducting himself as a Christian gentleman would; and so chary was he of his position and of his rights and duties under these circumstances that, in reply to a question that I put to him, he swore that he had never communicated to the forces or to the generals or to anyone else on either side of that controversy any information that could be valuable in a military sense. When Campos was there, Dr. Diaz got his permission and also, I may say, the permission of the Government of the United States to join with the Geneva Society of the Red Cross in establishing hospitals in Cuba. He came here and applied for a position in that benevolent institution under Miss Clara Barton, the same lady to whom De Lôme addressed a letter in February last. It was required in Cuba that they should change the style of the cross, that it should be a white cross instead of a red one, for some local reason, I do not know what.

Dr. Diaz was made vice-president of that mission. He went back and established a number of hospitals all through Cuba. He treated thousands of wounded and sick Spanish soldiers, and, with equal consideration, he treated and cared for the rebel soldiers, and also for their families. He got large medical supplies, and he was himself a surgeon, and performed skillful operations in Cuba, and amongst those the operation which saved the life of Delgado, of whom we have heard so much. This man, conducting himself in this way, after the Senate had passed a resolution recognizing the existence of a state of public war in Cuba, was preaching at night and in daytime in the city of Habana, when bombshells were thrown into his congregation and they were driven out. Still he behaved himself with that sort of propriety and dignity that belongs to his elevated character, for he fully appreciates it. He was arrested, together with his brother, and put in jail and kept incomunicado for as many, I think, as seven or eight days; and when he was discharged, without any crime being imputed to him, it was with an order of banishment from his church and from Cuba; and were he to return there now he would be at once arrested and executed.

Here is an American citizen, fully naturalized here, with the best purposes and intentions, a perfectly innocent man, who went back to the Island of Cuba upon the highest mission that the human mind can conceive of, and who has done untold good to those people, has introduced there the light of Protestant Christianity in a way, perhaps, to give offense to some other churches, but, at the same time, probably not in a way to offend against the sentiments and feelings of the American people, certainly not those of the members of the Southern Baptist Convention, who sent him there.

His arrest and banishment violate our treaties with Spain, but that grave offense has received no notice from our Government. When this Christian minister was in prison, our Government did not visit him.

Now, this is the man who was before the committee and who testified. I wish to call the attention of Senators who may not have known of this document, and who may wish to read it, to the fact that it is document 166 of the Fifty-fourth Congress, second session. There are copies in the document room. No man can read the statement of that noble divine and, if he is an American citizen, have any proper respect for his Government when he feels that it still lingers and halts in affording a remedy for these wrongs. I can not describe the wrongs that Dr. Diaz witnessed, in the presence of this audience, without offending the delicacy even of the men who are here, for they would leave the galleries and retire to the corridors should I spread the picture before the Senate. It is something that is absolutely unmentionable in the hearing of decent or civilized ears. Those are the people we are contending with.

Dr. Diaz knew this poor boy, Ona Melton. He sympathized with him, but he did not see him in the midst of his suffering, and did not, I believe, witness the trial that took place there. I wish to read now, and I must beg the pardon of the Senate for asking attention to this point, the proceedings of that trial as testified to by Mr. Frederick W. Lawrence, a correspondent of the New York Journal, I believe, who was present and saw it, and who was afterwards banished.

Mr. SPOONER. What is the number of the document?

Mr. MORGAN. It is Senate Document 166, Fifty-fourth Congress, second session. The Committee on Foreign Relations could have piled up a great deal of evidence here, sworn testimony, but we all felt that it was unnecessary to do so, because all of it was of one sort; it all ran in the same direction, and there was no occasion for multiplying evidence about a matter that everybody knows. Senator DAVIS was examining the gentleman, Mr. Lawrence, and he was going on to give a list of the gentlemen who had been banished from Cuba. In reply to a question as to what was the alleged cause, etc., of the banishment, he said:

Q. What was the alleged cause?
A. Sending false information to his paper. That has been the reason that General Weyler has alleged for the expulsion of all the correspondents whom he has expelled. There were four of us expelled—

But this list furnished by the President gives eight or nine names—

Q. Go on and give the next instance.
A. The case of Mr. Darling, an artist for Harper's Weekly, who has been arrested in territory that is not included in the Captain-General's edict, released each time, but detained from one hour to several hours—by several hours I mean eight or ten. I am not certain about the American citizenship of Mr. O'Leary, so I will not state his case. Mr. Creelman, of the New York Herald, was expelled at the same time I was; forbidden to remain longer on the island.
Q. Upon what charge?
A. Upon the charge of sending false information as to the state of affairs in Cuba. I was expelled for the same reason at the same time.
Q. Now, these cases are those of newspaper correspondents. I apply my main question to ill treatment of other American citizens, resident or temporary, of the island.
A. The cases of Alfred Laborde and Milton.
Q. Citizens of the United States?
A. Citizens of the United States.
Q. Is your information derived from what they told you?
A. No, sir.
Q. Who did you get it from?
A. From the testimony produced at the court-martial and from Vice-Consul Joseph Springer.
Q. With what were these two men charged?
A. They were charged with bringing a filibustering expedition into the Island of Cuba.
Q. Is that the case of the *Competitor?*
A. Yes, sir. Those two men, American citizens, were arrested, and, so far as the testimony of the men who captured them goes, had no arms upon their persons. They were brought to Habana, tried by general court-martial against the energetic protest of the United States consul-general there, condemned to death, and, as I am informed, their sentence delayed by the Madrid Government at the request of the Secretary of State, and still held in jail.
Q. Do you know whether they were assisted by counsel at their trial?
A. From the American point of view, they were not assisted by counsel at their trial; from the Spanish military point of view, they were.
Q. In what way?
A. They had a lieutenant in the navy, who asked no questions, who cross-

examined no witnesses. There were none produced, except Captain Butron and the other officers of the *Mensajerra*.

Q. Did this lieutenant advance by way of plea that these men were American citizens?
A. He stated in his plea that they were American citizens.
Q. Upon what grounds did he rest their defense?
A. He asked for mercy for Laborde, for the illustrious place his name had borne in the Spanish navy, and on account of the things his people had done for the Spanish Government.
Q. And the other man?
A. He asked for mercy for him, stating that he was not there for the purpose of fighting, but merely in his business as a newspaper correspondent.
Q. Do you know whether it appeared on that trial how far the *Competitor* was from the shore of Cuba when she was captured?
A. I do not remember.
Q. Do you know whether there was any evidence of that given on the trial?
A. At the trial there was no evidence given whatever.
Q. I mean as to the distance.
A. As to the distance or anything else.
Q. Have you any information as to the distance she was from the shore?
A. As to the exact distance, I do not know whether she was within the 3-mile limit or not.
Q. Was this trial secret or public?
A. Public.
Q. Did you attend it?
A. Yes, sir.
Q. Were the men in irons when tried?
A. No, sir.
Q. How long did it last?
A. From a little after 8 o'clock in the morning until afternoon.
Q. How many were tried?
A. Five, at once.
Q. How long was this after their arrest?
A. It was in the neighborhood of a week, more or less.
Q. Was any application made at the trial for postponement until they could communicate with their Government?
A. No, sir. Mr. Williams, however, saw them before the trial commenced and asked the judge-advocate in my presence what sort of a trial it was to be, and the judge-advocate replied, "A summary trial." Mr. Williams then replied, "I refuse to lend any official recognition to this trial. I protest against it," and left.

Mr. Williams was our consul-general at that time.

Q. So that no officer of the consular service of the United States was present at that trial?
A. No, sir.
Q. In what manner was this lieutenant appointed?
A. I do not know. If you care for presumption, I presume the judge-advocate appointed him.
Q. Was he appointed as deputy judge-advocate?
A. No; he was appointed as what they call "defensor." There was a prosecutor also. He made his plea in about the same way as one of our district attorneys would make a plea in this country.

That is the prosecutor.

Q. Well, this person was an officer in the Spanish navy, was he?
A. Oh, yes. He asked no questions, however. Neither the prosecutor nor the counsel for defense asked a single question of anybody. There was not a particle of testimony offered except the officers of the *Mensajerra*.
Q. Was there any interpreter present?
A. There was an interpreter present, but he did not make his presence known to the prisoners until they were asked whether they had anything to say in their own defense. These long statements were read by the judge-advocate in Spanish.
Q. These long statements of the prosecuting officer, you mean. Was the evidence given in Spanish and translated in their hearing?
A. No, sir.
Q. Did their defender communicate to them the substance of it?
A. He did not utter one single word to them.
Q. Can he speak English?
A. I did not hear him.
Q. Have you any reason to think he could speak the English language?
A. No, sir; I have every reason to think he could not.
Q. So that all this long harangue was delivered in Spanish?
A. Yes, sir.
Q. And then they were asked what they had to say?

A. Yes, sir; what they had to say in defense.
Q. Did he ask that in English?
A. He did not even do that. The presiding officer of the court-martial—there were ten of them, what we might call the jury—the presiding officer of that body said to Laborde in Spanish, "What have you to say?" He said a few words, and so it went until the last man was reached—William Gilday—and the presiding officer spoke to him and he did not understand him, and then the interpreter got up and said, "Do you wish to say anything?" Gilday arose and said, "All I have got to say is I do not understand one word that has been said to-day, for me or against me, and at any rate I appeal to both the British and American consuls."

That is the British man.

Q. Now, how many of these prisoners could not speak or understand Spanish?
A. I believe there were two who could not speak and understand Spanish.
Q. Which two?
A. Milton and Gilday. Laborde understood Spanish.

He calls him Milton. Melton is the proper name.

Q. Milton was the American and Gilday the naturalized American subject?
A. Yes, sir; I believe there is some question whether Gilday is a British subject or American. The British consul claims that he is a naturalized American, but he himself says he never renounced his allegiance to Great Britain.
Q. How long was it after they were asked whether they had anything to say before the trial terminated?
A. The trial terminated immediately upon the last man having made his statement.
Q. And when was it the defense summed up in their behalf, if at all?
A. Immediately after the prosecution.
Q. How long did it take him to conclude that summing up?
A. It took probably fifteen minutes.

By Senator MORGAN:

Q. But his appeal, as I understand you, was entirely for mercy and not for justification.
A. All for mercy, except you can call his plea for Milton that he was not there as a filibuster, but merely as a newspaper correspondent.

By Senator DAVIS:

Q. Did Milton undertake to give any account of why he was there?
A. Yes, sir.
Q. What account did he give?
A. He stated he came aboard the schooner as the correspondent of the Jacksonville Times-Union.
Q. Did he state he knew anything of the mission of the schooner?
A. He did not say. That is the statement that was made by him several days before the trial.
Q. What did Gilday have to say for himself?
A. He said he was a poor sailor earning his living, and he went aboard thinking the schooner was bound for Key West—I think it was for Sable Keys, going fishing; that he knew nothing of the nature of the business until after it started. Laborde claimed that his ship had been hired by some person for the purpose of going to Sable Keys for the purpose of fishing there, and he was simply held up by a revolver and told to go to Cuba.
Q. Laborde was the owner of the schooner?
A. No; he was the captain.

By Senator MORGAN:

Q. What did you ascertain to be the general feeling of the native Cubans you saw as to this rebellion or war?
A. The Cubans, all the natives of Cuba that I have seen who in the past have possessed any wealth at all, told me they had wrecked themselves to help along the war.
Q. I have seen statements in the papers about volunteer companies and regiments and perhaps brigades of native Cubans under the Spanish flag. Did you see anything of that sort there?
A. Yes, sir.
Q. To what extent, probably, were those enlistments?
A. Well, just giving a rough estimate—I never looked into the official records, but giving a rough guess, judging by the numbers of volunteers I saw in the streets, I should judge there were 3,000 volunteers.
Q. Were they volunteers for service in the field or for particular duty?
A. No, sir; they were volunteers for service in and around the outskirts of the city of Habana, guarding the banks, public buildings, theaters, and the like.

There that subject is dropped. No further attention, I believe, was paid to it in the examination of the witness. Dr. Diaz goes on to speak of it, but he speaks from information and not from actual observation. There are other matters in Dr. Diaz's testimony to which I should be glad to have the opportunity of referring, but this has all been printed in the RECORD heretofore, it has been printed in document form, and I do not feel authorized now to go through with all the statements that Dr. Diaz made.

There is Ona Melton still under that accusation and still in prison in Habana. I tried for a long time to get from the State Department, by resolution of the Senate, a statement of the facts in regard to Ona Melton, and I did not succeed until about the last days of the last Administration, and then only got what I believe to be a partial statement. But for the fact that there happened to be coming to Washington City a man who had written up the subject, a man of respectability, an honorable gentleman who was here and whom the committee ordered the Senator from Minnesota and myself to examine, we would have been still in the dark about that proceeding in Habana.

That proceeding is totally illegal—admitting, if you please, for the sake of the argument, the guilt of the parties—and violative of the treaty of 1795, which required, under the act of the Cortez of 1821, that a person, an American citizen, accused of insurrection or any crime against the political government of Spain, shall have his trial before a certain tribunal; shall be informed, before he is tried, of the nature of the accusation; shall have witnesses in his defense; shall have counsel employed by himself, and shall have free access to them on all occasions. A more flagrant, a more contemptuous, violation of treaty rights than is disclosed in this testimony can not be stated. Here we stand with Melton still in prison; no relief for him, no promise of relief, except the mere supplications that we send up here to each other to make a declaration of law under which the President of the United States would be compelled to demand his surrender.

Nothing, Mr. President, is done for that poor young fellow. I have seen letters that he has written, modest, earnest, supplicating letters, that he might be released from the horrors of that imprisonment; that he might be brought back to liberty. In my conception there is not a more innocent man on the earth than young Melton is to-day. The Spanish Government when it took the steps to condemn him to death, as it did, did not feel that it was necessary to produce evidence. The only thing that it proved about the poor fellow was that he was on board a ship where other men had come aboard, without his knowledge, with arms in their hands, and yet those men who came aboard came lawfully, or else Hamilton Fish and all the American publicists who have written upon subjects of this sort have entirely misunderstood the rights of American citizens.

In a letter which Mr. Fish wrote to Admiral Polo de Bernabé April 18, 1874, in reply to a communication that the admiral, who was minister to this capital, had written to him, informing him of certain orders that had been issued in respect of the Spanish marine affair and orders of the Captain-General, Mr. Fish took up the subject and replied upon the proposition that the admiral-minister had suggested to him. Among other parts of his reply which is pertinent to the point I am making, I will read this:

In regard to the second point thus stated by Admiral Polo's esteemed predecessor, the undersigned was constrained by due regard to universally recognized principles of international rights and duties to declare that in the absence of a recognized state of war it was no offense in the sailing vessels and steamers of the United States to carry arms and munitions of war for whomsoever it might concern.

This is in reference to the former rebellion, of which the present is a mere repetition, only it is with higher lights upon it and in more exaggerated form.

Mr. Fish continues:

The undersigned has uniformly said that no government can by the law of nations be held responsible for shipments of arms, munitions, or materials of war made by private individuals at their own risk and peril. If a state of war should exist, if Spain should be entitled to the rights of a belligerent, parties concerned in the shipment of arms and military supplies for her enemy would incur the risk of confiscation by her of their goods; but their act would involve no ground of reclamation against their government in behalf of Spain, and consequently no right to invoke the aid of that government in preventing the perpetration of the act. Such it is believed is the established law of nations, and such the received rule even when the shipment of arms and munitions is made from the territory of the country whose citizens may be the parties engaged in the introduction of these supplies for the use of one of the belligerents.

At another place he goes on to speak of the right of citizens of the United States, notwithstanding our very severe statutes upon that subject, to pass from these shores with any sort of war material, to land them on the Island of Cuba at any place that they can land, being responsible, if they are caught, only as smugglers, not responsible for treason, or rebellion, or insurrection because the arms may be used by men engaged in such conduct after they have been delivered in Cuba.

Here is a man engaged, according to our views of international law, as expressed, and specifically, under the terms of the treaty of 1795, in an enterprise that in itself is legally innocent, an enterprise for which the Government of Spain has no right to punish him except as it would punish a smuggler if he had been caught smuggling goods in there without paying the revenue. It has no such right, even under its own law—I speak of the law; I do not speak of the decrees of the Captain-General, for, Mr. President, as to us the decrees of the Captain.General are not laws when they contravene the treaty rights that are reserved to us under the treaty of 1795 and the subsequent modification of that agreement.

This innocent young man approached the Island of Cuba without any arms, on this mission of peace really, this mission of public education, which to him was a resource of living. He was captured, tried in the manner I have stated here, and condemned. The supreme court at Madrid reversed the decision and remanded his case more than ten months ago, and there he lingers in jail, and no President and no person raises a hand for the purpose of extricating him. Now, whether there are seventy-four prisoners in Cuba or seventy-four thousand, or whether there is but one, in the person of Ona Melton, this Arkansas youth, the flag of the United States, if it refuses to shelter him, is a disgraced rag.

No credit is attached to anything that is said by an American newspaper correspondent. No, sir; we have that mean vice in this country that we believe no man with an American tongue in his head unless he can corroborate his statements by somebody else, and if he can get a man from Great Britain to do it, then it all goes down all right. Here is a gentleman, Mr. Akers, who is the correspondent of the London Times, and who has been a commissioner of that paper for several years, having visited various parts of the world. He came here on his way to Europe and informed the State Department of his mission to Cuba and what he was going for. He was going to reside in Cuba and get information of the actual situation and communicate it to the London Times, and from time to time he did so. He gave impartial accounts, and some of them—most of them, indeed—were even more scathing in their criticism upon Spanish customs and usages and conduct in Cuba than those of the American correspondents who have been banished from the island on the pretense that they were making misrepresentations with regard to the situation in Cuba.

For the purpose of getting it before the Senate I desire to have the Secretary read a paper that was written by Mr. Akers to the editor of the New York World, and which appeared in that paper recently, some time during the last week. I desire to have the whole of it read, because it is a summary of the situation in Cuba. I trust at least that it will not fall upon dull ears when it reaches those gentlemen who have the habit of believing that everything British is right and that whatever a British man states must be the truth. The evidence, however, is of inherent force as to the rectitude of his statement. Will the Secretary please read as indicated?

The Secretary read as follows:

To the Editor of the World:

The end of the dry season is now at hand, and Spain has accomplished little toward the pacification of Cuba.

Certain gains have most certainly fallen to the Spaniards, the death of Maceo in December and the capture of Ruis Rivera a few days ago being the most notable. But at what cost has the campaign been conducted!

The provinces of Pinar del Rio and Habana and large portions of Matanzas and Santa Clara are one staring mass of cinders.

Desolation and extermination meet the eye at every point; ruin in the present, famine, disease, and death in the future, are all that the Cubans can hope for while Cuba remains under Spanish rule.

Under these circumstances I do not think that the death of this or that leader can bring victory any nearer to the Spanish arms. Where one such man as Ruis Rivera is lost to the insurgents a hundred spring up to take his place.

NO GREAT MILITARY GENIUS ESSENTIAL.

Moreover, it must not be forgotten that this guerrilla warfare needs not any great military genius to conduct it. It is, to a very great extent, "every man for himself and the devil take the hindmost." The only object in view is to keep the country in such a condition of unrest as to make imperative the presence of an enormous army of occupation. Small parties of 50 or 100 men scattered throughout the island can do this more effectively than a concentrated force of 20,000 or 30,000 men, upon which the Spanish commander-in-chief could at once mass greater numbers, equipped with superior armament.

General Weyler's policy of extermination and devastation is nothing short of the almost insane working of an ignorant and completely unbalanced mind.

To kill peaceful people on the technicality that they have neglected to obey the order to leave their homes and take up their residence in some town where no means of subsistence exist is inexcusable.

To devastate the whole Island of Cuba on the plea that by so doing all supplies will be shut off from the rebels only demonstrates the dense ignorance under which the Spanish general is laboring.

REBELS CAN GET ENOUGH FOOD FOR TEN YEARS.

The rebels can get food enough to live on for another ten years if necessary, while the cattle alone now roaming wild in the different districts will supply the insurgents with beef for a couple of years to come.

Hard living it may be, no doubt, but better subsist on the roots, the game, and the fish that are the natural products of the island than starve to death in crowded villages surrounded by Spanish soldiery. That, at least, is the idea dominating the bulk of the Cubans to-day, and Weyler's policy has helped that idea to take the practical form of joining the rebel ranks rather than obeying the order to come into the towns.

Of the Spaniards resident in Cuba there are few who approve of General Weyler's methods. Some doubtless do so because they fear with intense dread that the Cubans may win their independence, and when that time arrives treat the Spanish element in the future as the Cubans have been treated in the past.

Of course, if Cuba gains her independence, the Spaniards must make their choice of becoming Cuban citizens or retaining their Spanish nationality. If they elect the latter alternative, they naturally will lose all power to control public affairs.

CUBANS ALWAYS HUMANE.

Granted, however, that Cuban independence becomes un fait accompli, I do not believe, from my experience of the Cuban people, that any undue harshness would be shown toward the Spaniards. As a rule, wherever Spanish soldiers have been taken prisoners by the rebels they have been kindly treated, tended to if wounded, and often returned to the nearest Spanish military post without any condition being exacted.

The great majority of Spaniards with vested interests in the island condemn General Weyler and his practices in most unmeasured terms. Even the fear of being marked down as political suspects, with the prospect of transportation to an African penal settlement does not deter them from expressing openly their hatred of the régime now in vogue.

As for the foreigners resident in Cuba, they have but one feeling with regard to Weyler's methods of conducting the military operations. They consider Weyler and his actions as a reflex of the worst barbarities of the Middle Ages, far more brutal, indeed, than many of the most severe means employed by the Holy Inquisition to attain its ends.

And can they be blamed for passing such judgment on this fiend incarnate in human shape? Is there any precept advocated by God or man that justifies the wholesale slaughter of innocent men, women, and children on no other pretext than that they refuse to leave their homes and willingly submit to die slowly of starvation in such places as Weyler may order?

SLAUGHTER AND STARVATION.

The object of Weyler's present policy is to exterminate the Cuban people, a people composed of some 1,200,000 whites and 500,000 negroes or of mixed blood.

To kill every peaceful male inhabitant of the country is one of Weyler's methods; to drive the women and children into the towns to die of hunger is another.

General Weyler says that rations are issued to these poor wretches forced into garrison towns. I can only say that I have repeatedly asked about this reputed issue of rations from the poor people themselves, and the reply invariably is that there was some talk of this at first, but no such rations had ever been given. These people must beg for a little bread from day to day from neighbors better off than themselves, and when these sources are exhausted sit quietly down to watch their children and themselves waste slowly away, until a merciful death relieves them from their terrible sufferings.

In these circumstances, is it wonderful that foreigners in Cuba have small sympathy for Spain in her struggle against her colonists?

SPAIN'S "HEROISM" AND "NOBLENESS" UNMASKED.

A few pedantic individuals may talk of the heroic sacrifices and the noble efforts made by Spain to retain this last remnant of her once great colonial empire.

Is there anything heroic or noble in sending from Spain 200,000 raw and immature boys, not knowing the rudiments of a soldier's duty, to die of fever in some pestilential Cuban outpost?

Is there anything heroic or noble in shooting like dogs every prisoner of war taken in the field, or deporting thousands of men without show of trial to penal settlements because they are denounced as having sympathy with the rebellion?

Is there anything heroic or noble in reducing Cuba to ashes and plunging Spain into bankruptcy for no purpose whatever?

No. The truth is that the Spanish people are played upon by political cliques in Spain, and their quixotic feelings aroused for the single reason that certain politicians may benefit. It is time such criminal folly be ended, and nobody knows this better than the foreigner resident in Cuba.

DESPOTISM'S HEAVY HAND ON FOREIGNERS.

The cases are many in which the foreigner has fared as badly as the Cuban under this despotic and barbaric Government of Spain in Cuba.

There is the case of Ruis, done to death in the jail at Guanabacoa.

Henry D'Abregeon, a well-known Canadian, foully murdered by Spanish soldiers while lying sick in bed in his house in Cartagena.

Dr. Delgado, who was shot and left for dead.

The ill-fated prisoners of the *Competitor*, now nearly eleven months in the dungeons of the Cabana.

Verily, there is small reason for any love to be lost between the foreign resident in Cuba and the Spanish authorities, who, indeed, have little other thought of the foreigner than that he is a creature to be robbed and imposed upon on every possible occasion.

For the moment, the Spanish policy professes more leniency to American citizens in particular and more clemency toward the rebels in general. I say "professes" advisedly, for there is small proof that such a policy is to be adopted as the outcome of mature deliberation and the decision that the measures in the past have been of too severe a nature.

THE TIGER'S CLAWS ARE DRAWN IN.

The real reason for any momentary change is the advent to power of the McKinley Administration. Just now Spain is as full of smirks and smiles, of courtesies and tricks, as a coquette of six seasons at least, or, better said, perhaps, the treacherous weather of an English springtime.

Spain made Mr. Cleveland and Mr. Olney dance to the tune she piped.

I have the authority of Gen. Fitzhugh Lee, the United States consul-general at Habana, for stating that.

Not in one single case since he assumed the duties of the Habana consulate have American prisoners been accorded the privileges they are entitled to under the Spanish-American treaty and protocols. General Lee states that his efforts to obtain the full treaty rights for Americans were invariably thwarted by instructions emanating from Mr. Olney in Washington.

The object of Spain in making concessions in connection with American citizens is simply for the purpose of feeling the pulse of the new Administration.

If the wiles of the Spanish minister are as successful in entrapping Mr. McKinley and Mr. Sherman as they were Mr. Cleveland and Mr. Olney, then good-bye to any hope for justice to American citizens or protection to American property in Cuba.

God grant that Spain's efforts to mislead the United States Government may this time prove a failure!

Take, for example, the one question of the right of the Cubans to buy war material in this country. War material is simply an article of merchandise, and why should it not be shipped to Cuba?

SPAIN'S THIMBLE-RIGGING DIPLOMACY.

When the subject crops up, Spain says that this constitutes a breach of the neutrality laws, and yet in the same breath she declares there is no war in Cuba. If, however, any case arise in which all constitutional guaranties and treaty rights are ignored, the Spanish authorities assert their right to such action because a state of war exists.

If this latter assertion be true, then Cuban prisoners are entitled to be treated according to the customary usages of modern warfare; if there is not any state of war, there can be no objection to war material as merchandise being exported from this country to Cuba, as it can be to any other quarter of the globe.

The paramount question for those with interests in Cuba is what chance there may be for a speedy termination of the existing condition of affairs and the restoration of a lasting peace, established on a sound and firm basis. This happy consummation can not be reached by the promulgation of any reforms Spain may see fit to grant to the Cuban people.

WEYLER KILLED HOPE FOR REFORMS.

The time is passed when a measure of reform could have satisfied the craving for liberty possessed by the Cubans. Weyler's brutal policy of the past fourteen months has effectually killed any hope in this direction.

General Weyler, apparently with the support of the Madrid Government, is evidently of opinion that the proper way to get rid of the trouble is to exterminate the Cubans.

With all due deference to the Spanish commander-in-chief, I do not believe such a plan is feasible, even if the United States would quietly continue, as hitherto, standing by and allowing the experiment to be tried.

The Cubans are to-day better armed and equipped and with greater numbers in their fighting ranks than at any time since the revolt began. They can continue a guerrilla warfare on the present lines for years, and there is every indication that they are prepared to do so.

Spain, on the other hand, to maintain her present position, must send out reenforcements of at least 40,000 men during the current year to fill the gaps caused by sickness and the casualties of war. If the Spanish Government finds the resources of the mother country unequal to this further strain, then the alternative is to abandon the interior of the island and retain control only of the principal seaport towns and their immediate surroundings, and so nominally keep the Spanish flag flying over the Pearl of the Antilles.

DON QUIXOTE IN THE SADDLE.

It is on the rock of finance that Spain must inevitably come to grief over this Cuban matter. Her resources are already from a common-sense view too heavily mortgaged to allow of any further continuance of this disastrous struggle. But Spain puts common sense on one side and acts as did the wonderful creation of Cervantes in days gone by.

The spirit of Don Quixote governs every feeling of the average Spanish individual when his patriotism is questioned just as much to-day as it did five centuries ago. The fact that Spain is bankrupt and Cuba ruined does not, therefore, mean that there is a prospect of an end of the strife in Cuba in the very near future.

MORE PAPER, HEAVIER TAXES, UNPAID TROOPS.

The cost of the war for at least another year will be met by unlimited issues of paper money, by additional taxation in Spain, by every device that financial ingenuity can concoct, and finally by not paying the troops at all, or, at best, giving them only a pittance of what is due to them.

In this way the struggle will be maintained for another year or eighteen months unless unforeseen causes precipitate a finish. In the end the people of Spain will awake to the fact that the condition of their country does not allow them to maintain huge armies at great distances from home.

That the intervention of the United States Government should take place to bring to a close the pitiable scenes now enacted in Cuba admits of no shadow of reasonable doubt.

The past policy of this country has been to cry. "Hands off!" to any European interference in Cuban matters. This policy was reiterated in the strongest terms in Mr. Cleveland's last message to Congress.

Does not the enunciation of such a policy entail certain responsibilities? For my own part, I think it does, and my feeling in this matter is shared not only by every thinking foreign resident in Cuba, but also by the majority of Spaniards who have a stake in the island.

CUBANS A QUIET, PEACE-LOVING PEOPLE.

There is an idea lurking in the minds of many Americans, and also in those of nearly all Europeans, that the Cubans are a turbulent, quarrelsome people and require harsh measures to keep them in subjection.

Let me dispel that mistake once for all. The Cubans are a quiet, peace-loving race, the white population well educated and intelligent, the colored people always bright and cheerful. Both whites and blacks are hard working and industrious, far more so, indeed, than any other race I have seen living under similar climatic conditions.

If I may be permitted to give one word of advice to the people of this great country, it is to leave Armenia and the Turks to be dealt with by the European powers, and attend to their own Armenia, that lies but a stone's throw from their own shores.

C. E. AKERS.

The VICE-PRESIDENT. The hour of 2 o'clock having arrived, the unfinished business will be taken up.

Mr. MORGAN. I desire just a moment to put some papers in the RECORD, which I will not ask to have read. Then I will very cheerfully yield, without a motion to go on with the resolution, to the Senator from Minnesota [Mr. NELSON], who, I understand, desires to address the Senate on the subject of the bankruptcy bill. Can I have that indulgence?

Mr. HOAR. After the unfinished business is laid before the Senate, let it be laid aside informally for the purpose suggested by the Senator from Alabama.

Mr. MORGAN. It will take me but a moment.

The VICE-PRESIDENT. If there be no objection, that will be the order.

Mr. MORGAN. I have brought sworn evidence forward to-day from the American side of this question. I have heretofore put in the records of the Senate a large number of contributions from American correspondents, whose statements agree with that of Mr. Akers, and are more in detail and more particular, giving certain prominent facts that he undertakes to explain.

I now present and ask to have printed in the RECORD, without reading, a translation from La Lucha, a Spanish newspaper published in Cuba, under date of the 18th of January, 1897, for the purpose of showing some military orders that have been issued in Cuba recently, and also for the purpose of showing the distinct recognition there of the existence of war whenever it suits the purposes of the Spanish Government. I will send up the translation, and not the original text, which I hold in my hand:

In La Lucha of the 18th of January we see the following military decrees, showing that there is war in Cuba:

Boletin oficial de la Capitan General (official bulletin of the Captain-General). In the issue of the 15th of this month the following is published:

"ARMY OF OPERATIONS IN CUBA—GENERAL STAFF.

"[General order for the army of the 12th of January, 1897, given in Habana.]

"His excellency the general in chief has determined the following:

"First. His Excellency Pedro Pin Fernandez, general of division, will cease in the command of the division of Las Villas and will take charge of the division of Manzanillo y Bayamo.

"Second. His Excellency Julio Domingo Bazan, general of brigade, is appointed to the command of the first brigade of the division of Pinar del Rio (General Melguizo).

"Third. General of Brigade Eduardo Losas Berros is appointed chief of the second brigade of the trocha (Ciego de Avila).

"By order of his excellency this is published for general knowledge and compliance. The general of division, chief of staff, Andres Gonzalez Munoz."

The same issue of the bulletin contains the following decree as to the extraction of articles of commerce:

"ARMY OF OPERATION OF CUBA—GENERAL STAFF.

"The general in chief has seen fit to issue the following circular:

"In order to give compliance to article 2 of my decree of the 1st of this month as to the extraction of articles, the military authorities will proceed in the following manner:

"The taking out of provisions, clothes, and medicine from town will not be permitted unless the military authorities of the places to which the said articles are to be taken shall guarantee the buyer the necessity of the acquisition.

"For this purpose the military commander and the buyer will sign a duplicate invoice.

"In the place where the articles are bought the invoice shall be signed also by both the seller and the military authorities, one of the invoices to be kept by the latter, so that the merchandise may be examined and proved during the transportation, and when it shall have arrived at its destination the invoice shall be delivered to the military authority, who will cancel it and keep it as a matter of record.

"By order of his excellency this is published for general knowledge and compliance. The general of division and chief of staff, Andres Gonzalez Munoz."

In this same paper we have an official dispatch in which it is stated that Calixto Garcia, at the head of 5,000 rebels, besieged the town Jiguani and had an engagement with the Spanish General Bosch. A mere perusal of this paper, as well as of any copy published in the island, proves that there is constant warfare in every province.

The next is from the same sheet, translated from La Lucha, of date 26th January, 1897. It is a translation of certain telegrams which appeared in that paper, one of which relates to the surprise and capture of two prefecturas. I must explain for a moment that the prefecturas who were captured were parts of the civil government of the Cuban Republic, and were down in Las Villas, and also at Artemisa, a province of Pinar del Rio.

In La Lucha of the 26th of January, 1897, a Spanish paper published at Habana, under "Official telegrams," are the following:

"First. In Las Villas, the first guerrilla of Sagua killed the so-called Lieut. Col. Rafael Soccorro and Civil Governor Salvador Herrera.

"Second. From Artemisa, province of Pinar del Rio, we have the following headline: 'Prefecture surprised.'

"Third. Again, in the same province there is an account of a destruction by Colonel Ceballos of another prefecture.

"Fourth. There is still another destruction of a prefecture by the Spaniards, as can be seen in the sixth column of that paper."

All this shows from Spanish sources that the Cubans have a civil government established, and also from the engagements in this paper reported it can be seen that the war is being waged throughout the island.

This testimony that I put in now will be followed later on, when I next take the floor upon the joint resolution, if I have the opportunity to do so, by a copy of a statement made by a Cuban official, an official of the republic, who is the chief prefect of the most eastern of the provinces of Cuba, and who gives a complete account of the entire organization in that province and in some other provinces of the civil government there. I will only draw attention to it now as being supported by the telegrams which I have just put into the RECORD, because when I next take the floor I will have some remarks to make about the existence and the jurisdiction, the organization and the perfectness in its operations, of the civil government in Cuba, including the collection of taxes from the people, of which a very large amount has been paid to the government of the republic, and much of it sent here for the purpose of buying arms. I believe more than $400,000 has been sent to the United States from taxes collected by the Republic of Cuba for the purposes of buying arms, ammunition, and hospital supplies. The citizens of the republic who are refugees in the United States pay their taxes to the republic as cheerfully and as regularly as the tax collectors in Alabama collect theirs, and I suppose with more cheerfulness than our people pay their taxes, because they are of course urged to do it by motives of patriotism, not being under compulsion.

The civil government of Cuba, as I will be able to demonstrate by evidence that I intend to produce in connection with the evidence that I have put in now, is a thoroughly organized, complete, effectual government, administering justice, enacting laws, conducting a regular post-office, with postage stamps and mail carriers that carry letters through the entire length of the Island of Cuba and send them to the United States. I myself have received letters from Cuba with Cuban postage stamps and no other stamps on them. I do not know how it ever happens that they come through our mails, but I have the envelopes now in which those letters were inclosed. So I expect to show in the next attempt I make to explain this matter, which will be the final one, the existence in Cuba of a powerful civil government, as well as a thoroughly organized and very brave and powerful Cuban army.

* * * * * * *

April 13, 1897.

The VICE-PRESIDENT. The Senator from Alabama moves that the Senate proceed to the consideration of the joint resolution (S. R. 26) declaring that a condition of public war exists in Cuba, and that strict neutrality shall be maintained.

The motion was agreed to; and the Senate, as in Committee of the Whole, resumed the consideration of the joint resolution.

Mr. MORGAN. Mr. President, thus far in this discussion I have tried to confine the inquiry to the actual situation of citizens of the United States and their property in Cuba. I have not attempted to restate the facts disclosed and established in the former debates in both Houses of Congress, which prove that they have suffered almost beyond endurance from the illegal and barbarous treatment they have received from the Spanish authorities.

The case thus made out against Spain is a true bill of indictment which that Government has not attempted to deny.

With a feeling of confidence that no injustice has been done to her conduct or her motives in the terrible arraignment made by the American people on the facts that have become historic, I have attempted to show that our rights as a nation have been violated in the open, frequent, and defiant breach of our treaty agreements with Spain, and the rights of our people under those treaties, under the laws of nations, and the laws of humanity have been recklessly violated and abused.

Our Government has honestly employed all the power of our laws, which are of great severity, to shelter Spain from any unlawful aggression of our people. This sincere and expensive work has been responded to by Spain with constant reproaches of alleged neglect on our part to enforce our neutrality laws, while she has persistently violated our treaty rights, the law of nations, national comity, and the most elementary laws of Christian civilization, in her treatment of our people.

Under our treaties with Spain, we have the right to trade with every inhabitant of Cuba in every article that we can sell to Spaniards, so long as that island is in a state of peace; and our citizens residing there have the right, so long as Cuban ports are open, freely to import goods, without reference to the place of their residence, whether it is in Habana or in some rural village, or in the country. But these rights are denied to us in Cuba because Spain is waging war there.

This fast and loose way of dealing with questions that involve our people in prosecutions for felonies here as well as in Cuba, long imprisonments in Cuba that are intended for torture while awaiting trial and sentences to death, can not be tolerated at a less expense than that of our national dishonor.

We furnish the Spanish army and navy with all they need for war purposes, and, at the bidding of that Government, we arrest all who venture to send like supplies to the people of Cuba who are under arms.

We send our war ships out to sea to capture merchantmen belonging to our people who are suspected of carrying food, clothing, hospital supplies, or any material relief to the suffering Cubans.

These discriminations that violate our treaties and deprive our own people there of their treaty rights are attempted to be justified by the falsehood, which our Government does not deny, that war does not exist in Cuba, and yet, while affirming this falsehood, to which our Government is required to assent on the penalty of hostilities with Spain, we permit her to resort to all the measures that attend a state of war in her dealings with our people, that relate to commerce, to martial law, to imprisonment, trial, conviction, and sentence of death for alleged political offenses, such as insurrection, rebellion, enlistment in the Cuban armies, fighting in their ranks, and many other charges that are brought against them for the violation of the military orders of the Captain-General of Cuba.

Never before has any nation claimed the right in a time of peace to apply the laws of war to the trial and punishment of the citizens of a friendly power for offenses against the civil laws.

It is due to our people and to our self-respect that we should compel Spain to recognize the fact that war exists in Cuba, or else that she shall cease to resort to the laws of war and to military courts and procedure for the trial and punishment of our people for political offenses. No other than political offenses have been charged against any of the citizens of the United States who have been arrested in Cuba during the present war. Attempts to subvert the Government are the alleged basis of every arrest of our citizens that has been made in Cuba.

In the history of the world, the movements of organized masses of citizens to subvert bad governments by substituting better ones have been the great impulse to the development and security of the liberties of the people, and when the motive is just and the movement is assisted by numerous and patriotic bodies of the people, they always receive the approval of patriotic men everywhere, and are always repeated and persisted in until the reformation is finally complete. Such is the history of all essential liberties.

It is for this reason that, in the laws of nations, an insurrection rises to the proportion and dignity of a war when it is so strongly supported with numbers, resources, and arms as to compel the titular government to marshal armies and make open war in order to overcome the opposition.

However the pride of the Spanish monarchy may compel it to resent the fact, it is bound by the law of nations to the admission, in favor of the people of all countries, that the insurrection in Cuba has become an open and public war.

When that movement which began as an insurrection took the form of rebellion, as it did from the start, against the sovereignty of Spain, and grew in strength and widened the area of its military dominion until Spain was compelled to send greater armies to Cuba than Napoleon had at Austerlitz, and to send out the whole disposable strength of her navy, and to put the last possible strain upon her treasury and her credit to suppress that rebellion, she stands confessed before the world as being a party to a great public war, and all countries have the right, under the laws of nations, without giving her the least offense, to recognize the existence of open, public war in Cuba.

Our great Republic, while suffering in every sense from the existence of that war so near to our borders, so odious in its purposes, so inhuman in its conduct, and so injurious to our treaty rights, to the rights of our citizens, to our commerce, and the peace and welfare of our country, commiserates the wounded pride of the haughty monarchy, and has shown a degree of forbearance toward Spain that has encouraged her into excesses of cruelty to our own people that have become unbearable.

The great armaments of Spain have failed in their efforts to subdue her former subjects after two years of war attended with enormities of abuse at which all Christendom shudders, and still she demands that we shall silently admit that peace reigns in Cuba, while the only ruling authority she possesses there is the sword and the torch, the one bathed in the blood of innocence and the other lurid with the flames of extermination.

Our honorable and patient forbearance toward Spain is rapidly and deeply impressing our people with the conviction that our Government is more sympathetic toward this ancient Bourbon dynasty, now suffering the reactionary penalties of centuries of oppressive misrule, than it is toward our own people who are made to feel the cruelties of Spanish power in Cuba. It is time that we should convince mankind, and especially our own people, that no shelter can be found, either in our forbearance or our supposed weakness, for the inhuman barbarities of Spanish warfare in Cuba.

If it were possible to conceive that such deeds could be committed in Canada as I will now read from the sworn testimony of Dr. Diaz, it would be impossible to arrest the surging tide of volunteers who would rush into the Dominion to wipe off such a disgrace from the escutcheon of our great English-speaking family.

Dr. Diaz says in his sworn testimony before the Committee on Foreign Relations:

On the 12th day of September, 1895, I received authority from the inspector-general to organize and maintain sanitary delegations at different points throughout the Island of Cuba. I have now in my possession the original copy of said certificate of permission, signed officially.

The by-laws were approved on November 13, 1895, copy of which I hand you herewith. I would call special attention to article 2 of chapter 1, by which it will be seen I was permitted to constitute neutral camps.

I, with some other doctors and Christian people, some of whom were American citizens, organized the White Cross, in conformity with said by-laws.

While General Campos was in command the rules of civilized warfare were strictly enforced by his orders.

After General Weyler assumed command we were summoned before him and instructed not to treat or otherwise care for sick and wounded among the soldiers of the insurgents, as we had been permitted to do under the administration of General Campos.

Since the time General Weyler has been in command we have treated about 700 Spanish soldiers, each case being reported to him, at a cost to us of about $5,000, and before he assumed command we had treated about 1,300 Spanish soldiers.

During the time General Campos was in command our delegations treated the sick and wounded of both the insurgents and the Spanish alike.

During the prosecution of this work I have been a great deal out on the fields and have had good opportunities of making observations of the practices and character of the warfare of both armies.

I have seen the general order issued by Gen. Maximo Gomez directing that all prisoners captured from the Spanish army should be treated with proper consideration. That first they should be disarmed, then offered an opportunity to join the insurgent ranks. If they declined to do this voluntarily, then they must be released without parole and escorted to some point of safety. The same order further directed that Spanish prisoners who were either sick or wounded should be nursed and carefully treated until well, when, if they do not desire voluntarily to join the insurgent ranks, they must be released and conveyed under military escort to a point of safety. It was also ordered by General Gomez that no women should be molested or interfered with by any insurgent soldiers under penalty of death.

Those entire general orders are now in force and have been since the beginning of the insurrection. They are very positive, and severe penalties are provided for their violation.

From my personal observation I know these orders have been strictly enforced. I know of one instance where, in the town of Jamaica, an insurgent soldier violated these orders by laying his hands upon a woman with criminal intent. For this offense he was ordered to be shot, and I saw his body after he had been executed.

I have personal knowledge of this order in regard to the release of prisoners having been complied with.

At Peralego I saw General Maceo return to General Campos, at Ballamo, about 150 prisoners, and at Camaguani I saw Rego return to the Spanish authorities 100 prisoners.

I have also had opportunities for observing the methods of warfare and cruelties practiced by General Weyler. It is well known to the residents of Cuba that his record is one of cruelty and blood. I can substantiate the following incidents which have come under my own observation:

At Menocol farm, near Managua, on the 3d day of February, 1896, I was called to attend a woman who had been shot, the bullet entering her shoulder and ranging down her spinal column. I saw her at 4 p. m. The circumstances, as related to me by her husband, were as follows:

He was engaged plowing near his own home, and the woman, his wife, was in the field with him, dropping the seed. As soon as the Spanish soldiers, under command of General Ruiz, approached in view, they (the Spanish soldiers) commenced firing. Both the husband and wife lay down on the ground, and in that position she was shot. As the husband was lying down he held a small limb of a tree; this was struck with one of the shots. I treated the wound. They were noncombatants, unarmed, and pursuing their legitimate vocation in their own field; their only offense was that they were Cubans. There were at the time no insurgents within 20 miles of them.

On February 22, 1896, I was present at the city of Punta Braba, where a battle was fought between the insurgents and the Spanish under command of Captain Calvo. The insurgents retreated. The Spanish troops then went to Guatao, a suburb about 2 miles distant. The insurgents were not there and had not been there. The Spanish soldiers at once commenced to shoot private citizens indiscriminately on the streets or in their houses, wherever they found them, until they had killed six or seven men (noncombatants).

The soldiers then went into different homes and gathered together seventeen men; they tied these together two and two, binding their hands and arms together. Among the number was Mr. Ladislao Quintero, an American citizen, who they found in his own home, sick in bed. He informed the captain that he was an American citizen, and protested against being molested. Captain Calvo said he wanted him too, and forced him to go, bound with the others. When they were all tied, they were taken out together on the street and commanded to kneel down. After they had done so, then the whole company fired on them by command of the captain. The whole of the seventeen were killed except Mr. Quintero. He was wounded in the left arm, and the man to whom he was tied was killed with all the others. This all occurred at 7.30 p. m., on February 22, in the immediate presence of the wives and children of the unfortunate men. Mr. Quintero was about 21 years of age, born in Key West, Fla. The man to whom he was tied, Mr. Pedro Amador, was 17 years of age.

Mr. Pedro Amador was not killed by the gunshot wound he received, but one of the Spanish soldiers stepped forward to his prostrate body and beat him to death with the butt end of his gun while he was still tied to Mr. Quintero, the American citizen. I was present and saw this entire proceeding. When I returned to Habana, I learned that Mr. Quintero was in Morro Castle, a prisoner, where he remained until April 11 without having his wound dressed. On April 11 he was released.

I am informed by persons in Habana who have been prisoners in Morro Castle that there are in this prison as many as 100 prisoners confined in one small room; that in the morning they are furnished with only three pails of water. This is generally used up by 11 o'clock a. m., and they are not allowed any more until the following morning.

In the case of Mr. Edward Delgado, from Banao, an American citizen, who has a claim against the Spanish Government, his papers being on file in the Department of State at Washington, you will find by reference thereto that I was the physician who certified to his wounds. I am familiar with this case, and it is a very aggravated case of extreme cruelty to a private American citizen at his own home without provocation.

The following is only a few of the many cruel incidents that have occurred while I was present:

When the military courts inflicted the sentence of perpetual imprisonment in the cases of Messrs. Sabourin, Garcia, and others, the Captain-General protested against their leniency and asked for the infliction of the death penalty.

On the 12th of March I was called by the sanitary delegation of our society in the town of Calvario for the purpose of attending to the case of a young man of 19 years, who was wounded in the peaceful pursuit of his business— that of a milk dealer. He was driving into the town in his milk cart when two soldiers fired on him from an ambush without any warning, breaking his right leg.

I assisted in carrying the man to his home, and then made an examination of his wound and found that the bones of his leg had been fractured in such a manner that amputation was necessary. I found that the bullet used was an explosive one, made as follows: An outside covering of copper filled with lead, which results in the copper covering flattening against the lead and scattering it in such a manner as to destroy all surrounding tissues and compound the fractures of the bones.

On the 13th of March, at the corner of Reina and Aguila streets, Habana, I found a crowd collected around a prostrate man, and, as a member of the White Cross Society, I proceeded to render him whatever aid was necessary. I found the man dead, and counted and made an examination of his wounds. He had seventy-one bayonet wounds, seven of which were through the heart and several through the eyes. He also had four cuts with the machete on the head, the skull being fractured into small pieces. The ferocity of the soldiers was also shown by the marks in the sidewalk made by the point of the bayonet after having passed through the prostrate form of the man. The cause of the killing was as follows: The murdered man was in a drygoods store purchasing cloth when the two soldiers entered, and, after insulting the proprietor, took this man out and killed him in the manner related, saying he was an insurgent. The man had no arms whatever on his person, and could not, therefore, defend himself in any way. I wrote out a statement of his wounds and gave it to the judge in the case, who holds a position similar to that of coroner in this country.

On the 14th of the same month, I, as vice-president of the White Cross Society, received a report from the town of Artemisa, telling me that the Spanish troops under Gen. Suarez Inclan had bombarded an insurgent hospital, killing over fifty wounded men who were receiving treatment there, and that the surgeon had been compelled to flee to Habana hidden in a cart.

Upon his arrival at Habana he confirmed the report made to me. In Artemisa the ladies of our society had two hospitals, one for wounded Spaniards and one for wounded Cubans, the latter being the one bombarded, as told. The insurgent forces have entered the town of Artemisa several times, but have never disturbed the Spanish hospital, although they could have easily done so if they wished.

Another insurgent hospital in the town of Paso Real, Province of Pinar del Rio, was also destroyed by the Spaniards, killing all the wounded inmates. It is reported that at the time of destruction there were about 200 wounded Cubans in it.

The same thing was done with another hospital in Siguanea, Province of Santa Clara.

Notwithstanding the proclamation of the Captain-General that all those surrendering would be pardoned, Mr. Aleman, who surrendered, and who also had a wound in the hand, was shot a few days later, on the plea that his wound showed that he had been fighting.

In the woman's jail in Habana there is a lady who has been imprisoned for the last six months solely because she is suspected of being in sympathy with the insurgents' cause and because she has two brothers in the insurgent army. There are imprisoned, as rebel sympathizers, several children, the age of the youngest being 11 years.

When an armed force approaches any of the interior towns, there is great excitement and consternation until it is ascertained whether they are Spanish troops or insurgent forces. If insurgent forces, there is immediate tranquillity, as they do not destroy anything unless there are Spanish forces located there. But if the approaching troops turn out to be Spanish forces, there is great confusion and fear, as the Spaniards not only sack the town, but steal all they desire and also take all detachable woodwork to be used in building their huts. They destroy everything that comes in their way, take complete possession of the houses, violate women in many cases, and commit nuisances in the middle of the streets. They claim to go into the towns for the purpose of defending them against the insurgents, but on the approach of the latter they take refuge in the houses and do not come out until the town is set fire to by the insurgents for the purpose of driving them out. I have personally seen all this in more than ten cases.

On the 13th of March I went to the town of Caimito for the purpose of leaving medicines, bandages, etc. On arriving there I was informed that there were two wounded children at the farm known as "Saladriga." I went to their assistance, but found they had already received medical treatment. The eldest of these was 1 year and 6 months old, and had suffered a fracture of the right arm, caused by a bullet wound. The other was 3 months old, and had suffered a fracture of the lower jaw from a similar cause. I was informed that 2 miles from this place the insurgents had attacked a troop-laden train without success. The Spanish troops left the train to reconnoiter and took the road on which the insurgents had passed. On this road lived the mother of these two children. Fearing that some harm might befall them, she decided to seek shelter elsewhere. Upon her appearance at the door with two children in her arms, she was fired at, with the above results. These Spanish troops were under Commander Calixto Ruiz.

On the 19th of March I went with my brother Alfred to the town of Bainoa for the purpose of attending to Mr. Venancio Pino, 70 years of age, who was wounded at the same time as Mr. Delgado. I found that he had several slight bullet wounds in the head, but his right arm had been horribly fractured, necessitating amputation at the shoulder joint. The bone had been fractured into many pieces, and was caused by a bullet similar to the one in the case of the milk dealer spoken of before.

On the 8th of April, at the farms near the town of Campo Florida, the Spanish troop under Commander Fondevilla assassinated Mr. Ramon Castellanos, 19 years of age; Joaquin Medina, 14 years old; José J. Ochoa, 30 years, and a schoolmaster 35 years of age; Domingo Luzans, 36 years; Margarito Zarza, 50 years; Camilo Cejas, 40 years old; José Valdes, 14 years old; Manuel Martinez, 40 years old. These were buried at a point between the sugar estate of Tivo Tivo and the town, the Spaniards forcing the victims to dig their own graves before murdering them.

For the purpose of brevity, I will give the number of noncombatants assassinated each day. I have their names and can furnish them if required.

On the 9th of April, 4.

On the 15th, between Campo Florida and the sugar estate of Felicia, 10, whose corpses were left without interment.

On the same day, on the road between Guanabacoa and Bacuranao, 5 persons, 2 of whom were cousins of mine.

Over 100 persons were shot within a radius of 10 miles and not distant more that 6 miles from Habana, and within a period of fifteen days.

All of these were noncombatants.

The case against Julio Sanguily, the imprisoned American citizen, is purposely delayed so as to keep him incarcerated.

Mr. BACON. Will the Senator from Alabama please state from what he reads?

Mr. MORGAN. I am reading from the deposition before the Committee on Foreign Relations of Dr. Diaz, whose character you know probably personally as well as I do.

Mr. BACON. From the testimony before the committee?

Mr. MORGAN. Yes, sir; sworn to.

In the case of my brother and myself, we were persecuted for the reason that we were American citizens and had charge of American church institutions in Habana.

During the excitement attending the passage of the belligerency resolutions in Congress two dynamite bombs were placed in the church and exploded while we were holding service, but only resulted in the breaking of glass and causing a panic in the congregation. Our house was searched, but nothing incriminating was found, but we were arrested and imprisoned eight days, being released on the condition that we leave Cuba immediately. I would say that no charges were made against us. We immediately left Cuba.

Mr. Toledo, an American citizen employed as a Bible distributer by the American Bible Society, was imprisoned in the town of Jaruco, and has mysteriously disappeared, and it is believed that he has been murdered.

My brother and I are here for the purpose of laying these facts before your committee and to urge the honorable Senate to either recognize the belligerency of the Cubans or to have the United States intervene for the sake of humanity and civilization. Those are the only methods of putting a stop to these frightful barbarities.

Yours, respectfully, A. J. DIAZ.

Senator MORGAN. Do you swear to all that?

A. Yes, sir.

Senator MORGAN. Then please sign it.

The witness then signed the paper.

Before that time he had been conducted through a severe cross-examination by the Senator from Minnesota [Mr. DAVIS] and myself touching the memorandum from which I have just read.

What I have just read is only a sample of similar barbarities that have blackened the history of Spanish warfare in Cuba for the past two years. In the former ten-years war these infamous cruelties were less conspicuous only because they were less known. They alike interpret the inborn cruelty of Spanish rulers.

The same man, Weyler, who came out of that struggle with the odious name "hyena," uttered in scorn by every Cuban's tongue as the popular and just description of his character, is now Captain-General. He was then a subaltern, and his decrees now supply the law, from day to day, under which the people perish.

I would not recall this historic description that the people of Spanish origin have given to his public career, even to illustrate by a popular sobriquet the character of his conduct toward our own suffering people in Cuba, but from this bad eminence of his fame his inhumanity is as visible in Europe as it is in America.

Hear what a distinguished Frenchman, the genius and the soul of true liberty in France, says of Weyler in the April number of the Forum—Henri Rochefort.

Says M. Rochefort:

And it is possible that, after a long rule of pitiless suppression, the exuberance of the newly emancipated may be great at the beginning. And afterwards? Have not nations their periods of youth and maturity the same as individuals? Is it necessary to remind our Republicans of the motto of the Palatine Posnanie: "Better a stormy liberty than a calm of servitude?"

The cause of the Cuban insurgents is that of humanity. We see, too, even among the Spaniards themselves—whom it would be profoundly unjust to class as a mass with the Canovas and Weylers—the most respected men of the democracy, such as Pi y Margall, the former president of the republic, declare their sympathy for the brave, patriotic fighters, their abhorrence for the butcher general who maintains order by means of ambuscade, torture, the shooting of prisoners, and the violation and massacre of women. It would need volumes to recount the transgressions of this monster, whom, since the first insurrection, the Cubans had named "The Hyena," as they called his superior officer, Balmaceda, "The Tiger." The American continent has been aroused from one ocean to the other. From Hudsons Bay to Terra del Fuego there has been but a cry of horror against this miserable torturer and perjurer, who, always defeated by the heroic Maceo and threatened by him, even in the capital itself, has only been able to come to an end with his formidable adversary by having him murdered!

What a contrast to the conduct of the Cuban general, causing wounded Spaniards to be nursed and setting prisoners at liberty! If walls, which it is said to have ears, had also a voice, those of Morro Castle could tell a tale of numberless atrocities, the knowledge of which, by fragments, has reached even to us—the accumulation of suspects of all ages in underground places without air and without light; tortures similar to those Montjuich—crushing of the organs, deprivations of food and drink—inflicted upon prisoners to force them to betray their friends and pay rents; secret executions and drownings.

All this is done in the name of order, as it was also in the name of civilization that the Spaniards imported into Cuba the garrote, while the Americans, on the other hand, built railroads there.

Of this "order," which may be described as spoliation in time of peace and assassination in time of war, the Cubans will have no more at any price. It would be difficult to say they are wrong.

Weyler marches his great army of Spanish conscripts along the dark trail of inquisition, rapine, and murder, which has been carved by his genius for cruelty through the ashes and cinders left by the fires of extermination, and insolently spurns our petitions for the rights of civilized warfare in favor of our people in Cuba.

What it is our plain duty to demand of him, we pray for in vain. We take shelter under the pretext that our declaration that war exists in Cuba would expose our commerce to loss and our business interests to disturbance. Rochefort has seen the force of that objection, and has this to say about it:

While England, profiting by the lessons of history, endowed Canada, Australia, New Zealand, and the Cape with autonomous institutions, and allowed initiative action to freely take its course sheltered from official interference, giving over the country not to functionaries, to soldiers, and to priests, but to the civil and laboring population—the producers of all wealth—Spain persevered in the errors of the past. She had lost Mexico, Peru, Chile, Argentina, and Guatemala in less than fifteen years by the revolt of their exasperated inhabitants. But this lesson did not suffice. On the contrary, the colonies which still remained to it, notably Cuba, were ground down more cruelly than ever, and were obliged to pay for themselves and for those that had shaken off the yoke.

Robbed, gagged, having no influence where their interests were concerned, for all their rulers (one might say their convict keepers) were sent from the mother country, which chose, by preference, the ruined gamblers of the court, enjoying in reality, despite a seeming semiliberty of the press, no constitutional guaranties whatever, for the Captain-General assumed all power, as he does to-day, the Cubans, after patient endeavors to obtain pacifically the most indispensable reforms, realized that their only effective course was their resort to arms, and on October 10, 1868, the first insurrectional movement broke out at Yara.

I will not review this epoch, which endured for ten years—one year longer than the struggle of the Gauls against Cæsar. Half naked, almost without arms, led by chiefs that no peril daunted, no obstacle, however great, repelled, and who to-day meet again as old men in the new revolution, the Cubans inflicted upon their enemies a loss of 100,000 men and of nearly one thousand millions. And these, finally incapable to crush the rebellion, were forced to treat with it. The pact of Zanjon, concluded between Martinez Campos and the Cuban chiefs, stipulated a number of reforms: Administrative decentralization, admission to public office by competitive examination, establishment of new customs laws, creation of boards of works, representation in the Cortes on the basis of copyhold tenure; finally, and above all, cessation of a shameless system of malversation.

Of these clauses, some very flagrantly violated, others were put in force under conditions that worked to the disadvantage of the Cubans. Thus it was that a law of mercantile relations was enacted which, instead of reforming the customs system in a liberal sense, strengthened existing protection, compelling the island, without any kind of reciprocity, to supply itself with the costly and indifferent products of Spain. The presence of Cuban representatives in the Chamber and Senate of Madrid served only to demonstrate the complete futility of this measure, as the voices of these few men were drowned by ministerial majorities. In short, thefts and peculation became worse.

The Cubans could thus by experience convince themselves that the Liberals were no better than the Conservatives. The only rôle the one or the other assigned to them was, in fact, that of taxpayers.

Deceived, robbed, subjected to incessant arbitrary acts, eaten up by militarism and bureaucracy, hindered in the free cultivation of the most fertile soil in the world—for it was, above all, necessary to favor Spanish importation which has lost all its other outlets—the Cubans felt their misery all the more from having before their very eyes the picture of the great American Republic, so free, so prosperous.

They realized and knew that force alone could insure the success of their claims. It was at this moment that José Marti appeared.

The American continent is acquainted with the life and death of this man, as great as he was modest, whose every effort was devoted to the realization of that grand idea, "Cuba libre." An organizer of the first order, writer, counselor, indefatigable conspirator, the Antillian Mazzini prepared during ten years the elements and resources of the second revolution. It broke out on February 24, 1895, and has continued ever since.

Two years of desperate conflicts—ruinous for Spain, which is to-day on the verge of bankruptcy—have not weakened the efforts of the insurgent patriots. In the United States, better than anywhere else, one could follow day by day the varying fortune of this titanic duel—the landing of the two Maceo brothers, survivors of a family of heroes, both of whom were to find, a few months apart, the most glorious of deaths; the advent in the campaign of Maximo Gomez, the veteran of the ten years' insurrection; the death of Marti, fallen in ambuscade before seeing the triumph of his labor; the revolt deepening, spreading from the eastern to the western department, toward Pinar del Rio, and threatening Habana; the recall of Martinez Campos, powerless to conquer; his replacement by General Weyler, a wild beast with a human countenance; and, finally, the dissolution—greater each day—of the prestige and credit of monarchical Spain.

This is the state of things at present: The entire people of the United States have espoused the cause of those who are struggling with so much valor and abnegation to break so odious a yoke. Will the Federal Government show itself less generous than the great nation in the name of which it speaks? Will the American eagle allow the Spanish vulture to settle upon its prey?

I here insert a statement of our commerce with Cuba, which shows what we have lost in two years by the war that rages in that island:

Merchandise imported into and exported from the United States to Cuba for the years named.

IMPORTS.

	1894.	1895.	1896.
Free	$67,418,289	$17,684,765	$2,074,763
Dutiable	8,259,972	35,186,494	37,942,967
Total	75,678,261	52,871,259	40,017,730

EXPORTS.

	1894.	1895.	1896.
Domestic	$19,855,237	$12,533,260	$7,312,348
Foreign	270,084	274,401	218,532
Total	20,125,321	12,807,661	7,530,880

Imports decreased from 1894 to 1895, 30.2 per cent; and 1895 to 1896, 47.1 per cent.

Exports decreased from 1894 to 1895, 36.4 per cent; and 1895 to 1896, 62.6 per cent.

Imports and exports, United States and Cuba, for eight months ending February.

	1896.	1897.
Imports	$26,990,770	$6,755,591
Exports	5,423,189	5,494,777

Imports decreased, eight months in 1896 to 1897, 75 per cent.

What will be the value of our commerce with Cuba if this war should continue for ten years, as the former war did?

Up to date our losses in trade and in the value of our property in Cuba is more than the sum of $30,000,000. What have we done to make this enormous loss, and what can be done to restore this hitherto valuable trade?

Independent Cuba, with the right to regulate commerce with other countries, would soon add to the wealth of the world more than fourfold its former contributions, and would increase its population to four or five million. In this new development the United States, without any direct political control in Cuba, would naturally come in for a large share of the benefits.

With only one-eighth of its arable lands in cultivation the resources of Cuba would pay 6 per cent interest on a debt of $800,000,000, and would save to the people nearly one-half the money now extorted from them by Spanish taxation. At the end of this war, if it should close at once, the debt saddled on Cuba for the expense of butchering the native population, not including the devastation of the island, will be at least $300,000,000. I have here a letter I will read that states the debt at $400,000,000:

Hon. JOHN T. MORGAN.

SIR: Permit me to give you some facts anent the financial condition of Cuba, which so much occupies the attention of business men on said island, and, without doubt, interests the business men of the United States associated with the commerce of the Queen of the Antilles.

Four hundred million dollars is to-day the public debt which the governments of Spain have imposed upon Cuba during the brief period included between the years 1882 and 1896, as the following will show:

Gamazo loan of 1886, which absorbed former debts	$124,000,000
Fabié loan, 1890	175,000,000
Sums for satisfaction, according to the law of July 7, 1882	26,000,000
Loan of Spain of 1896 and charged to Cuba	50,000,000
Other debts (approximate calculation)	25,000,000

This colossal debt, supposing that it would not be increased, at 5 per cent interest, $20,000,000 each year. Cuba can not support a greater estimated expenditure than $17,000,000, that is to say, $10 per inhabitant. In order to meet said twenty millions of interest would necessitate an estimated expenditure of at least $37,500,000, and this would be absolutely impossible for Cuba.

The reforms projected by the Spanish Government do not satisfy even the pacific Cubans. These and many Spaniards, as well as the revolutionists, understand that with independence alone are they free from this suicidal debt and the payment of the large army which Spain must necessarily leave in Cuba to maintain armed peace, it being then possible for the Cubans to establish the estimated $17,000,000, and make with other countries commercial treaties necessary for the development of the riches of the country. The enormous estimates, the debt, and the impositions on the agriculture, industry, and commerce are the real causes of the wars in the island. The sums paid with that debt were acts on the part of Spain, not of Cuba.

After four hundred years of misgovernment, Spain persists in treating the Cubans like Indians, repeating the butcheries of the fifteenth and sixteenth centuries, for which purpose she has posted over the isle 200,000 soldiers, manipulated by the bloodthirsty Weyler, who persecutes the patriots, but can not defeat them, much less exterminate them, as the Spaniards desire. The Cubans constitute the educated element in the country, who are struggling for an honorable government, which Cuba has never had since her discovery in 1492.

Almost all the Cubans desire independence, and we must take into account that they constitute 90 per cent of the population of the island.

Respectfully, yours,

J. CROVVE.

JACKSONVILLE, FLA., *April 2, 1897.*

The interest on this debt would be a bagatelle as compared with the largess that is annually imposed upon Cuba of nearly $30,000,000 for the support of Spaniards of the Peninsula who are permitted to prey upon the industries of the country.

The absence of country roads, bridges, schoolhouses, churches, and all public improvements in Cuba is a condemnation of Spanish rule that needs no other statement to prove the fact that Spain rules in Cuba alone for the money that can be extorted from the people.

This is not an exceptional situation in colonial government by Spain. All her colonies have been destroyed by the tyranny and greed of the so-called mother Government.

All this wrong done to her own people, so far as it relates to their industrial prosperity, is no concern of ours in any political sense; yet it is a strong proof that almost any change in the government of Cuba will be to the commercial advantage of our people.

The furtive whisperings of diplomatic caution and admonition are listened to respectfully by the generous-hearted people of our country and are dutifully regarded, until their sense of justice and humanity is shocked by repeated acts of cruelty, or by some savage attack upon the liberties of the people and the rights of humanity; then they turn with one accord upon the oppressors, and are ready to make any sacrifice for the vindication of the oppressed.

The people of the United States are dangerously near to such a demonstration at this hour, and it is now far more difficult to restrain them than it is to prevent the shipment of arms to the rebels in Cuba. I fear that the near future has trouble in store for us.

If the land were continuous between us and Cuba, as it is toward Mexico or Canada, tens of thousands of our people would cross the border, and Cuba would be free in less than thirty days.

They would not delay until the diplomats could be informed, against their quibbling objections and their reluctant will, whether the Republic of Cuba has all the technical attributes of a government fully organized and equipped for the purposes of civil rule.

The sympathy that is born of a love of liberty and is turned into fierce indignation when Turkish cruelty unfetters the red hand of murder in Crete is native to our people, and is aroused in their hearts against Spanish cruelty, and will cause them to cross the Gulf of Mexico as the Greeks are crossing the waters of the Mediterranean Sea and the frontier of Macedonia to save suffering humanity from outrages that only Turks and Spaniards know how to inflict upon innocent people.

It is better that the oppressed people should have the unrestricted right of self-defense when despotism uses the sword and the torch to slay them and devastate their homes than that our great Republic should be compelled to ignore the truth that war exists in Cuba. It is better that we should confront Spain with the power and majesty of the laws of nations than to cover up her iniquities under a false disguise.

The belligerent rights of Cuba do not depend on the form or the efficiency of the civil government there. In the message of the President to the last session of Congress this objection to the recognition of the belligerency of the Cubans was urged as a prohibition upon any action on the part of the United States. Not only is it utterly illogical to say that belligerency depends on the form of civil government in Cuba, when open public war has been flagrant there for more than two years, but it is not true that such a government does not exist there.

War is a fact that does not depend upon the civil authority that may support it. Every revolution to overthrow the titular sovereignty in a state or province begins with insurrection, whether the rebellion is armed or is only a civil commotion. If it is armed rebellion, and if the resistance to it makes necessary the employment of armies and navies, the necessity for their use, when it is so serious as to displace the civil power of the sovereign, creates a state of war without reference to the nature or form of civil government which may be so displaced or adopted by the rebel power. Otherwise no insurrection could ever reach the condition of war until it had completely expelled the titular sovereignty and until the rebel power had been fully established and developed into organized government.

I repeat that war is a fact, and the proof of its existence is established when the whole military power of the parties engaged is called into the actual conflict of arms. This fact distinguishes open public war from partial or imperfect warfare. Spain and the people of Cuba both recognized in the beginning that open and desperate war existed in that island, and at once put forth their utmost military power in implacable hostility and deadly array.

This war was only the revival of the war of ten years—from 1868 to 1878—under the same generals on both sides and with the same classes of combatants. That war closed with the capitulation of the Republic of Cuba upon terms of settlement and with political conditions of vital importance, which were signed and duly celebrated by the warring powers in the treaty of Zanjon. Those conditions were afterwards broken by Spain, and the parties, for that cause, resumed the war that had already cost the lives of 100,000 men and the expenditure of $100,000,000 by Spain, and the destruction of property to a vast amount. The present war is only a second campaign of that first war of ten years.

In order to secure what General Grant considered the more important result the abolition of slavery in Cuba, he declined to recognize the belligerency of the contending parties in that war on the ground that only a portion of the island was included in the field of actual hostilities, while the rest of the island—more than two-thirds of its area—was free from all warlike disturbance.

Even under the pressure of this great policy, to which was linked the hope of Cuba's future independence, that was dear to his generous heart, General Grant did not withhold his indignant denunciation of the crimes against the laws of nations and of humanity that Balmaceda and Weyler had perpetrated upon the Cubans in the name of honorable warfare.

Hear what Martinez Campos, the general of the Spanish army and the author of the treaty of Zanjon, had to say about the reasons for its stipulations, which were admitted by the Spanish Crown.

An important document was addressed on May 19, 1878, by Gen. Martinez Campos to Mr. Canovas del Castillo, in which he says:

> The promises never fulfilled, the abuses of all sorts, the neglect of public improvements, the exclusion of the natives from all branches of the administration, and many other faults were the causes of the insurrection. The belief, shared in by all our governments, that the people should be terrorized into subjection, and that it was a point of dignity not to make concessions until the last shot had been fired—these factors, I believe, have kept up the insurrection. By the continuation of such a system we never would have come to an end, even though we had packed the island with soldiers. It is necessary, if we wish to avoid our ruin, to adopt frankly liberal measures. I believe that if Cuba can not constitute an independent state, she is more than

2777

prepared to constitute a Spanish province. And let there be a stop to the coming of officeholders—all Spaniards. Let the natives have their share, and give some stability to the tenure of office.

That statement summarizes the grounds upon which the present rebellion exists in Cuba. After making this treaty, Spain renewed with increased severity the same wrongs that caused Campos to inveigh so forcibly and so eloquently against her traditional policy of oppression toward the Cubans.

Her broken faith severed the last tie that bound the "faithful island" to Spain.

When this second campaign was opened to enforce the treaty that ended the first campaign, the negroes had been emancipated in law, only to be placed under a worse servitude in fact, and they united with the republic in arms as the only hope of the assertion of their liberties. This combination greatly increased the power of the republic, which has effectually driven the royal power within the towns and cities that are fortified, and has forced it to take shelter under the guns of the army and navy.

The country is open and free from enemies of the republic throughout the entire island, except in the parts through which marching columns of soldiery or ships of war command it for short periods. Farming, stock raising, factories, and all other industries of the people are in successful operation and without interruption, except from occasional irruptions or invasions of Spanish soldiery. In truth, the Spanish forces in Cuba are in a state of siege in an enemy's country in every place where they are found in important numbers.

In comparison with the first campaign, from 1868 to 1878, this second campaign is more than five times as strong and more successful than that was. Again, it is urged that the republic is not in possession of any seaport and has no ships of war.

Switzerland and Poland have often engaged in public wars, and neither State has ever had a port or a ship of war, and the whole of Spanish America conquered their independence without a fleet on the oceans.

In the second campaign of this war, as in the first, Cisneros is president of the republic, duly elected by delegates from the army of the republic, who were appointed by the people that comprised the army.

In the second election of Mr. Lincoln the armies in the field voted for and elected the electors of the States in which they were resident at the time of enlistment. Shall we be heard to assert that civil authority can not emanate from armies in the field?

In the outset of this campaign the Republic of Cuba was reorganized under a written provisional constitution, suited to the condition of the people and made obligatory by oaths of allegiance. All the proceedings of the convention that ordained that government and its general acts of legislation have been presented by Estrada Palma, the authorized commissioner of the republic to the Government of the United States, and they have been sent to the Senate and printed by its order. They have been examined and reported upon by the Committee on Foreign Relations as the constitutional basis of the republic.

As to all these formalities our Government has been duly informed. They are exact, complete, and wise declarations of constitutional laws, and are entitled to full faith and credit as such.

This organic law, and the statutes enacted in pursuance of its provisions, creates revenues by taxation and collects them, provides for the organization of prefectures and prescribes the duties of prefects, provides for postal facilities, creates a judiciary, and issues commissions to all officers, civil and military, in the republic.

I will not again repeat these laws and ordinances that have already been printed in the CONGRESSIONAL RECORD and in executive documents, but will content myself with a mere reference to them.

It is indeed strange, in view of these facts, that the President should have ignored their existence when he assumed in his message to Congress that there was no sufficient proof that an organized civil government had been established by the revolutionists in Cuba.

But the greatest stress seems to be laid upon the assertion made by him that no actual civil government is maintained in Cuba by the revolutionary party. In the meager information that has been obtainable by private persons, and in the almost studied silence of our consular reports on this subject, we have been deprived of the authentic facts that have been easily in reach of our Government. Yet there is abundance of proof to show that a well-organized, efficient, and vigorous republic exists in Cuba, and that its official entourage is as capable of conducting a state to a high and noble destiny and its people to the enjoyment of peace and prosperity as is found among the average governments of the American Republics.

The debates published in the CONGRESSIONAL RECORD abound in these clear and unimpeachable proofs, none of which have been contradicted.

But there are other proofs at hand, some of which I will now present. I will ask the Secretary to read a copy of the last annual report made by the governor of Oriente to the government of the Republic of Cuba for the year 1896.

The Secretary read as follows:

[Seal (which says, "Republic of Cuba, state of Oriente, office of the governor").]

General report for the year 1896.

To the government council of the Republic of Cuba, the civil governor of Oriente:

In a session held on the 12th of January, 1896, and on motion of the vice-president, Maj. Gen. Bartolomé Massó, who at that time was occupying pro tempore the secretaryship of the interior in the government council of the republic, I was appointed civil governor of the state of Oriente.

It is a year since you confided to my patriotism the labor of organization and the civil government of a territory which, on account of its history and size, is the most conspicuous of the island.

It seems to me proper, therefore, that I should report the result of my work to the supreme powers of the republic and submit to its judgment the appreciation of the difficult task of so many faithful citizens who have cooperated fervently to the cause of independence.

I.

Before entering fully into this report, I may be pardoned if I submit certain considerations as to the condition of affairs in Oriente at the beginning of the year 1896.

It is a curious fact for our history that on the very 24th of February, 1895, Gen. Bartolomé Massó appointed in Gua Citizen Francisco Martinez as prefect of La Gloria.

He thus gave proof, from the very inception of the revolution, of its democratic tendencies. The civil authorities, owing to the natural weakness of the war at that time, could not discharge their duties free from the direct action of the military chiefs, until the government, constituted in September, 1895, returned from Las Villas and entered this territory.

Nevertheless, the original organization, so quickly established in each district by the first leaders of the movement, continued to grow, and indeed it can be said that the primitive structure has been the basis of the future organizations, although it has been corrected and adapted to conform to the favorable conditions which have followed. The importance of this organization can not be underestimated when we consider that the civil government is the immediate representative of a sovereign people.

The territorial division was very deficient; this was due perhaps to the want of stability of our frontiers, which were continually invaded by columns operating at will without finding any resistance worth mentioning, for the contingent of the invading army took the best arms and ammunition of the troops of this territory, where, until then, only small expeditions had landed. The first of importance arrived on our shores on the 24th of March, 1896, under the command of Gen. Calixto Garcia. It can be seen, therefore, that this first problem was an arduous one.

The personnel was not up to the requirements. Some of the offices were held by country people of little instruction, and the subordinates in the prefectures and their clerks were not capable of fulfilling their responsible duties, which included judicial functions, notary business, administration, and police.

The interior roads for communication were not subject to system, nor to a perfect plan, the result of a thorough study of the different lines and their several branches, but they were drawn at random, and were far from satisfying the exigencies of rapidity and precision, so indispensable to military operations. The original personnel was still more deficient in this branch. The workshops, except in Tunas (and this due to the activity of Luis Marti, then lieutenant-governor of that district), failed to yield any positive results to the army. The scarcity of salt, with the exception of the foregoing district, could only be lessened with the small quantities of that article which through private sources were obtained from the towns occupied by the enemy.

Public education did not exist, nor was the provisioning of the army properly attended to.

A period of general expectancy followed after the withdrawal of the contingent. On its success it was thought that the success of the war depended.

The so-called policy of moderation of Captain-General Arsenio Martinez Campos still kept in the towns many men and families who, sympathizing with the revolution, were not decided to come to it, not for fear of the enemy, but thinking that they would have to pass through the same hardships as in the last war.

The archives and the public offices, without order or system, were useful only to provide information to the headquarters. Our legislation then commencing, and very limited at that, hardly responded to actual necessities.

Finally, and as a culmination of such disequilibrium, the defenseless zones, without guards or police, were constantly exposed to abuses and disorders, to invasion or surprise.

Such was the condition of things in Oriente, and therefore the future of its government did not appear to be very bright.

II.

After the defeat of the Spaniards at Cauto, in the engagement of Maibio, on the 2d of February, 1896, I asked permission of the government council to make my first inspection trip to Cape Cruz, near Manzanillo.

I had matured a plan of organization inspired by the purest patriotism, based on the famous motto of the French republicans: "Liberty, equality, and fraternity."

Since then I have constantly inspected this vast territory without being deterred by any difficulties whatever. I have found everywhere support and aid from the military authorities, who vied with each other in their desire to give strength and prestige to the civil government, and the relations of the civil with the military authorities have been most cordial. In view of these facts, and in what refers to this Government, the assertions made by certain foreign authorities are of no value. These assertions are due to the calumnies of our enemies, or perhaps to the superficial information of their own officials.

In compliance with the laws, this Government has issued a series of "Regulations for the interior organizations of the prefectures;" also, "Regulating the relations of the prefectures and districts among themselves," "Rules for workshops," "Post-offices and cattle." Sanitary measures have been decreed, as well as those referring to commerce and on other points, in order to better carry out the general laws of the republic. Public instruction has been temporarily provided for; numerous families of Cuban patriots are already reaping benefit from it.

The government of the east has seen order and uniformity established throughout its jurisdiction, and by dint of perseverance and patriotism has attained a degree of perfection which can be judged from the positive facts hereinafter stated.

The territorial division is the result of a detailed study, enlightened by observation, on the very ground of the necessity, and by the opinion of those interested, and of impartial experts.

As much can be said of the postal organization. The route consists of three mail lines, with branches radiating in all directions. A selected personnel, with commendable activity and zeal, has assured a considerable regularity and rapidity. As to the workshops and salt works, the details that you will find in this report are eloquent enough. I will say nothing of the territorial guards, a strictly civil institution, which protects the roads and prefectures; but I must mention as a model of valor and discipline the one operating in the district of Tunas, actually besieging the town, which it frequently fires upon.

I will here state that the situation of the enemy here is most precarious. He is confined to the towns, and exercises no control but over the limited surroundings of its fortresses. Consequently there is great misery and starvation, crime and immorality, in the enemy's territory. On the other hand, if we were to count only with the district of Manzanillo, to which I refer because in times of peace it was a cattle-raising country, we would have provisions in abundance for all the revolution.

Still more, this government has not had to deal with a single case of criminal homicide, nor a single theft of importance, nor a single case of banditism, the curse and terror of colonial days.

III.

From the River Jobabo to the point brightened by the rays of the lighthouse of Maise, about 300,000 souls live under the Cuban flag.

From this there should be excluded the five divisions of the first and second army corps, which fight bravely for the independence of Cuba; 4,000 civil employees, the members of the territorial guards, and the new immigration of the last months.

Holguin alone has more than 40,000 inhabitants, of which 9,200 are in one of its prefectures. Of this population the males work on the lands of the state fifteen days out of every month. Their labor is exclusively devoted to provide the army and certain public charges. The rest of their time is devoted to their affairs, such as the maintenance of their families, commerce in small scale of products and manufactures, on which the officers of the treasury collect a moderate duty.

The workshops throughout the districts have rendered excellent service in the matter of arms, carpenter work, saddlery, foundry, ropes, and shoes. Owing to the system in vogue until a short time ago, the labor of the artisans could not be fully estimated. The demand having increased, the production has been considerably augmented.

In the last months about 1,000 saddles have been manufactured, 20,000 pairs of shoes, and a great quantity of ammunition belts and straps, as can be seen by the last statements and receipts of the army.

The workshops of Mayari, Tunas, Holguin, and Manzanillo have specially distinguished themselves. The last-named district has contributed 2,225 pairs of shoes and other articles of prime necessity, produced by a relatively small number of workmen.

With the recent regulations, a minimum production of 8,000 pairs of shoes per month is assured. This does not include other articles manufactured in the workshops.

The salt produced in all the territory during the year that has just expired may be calculated at 30,000 quintals, of which 12,000 are due to the extraordinary activity of Luis Marti, lieutenant-governor of Holguin. In this amount are not included the several quantities that he has given to his neighbors.

The salt works have been definitely organized by this government, and it is calculated by exports that they will yield 500 quintals per month, those of Bayamo 700, and those of Manzanillo 25 to 30 quintals a day.

Similar results I purpose to obtain with the elements which exist in each of the remaining districts. In the general list of civil employees and in the detailed reports, which at present are being prepared for the department of the interior, the government council may inform itself with greater accuracy of our work.

Finally, it can be guaranteed that the invincible fraction of the army of liberty, which, thoroughly equipped and commanded by illustrious veterans, gives battle and triumphs daily—it can be guaranteed that, aided by the solid governmental and administrative mechanism, this extreme end of the island can never see its power diminished, even if all the troops of Spain in Cuba would attempt to conquer the aspirations of the people.

IV.

In the labor of organization and government the name of Luis Marti shines with commendable perseverance. As a reward to his extraordinary services to the army, the general in chief conferred on him the rank of lieutenant-colonel. I can only ask you to give a vote of thanks to this model officer.

The others have labored faithfully with increasing fervor and perseverance. To mention one would necessitate to mention all. The general statements speak of each one. Yet they do not say anything of those who accompany me day and night, who share with me the fatigues of eternal march; of those who, from the rising of the sun to the advanced hours of night, bend over the table of work, never rest, preaching the doctrine of love and perseverance—they have come to know by memory the creed of independence. For them there are no discouragements, no sufferings, no fear, no ambitions. They reflect an immaculate patriotism, always rebellious to the domination of Spain.

Contemplate, then, government councilors, the favorable condition of affairs in Oriente, which for many years was one of gold and blood, to-day the guarantor of the Cuban revolution.

Country and liberty.

Residence of the governor, 22d of January, 1897.

CARLOS MANUEL DE CESPEDES.

Mr. MORGAN. That is an interesting paper to inquirers after the truth, and it has been easily within the power of our Government to get others from three or four of the departments of the republic equally as explicit and important.

I now read a letter from a gentleman who has been in the field with President Cisneros for nearly two years:

NEW YORK, April 9, 1897.

DEAR SIR: It has been my privilege and pleasure to spend the greater part of the past two years with the "provisional government" in the capacity of a war correspondent, both for the World and the New York Herald. I am of course personally acquainted with President Salvador Cisneros and with the members of his cabinet, and am thoroughly familiar with the efficient work done by that most potent, although unrecognized, insurgent government. I can testify not only to its existence, but to the support given it by the people of Cuba libre. I am not a Cuban, but an American, born of American parents in the State of Louisiana. The foreign editor of the Herald, Mr. Jackson, the managing editor of the New York World, Mr. Bradford Merrill, and Col. Robert G. Ingersoll will, I am sure, vouch for my integrity. Now, if my testimony before the Committee on Foreign Relations, or anyone else, will be of service in aiding a just cause, I will gladly come to Washington at any time and place myself at your disposal.

I will now read the part of it which relates to Cisneros's operations:

Inclosed you will find the proof sheets of an article descriptive of President Cisneros and his cabinet, together with some details which may prove of interest. In my estimation the collection of taxes and the establishment of public schools by the insurgent government of the Cuban Republic are very significant facts. In the capacity of a correspondent I accompanied the tax collectors throughout most of the province of Puerto Principe and witnessed the orders cheerfully given by the planters and cattle raisers of that province. These orders were converted into drafts and have been honored by the banks of New York City:

I have myself seen thousands of dollars thus paid into the treasury of the Republic of Cuba. To my certain knowledge over $400,000 of money thus collected has been forwarded to this city. The civil governor of the department of Camaguey or Puerto Principe is young Bernabe Sanchez, son of the English consul at Nuevitas, and himself worth over a million dollars. I have ridden with him over hundreds of miles of territory and noted the excellent work done under his direction.

I have seen the establishment of public schools for the first time in Cuba, and have watched the distribution of pamphlets and proclamations issued by the civil government for the purpose of encouraging and enlightening the poor people of Cuba libre. It would take a volume to tell of all the excellent work done by the civil government of the Cuban Republic.

I will read a portion of his article, the proof sheets of which he sent to me, which will appear to-morrow, if it has not done so to-day, in the New York Herald:

It is a favorite assertion of the enemies of Cuban independence that there exists among the insurgents in Spain's war-ridden colony no practical system of government. Such a view of the present state of the Cuban Republic is, as can be shown from personal observation by the writer, wholly untenable.

Salvador Cisneros is the president and chief executive of the Cuban Republic, rightly so called. It has fallen to the writer's lot to dwell in the tents of President Cisneros and to study attentively the admirable system of rule by him established throughout his native island.

PRESIDENT IN FACT.

Although known as the Marquis of Santa Lucia, Salvador Cisneros is, by temperament and tuition, a democrat. In spite of his being descended from a long line of Spanish nobility, he was born a democrat. In 1846 he first came to this country to study the great principles which underlie the foundation of this Republic. To give Cuba a government like it is the ambition of his life. He is far from being, as some people in this country are inclined to believe, a president in name only—a mere figurehead. He is a president in fact, the executive head of the million and a quarter of people on the island who are either farming or fighting for the success of the "army of liberation."

As in the United States, the president is the commander-in-chief of the forces on land and sea, and on his shoulders rests the actual responsibility for the conduct of the war and the establishment of a permanent and enduring republic. Although Cisneros is a man of pronounced character and marked independence, he is far from being a dictator. Between him and Generals Gomez and Garcia there is a degree of mutual dependence and cooperation which has made the revolution almost free from the hitches and blunders which have occurred in similar uprisings in many of the South and Central American countries. Of jealousies among the leaders there have been none. The cause of liberty is too sacred to permit it. Occasional differences of opinion and friendly clashes are unavoidable, but the one great end in view enforces harmony in all branches, civil and military.

The constitution of the Republic of Cuba is constructed along the same lines as our own. The broad principles of democracy which inspired Thomas Jefferson are to be found all through its text. Salvador Cisneros saw that they were incorporated in it, and has placed copies of the document in the hands of every "prefecto" and "subprefecto," with instructions to read them to the free people of "Cuba Libre."

No sooner did the first notes of battle come down from the hills of Oriente than this old veteran made preparations to go to the front. He had sacrificed everything—lands, wealth, position, and title—on the altar of liberty, and when General Gomez crossed the frontier into Camaguey, Salvador Cisneros was there to welcome him. This patriotic old man of 70 years had mounted his horse and ridden out of the city of Puerto Principe, with fifteen companions, eager to devote the remainder of his life to the freedom of his country.

HOW INSURGENT CUBA IS ADMINISTERED.

The people, through the assembly convened in the following September, elected him president of the provisional government, and in that capacity he has worked quietly and faithfully for nearly two years. The result of this labor may not be apparent to the outside world, but its benefits are most obvious to a traveler through the interior of Cuba.

The entire island has been divided, first, into what are known as civil districts, with a civil governor over each. These civil districts are divided into "prefectos" and "subprefectos," the latter usually about 3 miles square, and officers known as "prefectos" and "subprefectos," appointed by the government, are in charge of their respective territories.

Each has his official seal and functions carefully prescribed by the constitution. It is his duty to instantly notify the nearest body of insurgent troops of the approach and strength of any Spanish column and to furnish "practicos," or guides, whenever called upon. If an insurgent force camps in his district, it is his duty to furnish, so far as possible, any food they may need.

To all complaints or requests for food, clothes, or medicines, coming from families whose fathers or sons may be fighting for "Cuba libre," he must lend an ever-willing ear, and if it is impossible to satisfy the requirements of the case, it is his duty to inform his "prefectura," and he in turn relies upon the support of the civil governor.

The PRESIDING OFFICER (Mr. PASCO in the chair). The hour of 2 o'clock having arrived, it is the duty of the Chair to lay before the Senate the unfinished business, which will be stated.

The SECRETARY. A bill (S. 1035) to establish uniform laws on the subject of bankruptcies throughout the United States.

Mr. MORGAN. Unless there is objection, I will proceed to the close of my remarks, which will not take me long. I wish to say now that at the close of my remarks to-day I will have nothing further to urge in favor of this resolution. The parts of four days I have occupied this floor have been purposely occupied in a presentation of the facts and the law as I have gathered them and as I understand them as a necessary foundation for this very important movement.

The Senate of the United States can not afford to pass a resolution of this gravity without having a proper, firm foundation to support its action. The people of the United States require it, and it is due from the Senate that they should receive that kind of investigation of this great issue. I have been compelled, contrary to my personal comfort and my wishes, to devote a great deal of time in putting upon the records of the country those facts which have not hitherto fully and authentically appeared. Some of the facts that I am now stating to the Senate are new to us, and have been sought for by this body on former occasions when this matter has been up for consideration.

The PRESIDING OFFICER. The request is that the pending order be informally laid aside, in order that the Senator from Alabama may conclude his remarks. The Chair hears no objection, and the Senator from Alabama will proceed.

Mr. MORGAN. The article of Mr. Reno proceeds as follows:

If this official is unable to cope with the difficulty, he must appeal to the secretary of the interior, and lastly to the president of the republic. The latter is easily approached at all times by the poorest peasant in the land, and is simply worshiped by the people at large.

The carrying and distribution of mail matter by means of mounted messengers, who traverse the interior, is both efficient and rapid. President Cisneros told me that twenty-four hours after the passage of the concurrent resolution by our Congress last spring the news was received by him at his headquarters in Najassa, province of Camaguey.

A MOVABLE SEAT OF GOVERNMENT.

Strange as it may seem, the "Marques" (the name by which he is most frequently called) becomes most restless if long compelled to remain in camp at any one place. He loves to travel about; to visit the civil governors and prefectos of different districts; to talk with the people, or, better still, to accompany the forces of Gomez or Garcia, and watch the military movements from day to day.

With an escort of only fifty men, he has many times made the trip from Santa Clara to Santiago de Cuba and back again. And it is this penchant for moving about and changing camp which has given rise to the absolutely groundless report that the provisional government was being driven by the Spanish forces from one part of the island to another, and was always in danger of capture.

During the month of July last there were laid before President Cisneros the advantages which, it was thought, would accrue should he see fit to establish a permanent headquarters or seat of government at some given place—Najassa, Cubitas, or even in the mountains of the "Oriente."

Generals Garcia and Rabi supported these suggestions most heartily, but the Marques, while he admitted that such a permanent location of the government could be easily defended, and that a certain increase of dignity might follow, still did not take kindly to the idea. The provisional government had traveled about and shared the dangers of battle during the "ten-years war," and he saw no sufficient reason to change his tactics.

"We are doing good work," he said. "You have seen the evidences of our administration on every hand, and you found no difficulty in reaching us, nor will anyone else. If the United States or any country will send an agent, officially or socially, to visit and inspect the administration and execution of our laws in 'Cuba libre,' we will not only conduct him here, but we will entertain him so long as he cares to stop, and provide for his return in safety whenever he may wish to depart."

There is a quiet and unconscious dignity about Salvador Cisneros's life in the woods which seems almost pathetic. Seated on a leather camp stool, or more frequently standing, he receives the constant stream of officers and messengers who come to bring reports from civil governors and commanders in different parts of the island. These are duly filed and copied by his two secretaries, Manolo and Diego Betancourt. Long after dark these industrious brothers may be seen recording in huge government ledgers the events of the day. Yellow home-made wax candles, with the lower half coiled into a base, furnish a weird light by which the struggles of patriotic and desperate people are transmitted to the pages of Cuba's history.

Nothing but a canvas shelter stretched over a ridge pole protects the president's white hairs from the sun and storms of the Tropics. Front, back, and sides of the tent are all open to the elements, but no one ever heard a complaint from within. A folding table, surrounded by four camp stools, occupies the center of this White House of the woods. Several chests, in which are kept the government records, furnish additional seats when required. Two linen cloth hammocks swing upon either side of the tent.

One of them is occupied by the "Marquis," the other by Vice President Bartolomé Masó, a singular, quiet little man of remarkable learning and capacity, whose self sacrifice and devotion to the cause of Cuban liberty have won for him the esteem and gratitude of the whole island. Even the enemy respects and admires Masó, for before taking the field against Spain he insisted on paying off a debt of $10,000 owed to Spaniards. The vice president, unlike Cisneros, does not speak English, although he understands it if spoken slowly and distinctly. The only other occupant of this humble shelter is [illegible], the adopted son of the president, and the youngest soldier in the Cuban army.

YOUNGEST SOLDIER IN THE CUBAN ARMY.

Two years ago this spring, a bright faced boy of 13 years rode up to the president's headquarters in Najasa. He had left his home in the city of Puerto Principe and sought the insurgent camp.

"Señor Marquis," he said, "the Spaniards have killed my father. There is no one of us left but me to fight for Cuba. But if I could have a gun, I'd like to take my father's place."

And he got the gun, together with the love and protection of Salvador Cisneros. A pile of [illegible] palmetto or grass [illegible] answered as a bed for this infant soldier of the republic until a few months ago, when the president concluded to send him to New York to be educated.

The marquis is tall and stately in his bearing, but most democratic in his dress. A light suit of home manufactured linen clothes his tall, spare form, which is very like our recollection of Abraham Lincoln's. A pure white "jipijapa" protects his fine, almost classical face from the sun. A neatly trimmed silver white beard and mustache add a softening effect to his rather stern, weather bronzed features.

The erect, commanding figure of the marquis, afoot or on horseback, seems to deny the seventy two years which have passed over his head.

HARDSHIP AND PRIVATIONS OF THE PRESIDENT.

Salvador Cisneros is a soldier, every inch of him. At the siege of Zanja I saw him come out onto the field, ride up his horse alongside the rapid fire field pieces, and calmly watch the effect of the fire, while Mauser balls were cutting down men on all sides of him. Poor Osgood, the American who met his death while serving the cannon, protested against this unnecessary exposure, but the brave old man replied, "We have many men with us who have never before been under fire; they must be taught by example that a soldier should ignore the chances of death."

And yet this old warrior has all the tender heart of a woman. After listening one day to my description of the death of a notable lieutenant who had led a charge on horseback in the "Cabanas," the tears stood in the marquis's eyes as he murmured, "Too bad, too bad! Were not liberty so precious a thing it would be dearly bought, even at the cost of that poor fellow's life. Every drop of blood spilled seems wrung out of my own heart."

Every hardship, privation, and danger of the war has been shared by President Cisneros from the beginning. Such luxuries as bread and butter are entirely unknown. A poor substitute for the former, called "casabe," drifts into camp occasionally, but seldom lasts more than a day. Coffee is worth almost its weight in silver, and hard to get at any price. A drink called "canchanchara," made by slightly scorching honey over the camp fire and afterwards adding boiling water, usually takes its place. If honey can not be obtained, brown sugar in cakes called "raspadura" answers very well. Fresh beef and green bananas ("platanos") are almost always on hand and in plenty. Sweet potatoes ("boniatos") are abundant in some parts of the island.

I remember that in Najasa last summer we lived for five days on beef and mangoes. The president reminded me one morning that I had not eaten at his table for several meals, and I was obliged to tell him that his table had become really too bad. That evening it was my privilege to send the "marquis" a young roast pig, 10 pounds of honey, and some fresh eggs I had been foraging.

THE PRESIDENT'S CABINET.

Surrounding the president's tent are those of his cabinet. 'Tis needless to say that they shelter men of culture and refinement. They were the choice of the assembly elected by the people of Cuba, and are all devoted to the common cause of liberty at any price.

Colonel Mendoza, acting secretary of war in General Roloff's absence, is a bright and most industrious officer of the government. Quarters are coming and going from his headquarters at all hours of the day, and often until far into the night. The Colonel has some knowledge of English and is very proud of his accomplishment, although his speaking vocabulary is confined to a few phrases. The favorite of these is "Poor Cuba!" and this is made to serve on all occasions, sublime or ridiculous. I remember one morning, just previous to a review of the forces by the late Gen. Serefin Sanchez, Colonel Mandulay, who is the personification of military tidiness, swung himself gracefully into the saddle. The manner of the mount would do credit to one of the Queen's guards, but there came over his countenance a change, an anxious, distressed look, which portended trouble. There was. The back seam of his long-enduring trousers had split from one end to the other. With rare forbearance he indulged simply in a long-drawn sigh and his favorite exclamation "Poor Cuba!" and immediately sought the tentmaker for a needle and twine.

One of the most important and imposing personages of the camp is Colonel Betancourt, governor, quartermaster, sanitary inspector, and "all round boss." He deals out the coffee (if there happens to be any), the raspadura, and the manteca de vaca (beef suet). He sees that the beeves driven into camp each day are killed and the meat fairly apportioned to each mess. Great bonfires are built over the refuse the moment the meat is taken from the bones, so that there is no opportunity for disease germs to be engendered.

The sanitary rules of insurgent camps are rigidly enforced in all parts of the island, which accounts for the almost total absence of disease. Camp, whenever possible, is made by some running stream, and guards are at once posted to see that no bathing or washing of horses is indulged in above the spot where drinking water is obtained.

Colonel Betancourt is a great gun in camp, but when stakes are pulled up and hammocks pulled down, you will observe a shade of anxiety spreading over his naturally serene countenance. But a still deeper one comes over the face of the little mule which has to carry the colonel's 300 pounds of adipose tissue to the next stopping place. He at first appears inclined to rebel, but after reflection a change comes over the spirit of his dream. His ears resume an angle of resignation and in his eyes you easily read, "It is for Cuba, poor Cuba! I will bear my burden with the rest; but Colonel Betancourt is pretty heavy."

In going over the road this patient little beast usually picks out a rut in which to walk, so that often all six feet touch the ground at once.

There is a peculiar mingling of the picturesque and the pathetic in the nomadic life of the insurgent government. The cluster of white canopies reflecting back the soft, pure light of a tropical moon; the long, graceful plumes of royal palms, gently fanning the tired patriots into slumber; the sweet little night song of the mocking bird, all help to form a picture of joy and content, and were it not for the distant roar of musketry, which comes from the lines of a harassed Spanish column on the other side of the hills, one could easily imagine himself in a land of perpetual peace.

GEORGE RENO.

Now, in further support of that statement, I will read again from the deposition of Dr. Diaz the following brief extract:

By Senator DAVIS:

Q. Gomez is commander in chief over all?
A. Yes, sir.

By Senator MORGAN:

Q. And that is the military organization?
A. Yes, sir.
Q. Let us know something about the civil organization. Did you meet any civil officers?
A. Yes, sir; Mr. Portuondo.
Q. What is his office?
A. He is secretary of the interior.
Q. He belongs to the general government of the Cuban Republic?
A. Yes, sir.
Q. I want you to speak of the local officers—the prefects and subprefects. Do you know anything about them?
A. Yes, sir.
Q. What is a prefect?
A. He is the man in charge to find supplies for the families of insurgents in every place there.
Q. Sort of a commissary?
A. Yes, sir; if the families need something to eat, for instance, he brings food, cattle, etc.
Q. Takes care of the families of the men in the army?
A. Yes, sir; and if the men are sick or wounded the prefects take care of them.

Q. They take care of the sick and wounded, and subprefects have smaller districts?
A. They have smaller districts.
Q. Now, who are the tax collectors there?
A. There are tax collectors, too; I know, personally, Mr. Menocal.
Q. A cousin of our Menocal here?
A. A brother, I think.
Q. Is he a tax collector?
A. Yes; they divide themselves into different places and collect all the revenue.
Q. Do they collect revenue from the people?
A. Oh, yes. Sometimes they have no place to put the money. Sometimes Gomez has mules loaded with money—going from one place to another with money.

By Senator DAVIS:
Q. Do they collect supplies in kind?
A. The prefects do, but these are the tax collectors.

By Senator MORGAN:
Q. Do the people of Cuba voluntarily and freely pay taxes to the Cuban Government, or are they forced to do it?
A. No, sir; they freely do it. They pay taxes where the Cubans have no control over it.

By Senator DAVIS:
Q. Now, over this territory have the Spanish any tax collectors?
A. Not one.

By Senator MORGAN:
Q. Have they any judges?
A. Not one.

By Senator DAVIS:
Q. Any civil officers at all?
A. No. In the larger towns is the only place. In the smaller places they have nothing of the kind—no mayors, no aldermen.

On the 6th of this month (April), Mr. Guerra, of 192 Water street, New York, sent me the following telegram:

NEW YORK, *April 6, 1897.*

Senator MORGAN:

As treasurer for Republic of Cuba abroad and as agent for the secretary of the treasury, I have received in payment of taxes on rural property and products $141,182, paid me by commercial houses in this country by agreement with the treasury officers in the Republic of Cuba.

BENJ. J. GUERRA, *192 Water Street.*

The number of the factories in the republic and the variety of their productions gives the highest assurance of the thrift and industry of the native Cubans and of their ability in times of peace to gather from the resources of that wonderfully rich island great wealth in agricultural products, in mines and minerals, in valuable woods, and the finest fruits.

Its waters abound in fish, and its plains and mountains furnish food in abundance for raising great numbers of domestic animals. These resources of a country in which famine has never appeared will furnish an abundant commissariat to supply the Cuban armies for many years. Living at home upon their own food supplies, which the soil provides almost without labor, the Cubans force Spain to import all the subsistence of their armies from abroad. They have never had rations for twenty days in their reserved stores and are exposed to the danger of light and swift cruisers which would intercept their ships on the seas, with even greater success than they now land cargoes of war supplies on a coast that it is impossible for Spain to protect.

It is this feature of belligerent rights that causes Spain to dread that any nation should rise up and declare the truth, so shamefully denied, that war exists in Cuba. Alarmed at the vote of the

Senate last week, Spain has granted belligerent rights to General Rivera, who was wounded and captured recently in Pinar del Rio, and has concluded, at least, not to kill him at once. If the rights of war are granted to the distinguished leaders of insurrection by the voluntary act of Spain, why are they not due to every soldier in the Cuban army and to every citizen of the United States who is charged with the intention of aiding Cuba with arms, as these high officers have done?

I am aware that Mr. De Lôme is quoted by an interviewer as having stated that "Rivera's punishment largely depends upon the conduct of Cuban sympathizers in the United States." If it has come to this, that the issue of life or death to a Spanish subject found in arms and fighting for liberty is to depend upon the sympathies or the conduct of our people, and that Rivera is held as a hostage for our good conduct, it is time that we had put an end to this badgering by stating our real attitude toward the Cuban people in a way to comport with our national rights and our integrity of character.

This form of dealing with Rivera, by holding the sword suspended over him by a thread that we are challenged to break, is not misunderstood by our people. They know that Spain has at last discovered that it is her duty, and her only course of self-preservation—that she must confess that public war exists in Cuba, and that those who are engaged in it on either side are not outlawed felons who are worthy of death or of any punishment that is not sanctioned by the laws of nations as they properly apply to civilized warfare. Spain has evidently reached this conclusion, and has put it in practice in the case of General Rivera.

This new departure happened on the heels of the unanimous vote of the Senate protesting against his execution, as Sanguily's release from prison, under an alleged parole, followed a vote of the Senate for the consideration of the causes of his long and horrible imprisonment, and his second sentence to imprisonment for life, in chains.

These votes in the Senate only expressed our convictions, which, fortunately, became also the convictions of the Spanish Government, and while we were holding these matters under debate Spain recognized the belligerency of the Cubans by throwing open the doors of Sanguily's dungeon and accepting his parole, and by suspending capital proceedings against General Rivera.

What is now left for us to do is to formally declare the belligerency of the warring hosts in Cuba, which Spain has thus tacitly acknowledged.

If we leave Spain to play fast and loose upon this question, and to putter with us in a double sense, we shall soon find that we have been deceived into a dilemma, either horn of which she will take at pleasure. Already it is announced that Major Sandoval, a member of Weyler's staff, is to be here, if he has not already arrived, to wage war in our courts, with the aid of the Pinkerton detectives, so long in Spain's service, against a Cuban junta that is alleged to exist in the United States. I hope he will come on a less intrusive mission.

If he comes on that mission, it may occur to our Government to inquire by what authority Weyler can transfer his hostilities to our soil and prosecute the pleas of the United States against Cubans who, equally with Spanish subjects, are enjoying the shelter of our national hospitality. Our laws of neutrality were no more enacted for the service of Spain than for that of Canada or Mexico.

They were enacted to regulate the conduct of our own people, through the judicial or executive agencies of our own Government.

We do not need Spanish military assistance in the administration of our laws, being ourselves quite equal to that duty, and a proper sense of self-respect will, I hope, cause us to dismiss Major Sandoval from further attendance after his complaint has been respectfully heard, if he is here as a Spanish military officer for any such purpose. If he comes to complain that we are unfaithful to our treaty obligations, or to our duties under the laws of nations, and is properly empowered, he is entitled to a most candid and respectful audience at the Department of State.

If he comes as Weyler's aid to prosecute our people, or our guests, for the violation of our own laws, in our open courts, let him first be held to explain why his Government, and under Weyler's orders, has persistently refused trial to our people arrested in Cuba in the manner provided by Spanish law with reference to civil or political offenses and pledged to them in our treaties.

Let him account for the military arrest, the deadly silence of the incomunicado, the solitary inquisition, the torments of thirst and beatings of men in chains, and the nights in prison without the privilege of sleeping on the floors of the filthy dungeons or of a blanket to wrap the bodies of the victims crowded into black holes like those of Calcutta and Ceuta. If his mission is peace and mercy, let him explain such deeds, many times repeated all over Cuba, as I have read from the sworn testimony of Dr. Diaz, a most worthy and truthful Protestant divine.

I could multiply statements such as I have read until Weyler even would shudder at his own cruelties, but it is needless to recall this dark record of inhumanity. It is graven indelibly on millions of hearts. I have cited these instances of outrage only to illustrate the insolence of a government that has inflicted them in their effort now to inflict other punishments, under our laws, upon the Cuban patriots after they are at last compelled by the judgment of all civilized people to accord to them, in Cuba at least, the pretense of belligerent rights.

A large amount of money is being expended in the United States, both by Spain and Cuba, for war purposes. Spain also expends large sums in support of a secret detective force in our country, through which she prosecutes clandestine war against the Cuban people as effectively as she does from her picket posts and skirmish lines in that island. This is excused because of the comity supposed to be due to her titular sovereignty, when she can not open a court or collect taxes at a distance of 10 miles from her military posts in Cuba. A Pinkerton detective force in the pay of the Cuban people in Habana would be shot to death as fast as they could be caught; and a banished citizen of the United States who should return to Cuba under the guaranty of our treaties would be subjected to a like fate.

We do not claim mutuality in the Spanish privilege of murder, but we do claim that we shall not be made accessory to Spanish atrocities by lending our courts to them to facilitate their perpetration upon the friends of liberty and human rights in Cuba.

When they have declared that public war exists in Cuba, then the laws of nations will open our courts alike to both parties on equal terms, and the use of our statute laws to punish Cuban patriots for the same acts that Spain can now perform with impunity will cease.

A Spanish man-of-war can now convoy a ship from the port of New York loaded with war material to destroy the King's subjects in arms, or in rebellion, or suspected of political crimes in Cuba, and to intercept her in such a voyage would invite condign punishment. As she passes our forts, they exchange salvos in honor of the flag that covers this engine of war and these conspirators against the million of people who are fighting in open war for life, country, and liberty.

And all this is done because our Government, through obeisance to a chronic despotism, lowers its flag to a tyrant that despises justice and scorns to recognize the fact that it can be successfully driven into public and acknowledged war by its persecuted subjects.

The next ship that sails from our great port may be loaded with food, munitions of war, and hospital stores for those starving rebels and their sick and wounded defenders.

Under the laws of nations both vessels can depart from our shores in peace, if public war exists in Cuba, but if the monstrous falsehood is adopted by our Government that all the naval power of Spain and 150,000 soldiers are not in the field making war upon her subjects until Spain chooses to declare that war exists, our war vessels will open their guns on that messenger of mercy and sink her to the bottom of the seas.

The glory of our Republic will cease to attract the love of our people when it becomes the ally of Spain in the support of a falsehood that crushes every hope of liberty and denies to humanity the helping hand of charity.

If this were a new struggle provoked by some recent and insufficient cause, our refusal to recognize the fact that war exists in Cuba might furnish us with a plausible excuse for our present course. But it is only an episode in a long struggle for liberty. The foundation of the Republic of Cuba was laid in Spain by the constitution of 1812, which was extended to Cuba, and gave to her people their first and only impulse of prosperity, confidence, and self-reliance.

Later, and before 1836, those constitutional rights had been revoked, and Cuba was relegated to the irresponsible despotism of the Captain-Generalcy, with power given him as a viceroy to suspend the laws and supplement them with his decrees, to levy and collect taxes, to confiscate property, and to inflict death by military order. In this authority he was supported by a standing army of at least 18,000 men, whose sole service was to keep the people of Cuba in subjection. Their whole career was that of an enslaved and subdued race.

Mr. Ballou, of Massachusetts, in 1854 visited Cuba with his invalid wife, and, after a long stay, he returned and wrote a book of great interest, from which I will read some quotations that show the condition of that country at that period, that we may trace the parallel to this day and understand the causes of the struggle that now engages the sympathy of all Christendom.

As I read from this author, we will see the fountain—the same from which our fathers drank—of constitutional liberty from which the Cubans received the inspiration that now refreshes the Republic of Cuba with the hope of that right of self-government to which we owe our independence, our strength, our happiness, our prosperity, and the glory of our national renown. We will see also how we are responsible for having held Cuba in the chains of Spanish despotism, when Mexico, led by Victoria, and

Colombia, led by Bolivar, were forbidden by us, in combination with France and England, from striking those fetters from this Queen of the Antilles.

I make no excuse, Mr. President, for reading from this able gentleman in private life, who in 1854 was in Cuba, having gone from Massachusetts to that country, and who, on his return, felt that it was incumbent upon him to make some statements to his fellow-countrymen in regard to the situation of the Cubans.

It is not a pleasant remembrance that the truth of history forces us to recall that Bolivar and Victoria would have secured national independence in Cuba in 1823 but for the slavery question in the United States and our dread of Great Britain and France, which caused us to interpose and warn them off from Cuba with their armies, and to forbid Colombia and Mexico to aid those people in their effort to escape from Spanish domination, as they had so recently done.

Our responsibility for the sufferings of Cuba under the Spanish yoke for the past seventy years is not a light thing either to them or to our people. There is a retribution for our wrong that it is unpleasant to suffer.

Mr. Ballou says:

When the French invasion of Spain in 1808 produced the constitution of 1812, Cuba was considered entitled to enjoy its benefits, and the year 1820 taught the Cubans the advantage to be derived by a people from institutions based on the principle of popular intervention in public affairs. The condition of the nation on the death of Ferdinand VII obliged Queen Christina to rely on the Liberal party for a triumph over the pretentions of the Infante Don Carlos to the crown and to assure the throne of Donna Isabella II, and the estatuto real (royal statute) was proclaimed in Spain and Cuba.

The Cubans looked forward, as in 1812 and 1820, to a representation in the national congress and the enjoyment of the same liberty conceded to the Peninsula. An institution was then established in Habana, with branches in the island, called the Royal Society for Improvement, already alluded to in our brief notice of Don Francisco Arranjo. The object of this society was to aid and protect the progress of agriculture and commerce, and it achieved a vast amount of good. At the same time the press, within the narrow limits conceded to it, discussed with intelligence and zeal the interests of the country, and diffused a knowledge of them.

In 1836 the revolution known as that of La Granja, provoked and sustained by the progressionists against the moderate party, destroyed the "royal statute" and proclaimed the old constitution of 1812. The queen-mother, then Regent of Spain, convoked the constituent Cortes and summoned deputies from Cuba.

Up to this time various political events, occurring within a brief period, had disturbed but slightly and accidentally the tranquillity of this rich province of Spain. The Cubans, although sensible of the progress of public intelligence and wealth under the protection of a few enlightened governors and through the influence of distinguished and patriotic individuals, were aware that these advances were slow, partial, and limited, that there was no regular system, and that the public interests, confided to officials intrusted with unlimited power and liable to the abuses inseparable from absolutism, frequently languished or were betrayed by a cupidity which impelled despotic authorities to enrich themselves in every possible way at the expense of popular suffering.

Added to these sources of discontent was the powerful influence exerted over the intelligent portion of the people by the portentous spectacle of the rapidly increasing greatness of the United States, where a portion of the Cuban youths were wont to receive their education and to learn the value of a national independence based on democratic principles, principles which they were apt freely to discuss after returning to the island.

There also were the examples of Mexico and Spanish South America, which had recently conquered with their blood their glorious emancipation from monarchy. Liberal ideas were largely diffused by Cubans who had traveled in Europe, and there imbibed the spirit of modern civilization. But, with a fatuity and obstinacy which has always characterized her, the mother country resolved to ignore these causes of discontent, and, instead of yielding to the popular current and introducing a liberal and mild system of government, drew the reins yet tighter, and even curtailed many of the privileges formerly accorded to the Cubans. It is a blind persistence in the fated principle of despotic domination which has relaxed the moral and political bonds uniting the two countries, instilled gall into the hearts of the governed, and substituted the dangerous obedience of terror for the secure loyalty of love. This severity of the home Government has given rise to several attempts to throw off the Spanish yoke.

The first occurred in 1823, when the Liberator, Simon Bolivar, offered to aid the disaffected party by throwing an invading force into the island. The conspiracy then formed by the aid of the proffered expedition, for which men were regularly enlisted and enrolled, would undoubtedly have ended in the triumph of the insurrection had it not been discovered and suppressed prematurely, and had not the Governments of the United States, Great Britain, and France intervened in favor of Spain.

In 1826 some Cuban emigrants, residing in Caracas, attempted a new expedition, which failed, and caused the imprisonment and execution of two patriotic young men, Don Francisco de Aguero y Velazco and Don Bernabe Sanchez, sent to raise the department of the interior. In 1828 there was a yet more formidable conspiracy, known as El Aguila Negra (the black eagle). The efforts of the patriots proved unavailing, foiled by the preparation and power of the Government, which seems to be apprised by spies of every intended movement for the cause of liberty in Cuba.

Here we see, Mr. President, that in 1823 Bolivar, the great deliverer of South America, had formed a combination with Victoria, the President of Mexico, for the purpose of driving out the Spanish authority from Cuba, as it had already been driven out from all the other Spanish-American states.

If we had not then prevented this noble and generous movement, Cuba would be to-day, as she will soon be, the nineteenth great republic of the Western Hemisphere and the central glory of the southern seas.

It is time that we had begun to redeem our own great error by taking Cuba by the hand and lifting her from beneath the foot of Weyler and placing her, in honor, upon the beautiful throne that God built for the Queen of the Antilles—the throne of liberty, supported by the independence of the people. Let us glance for a moment at the results of our fatal blow at Cuban independence. The legitimate fruit of this painful intervention was the Captain-Generalcy, in the hands of Tacon, whose successor, Weyler, has at last brought Tacon's usurpations to that excess of depravity at which the whole world is in revolt. I will read from the same author, Mr. M. M. Ballou:

Although the royal proclamation which announced to Tacon the establishment of the constitution in Spain intimated forthcoming orders for the election of deputies in Cuba to the general Cortes, still he considered that his commission as Captain-General authorized him, under the circumstances, to carry out his own will and suppress at once the movement set on foot by General Lorenzo on the ground of its danger to the peace of the island and the interests of Spain.

The royal order which opened the way for his attacks upon the Cuban people, after a confused preamble, confers on the Captain-General all the authority appertaining in time of war to a Spanish governor of a city in a state of siege, authorizing him in any circumstances and by his proper will to suspend any public functionary, whatever his rank, civil, military, or ecclesiastical, to banish any resident of the island without preferring any accusations, to modify any law or suspend its operations, disobey with impunity any regulation emanating from the Spanish Government, to dispose of the public revenues at his will, and, finally, to act according to his pleasure, winding up with recommending a moderate use of the confidence evinced by the sovereign in according power so ample.

Although the Captains-General of Cuba have always been invested with extraordinary power, we believe that these items of unlimited authority were first conferred upon Vivez in 1825, when the island was menaced by an invasion of the united forces of Mexico and Colombia. In these circumstances, and emanating from an absolute authority like that of Ferdinand VII, a delegation of power which placed the destinies of the island at the mercy of its chief ruler might have had the color of necessity; but to continue such a delegation of authority in time of peace is a most glaring and inexcusable blunder.

Here we find ourselves responsible also for the enlarged powers of the Captain-General, which were conferred by this royal order for the purpose of checking and putting down the combination between Victoria and Bolivar, when they were about to enter the Island of Cuba to release her from Spain's dominion and were prevented by the intervention of the Government of the United States.

We have some responsibilities about this matter, Mr. President, that we had better begin at least to consider. We are now trying to find out exactly our bearings with reference to this question, and I hope we shall be sincere and dutiful in our belated work. This writer, Mr. Ballou, portrays the policy of Spain toward Cuba and its execution through the office of Captain-General in the following clear manner, so that we have only to compare the present with the past to see that in the hands of this vice-royal autocrat Spain has lodged a power that wars against Christian civilization with far greater excess of cruelty than that which Turkey visits upon the Christians in Crete or Armenia.

He further writes:

We have seen that the office of Captain-General was established in 1589, and, with a succession of incumbents, the office has been maintained until the present day, retaining the same functions and the same extraordinary powers. The object of the Spanish Government is, and ever has been, to derive as much revenue as possible from the island; and the exactions imposed upon the inhabitants have increased in proportion as other colonies of Spain in the western world have revolted and obtained their independence. The imposition of heavier burdens than those imposed upon any other people in the world has been the reward of the proverbial loyalty of the Cubans; while the epithet of "ever faithful" bestowed by the Crown has been their only recompense for their steady devotion to the throne. But for many years this lauded loyalty has existed only in appearance, while discontent has been fermenting deeply beneath the surface.

The Cubans owe all the blessings they enjoy to Providence alone, so to speak, while the evils which they suffer are directly referable to the oppression of the home Government. Nothing short of a military despotism could maintain the connection of such an island with a mother country more than 3,000 miles distant; and accordingly we find the Captain-General of Cuba invested with unlimited power. He is in fact a viceroy appointed by the Crown of Spain, and accountable only to the reigning sovereign for his administration of the colonies.

His rule is absolute. He has the power of life and death and liberty in his hands. He can, by his arbitrary will, send into exile any person whatever, be his name or rank what it may, whose residence in the island he considers prejudicial to the royal interests, even if he has committed no overt act. He can suspend the operation of the laws and ordinances, if he sees fit to do so; can destroy or confiscate property, and, in short, the island may be said to be perpetually in a state of siege.

Mr. Ballou thus describes the power with which in 1854 the Captain-General maintained his authority in Cuba:

The Spanish Government supports a large army on the island, which is under the most rigid discipline and in a state of considerable efficiency. It is the policy of the home Government to fill the ranks with natives of old Spain in order that no undue sympathy may be felt for the creoles, or islanders, in case of insurrection or attempted revolution. An order has recently been issued by Pezuela, the present governor-general, for the enrollment of free blacks and mulattoes in the ranks of the army, and the devotion of these people to Spain is loudly vaunted in the Captain-General's proclamation. The enlistment of people of color in the ranks is a deadly insult offered to the white population of a slaveholding country—

This is an abolitionist who is writing—

a sort of shadowing forth of the menace, more than once thrown out by Spain, to the effect that if the colonists should ever attempt a revolution she would free and arm the blacks, and Cuba, made to repeat the tragic tale of Santo Domingo, should be useless to the creoles if lost to Spain. But we think Spain overestimates the loyalty of the free people of color whom she would now enroll beneath her banner. They can not forget the days of O'Donnell (governor-general), when he avenged the opposition of certain Cubans to the illicit and infamous slave trade by which he was enriching himself by charging them with an abolition conspiracy in conjunction with the free blacks and mulattoes, and put many of the latter to the torture to make them confess imaginary crimes, while others, condemned without a trial, were mowed down by the fire of platoons. Assuredly the people of color have no reason for attachment to the paternal Government of Spain.

And in this connection we may also remark that this attempt at the enrollment of the blacks has already proved, according to the admission of Spanish authority, a partial failure, for they can not readily learn the drill, and officers dislike to take command of companies.

We turn now to the condition of the people of Cuba in 1854, as it is described by Mr. Ballou. He says:

We have thus dilated upon the natural resources of Cuba and depicted the charms that rest about her; but every picture has its dark side, and the political situation of the island is the reverse in the present instance. Her wrongs are multifarious, and the restrictions placed upon her by her oppressors are each and all of so heinous and tyrannical a character that a chapter upon each would be insufficient to place them in their true light before the world. There is, however, no better way of placing the grievances of the Cubans, as emanating from the home Government, clearly before the reader than by stating such of them as recur readily to the writer's mind in brief:

She is permitted no voice in the Cortes; the press is under the vilest censorship; farmers are compelled to pay 10 per cent on all their harvest except sugar, and on that article 2½ per cent; the island has been under martial law since 1825; over $23,000,000 of taxes are levied upon the inhabitants to be squandered by Spain; ice is monopolized by the Government; flour is so taxed as to be inadmissible; a creole must purchase a license before he can invite a few friends to take a cup of tea at his board; there is a stamped paper, made legally necessary for special purposes of contract, costing $8 per sheet; no goods, either in or out of doors, can be sold without a license; the natives of the island are excluded entirely from the army, the judiciary, the treasury, and the customs; the military Government assumes the charge of the schools; the grazing of cattle is taxed exorbitantly; newspapers from abroad, with few exceptions, are contraband; letters passing through the post are opened and purged of their contents before delivery; fishing on the coast is forbidden, being a Government monopoly; planters are forbidden to send their sons to the United States for educational purposes; the slave trade is secretly encouraged by Government; no person can remove from one house to another without first paying for a Government permit; all cattle (the same as goods) that are sold must pay 6 per cent of their value to Government; in short, every possible subterfuge is resorted to by the Government officials to swindle the people, everything being taxed, and there is no appeal from the decision of the Captain-General.

This New England abolitionist, Mr. Ballou, had scant sympathy for the Cubans, all of whom were slaveholders in 1854; yet their political enslavement to Spanish oppressors was so terrible in the view he had of their wrongs that he forgot the slaves in his compassion for their masters, the white race; and he thus speaks of them and the beautiful island, another Eden, where the sting of the serpent is forever wounding his victim, while the promise of death is delayed to protract his sufferings indefinitely:

> It is a goodly sight to see
> What Heaven hath done for this delicious land!
> What fruits of fragrance blush on every tree!
> What goodly prospects o'er the hills expand!

If it were possible to contemplate only the beauties that nature has so prodigally lavished on this Eden of the Gulf, shutting out all that man has done and is still doing to mar the blessings of Heaven, then a visit to or residence in Cuba would present a succession of unalloyed pleasures equal to a poet's dream. But it is impossible, even if it would be desirable, to exclude the dark side of the picture. The American traveler particularly, keenly alive to the social and political aspects of life, appreciates in full force the evils that challenge his observation at every step and in every view which he may take.

If he contrast the natural scenery with the familiar pictures of home, he can not help also contrasting the political condition of the people with that of his own country. The existence, almost under the shadow of the flag of the freest institutions the earth ever knew, of a government as purely despotic as that of the Autocrat of all the Russias is a monstrous fact that startles the most indifferent observer. It must be seen to be realized. To go hence to Cuba is not merely passing over a few degrees of latitude in a few days' sail. It is a step from the nineteenth century back into the Dark Ages.

In the clime of sun and endless summer, we are in the land of starless political darkness. Lying under the lee of a land where every man is a sovereign is a realm where the lives, liberties, and fortunes of all are held at the tenure of the will of a single individual, and whence not a single murmur of complaint can reach the ear of the nominal ruler, more than a thousand leagues away in another hemisphere.

In close proximity to a country where the taxes, self-imposed, are so light as to be almost unfelt is one where each free family pays nearly $400 per annum for the support of a system of bigoted tyranny, yielding, in the aggregate, an annual revenue of $25,000,000, for which they receive no equivalent—no representation, no utterance, for pen and tongue are alike proscribed, no honor, no office, no emolument, while their industry is crippled, their intercourse with other nations hampered in every way; their bread literally snatched from their lips, the freedom of education denied, and every generous, liberal aspiration of the human soul stifled in its birth. And this in the nineteenth century and in North America.

Such are the contrasts, broad and striking, and such the reflections forced upon the mind of the citizen of the United States in Cuba. Do they never occur to the minds of the creoles? We are told that they are willing slaves. Spain tells us so, and she extols to the world with complacent mendacity the loyalty of her "siempre fielissima Isla de Cuba." But why does she have a soldier under arms for every four white adults? We were about to say white male citizens, but there are no citizens in Cuba. A proportionate military force in this country would give us a standing army of more than a million bayonets, with an annual expenditure, reckoning each soldier to cost only $200 per annum, of more than $200,000,000.

And this is the peace establishment of Spain in Cuba—for England and France and the United States are all her allies, and she has no longer to fear the roving buccaneers of the Gulf who once made her tremble in her island fastnesses. For whom, then, is this enormous warlike preparation? Certainly for no external enemy; there is none. The question answers itself—it is for her very loyal subjects, the people of Cuba, that the Queen of Spain makes all this warlike show.

It is impossible to conceive of any degree of loyalty that would be proof against the unparalleled burdens and atrocious system by which the mother country has ever loaded and weighed down her western colonists. They must be either more or less than men if they still cherish attachment to a foreign throne under such circumstances. But the fact simply is, the creoles of Cuba are neither angels nor brutes. They are, it is true, a long-suffering and somewhat indolent people, lacking in a great degree the stern qualities of the Anglo-Saxon and the Anglo-Norman races, but nevertheless intelligent, if wanting culture, and not without those noble aspirations for independence and freedom, destitute of which they would cease to be men, justly forfeiting all claim to our sympathy and consideration.

During the brief intervals in which a liberal spirit was manifested toward the colony by the home Government the Cubans gave proof of talent and energy, which, had they been permitted to attain their full development, would have given them a highly honorable name and distinguished character. When the field for genius was comparatively clear, Cuba produced more than one statesman and man of science who would have done honor to a more favored land.

But these cheering rays of light were soon extinguished and the fluctuating policy of Spain settled down into the rayless and brutal despotism which has become its normal condition and a double darkness closed upon the political and intellectual prospects of Cuba. But the people are not, and have not been, the supine and idle victims of tyranny which Spain depicts them. The reader who has indulgently followed us thus far will remember the several times they have attempted, manacled as they are, to free their limbs from the chains that bind them. It is insulting and idle to say that they might have been free if they had earnestly desired and made the effort for freedom.

Who can say what would have been the result of our own struggle for independence if Great Britain at the outset had been as well prepared for resistance as Spain has always been in Cuba? Who can say how long and painful would have been the struggle if one of the most powerful military nations of Europe had not listened to our despairing appeal and thrown the weight of her gold and her arms into the scale against our great enemy?

I will insert in my remarks a further extract from Mr. Ballou's book without delaying the Senate to read it.

When it is compared with what we know and so painfully feel as to the present condition of Cuba and its long-suffering and brave people, and connect the present with the ten years' war which occurred twenty-four years after Mr. Ballou wrote his book, and then twenty years to the opening of the present war, we see a chain of political cause and effect into whose links there is woven the same undying love and devotion to the liberty of self-government that inspired our fathers in their Revolutionary struggle.

It is a cause that will not die, even if we, its natural guardians, should banish it from our hearts to make room for the depravity of that royal slavery that some seem to crave who still claim to be Americans. The people of Cuba still pray for the boon of our liberty and independence, and are even willing to perish in the fires of Spanish inquisition if, in such a death, they can secure these blessings for their children. Let us reflect that it was in 1854 that Mr. Ballou wrote these prophetic words:

> If Cuba lies at present under the armed heel of despotism, we may be sure that the anguish of her sons is keenly aggravated by their perfect understanding of our own liberal institutions and an earnest, if fruitless, desire to participate in their enjoyment. It is beyond the power of the Spanish Government to keep the people of the island in a state of complete darkness, as it seems to desire to do. The young men of Cuba educated at our colleges and schools, the visitors from the United States, and American merchants established on the island are all so many apostles of republicanism and propagandists of treason and rebellion. Nor can the Captains-General, with all their vigilance, exclude what they are pleased to call incendiary newspapers and documents from pretty extensive circulation among the "ever faithful."
>
> That liberal ideas and hatred of Spanish despotism are widely entertained among the Cubans is a fact no one who has passed a brief period among them can truthfully deny. The writer of these pages avers from his personal knowledge that they await only the means and the opportunity to rise in rebellion against Spain. We are too far distant to see more than the light smoke, but those who have trodden the soil of Cuba have sounded the depths of the volcano. The history of the unfortunate Lopez expedition proves nothing contrary to this. The force under Lopez afforded too weak a nucleus, was too hastily thrown upon the island, too ill prepared, and too untimely attacked to enable the native patriots to rally round its standard and thus to second the efforts of the invaders.
>
> With no ammunition nor arms to spare, recruits would have only added to the embarrassment of the adventurers. Yet had Lopez been joined by the brave but unfortunate Crittenden, with what arms and ammunition he possessed, had he gained some fastness where he could have been disciplining his command until further aid arrived, the adventure might have had a very different termination from what we have recorded in an early chapter of this book.

Mr. President, the conditions in Cuba have not changed for eighty years as to the determination of those people to lift themselves to that plane of liberty that all Spanish America has reached, upon which we were the first to raise the banner of redemption from the power of European monarchy. In that period they have suffered more than all the republics of America for the cause so dear to them all. What they suffer to-day is only the repetition of agony from which they have never been free.

Until Weyler came its most dreadful pangs had not been felt. Now it seems that by a supreme effort of the writhing victim the hold of the oppressor is to be broken.

We had France to help us in our travail, but Cuba has found no friend such as France was to us.

That Cuba will be free is written in the stars that glow in the unfailing light of the Southern Cross, to which her children turn their eyes with a faith that grows stronger and a hope that grows brighter as the night of their sorrows grows darker and darker.

As an appendix to my remarks I present a paper entitled "The surrender of Guaimaro," for the purpose of showing the treatment of prisoners of war by the Cubans in contrast with the treatment of such prisoners by the Spaniards.

The PRESIDING OFFICER. The document will be printed as an appendix, in the absence of objection.

APPENDIX.

THE SURRENDER OF GUAIMARO.

[Minutes of the surrender of Guaimaro.]

In Guaimaro, on the 28th of October, 1896, there being present in the garrison quarters of this town Col. G. Menocal, of the Cuban army, chief of staff of the military department of the east, and Capt. José Rosario Baez, of the Spanish army, the latter said that his situation being unbearable, owing to the siege of this fortified town, since the 17th instant, by the forces under Maj. Gen. Calixto Garcia Iniguez, chief of the department, he surrenders the fortified town under the conditions offered respecting his life and those of his troops under him, the officers and other forces which defended the forts of the town having given up in the same manner.

Rosario is to give his own arms and his property and that of his subordinates. Rosario delivers 40 Mauser rifles, 8 boxes of ammunition of the same, 2 bugles, and $1,580.40 in silver, which, he says, was given him as a deposit by the commissary of war.

Mr. Garcia Menocal, representing Maj. Gen. Calixto Garcia Iniguez, ratifies the above conditions and acknowledges receipt of the fortified town and the effects and money mentioned, stating that when Captain Rosario surrendered the Cuban forces were in possession of the fortifications and troops that defended them and occupied the town.

And so that it shall appear from the proceedings, they sign two of the same tenor.

M. C. MENOCAL.
JOSE ROSARIO,
Chief of Department.
Maj. MANUEL RODRIGUEZ.

In the free town of Guaimaro, on the 28th day of the month of October, 1896, Drs. Eugenio Molinet, colonel, chief of the sanitary department of the army of liberation of Cuba, and Fernando Perez de la Cruz, physician of the first class of the sanitary corps of the Spanish army, having come together, agreed to draw the following minutes, in which it is stated that at 2 o'clock in the morning of the same day, and before the surrender of the garrisons, neutrality was granted to the hospital of Guaimaro, in conformity to what was determined in the international congress which took place in Geneva, in which it was declared in a solemn manner that the wounded, field hospitals, and sanitary employees would be respected.

This neutrality was granted not only on account of the petition made by the head of the hospital, but also because of the desires of Maj. Gen. Calixto Garcia Iniguez, chief of the military department of the east, who desires that it shall be known that it is his firmest intention to respect the treaty above referred to, although the Spanish Government has not wished to accept said treaty with respect to the Cuban army.

At the request of Dr. Fernando Perez de la Cruz, he was left in charge of the cure of the sick and wounded of the said hospital, leaving him all the means which he deemed necessary for the care of his sick and wounded. He was also offered all the means, personal as well as medical, of the Cuban army. The said doctor of the Spanish army was provided with all the means to transport his sick and wounded to a place where they can be gathered by forces of his army.

And so that it shall appear from the proceedings, we sign the present minutes in duplicate.

Country and liberty!

DR. E. MOLINET.
FERNANDO PEREZ DE LA CRUZ.

In the cattle farm "El Platano," State of Camaguey, on the 2d of November, 1896, Dr. Eduardo Padro, lieutenant-colonel of the sanitary department of the army of liberation of Cuba, and Dr. Manuel Huelva Romero, physician of the first class of the Spanish army, being present, Dr. Padro said that by order and representation of Maj. Gen. Calixto Garcia Iniguez, chief of the military department of the east, and by virtue of a communication that said superior chief has sent and was sent to the chief of the Spanish army, Adolfo Jimenez Castellanos, in regard to the universal laws of war that the Cuban army observes, although they are not observed by the Spanish army, he delivered by this act to Dr. Huelva 22 sick and wounded, 5 sanitary employees, 4 civilians, Dr. Fernando Perez de la Cruz, and an officer of the first class of the military department, Julio Perez Pitarch, said individuals being all taken prisoners in the field hospital of the Spanish army, to which they belonged, in the capture of the town of Guaimaro by the Cuban forces, under the orders of Maj. Gen. Calixto Garcia Iniguez, which took place on the 28th of last October. And Dr. Manuel Romero said that in representation of the Spanish general, Don Adolfo Jimenez Castellanos, and, in conformity with what has been declared by Dr. Padro, he admits the receipt of the sick, wounded, and other prisoners mentioned, declaring that among the wounded there is a chief and an officer, and in order that it shall appear from the proceedings for its proper use, they drew up the present minutes, making two of the same tenor.

Dr. EDUARDO PADRO.
Dr. MANUEL HUELVA.

Mr. MORGAN. To-morrow, in the morning hour, I will ask that the joint resolution be laid before the Senate, being aware that some of the Senators in favor of the measure desire to speak upon it, and I shall have the hope of getting the joint resolution to a vote within a few days.

* * * * * * *

May 4, 1897.

Mr. ALLISON. If the routine business is closed, I move that the Senate proceed to the consideration of the sundry civil appropriation bill.

Mr. MORGAN. Before that motion is put, I desire to ask the Senator from Iowa whether since yesterday there has been any very great emergency for pushing this bill to the front. The Senator yesterday at my suggestion very kindly consented to give notice that he would move to take up this appropriation bill to-day at 2 o'clock. Now, it seems that he is moving it to the front, and I suppose—I hope it is not true—but I suppose the Senator is doing that in order to prevent me from calling up Senate joint resolution No. 26 on the subject of Cuba. I should like to know whether the Senator desires to displace that order with his present motion—whether that is his purpose?

Mr. ALLISON. The Senator from Alabama is usually able to discern my motives, but in this instance he happens to be mistaken. I refrained from suggesting to the Senate yesterday that I would call up the appropriation bill in the morning hour to-day, understanding that the Senator from Missouri [Mr. VEST] had some resolution that he wished to make some observations upon this morning, and also the Senator from Arkansas [Mr. BERRY]. In order to make my pathway as clear as possible, I saw those Senators and asked them if they would not allow me to go on with the appropriation bill this morning. I did not know that there was any special interest in the matter of Cuba that required the occupation of the morning hour this morning, and I did not suppose that that question would be before the Senate to-day. So the Senator from Alabama is wholly mistaken as to any view I may have had on the subject.

Mr. MORGAN. I wish to ask the unanimous consent of the Senate that I may be indulged for a few moments in making an appeal to the Senator from Iowa.

I have intended, as my conduct has very clearly shown, to press the joint resolution as rapidly as I could before the Senate. My purpose has not been in the slightest degree personal, nor has it been any other than a desire on my part to prevent the continuance of a condition in Cuba that is absolutely unbearable in the sight of God and man. That is to say, I have authentic information, which I can submit to the Senator from Iowa, and which he will not doubt when I do it, that American citizens as well as Cubans are being penned up and have been penned up in the cities and towns of Cuba by the order of General Weyler as a military movement, and that they are now literally starving to death in numbers for the want of provisions and supplies.

I apprehend that the delays, which have been great in this matter, and such as it has been impossible for me to control, have a direct reference to the fact that the Spanish Government is now attempting in monetary circles in Europe to negotiate a loan for the purpose of paying the interest upon a bonded debt which falls due now within a few days. Failing to do that, Spain will probably not conduct the war, even during the wet season, against Cuba. Her power in Cuba is going into a state of rapid dilapidation, and unless she can delay action in the Senate of the United States, through which we will give an expression again to that which heretofore we have so solemnly expressed with respect to the rights of belligerency between Spain and Cuba in that island, she will not be able to sell her bonds in the European market.

I do not wish, Mr. President, to contribute to the form of war which is prevailing in Cuba to-day, with cruelties that are destroying innocent men, women, and children, by facilitating this operation of Spain in the money markets of Europe. That is my reason for urgency in the passage of the joint resolution. I think I know what the opinion of the Senate is, and unless the Senate has been able to abandon its solemnly declared opinion of a year ago, in view of the fact and in consequence of the fact that the horrors of war in Cuba have been continually multiplied and increased, I can not doubt what the vote of the Senate will be upon the joint resolution when it is again taken up and brought to a vote. Not having any doubt about that, I do not wish that the men who are concerned in financial affairs in Europe shall be deceived by the delays which occur in this body in respect to the sentiments of the Senate of the United States. I think I can anticipate what that expression will be very clearly. If we could vote the resolution through this body to-day, Spain could not sell her bonds in the markets of Europe. If we delay until to-morrow, or a week hence, or two weeks hence, she may be able to inveigle the money powers of Europe into taking her bonds and restrengthening her credit so as to continue this campaign of starvation, murder, and cruelty for some time longer, perhaps for a year hence.

Now, under these conditions and in this situation I would not feel at all satisfied with myself, having offered the resolution, if I did not press it upon the attention of the Senate of the United States constantly and as often as I have the opportunity, in order to cut Spain off (for that is my purpose) from a resort to a credit that really is fictitious amongst the money lenders of Europe to get money in that way for the purpose of continuing this horrible crime against humanity.

I would gladly, Mr. President, retire from the contemplation of this subject, from any contact with it or any responsibility for it, if I could do so with a clear conscience. I would avoid the labor and responsibility and the acrimonious things that are said about me in this connection if I could possibly do so.

But, sir, I still have a heart in my bosom; I still have sympathy for suffering humanity; I still have respect for people who fight for liberty, and I still have contempt and abhorrence for those methods of warfare in the Island of Cuba which have made that man Weyler the most thoroughly condemned and despised man that now lives in the world. So I have thought that I would appeal to the Senator from Iowa if he could not postpone the appropriation bill until the hour of 2 o'clock, that perchance we might get at least nearer to a vote, if we do not reach a vote by that hour, upon the joint resolution.

Mr. ALLISON. I appeal to the Senator from Alabama to allow me to go on with the consideration of the appropriation bill for the reasons which I have already stated and for other reasons of public concern. This appropriation bill has been upon the table of the Senate for some time, because I have been occupied in another matter of public interest wherein it was supposed to be of great importance that the measure should be brought to the attention of the Senate. This is the first moment in three weeks in which I have been able to bring the bill before the Senate. This matter relating to Cuba has been under consideration here for two or three weeks. During the last week it was not pressed with any great vigor, at least so far as the public sessions of the Senate are concerned. I desire very much to have the appropriation bill disposed of now, in order that I may for a few days absent myself from the Senate. That is the only personal reason why I urge it now. I have no doubt the Senator from Alabama will have an early opportunity to bring forward his resolution and secure a vote on it. I certainly will interpose no impediment in the pathway of a vote.

Mr. MORGAN. The Senator from Iowa says or intimates that there has been no attempt on my part——

Mr. ALLISON. No; I do not intimate that.

Mr. MORGAN. To press the Cuban resolution during the last week or ten days.

Mr. ALLISON. I do not intimate that.

Mr. MORGAN. Out of a spirit of honorable and just indulgence to one solitary Senator on this floor, which I conceived it to be my duty to do, I have allowed this measure to pass from day to day, and when that Senator returned to the Senate yesterday morning he still said he was not prepared, and the matter went over again, with the understanding that the appropriation bill which the Senator from Iowa is now pressing at the hour of a quarter to 1 o'clock would not be called until 2 o'clock to-day.

Well, I know that the Senator has always been faithful, zealous, able, honorable, and patriotic in the discharge of every duty the Senate has ever imposed upon him, and I know that as a rule no measure can properly be antagonized to an appropriation bill when there is any emergency whatever for the passage of the appropriation bill. There is no emergency now for the passage of the sundry civil appropriation bill, for it will not take effect until the beginning of the next fiscal year, which is some time off yet. There being no emergency for that, and there being an emergency in respect of the Cuban resolution, I thought that I would ask the Senator if he would not yield in favor of my effort to relieve those people in Cuba for a while, to say the least of it.

There is at present no urgent necessity for the passage of the appropriation bill. But, sir, I will not antagonize an appropriation bill. Senators can take their responsibility. It will be but a few days until I think they will all be shocked with the idea that they have interposed objections to this measure, when, by declining to do so, they could have saved many human lives, and amongst them the lives of American citizens.

www.ingramcontent.com/pod-product-compliance
Lightning Source LLC
Chambersburg PA
CBHW031955230426
43672CB00010B/2163